WECHSLER ADULT INTELLIGENCE SCALE®– FOURTH EDITION

Technical and Interpretive Manual

David Wechsler

WAIS–IV Research Directors

Diane L. Coalson
Susan Engi Raiford

Table of Contents

Chapter 3.
WAIS–IV Research Procedures, Standardization, and Norms Development 25

List of Tables

List of Figures

Acknowledgments

The publication of the *Wechsler Adult Intelligence Scale–Fourth Edition* (WAIS–IV) involved the collaboration of a large number of individuals over a period of 4 years. Their hard work and dedication resulted in an extraordinary achievement—a significant improvement to an already outstanding intelligence scale. We would like to acknowledge this team for their hard work, ingenuity, and skill.

The WAIS–IV advisory panel members are greatly appreciated for their expertise and guidance throughout development. Drs. Gordon Chelune, C. Munro Cullum, Gerald Goldstein, Jacques Grégoire, Joel Kramer, Glenn Larrabee, Jennifer Manly, Scott Millis, Donald Saklofske, and Timothy Salthouse challenged us and provided crucial insight and advice at every phase. We are highly indebted to this advisory group for their clinical wisdom, way-finding abilities, and patience.

Dr. Jianjun Zhu, director of Psychometrics, played a critical role throughout the project. We are indebted to him for serving as a respected mentor, strategist, critical thinker, and scientist, and for sharing his experience from 15 years of Wechsler intelligence scale development. His contributions are far too numerous to mention. Thanks go to Dr. Tom Cayton, senior director of the Psychological Measurement Group, for his unwavering support of the project and team members, sage advice, and clinical expertise. We thank Dr. Judy Chartrand for her support in the same role during the tryout research phase. We are grateful to Mark Daniel, senior scientist, for his review of the Technical and Interpretive Manual and for his guidance during the closing days of this project. We appreciate Dr. Larry Weiss, vice president of Test Development, for his creativity and involvement in providing feedback and guidance throughout the project. We are also sincerely grateful for the support and counsel of Dr. Aurelio Prifitera, group president and CEO of Clinical Assessment/Worldwide.

Dr. Amy Gabel, national director of Clinical Sales and Training, shared her extensive clinical expertise and served as a direct link to practicing clinicians in the field. A number of clinical measurement consultants also provided their expertise. Drs. Sandra Adams, Diane Donaldson, Peter Entwistle, Sherry Eyer, John Hanson, Gloria Maccow, Patrick Moran, Gail Rodin, David Schwartz, Donna Smith, and Christina Sparks provided suggestions for meeting customer needs and offered critical insights throughout the phases of test development.

Several experts and consultants, who provided reviews of the WAIS–IV at each stage of development, are credited in Appendix F. Dr. Steven Hardy-Braz served as the expert consultant to represent the assessment needs for the deaf and hard of hearing population and provided all related manual content. Dr. Vernon Neppe provided invaluable and timely consultation on psychopharmacological issues prior to the standardization phase.

We are indebted to an outstanding team of research analysts on the development team for their ongoing contributions to the project from initiation to publication. Stephanie Tong, senior research analyst, trained sampling and scoring staff, reviewed hundreds of test protocols, drafted portions of the Administration and Scoring Manual, developed and refined items for the Comprehension subtest, and reviewed final test components. Imelda G. Martinez, senior research analyst, closely monitored the sample to prioritize scoring according to stratification, created the scoring materials, trained and supervised scorers, ensured quality of the data, and developed and refined items for the Visual Puzzles subtest. María R. Muñoz, senior research analyst, participated in tedious scoring studies, literature reviews, and cross-component review; developed and refined items for the Vocabulary subtest; and reviewed hundreds of test protocols. Erik M. Gallemore, research analyst, made noteworthy contributions to the standardization and final phases in the areas of cross-component review, protocol review, and quality assurance of data and tables. Amy Harrell-Medellin, research analyst, made outstanding contributions to tryout case review, item development and refinement, art coordination and tracking, and the standardization edition of the examiner training CD.

Frances Frey, research director, commented on drafts of the Technical and Interpretive Manual, reviewed scoring rubrics for the Verbal Comprehension subtests, and provided her expertise in protocol review. Dr. Paul Williams, research director, developed an innovative item type that evolved into the Figure Weights subtest.

The overlapping development of the WAIS–IV and the forthcoming *Wechsler Memory Scale–Fourth Edition* (WMS–IV) required close collaborative effort across two development teams. We wish to thank the WMS–IV research directors: Drs. Jim Holdnack and Lisa Drozdick. Dr. Holdnack, senior research director, was integrally involved in the early planning and provided important input and feedback at several stages, and his comments on the final data shaped numerous sections of the Technical and Interpretive Manual. Dr. Drozdick, research director, was critical to the planning and implementation of the co-norm and offered important insights into clinical case selection and review. Dr. Drozdick also assumed primary responsibility for the WAIS–IV scoring assistant during the final phase of development. Research analyst Jayme Lyon and senior research analysts Andre Lane, Elsa Tijerina, and Mary Sichi worked collaboratively with the WAIS–IV research analysts to track and to oversee case check-in of the linked WMS–IV cases and the shared concurrent validity cases.

We are grateful to Dr. Xiaobin Zhou, psychometrician, for her statistical consultation as we addressed numerous research questions throughout the standardization and final assembly and evaluation phases, as well as her skillful planning and efficient implementation of the normative and psychometric analysis process. We also acknowledge her invaluable sample refinement efforts and her innovative work on the software programs used for scoring studies. Monica Minter and Rencan Yan, statistical analysts, assisted Dr. Zhou in preparing the final normative data and in performing the extensive psychometric analysis of the final data set. Consulting and auditing by Dr. Hsin Yi Chen, senior psychometrician, further ensured the quality of psychometric results. We greatly appreciate Dr. Eric Rolfhus, Dr. Troy Courville, and other members of the psychometric team for their contributions during the pilot and early tryout phases.

Leanne Smith, senior Sampling analyst, diligently tracked the sampling matrix and performed study management. Special mention is given to the Sampling Department's management team, including Hector Solis, recruiting manager, Ruth Mendez, operations manager, and Victoria Locke, Sampling director. Other essential members of the Sampling team included: Greg Hudack and Jennifer Romig, project leads/recruiting coordinators; Darrell Stiffey, clinical lead and recruiting coordinator; Mylene Bagalawis, Mike Kelly, and Cat Ruiz, recruiting coordinators; Tracy Cowan, Jane McDonald, and Jennifer Hervey; clinical recruiting coordinators; Jo-Ann Cuellar, Sampling analyst; Colleen McAndrew and Rene Martinez, clinical case reviewer project leads; Cynthia Jackson, Karla Peterson, and Mario Thomas, examiner contact project leads; Eloisa Kirkwood, Gloria Angel, and Jennifer Austerman, Sampling case check-in reviewers; and Darlene Griffin, Jennifer Ches, Lauren Miles, Mitzi Roberts, Nell Montgomery, Stacy Bridges, David D. Mayfield, Jennifer Ramirez, Judith Collard, and Julie C. Schweers, Sampling operations team.

Harriet Wiygul, senior editor, worked tirelessly to refine the quality of the publication manuals and other printed materials throughout the project. Her intimate familiarity with the Wechsler intelligence scales, her planning and implementation of the collaborative editorial process throughout the entire project, and her proactive preparation of final components facilitated timely progression through a challenging project timeline. Special thanks to Alanna Carmichael, senior editor, for her careful attention to references. Our thanks also to Weslea Miller, senior editor, and Anne Trominski, editor, who lent their able assistance on the final manuals.

The production and manufacturing of test materials was completed on schedule thanks to the hard work and creativity of Jeann Kincaid, manager of Clinical Production, and Robin Espiritu, Manufacturing manager. These individuals ensured that the WAIS–IV would be highly usable, attractive, and of course, published on time. A special thanks goes to Mark Cooley, designer, for providing the artists with clear explanations of art functions and requirements during the research phases. We also appreciate his design of the final Record Form. We extend our gratitude to David Mellott and the excellent staff of DKM Productions, Ltd. for page composition on all phases of the WAIS–IV.

Sincere thanks are due to our scoring team. David Quintero, supervisor, clinical handscoring, and lead scorers Glenna Simmons and Irvin Salvador are thanked especially for performing a very demanding job. We thank Matt Morris, manager, software development along with Glen Larson, programmer analyst, for providing scoring system and sampling matrix support. Mary Mata, Evangelina Souza, and Sylvia Mendez verified the data in the numerous tables in both manuals.

The WAIS–IV project team was fortunate to have Stephanie Torres, project manager, to manage project timeline, budget, and cross-functional group coordination. Her perseverance, helpfulness, and organizational and problem-solving skills set a pleasant, cooperative tone that facilitated a strong approach to teamwork. Ray Blom, senior project manager, and Lauretta Bateman, project manager, oversaw timeline, budget, and cross-functional group coordination toward the end of a complex standardization phase through final publication.

Clay Richey, product line manager, coordinated customer research and interviews to address several questions relevant to customer priorities, usability, and flexibility. We are also grateful to David Shafer, product line manager, who served a similar function earlier in the project. We wish to thank our talented marketing group: Janet Ward, Clinical Marketing manager, and Brittany Drew, associate Marketing manager.

We thank the literally thousands of examinees who assisted with this endeavor. Obviously, this revision could not have been done without them. We also wish to thank the many examiners, sites, and site coordinators who made this project possible. Finally, we are most indebted to Dr. David Wechsler, whose clinical acumen and lifelong dedication to cognitive assessment provided us an extraordinary foundation on which to build.

Diane L. Coalson, PhD
Susan Engi Raiford, PhD

WAIS–IV Research Directors

Chapter 1

Introduction to the WAIS–IV

The *Wechsler Adult Intelligence Scale–Fourth Edition* (WAIS–IV) is an individually administered, comprehensive clinical instrument for assessing the intelligence of examinees ages 16 years 0 months through 90 years 11 months (16:0–90:11). It is a revision of the *Wechsler Adult Intelligence Scale—Third Edition* (WAIS–III; Wechsler, 1997a). The WAIS–IV provides composite scores that represent intellectual functioning in specified cognitive areas (i.e., Verbal Comprehension Index, Perceptual Reasoning Index, Working Memory Index, and Processing Speed Index), and a composite score that represents general intellectual ability (i.e., Full Scale IQ).

Historical and Current Trends in Intelligence Testing

The most prevalent theory of intelligence in the early 20th century emphasized a single, underlying construct of intelligence as largely responsible for an individual's performance on all mental tasks. Spearman (1904) originally identified this construct as the *g*-factor. Although his theory of intelligence incorporated more specific factors, early intelligence tests emphasized the classification of individuals based on their overall level of cognitive functioning (Beres, Kaufman, & Perlman, 2000; Goldstein & Hersen, 2000).

In response to a French government commission, Binet and Simon published an intelligence scale in 1905 that was aimed at developing methods to identify children who would not benefit from regular education. Following a series of refinements to the scale made in the early 1900s, Terman and his colleagues at Stanford (Terman, 1916) introduced a well-standardized revision and extension of the scale to the United States. Although the methodology for test development was improving during this time, the primary focus of intelligence testing continued to be the identification of intellectual deficiency.

The entry of the United States into World War I created a need for intelligence measures to screen recruits. The Army Alpha, which included a large verbal component, was created to serve this purpose. The limited literacy of some recruits presented the need for a nonverbal measure of intelligence, and the Army Beta was subsequently developed (Thorndike, 1997). Addressing the need for verbal and nonverbal measures of intelligence, Wechsler's original intelligence test, the *Wechsler–Bellevue Intelligence Scale* (WB; Wechsler, 1939), yielded scores for both verbal and performance scales in addition to an overall composite score. The WB was also innovative because it provided deviation IQ scores that were based on standard scores computed with the same distributional characteristics at all ages.

In the 1950s, intelligence testing began to focus on measuring more discrete aspects of an individual's cognitive functioning. Concurrent advances in factor-analytic techniques were applied to measures of mental abilities to further clarify the nature of intelligence. Cattell, a student of Spearman, introduced the theory that intelligence was composed of two general factors: fluid intelligence (*Gf*) and crystallized intelligence (*Gc*; Cattell, 1941, 1957). Horn later expanded on Cattell's original *Gf-Gc* theory to include visual perception, short-term memory, long-term storage and retrieval, speed of processing, auditory processing ability, quantitative ability, and reading and writing ability factors (Horn, 1985, 1988, 1991; Horn & Noll, 1997). As researchers identified more discrete domains of intelligence, the interpretation of intelligence tests began to emphasize the individual's performance in more narrow domains of cognitive functioning, as well as possible differences in the developmental trajectories of these domains (Carroll, 1993; Goldstein & Hersen, 2000; Kaufman & Lichtenberger, 2006; Keith, 1985, 1990).

Much of the debate over intellectual assessment during the last 70 years has focused on the existence of an underlying, global aspect of intelligence that influences an individual's performance across cognitive domains (Gustafsson & Undheim, 1996; Jensen, 1998). Based on the most comprehensive factor-analytic investigation of cognitive ability measures to date, Carroll (1993, 1997) concluded that the evidence for a general factor of intelligence was overwhelming. Thus, the trend toward an emphasis on multiple, more narrowly defined cognitive abilities has not resulted in rejection of an underlying, global aspect of general intelligence. Despite continuing debate over the existence of a single, underlying construct of intelligence, the results of factor-analytic research converge in the identification of 8 to 10 broad domains of intelligence (Carroll, 1993, 1997; Horn & Noll, 1997). Currently, intelligence is widely viewed as having a hierarchical structure, with more specific abilities comprising several broad cognitive domains.

For a more comprehensive review of historical and contemporary developments in intelligence theory, consult Sternberg's (2000) *Handbook of Intelligence* and Goldstein and Beers (2003) *Comprehensive Handbook of Psychological Assessment, Volume 1: Intellectual and Neuropsychological Assessment.*

Wechsler Scales in Historical and Theoretical Perspective

The evolution of the *Wechsler Adult Intelligence Scale–Fourth Edition* (WAIS–IV) began with the WB. Wechsler based this test on the premise that intelligence is a *global* entity because it characterizes the individual's behavior as a whole, and it is also *specific* because it is composed of elements or abilities that are distinct from each other. Based on his clinical expertise, Wechsler selected and developed subtests that highlighted the cognitive aspects of intelligence he thought were important to measure: verbal comprehension, abstract reasoning, perceptual organization, quantitative reasoning, memory, and processing speed. All of these areas have been confirmed as important aspects of cognitive ability in more contemporary theories and measures of intelligence (Carroll, 1993, 1997; Horn, 1991).

Research indicates that intelligence is composed of specific abilities that appear to cluster into higher-order cognitive ability domains (Carroll, 1993; Keith, 1990). Some researchers have presumed that because Wechsler split subtests into verbal and performance tasks, he assumed a two-factor structure of intelligence. However, Wechsler (1958) clarified the practical purpose of the split by noting:

> [The grouping of subtests into Verbal and Performance areas]. . . does not imply that these are the only abilities involved in the tests. . . . The subtests are different measures of intelligence, not measures of different kinds of intelligence, and the dichotomy of Verbal and Performance areas is only one of several ways in which the tests could be grouped. (p. 64)

More recent revisions of the Wechsler intelligence scales have enhanced the measure of more discrete domains of cognitive functioning (e.g., working memory, processing speed) while continuing to provide a reliable measure of global intelligence (i.e., FSIQ). Although there are distinct advantages to the assessment and division of more narrow domains of cognitive functioning, several issues deserve note. First, cognitive functions are interrelated, functionally and neurologically, making it difficult to measure a pure domain of cognitive functioning. Even traditional measures of narrow domains, such as processing speed, involve the ability of individuals to comprehend verbal instruction, discriminate between visual stimuli, process the information, and indicate their response by performing a motoric function. Although the results of factor analytic studies suggest the presence or absence of a measured domain, the results may not capture the variety of cognitive abilities required to complete a subtest task. Subtest factor loadings differ based on the composition and combination of subtests, so claims about what a subtest measures also vary based on the mix of subtests included in the analysis.

Second, it is ecologically valid to include subtests that require the use of multiple cognitive abilities. Cognitive tasks are rarely, if ever, performed in isolation. As Wechsler (1975) noted:

> . . . the attributes and factors of intelligence, like the elementary particles in physics, have at once collective and individual properties, that is, they appear to behave differently when alone from what they do when operating in concert. (p.138)

The ecological validity of general intelligence is supported by the evidence of its ability to predict such things as job performance and overall psychological well-being. Measures of more specific domains of cognitive and personality functioning do not show the same degree of predictive ability (Gottfredson, 2008). Measuring psychometrically pure factors of discrete domains may be useful for research, but it does not necessarily result in information that is clinically rich or practical in real world applications (Zachary, 1990).

Third, it would be unreasonable to expect any single measure of intelligence to adequately test all domains in a meaningful and practical way (Carroll, 1997). Wechsler was successful in selecting measures that sampled a wide variety of domains (e.g., verbal comprehension, perceptual organization, memory), which have since proven to be important aspects of cognitive functioning and have been included as more discrete domains in revisions of the Wechsler scales. He also realized the possibility of obtaining invalid test results when examiners or examinees became fatigued. He selected a sufficient number of subtests to provide clinically meaningful information regarding an individual's cognitive functioning in a reasonable time period. Wechsler believed that other related factors, such as academic achievement and motor skills, may influence performance on intelligence tests but are best measured by instruments designed specifically to assess these domains. His sensitivity to the practical aspects of intelligence testing is evidenced in his development of a separate memory scale (Wechsler, 1945).

Finally, performance on measures of cognitive ability reflects only a portion of what comprises intelligence. Wechsler (1944) defined intelligence as the "capacity of the individual to act purposefully, to think rationally, and to deal effectively with his environment" (p. 3). He avoided defining intelligence in purely cognitive terms because he believed that these factors only comprised a portion of intelligence. Wechsler was keenly aware that the results of factor-analytic studies accounted for only a portion of what comprises intelligence, and he believed that another group of attributes contributed to intelligent behavior. These attributes included planning and goal awareness, enthusiasm, field dependence and independence, impulsiveness, anxiety, and persistence. Such attributes are not directly tapped by standardized measures of intellectual ability, yet they influence an individual's performance on these measures and his or her effectiveness in daily living and meeting the world and its challenges (Wechsler, 1975).

The clinician should view each individual as unique and take into account attributes other than intelligence when interpreting test results (Kaufman & Lichtenberger, 2006; Matarazzo, 1972, 1990). It is widely recognized that individuals with similar test scores may not cope equally well with similar environmental challenges for reasons unrelated to their cognitive abilities. Conversely, because factors unrelated to intelligence influence test performance, individuals with different underlying levels of intellectual ability could achieve similar scores. The task of assessing an individual's intelligence necessarily involves more than simply obtaining his or her scores on measures of intelligence. As Wechsler (1975) noted:

What we measure with tests is not what tests measure—not information, not spatial perception, not reasoning ability. These are only a means to an end. What intelligence tests measure is something much more important: the capacity of an individual to understand the world about him and his resourcefulness to cope with its challenges. (p. 139)

Further support of a theoretical basis in the Wechsler scales is evident in the appearance of the same or similar subtests in other measures of intelligence, and the high correlation of Wechsler intelligence scales with other measures of cognitive ability. Many of the original subtests (e.g., Block Design and Vocabulary) continue to appear in a modified form on current measures of intellectual ability with claims of strong foundations in intelligence theory. Similarly, evidence of the scale's validity is supported by its correlations with other measures of cognitive ability (e.g., *Kaufman Adolescent and Adult Intelligence Test* [Kaufman & Kaufman, 1993]; *Stanford-Binet Intelligence Scales, Fifth Edition* [Roid, 2003]; *Woodcock-Johnson III Tests of Cognitive Abilities* [Woodcock, McGrew, & Mather, 2001]). The high correlations between the Wechsler intelligence scales and other measures of intellectual ability indicate that these instruments are measuring similar constructs.

Almost 70 years of research support the practical and clinical utility of the Wechsler scales across a wide range of settings and purposes. Again and again, the scales have demonstrated their clinical utility for such purposes as the identification of intellectual disability and learning disorders, placement in specialized programs, clinical intervention, and neuropsychological evaluation (Beres et al., 2000). With such overwhelming evidence of clinical utility, it is hard to accept, as some have asserted, that "it is a matter of luck that many of the Wechsler subtests are neurologically relevant" (McFie, 1975, p. 14), or that Wechsler did not have remarkable insight into the nature of intelligence when selecting and developing the subtests for his scales.

Cognitive Ability Test Performance From Adolescence to Adulthood

The WAIS–IV age range (i.e., 16:0–90:11) encompasses profound changes in cognitive abilities. These changes have been described by numerous authors, including Kaufman and Lichtenberger (2006), Lezak, Howieson, and Loring (2004), and Salthouse (2004), among others. Age-related declines in processing speed, executive functioning, sensory acuity, psychomotor ability, working memory, attention, memory, and a host of other variables are interrelated and likely influence results of studies that examine age-related cognitive decline. Understanding age-related cognitive decline and determining cause and effect is therefore quite difficult (Kaufman & Lichtenberger).

Although age-related declines in cognitive test performance appear as early as ages 20–29 (Kaufman, 2000; Salthouse, 2004), the most striking changes are observed following age 55. Declines in cognitive test performance do not necessarily translate to impaired daily activities (see Lezak et al., 2004). Salthouse also notes that the everyday consequences of cognitive decline can be minimized by numerous other factors, such as experience, adaptation to the environment, and conative variables (e.g., motivation and persistence) that Wechsler also viewed as important to intellectual functioning (Tulsky et al., 2003). Cognitive test performance must therefore be interpreted in the context of behavioral observations and other available data. Normative data should reflect the individual's performance relative to his or her same-age peers to prevent interpretive errors (Lezak et al., 2004).

Age-related cognitive decline differs according to cognitive domain. Over the ages spanned by the WAIS–IV, verbal abilities appear to rise gradually and slightly beginning at age 16, peak at approximately age 50, and show small, gradual decreases after age 55 (Kaufman, 2000; Ryan, Sattler, & Lopez, 2000; Salthouse, 2004). Relative to other abilities, verbal ability is relatively preserved across the WAIS–IV age range (Kaufman; Kaufman & Lichtenberger, 2006; Salthouse).

Performance on perceptual tasks involving visual perception, visuospatial abilities, and fluid reasoning rapidly and steadily declines with age. Performance on such measures begins to decline in the mid-30s (Kaufman, 2000; Kaufman & Lichtenberger, 2006; Ryan et al., 2000), with more precipitous drops beginning between ages 50 and 60 (Salthouse, 2004). Some have argued that this decline is related to slowed processing speed because many measures of visuospatial ability and reasoning are timed (see Lezak et al., 2004 and Kaufman & Lichtenberger, 2006 for discussion). However, the decline is also evident on untimed reasoning tasks and perceptual tasks that do not award bonus points for speed (Kaufman; Kaufman & Lichtenberger; Ryan et al.; Salthouse). Furthermore, some timed tasks involving working memory do not show such precipitous decline as timed perceptual tasks (Kaufman & Lichtenberger).

Tasks involving working memory appear to decline less precipitously with age, and the decline begins at an older age relative to perceptual tasks: that is, the decline begins after age 45 (Kaufman, 2000; Kaufman & Lichtenberger, 2006; Ryan et al., 2000). The WAIS–IV working memory tasks are verbal in mode of presentation; it is therefore noteworthy that differential decline of verbal and visuospatial working memory tasks has been observed in healthy aging adults, with visuospatial tasks evidencing a greater decline than verbal tasks (Jenkins, Myerson, Joerding, & Hale, 2000).

Among the abilities measured by the WAIS–IV, declines in processing speed performance are most consistently related to aging (Kaufman & Lichtenberger, 2006; Lezak et al., 2004). A steady decrease in processing speed performance begins at age 20, followed by a more precipitous drop beginning at age 35 (Kaufman, 2000; Kaufman & Lichtenberger; Ryan et al., 2000). Related research indicates that declines in processing speed ability may be related to age-related differences in other measures of cognitive ability, such as fluid reasoning and working memory (Lindenberger, Mayr, & Kliegl, 1993; Salthouse, 1996, 2000; Salthouse & Ferrer-Caja, 2003).

The WAIS–IV addresses a broad range of ages, and ensuring that a test meets the needs of individuals ages 16–90 is a challenging task for test developers. Many functions, including hearing, visual acuity, psychomotor ability, response speed, and visual processing speed, decline with increasing age (Lezak et al., 2004; Storandt, 1994). The WAIS–IV was designed to reduce the potential impact of these declines on test performance in order to provide a clear sense of an adult's intellectual functioning. Specific design goals related to these functional declines are described in chapter 2.

WAIS–IV Structure, Content, and Revision Goals

The Wechsler intelligence scales have been frequently revised over the last 70 years to incorporate advances in the field of intellectual assessment and to update norms to reflect population changes, as well as to meet the practical and clinical needs of contemporary society. The development of the WAIS–IV continues this trend. The chapter begins with an overview of the WAIS–IV predecessors. The revised structure of the WAIS–IV, as well as the revised subtest content, are then reviewed. The chapter concludes with a review of the goals that guided this revision of the scale.

Predecessors of the WAIS–IV

The original *Wechsler Adult Intelligence Scale* (WAIS; Wechsler, 1955) was an extension and modification of the WB. Whereas the WB provided norms derived from testing adults in a small geographic area, the WAIS provided adult norms derived from a nationally stratified sample based on U.S. Census Bureau data. The WAIS retained all 11 WB subtests (i.e., Information, Comprehension, Arithmetic, Similarities, Digit Span, Vocabulary, Digit Symbol, Picture Completion, Block Design, Picture Arrangement, and Object Assembly); however, a number of items were dropped, many new items were added, and changes were made to administration and scoring rules. The subtests were organized into Verbal and Performance scales, and scores for Verbal IQ (VIQ), Performance IQ (PIQ), and Full Scale IQ (FSIQ) were provided.

The *Wechsler Adult Intelligence Scale—Revised* (WAIS–R; Wechsler, 1981) retained all 11 subtests from the first edition. A number of items were dropped, many new items were added, and changes were made to administration and scoring rules (e.g., increased teaching and prompts, awarding bonus points for quick, perfect performance). No new subtests were introduced, and the revised instrument continued to provide VIQ, PIQ, and FSIQ scores. The older age groups (65–69 and 70–74) were more closely matched to the census data than comparable groups in the WAIS.

The *Wechsler Adult Intelligence Scale—Third Edition* (WAIS–III; Wechsler, 1997a) retained all 11 subtests from the WAIS–R and introduced three new subtests: Matrix Reasoning, a measure of perceptual organization (now termed *perceptual reasoning*); Letter–Number Sequencing, a measure of working memory; and Symbol Search, a measure of processing speed. Two new optional procedures, Digit Symbol—Incidental Learning and Digit Symbol—Copy, were included. In addition to the traditional VIQ, PIQ, and FSIQ scores, the WAIS–III introduced four new index scores representing more narrow domains of cognitive function (i.e., the Verbal Comprehension Index, the Perceptual Organization Index, the Working Memory Index, and the Processing Speed Index).

Structure of the WAIS–IV

The four-index framework of the WAIS–IV is similar to that introduced in the *Wechsler Intelligence Scale for Children–Fourth Edition* (WISC–IV; Wechsler, 2003). Like the WISC–IV, the WAIS–IV provides a measure of general intellectual functioning (FSIQ) and four index scores. The dual IQ (Verbal and Performance) and index score structure of the WAIS–III is no longer utilized. The new framework is based on current intelligence theory and supported by clinical research and factor-analytic results (see chapter 5 for factor-analytic support).

The test framework of the WAIS–IV is organized into four index scales: Verbal Comprehension, Perceptual Reasoning, Working Memory, and Processing Speed. The subtests within a scale are used to derive the corresponding index score (i.e., Verbal Comprehension Index, Perceptual Reasoning Index, Working Memory Index, Processing Speed Index). Each index scale contributes to the Full Scale, which is used to derive the FSIQ. Figure 2.1 depicts the test framework of the WAIS–IV, including the subtest composition of the scales.

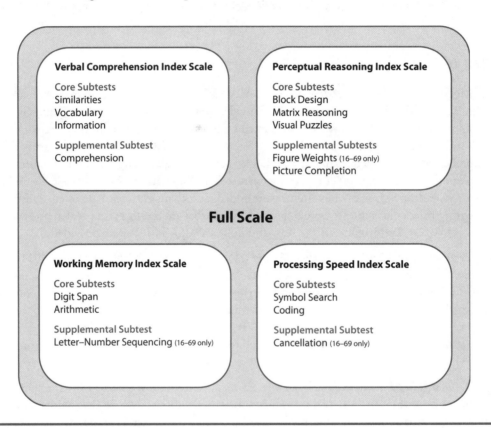

Figure 2.1   Test Framework of the WAIS–IV

Subtests are identified as core or supplemental. Core subtests are administered when composite scores are desired. Supplemental subtests extend the range of cognitive skills sampled, provide additional clinical information, and enable the practitioner to complete additional discrepancy analyses. When necessary, supplemental subtests can also be used as substitutes for core subtests when deriving composite scores. Table 2.1 provides a list of core and supplemental subtests, along with their abbreviations.

Table 2.1   Abbreviations for WAIS–IV Subtests

Core Subtest	Abbreviation
Block Design	BD
Similarities	SI
Digit Span	DS
Matrix Reasoning	MR
Vocabulary	VC
Arithmetic	AR
Symbol Search	SS
Visual Puzzles	VP
Information	IN
Coding	CD

Supplemental Subtest	Abbreviation
Letter–Number Sequencing	LN
Figure Weights	FW
Comprehension	CO
Cancellation	CA
Picture Completion	PCm

The Verbal Comprehension scale includes three core subtests (Similarities, Vocabulary, and Information) and one supplemental subtest (Comprehension). The Perceptual Reasoning scale includes three core subtests (Block Design, Matrix Reasoning, and Visual Puzzles) and two supplemental subtests (Figure Weights and Picture Completion). The Working Memory scale includes two core subtests (Digit Span and Arithmetic) and one supplemental subtest (Letter–Number Sequencing). The Processing Speed scale includes two core subtests (Symbol Search and Coding) and one supplemental subtest (Cancellation).

Whenever possible, core subtests should be administered when composite scores (e.g., Verbal Comprehension Index, Perceptual Reasoning Index, FSIQ) are desired. Occasionally, the scores obtained on core subtests may be invalidated due to factors such as administration errors, recent exposure to test items, physical limitations or sensory deficits, or response sets (e.g., the examinee provides the same response or says "I don't know" to all items on a subtest).

When the score for a core subtest is invalid, the score for a supplemental subtest may be substituted when deriving composite scores. Letter–Number Sequencing, Figure Weights, and Cancellation are supplemental subtests only for examinees ages 16:0–69:11. Scores for these supplemental subtests are not available for examinees ages 70:0–90:11. Chapter 2 of the Administration and Scoring Manual provides guidelines regarding the substitution of supplemental subtests for core subtests when deriving composite scores.

Composite Scores

Users of the WAIS–III should note the change in terminology for composite scores. These modifications in nomenclature are designed to more accurately reflect the configuration of contributing subtests and the cognitive abilities assessed by each composite. The VIQ and the PIQ have been replaced with Verbal Comprehension Index (VCI) and Perceptual Reasoning Index (PRI), respectively. ***The terms VCI and PRI should be substituted for the terms VIQ and PIQ in clinical decision-making and other situations where VIQ and PIQ were previously used.*** The VCI is composed of subtests measuring verbal abilities that require reasoning, comprehension, and conceptualization, and the PRI is composed of subtests measuring nonverbal reasoning and perceptual organization. The Working Memory Index is composed of subtests measuring working memory (specifically, simultaneous and sequential processing), attention, and concentration. The Processing Speed Index is composed of subtests measuring the speed of mental and graphomotor processing. Abbreviations for the WAIS–IV composite scores are shown in Table 2.2.

Table 2.2   Composite Score Abbreviations

Composite Score	Abbreviation
Verbal Comprehension Index	VCI
Perceptual Reasoning Index	PRI
Working Memory Index	WMI
Processing Speed Index	PSI
Full Scale IQ	FSIQ

In addition to the five composite scores, the General Ability Index (GAI) is included as an optional composite score. The GAI is derived from the sum of scaled scores for the three Verbal Comprehension and three Perceptual Reasoning subtests, providing a summary score that is less sensitive than the FSIQ to the influence of working memory and processing speed.

In general, the FSIQ is considered the most valid measure of overall cognitive ability. Working memory and processing speed are vital to the comprehensive evaluation of cognitive ability, and excluding measures of these abilities from a summary score reduces its breadth of construct coverage. In the presence of neuropsychological deficits, however, performance on the Working Memory and Processing Speed subtests that contribute to the FSIQ is more likely to be impaired than performance on the Verbal Comprehension and Perceptual Reasoning subtests. In these situations, impaired performance on the Working Memory and Processing Speed subtests may mask actual differences between general cognitive ability (represented by the FSIQ) and other cognitive functions (e.g., memory). The GAI was developed specifically to help clinicians with the identification of relative strengths and weaknesses that are based on comparisons between ability and other cognitive functions. The GAI does not replace the FSIQ, but it should be reported and interpreted along with the FSIQ and all index scores, including the WMI and PSI. Refer to Appendix C for additional discussion on the appropriate use and interpretation of the WAIS–IV GAI.

Process Scores

The Boston Process Approach to neuropsychological assessment was pioneered by Heinz Werner (1937) and articulated by Edith Kaplan (1988), who noted that often in neuropsychological evaluations, qualitative interpretation of test performance, analysis of errors, and testing of the limits are as important as the quantitatively derived scores. The process approach to the use of the Wechsler scales was first introduced with the *WAIS–R as a Neuropsychological Instrument* (Kaplan, Fein, Morris, & Delis, 1991), and more recently applied to the assessment of children in the *Wechsler Intelligence Scale for Children–Fourth Edition Integrated* (Wechsler et al., 2004).

The WAIS–IV provides one process score for Block Design, six process scores for Digit Span, and one process score for Letter–Number Sequencing. These scores are designed to provide more detailed information on the cognitive abilities that contribute to an examinee's subtest performance. Derivation of these scores is based on the examinee's performance on the corresponding subtests, eliminating the need for additional administration procedures. ***Process scores may not be substituted for any subtest score nor contribute to any composite score.*** Table 2.3 lists the process scores and their abbreviations.

Table 2.3   Process Score Abbreviations

Process Score	Abbreviation
Block Design No Time Bonus	BDN
Digit Span Forward	DSF
Digit Span Backward	DSB
Digit Span Sequencing	DSS
Longest Digit Span Forward	LDSF
Longest Digit Span Backward	LDSB
Longest Digit Span Sequence	LDSS
Longest Letter–Number Sequence	LLNS

The BDN process score is based on the examinee's performance on the Block Design subtest **without** additional time bonus points for rapid completion of items. The DSF, DSB, and DSS process scores reflect an examinee's performance on the three Digit Span tasks; the LDSF, LDSB, and LDSS process scores represent the number of digits recalled on the last correctly completed trial of the Digit Span Forward, Backward, and Sequencing tasks, respectively. The LLNS process score represents the number of digits and letters recalled on the last correctly completed trial of the Letter–Number Sequencing subtest. Additional information on the theoretical rationale and interpretation of process scores is presented in chapter 6.

Subtest Content of the WAIS–IV

General Changes to Subtest Content

A number of modifications to the WAIS–III are represented in the WAIS–IV, including changes to subtest content and administration and scoring procedures. Examiners need to become familiar with these changes in order to provide a standard administration of the scale.

Deleted Subtests

Two subtests from the WAIS–III were dropped in this revision: Picture Arrangement and Object Assembly. The removal of these subtests reduces the emphasis on motor demands and time bonus points. Two optional procedures, Digit Symbol—Incidental Learning and Digit Symbol—Copy, were also deleted in this revision.

Retained Subtests

The 12 subtests retained from the WAIS–III are Block Design, Similarities, Digit Span, Matrix Reasoning, Vocabulary, Arithmetic, Symbol Search, Information, Coding, Letter–Number Sequencing (for ages 16:0–69:11), Comprehension, and Picture Completion. Although the subtests were retained, the item content and administration and/or scoring procedures were revised.

New Subtests

Three new subtests were developed for the WAIS–IV. Visual Puzzles was developed as a Perceptual Reasoning subtest designed to measure nonverbal reasoning and visual perception. A visual variation of the Object Assembly subtest, it is similar to other tasks that are strong measures of nonverbal reasoning and visual perception (e.g., Likert & Quasha, 1995). Figure Weights was developed as a Perceptual Reasoning subtest for ages 16:0–69:11 designed to measure quantitative and analogical reasoning. Cancellation was developed as a supplemental

Processing Speed subtest for ages 16:0–69:11 based on existing versions of similar tasks (e.g., Bate, Mathias, & Crawford, 2001; Geldmacher, Fritsch, & Riedel, 2000; Wechsler, 2003; Wojciulik, Husain, Clarke, & Driver, 2001).

Table 2.4 provides a summary of the subtest modifications from the WAIS–III to the WAIS–IV.

Table 2.4   WAIS–IV Subtest Modifications

	New Subtest	Administration	Recording & Scoring	New Items
Block Design		✓	✓	✓
Similarities			✓	✓
Digit Span		✓	✓	✓
Matrix Reasoning		✓	✓	✓
Vocabulary			✓	✓
Arithmetic		✓	✓	✓
Symbol Search		✓	✓	✓
Visual Puzzles	✓			
Information			✓	✓
Coding			✓	✓
Letter–Number Sequencing		✓	✓	✓
Figure Weights	✓			
Comprehension			✓	✓
Cancellation	✓			
Picture Completion			✓	✓

Subtest Description and Rationale

Verbal Comprehension Subtests

Similarities

Similarities is a core Verbal Comprehension subtest. The examinee is presented two words that represent common objects or concepts and describes how they are similar. It is designed to measure verbal concept formation and reasoning. It also involves crystallized intelligence, abstract reasoning, auditory comprehension, memory, associative and categorical thinking, distinction between nonessential and essential features, and verbal expression (Groth-Marnat, 2003; Kaufman & Lichtenberger, 1999, 2006; Sattler, 2008b).

The Similarities subtest has 18 items, 12 of which are new. Scoring criteria for retained items were revised. A sample item has been added to provide corrective feedback if necessary before beginning the test items. In addition, corrective feedback is now provided for an incorrect response to the start point item and the subsequent item. All items are now scored 0, 1, or 2 points to extend the floor of the subtest.

Vocabulary

Vocabulary is a core Verbal Comprehension subtest. For picture items, the examinee names the object presented visually. For verbal items, the examinee defines words that are presented visually and orally. Vocabulary is designed to measure an examinee's word knowledge and verbal concept formation. It also measures an examinee's crystallized intelligence, fund of knowledge, learning ability, long-term memory, and degree of language development. Other abilities that may be used by the examinee during this task include auditory comprehension and verbal expression (Groth-Marnat, 2003; Kaufman & Lichtenberger, 1999, 2006; Sattler, 2008b).

The Vocabulary subtest has 30 items, including 3 new picture items and 27 verbal items. The picture items were developed to extend the floor of the subtest. Six verbal items are new, and 21 verbal items were retained from the WAIS–III. Scoring criteria were revised for retained verbal items.

Information

Information is a core Verbal Comprehension subtest. The examinee answers questions that address a broad range of general knowledge topics. It is designed to measure an examinee's ability to acquire, retain, and retrieve general factual knowledge. It involves crystallized intelligence and long-term memory. Other skills that may be used include verbal perception, comprehension, and expression (Groth-Marnat, 2003; Kaufman & Lichtenberger, 1999, 2006; Sattler, 2008b).

The Information subtest has 26 items. Eleven items are new, and 15 items were retained from the WAIS–III with little or no change in wording. Scoring criteria for retained items were revised.

Comprehension

Comprehension is a supplemental Verbal Comprehension subtest. The examinee answers questions based on his or her understanding of general principles and social situations. It is designed to measure verbal reasoning and conceptualization, verbal comprehension and expression, the ability to evaluate and use past experience, and the ability to demonstrate practical knowledge and judgment. It also involves crystallized intelligence, knowledge of conventional standards of behavior, social judgment, long-term memory, and common sense (Groth-Marnat, 2003; Kaufman & Lichtenberger, 1999, 2006; Sattler, 2008b).

The Comprehension subtest has 18 items. Nine new items were added, and nine items were retained from the WAIS–III with little or no change in wording. Scoring criteria for retained items were revised. All items are now scored 0, 1, or 2 points to extend the floor of the subtest.

Perceptual Reasoning Subtests

Block Design

Block Design is a core Perceptual Reasoning subtest. Working within a specified time limit, the examinee views a model and a picture, or a picture only, and uses red-and-white blocks to re-create the design. It is designed to measure the ability to analyze and synthesize abstract visual stimuli. It also involves nonverbal concept formation and reasoning, broad visual intelligence, fluid intelligence, visual perception and organization, simultaneous processing, visual-motor coordination, learning, and the ability to separate figure-ground in visual stimuli (Carroll, 1993; Groth-Marnat, 2003; Kaufman & Lichtenberger, 1999, 2006; Sattler, 2008b).

The Block Design subtest has 14 items. Ten items from the WAIS–III were retained, and four new items were added to improve the difficulty gradient. Instructions have been shortened to reduce testing time and to increase user-friendliness, and all items are presented in the Stimulus Book (i.e., the WAIS–III model-only items are now administered using both a model and a visual stimulus). The number of items with time bonus points (i.e., 6) has been reduced relative to the number of time bonus items on the WAIS–III Block Design subtest (i.e., 8). In addition, the BDN process score was included to reflect performance without additional time bonus points.

Matrix Reasoning

Matrix Reasoning is a core Perceptual Reasoning subtest. The examinee views an incomplete matrix or series and selects the response option that completes the matrix or series. It involves fluid intelligence, broad visual intelligence, classification and spatial ability, knowledge of part-whole relationships, simultaneous processing, and perceptual organization (Groth-Marnat, 2003; Kaufman & Lichtenberger, 1999, 2006; Sattler, 2008b).

Only two item types are retained on the WAIS–IV version of this subtest, compared to the four item types included in the WAIS–III. The number of item types was reduced to allow for effective and efficient teaching. Explicit instructions are included for all examinees to teach the problem-solving strategy for successful performance.

The Matrix Reasoning subtest has 26 items. Twelve items from the WAIS–III were retained, and 14 items are new.

Visual Puzzles

Visual Puzzles is a core Perceptual Reasoning subtest. Working within a specified time limit, the examinee views a completed puzzle and selects three response options that, when combined, reconstruct the puzzle. It is a new subtest designed to measure nonverbal reasoning and the ability to analyze and synthesize abstract visual stimuli. Similar measures, such as Object Assembly and the *Revised Minnesota Paper Form Board Test* (Likert & Quasha, 1995), involve visual perception, broad visual intelligence, fluid intelligence, simultaneous processing, spatial visualization and manipulation, and the ability to anticipate relationships among parts (Carroll, 1993; Groth-Marnat, 2003; Kaufman & Lichtenberger, 1999, 2006; Likert & Quasha, 1995; Sattler, 2008b).

The Visual Puzzles subtest has 26 items.

Figure Weights

Figure Weights is a supplemental Perceptual Reasoning subtest for ages 16:0–69:11. Working within a specified time limit, the examinee views a scale with missing weight(s) and selects the response option that keeps the scale balanced. It is a new subtest designed to measure quantitative and analogical reasoning. Quantitative reasoning tasks involve reasoning processes that can be expressed mathematically, emphasizing inductive or deductive logic (Carroll, 1993). Although Figure Weights involves working memory to some extent, it reduces this involvement relative to typical quantitative tasks (e.g., the Arithmetic subtest) through the visual presentation of items in a stimulus book.

The Figure Weights subtest has 27 items.

Picture Completion

Picture Completion is a supplemental Perceptual Reasoning subtest. Working within a specified time limit, the examinee views a picture with an important part missing and identifies the missing part. It is designed to measure visual perception and organization, concentration, and visual recognition of essential details of objects (Groth-Marnat, 2003; Kaufman & Lichtenberger, 1999, 2006; Sattler, 2008b).

All artwork for this subtest has been redrawn and enlarged. Scoring criteria were reviewed and modified to distinguish between those verbal responses that deserve credit, and those that require clarification with a pointing response.

The Picture Completion subtest has 24 items, including 15 retained items from the WAIS–III.

Working Memory Subtests

Digit Span

Digit Span is a core Working Memory subtest composed of three tasks: Digit Span Forward, Digit Span Backward, and Digit Span Sequencing. For Digit Span Forward, the examinee is read a sequence of numbers and recalls the numbers in the same order. For Digit Span Backward, the examinee is read a sequence of numbers and recalls the numbers in reverse order. For Digit Span Sequencing, the examinee is read a sequence of numbers and recalls the numbers in ascending order.

The shift from one Digit Span task to another requires cognitive flexibility and mental alertness. Digit Span Forward involves rote learning and memory, attention, encoding, and auditory processing. Digit Span Backward involves working memory, transformation of information, mental manipulation, and visuospatial imaging (Groth-Marnat, 2003; Reynolds, 1997; Sattler, 2008b). Digit Span Sequencing is similar to other tasks that are designed to measure working memory and mental manipulation (MacDonald, Almor, Henderson, Kempler, & Andersen, 2001; Werheid, Hoppe, Thöne, Müller, Müngersdorf, & Cramon, 2002).

Digit Span Sequencing was developed to increase the working memory demands of the Digit Span subtest relative to the previous version, in response to research indicating different cognitive demands for the Digit Span Forward and Digit Span Backward tasks (e.g., Banken, 1985; Reynolds, 1997). The total raw score for Digit Span is now based on Digit Span Forward, Digit Span Backward, and Digit Span Sequencing. Digit Span Forward must be administered, as pilot study data indicated the omission of this task results in lower Digit Span Backward scores for some examinees (possibly due to the loss of instructional progression). Retaining Digit Span Forward also ensures sufficient floor items for examinees with intellectual disability or general intellectual deficiency.

Each item of Digit Span Forward, Digit Span Backward, and Digit Span Sequencing is composed of two trials with the same span length. There are 8 items in each task. Eleven trials from the WAIS–III were retained in Digit Span Forward and 5 were retained in Digit Span Backward. Five trials for Digit Span Forward and nine trials for Digit Span Backward were modified to more evenly distribute the use of each of the nine digits and to minimize or eliminate intratrial repetition of digits with phonetic similarity (i.e., the number 9 and the number 5). Two new trials were developed for Digit Span Backward to extend the floor of the task. The three-digit sample item for Digit Span Backward was eliminated in favor of a two-digit sample item to provide the examinee additional opportunity to shift instructional set before increasing span length.

The DSF, DSB, DSS, LDSF, LDSB, and LDSS process scores were added to provide additional information about the examinee's Digit Span performance (e.g., Banken, 1985; Harvey, Reischenberg, Romero, Granholm, & Siever, 2006).

Arithmetic

Arithmetic is a core Working Memory subtest. Working within a specified time limit, the examinee mentally solves a series of arithmetic problems. It involves mental manipulation, concentration, attention, short- and long-term memory, numerical reasoning ability, and mental alertness. It may also involve sequential processing; fluid, quantitative, and logical reasoning; and quantitative knowledge (Groth-Marnat, 2003; Kaufman & Lichtenberger, 1999, 2006; Sattler, 2008b).

The Arithmetic subtest consists of 22 items. Twelve items involve the same numerical calculations as items on the WAIS–III: The content of 11 of these items was revised to eliminate references to currency and to English system units of measurement. These modifications were designed to increase applicability across different cultures and countries and to eliminate modifications necessitated by changing consumer price indexes. The content of one item from the WAIS–III was retained and slightly reworded to improve clarity. The three WAIS–III items that required presentation of blocks were eliminated in favor of new picture items. Nine new items were developed to improve the floor, ceiling, and difficulty gradient. All items were reviewed and revised, as necessary, to increase working memory demands while simultaneously holding constant or reducing the mathematical knowledge required to complete the subtest. Explicit instruction on requesting repetition is now given to all examinees. Time bonuses were eliminated.

Letter–Number Sequencing

Letter–Number Sequencing is a supplemental Working Memory subtest for ages 16:0–69:11. The examinee is read a sequence of numbers and letters and recalls the numbers in ascending order and the letters in alphabetical order. The task involves sequential processing, mental manipulation, attention, concentration, memory span, and short-term auditory memory. It may also involve information processing, cognitive flexibility, and fluid intelligence (Crowe, 2000; Groth-Marnat, 2003; Kaufman & Lichtenberger, 1999, 2006; Sattler, 2008b).

The Letter–Number Sequencing subtest consists of 10 items with three trials each. One trial from the WAIS–III was retained, and the remaining 29 trials are new. Trials for initial items were revised to improve the floor by incorporating the use of smaller numbers and letters close to the beginning of the alphabet, both of which are more likely to be automatized. Trials were also revised to improve the difficulty gradient of the subtest, to more evenly distribute the use of numbers and letters, and to eliminate intratrial repetition of numbers and letters with phonetic similarities (e.g., the letter *B* and the letter *C*, the letter *B* and the number *3*). The examinee is now taught the task in a stepwise manner (i.e., first, to repeat numbers before letters, and second, to sequence the repeated numbers and letters). As a result, the subtest includes two new demonstration items and two new sample items.

The LLNS process score was added to provide additional information about the examinee's Letter–Number Sequencing performance.

Processing Speed Subtests

Symbol Search

Symbol Search is a core Processing Speed subtest. Working within a specified time limit, the examinee scans a search group and indicates whether one of the symbols in the target group matches. In addition to processing speed, the subtest involves short-term visual memory, visual-motor coordination, cognitive flexibility, visual discrimination, psychomotor speed, speed of mental operation, attention, and concentration. It may also measure auditory comprehension, perceptual organization, fluid intelligence, and planning and learning ability (Groth-Marnat, 2003; Kaufman & Lichtenberger, 1999, 2006; Sattler, 2008b).

The Symbol Search subtest was revised to require examinees to mark the selected search group symbol or the NO box to allow for additional qualitative observation of examinee errors (e.g., marked a similar symbol, marked a rotated symbol in error). Verbatim instructions have been simplified, and symbols were enlarged to reduce visual acuity demands.

The Symbol Search subtest has 60 items.

Coding

Coding is a core Processing Speed subtest. Using a key, the examinee copies symbols that are paired with numbers within a specified time limit. In addition to processing speed, the subtest measures short-term visual memory, learning ability, psychomotor speed, visual perception, visual-motor coordination, visual scanning ability, cognitive flexibility, attention, concentration, and motivation. It may also involve visual sequential processing and fluid intelligence (Groth-Marnat, 2003; Kaufman & Lichtenberger, 1999, 2006; Sattler, 2008b).

Two symbols were retained from the WAIS–III but were paired with different numbers on the key. Four new symbols were introduced to replace more complex symbols. The total number of sample items was increased from four to six to allow additional practice and to ensure exposure to all nine number-symbol pairings prior to proceeding with test items. To enhance the equal item difficulty that is recommended for measures of processing speed, each number now appears twice within each row. The total number of test items was increased from 133 to 135 to accommodate this equal distribution. The symbols and numbers were enlarged to reduce visual acuity demands, and the boxes used to record responses were slightly enlarged to reduce fine motor demands.

Cancellation

Cancellation is a supplemental Processing Speed subtest for ages 16:0–69:11. Working within a specified time limit, the examinee scans a structured arrangement of shapes and marks target shapes. It is similar to previously developed cancellation tasks designed to measure processing speed, visual selective attention, vigilance, perceptual speed, and visual-motor ability (Bate, Mathias, & Crawford, 2001; Geldmacher, Fritsch, & Riedel, 2000; Sattler, 2008b; Wojciulik et al., 2001). Cancellation tasks have been used extensively in neuropsychological settings as measures of visual neglect, response inhibition, and motor perseveration (Adair et al., 1998; Geldmacher et al., 2000; Lezak et al., 2004; Na, Adair, Kang, Chung, Lee, & Heilman, 1999). Relative to the WISC–IV version of Cancellation, the decision-making component of the WAIS–IV Cancellation subtest was designed to place more complex cognitive demands on examinees: The decision-making component requires examinees to discriminate both the color and the shape of stimuli.

The Cancellation subtest has two items.

Revision Goals for the WAIS–IV

Revision goals were based on almost 70 years of research with the Wechsler intelligence scales; advice from experts in the fields of neuropsychology, clinical psychology, adult cognitive development, and school psychology; market research and examiner surveys; and an extensive review of literature in the areas of intelligence theory, intellectual assessment, adult cognitive development, and cognitive neuroscience. The five primary revision goals were to:

- update theoretical foundations,
- increase developmental appropriateness,
- increase user-friendliness,
- enhance clinical utility, and
- improve psychometric properties.

Update Theoretical Foundations

Recent versions of the Wechsler intelligence scales (i.e., *Wechsler Preschool and Primary Scale of Intelligence—Third Edition* [WPPSI–III; Wechsler, 2002b], WISC–IV) have introduced new subtests to improve measurement of fluid reasoning, working memory, and processing speed. The WAIS–IV continues to build upon this work.

Fluid Reasoning

Several theories of cognitive functioning emphasize the importance of fluid reasoning (Carroll, 1997; Cattell, 1943, 1963; Cattell & Horn, 1978; Sternberg, 1995). Tasks that require fluid reasoning involve the process of "manipulating abstractions, rules, generalizations, and logical relationships" (Carroll, 1993, p. 583). In addition to retaining subtests that require fluid reasoning ability (e.g., Similarities and Matrix Reasoning), the WAIS–IV incorporates an additional subtest, Figure Weights, to enhance the measurement of this domain.

Working Memory

Working memory is the ability to actively maintain information in conscious awareness, perform some operation or manipulation with it, and produce a result. Contemporary research has shown that working memory is an essential component of fluid reasoning and other higher order cognitive processes (Buehner, Krumm, Ziegler, & Pluecken, 2006; Kaufman & Lichtenberger, 2006; Ribaupierre & Lecerf, 2006; Salthouse & Pink, 2008; Unsworth & Engle, 2007).

Arithmetic items were revised to decrease demands on verbal comprehension and mathematical knowledge, thus increasing demands on working memory. To increase the working memory demands of the Digit Span subtest, a new task, Digit Span Sequencing, was added to the traditional Forward and Backward tasks. Based on research indicating greater demands on working memory for Digit Span Backward than Digit Span Forward (e.g., de Jonge & de Jong, 1996; Reynolds, 1997), separate process scores were included for these tasks, as well as for Digit Span Sequencing.

Processing Speed

Contemporary research has shown that the speed of information processing is dynamically related to mental capacity (Kail & Salthouse, 1994), reading performance and development (Kail & Hall, 1994), reasoning by the conservation of cognitive resources, and the efficient use of working memory for higher order fluid tasks (Fry & Hale, 1996; Kail, 2000). Processing speed has been identified as an important domain of cognitive functioning in factor-analytic studies of cognitive abilities (Carroll, 1993, 1997; Horn & Noll, 1997), and measures of this domain are included in the WAIS–III, WPPSI–III, and WISC–IV. Moreover, processing speed is sensitive to such neurological conditions as epilepsy, Attention-Deficit/Hyperactivity Disorder, and traumatic brain injury (Donders, 1997).

Processing speed may be especially important to assess in adults because of its relationship to aging (Finkel, Reynolds, McArdle, & Pederson, 2007; Kaufman & Lichtenberger, 2006; Salthouse, 1996, 2000; Salthouse & Ferrer-Caja, 2003). The role of processing speed is believed to be critical in older adults, as the effects of decline appear to be dynamically related to changes in other areas of cognitive performance, including memory and spatial ability (Finkel et al., 2007).

Cancellation, a new subtest on WAIS–IV, was developed to provide a supplemental Processing Speed subtest for ages 16:0–69:11. Similar subtests have been extensively used as part of a comprehensive neuropsychological evaluation.

Increase Developmental Appropriateness

Kaufman and Lichtenberger (2006), Lezak et al. (2004), and Storandt (1994) described the sensory and psychomotor changes that accompany the aging process and concluded that many functions, including hearing, visual acuity, response speed, and visual processing speed decline significantly in the older adult. Several of the WAIS–IV revision goals were directed at addressing these issues for older adults, as well as for younger examinees with similar difficulties.

Explicit Instructions for All Examinees

The use of relatively non-explicit instructions may adversely affect some examinees' understanding of task requirements. During the research phases of development, it was noted that some examinees (e.g., older adults, individuals with intellectual disability, and adults with limited educational opportunities) had less exposure to the task demands of some subtests (e.g., Matrix Reasoning, Figure Weights) than other examinees. Furthermore, a growing body of research suggests older adults experience age-related reductions in attentional resources (Kaufman

& Lichtenberger, 2006). Such decline may result in a need for more explicit instructions and additional teaching and practice opportunities when learning a subtest task.

For these reasons, subtest instructions were modified to ensure that *all* examinees receive the same level of instruction for some subtests, regardless of their performance on sample items. For example, the problem-solving approach for Matrix Reasoning is described whether a correct or incorrect response is provided on the sample item. Subsequent to the modifications, data indicated that the performance of some examinees had been limited by their understanding of the subtest task, rather than their cognitive ability (i.e., examinees' performances improved with additional instruction). The use of standardized, explicit instructions for all examinees ensures that different levels of instruction and different experience with item types do not contribute to differential performance among individuals.

Instructions to clarify the subtest task demands often involve the administration of demonstration and sample items. Demonstration items are completed by the examiner and are designed to explain and to illustrate the subtest task. Sample items are completed by the examinee and allow for practice before proceeding to the test items. Sample items often provide additional opportunities for explaining the task based on the examinee's performance. For those subtests without demonstration or sample items (e.g., Vocabulary and Comprehension), corrective feedback is provided if the examinee does not obtain perfect scores on start point items.

Emphasis on Time Bonuses

Overemphasizing quick task completion may be especially problematic for older adults due to decline in motor functioning and slowed cognitive processing (Lezak et al., 2004; Salthouse, 2004). Related research suggests that some cultures may emphasize the speed of performance to different degrees (Armour-Thomas & Gopaul-McNicol, 1997). The implementation of time limits on some subtests is appropriate and necessary to limit the overall testing time, minimize examinee frustration, and ensure an appropriate range of item difficulty. However, limiting the number of items with time bonus points reduces the possible confound of timed performance on those subtests that are not specifically designed to measure processing speed. For this reason, the number of Block Design items with time bonus points was reduced and the use of time bonuses on Arithmetic was eliminated altogether.

Auditory Discrimination Demands

For any examinee, the examiner should ensure that adequate hearing ability is present prior to administering the WAIS–IV. It is especially important that the examiner address the proper use of assistive listening devices, if applicable.

To reduce possible auditory confounds, the use of phonetically similar digits was minimized as much as possible on Digit Span (i.e., the use of *5* and *9* was necessary for the nine-digit trials of Digit Span Forward). Phonetically similar numbers and letters were eliminated within trials of the Letter–Number Sequencing subtest.

Visual Acuity Demands

Similar to the reduction of auditory discrimination demands, one objective of the WAIS–IV revision was to reduce demands on visual acuity. All of the stimulus book artwork for retained subtests (e.g., Block Design and Picture Completion) was enlarged relative to that of the WAIS–III. Visual acuity issues also were considered when developing artwork for the new subtests with visual stimuli. Similarly, the symbols used in Response Booklet 1 for Symbol Search and Coding are simpler and larger than those used in the WAIS–III versions of these subtests.

Motor Demands

Subtests with motor demands may underestimate the cognitive ability of examinees with motor difficulties and other physical problems (e.g., arthritis, hand tremors). Some examinees can have other physical limitations that may affect performance on subtests with motor demands. For example, use of an oxygen delivery system by an examinee with chronic obstructive pulmonary disease could impede upper body movement. The Picture Arrangement and Object Assembly subtests of the WAIS–III were replaced with new measures of perceptual reasoning that have no motor demands: Visual Puzzles and Figure Weights. Although all WAIS–IV Processing Speed subtests require motoric responses, additional steps were taken to reduce the motor demands of these measures. Relative to Coding, the new Cancellation subtest has reduced demands on fine motor skills and may be substituted as a measure of processing speed for examinees (ages 16:0–69:11) with motor difficulties. Enlarged spaces for examinee responses are provided on Symbol Search and Coding, and four new symbols were selected for the Coding subtest to replace more complex symbols used in the WAIS–III version.

Increase User-Friendliness

Testing Time

The WAIS–III required administration of 13 subtests to obtain the four index scores and FSIQ, with a reported average testing time of 80 minutes. The WAIS–IV requires administration of 10 subtests to obtain the four index scores and FSIQ, with an average testing time of 67 minutes. Administration time of the WAIS–IV varies with the number of subtests administered and the characteristics of the individual, such as age, ability level, motivation, and attention.

More detailed information about testing time is reported in Tables 2.2 and 2.3 of the Administration and Scoring Manual. Table 2.2 provides the time required by various percentages of the normative, Intellectually Gifted, and Intellectual Disability samples to complete the 10 core subtests of the standardization edition. To evaluate whether the testing times for the standardization and final editions were similar, 37 examinees were tested with a beta edition of the WAIS–IV, which included final item sets, start points, and discontinue rules. Table 2.3 in the Administration and Scoring Manual provides the time required by various percentages of the beta sample to complete the 10 core subtests, as well as the 15 core and supplemental subtests. Although the beta sample was not fully stratified on demographic variables, testing times for this sample were consistent with or shorter than those of the normative sample.

In addition to measuring cognitive ability with the WAIS–IV, measurement of such domains as memory, social-emotional functioning, adaptive behavior, or achievement may be necessary. Reduced testing time on the WAIS–IV gives the examiner additional time to measure these important domains with instruments that are designed specifically for their respective purposes.

Discontinue Rules

The discontinue rules for most retained subtests were substantially reduced. For example, the WAIS–III discontinue rule for Vocabulary was 6 consecutive scores of 0 but was reduced to 3 consecutive scores of 0 on the WAIS–IV. The discontinue rules for new subtests were also set to minimize the required number of consecutive scores of 0. The shortened discontinue rules allowed for reduced overall testing time.

Design of Test Materials

The design of some test materials was modified to improve ease of administration and scoring, as well as organization of manual content. The layout of the stimulus books was changed so that pages are turned toward the examinee, which reduces reaching distance for the examiner and possible interference with the examinee's line of vision. The design and organization of manual content, including the order of normative tables in the appendixes, is similar to that of more recent Wechsler intelligence scales. Unlike the combined *WAIS–III/WMS–III Technical and Interpretive Manual*, this manual contains psychometric and technical information for the WAIS–IV only. The Record Form was redesigned to reduce the occurrence of administration and scoring errors. It also incorporates design and organization elements introduced in more recent Wechsler scale record forms, including abbreviated versions of the administration and scoring rules for each subtest and consistent layouts for summary pages.

Enhance Clinical Utility

Special Group Studies

To enhance the scale's clinical utility, 13 special group studies were conducted during WAIS–IV standardization. The studies, which are described in chapter 5, provide initial evidence of clinical validity for the following special groups: Intellectually Gifted, Intellectual Disability-Mild Severity, Intellectual Disability-Moderate Severity, Borderline Intellectual Functioning, Reading Disorder, Mathematics Disorder, Attention-Deficit/Hyperactivity Disorder, Traumatic Brain Injury, Autistic Disorder, Asperger's Disorder, Major Depressive Disorder, Mild Cognitive Impairment, and Probable Dementia of the Alzheimer's Type-Mild Severity.

Statistical Linkage to Measures of Memory

Because memory and intellectual ability are often tested concurrently, the WAIS–IV provides validity studies with the *Wechsler Memory Scale–Third Edition* (WMS–III; Wechsler, 1997b) and the *Children's Memory Scale* (CMS; Cohen, 1997). These pairings enhance the clinical utility of the WAIS–IV by providing more complete information on the relationship between intellectual and memory functioning. Chapter 5 provides details of the WAIS–IV correlational studies with the WMS–III and the CMS.

Like their predecessors, the WAIS–IV and the forthcoming *Wechsler Memory Scale–Fourth Edition* (WMS–IV; Wechsler, in press) research programs overlapped during the standardization stages to allow co-norming. The linkage provides a more complete picture of cognitive functioning in the areas of intellectual ability and memory, and allows for direct comparison of intelligence and memory through normative information. The linkage additionally enables prediction of memory scores on the basis of intellectual ability scores and interpretation of memory scores in the context of intellectual ability scores. Information regarding the co-normative sample, correlations between measures, and analyses relevant to concurrent use of the two scales (e.g., ability-memory discrepancy comparisons and ability-memory contrast scores) will be reported in the *WMS–IV Technical and Interpretive Manual* (Wechsler, in press).

Statistical Linkage to a Measure of Achievement

A sample of examinees, aged 16:0–19:11 and currently enrolled in high school, was administered both the WAIS–IV and the WIAT–II. The linkage provides a more complete picture of cognitive functioning in the areas of intellectual ability and academic achievement, and enables prediction of achievement scores on the basis of intellectual ability scores for examinees ages 16:0–19:11 currently enrolled in high school. Details of the WAIS–IV/WIAT–II linking study, as well as other validity studies, are presented in chapter 5. See chapter 6 and Appendix C for additional information on performing and interpreting ability-achievement discrepancy comparisons.

Statistical Linkage to WAIS–IV/WMS–IV Advanced Clinical Solutions

A sample of examinees aged 16:0–19:11 was administered both the WAIS–IV and the *WAIS–IV/WMS–IV Advanced Clinical Solutions* (Pearson, in press). This linkage provides a number of features that may be particularly useful for practitioners working with special populations (e.g., older adults and neuropsychologically impaired individuals), including demographically adjusted norms; methods for predicting premorbid intellectual functioning; and measures of insufficient effort, executive function, social perception, and daily living skills. Information regarding the linking study will be reported in the *WAIS–IV/WMS–IV Advanced Clinical Solutions Manual* (Pearson, in press).

Improve Psychometric Properties

Norms

Over time, items and scoring rules may become outdated. Outdated items were revised or removed and new items were incorporated to reflect more contemporary ideas and situations. Scoring rules for subtests requiring verbal responses were based on iterative scoring studies throughout development for both new and retained items. Research also suggests that older norms produce inflated scores on intelligence measures (Flynn, 1984, 1987, 1999, 2007; Flynn & Weiss, 2007; Matarazzo, 1972). Test scores should be based on normative information that is both contemporary and representative of the relevant population.

The WAIS–IV normative data was established using a sample collected from March 2007 to April 2008. The sample was stratified on key demographic variables (i.e., age, sex, race/ethnicity, self or parent education level, and geographic region) according to the October 2005 U.S. census data. A complete description of the sampling matrix is provided in chapter 3.

Evidence of Reliability and Validity

A number of concurrent studies were conducted to provide additional evidence of the scale's reliability and validity. Retest data are reported for all ages and for four separate age groups (16–29, 30–54, 55–69, and 70–90). Evidence of the convergent and discriminant validity of the WAIS–IV is provided by correlational studies with the following instruments: WAIS–III, WISC–IV, WMS–III, CMS, WIAT–II, *Brown Attention-Deficit Disorder Scales* (Brown ADD; Brown, 1996), *Delis–Kaplan Executive Function System* (D–KEFS; Delis, Kaplan, & Kramer, 2001), *California Verbal Learning Test—Second Edition* (CVLT–II; Delis, Kramer, Kaplan, & Ober, 2000), and *Repeatable Battery for the Assessment of Neuropsychological Status* (RBANS; Randolph, 1998).

Additional evidence of construct validity was provided through a series of confirmatory factor-analytic studies and mean comparisons using special group samples and matched control samples. Detailed descriptions and results of reliability and validity studies are presented in chapters 4 and 5, respectively.

Floors and Ceilings

Attention to the floors and ceilings of subtests ensures an adequate range of scores to represent a broad range of cognitive ability, from extremely low (i.e., $40 \leq \text{FSIQ} \leq 69$) to very superior (i.e., $130 \leq \text{FSIQ} \leq 160$). To adequately measure this range of ability, items of both low and high difficulty were added to retained subtests as necessary. For example, picture items were added to extend the floor of the Vocabulary subtest, and more difficult items were added to extend the ceiling of the Information subtest. Data were collected on individuals diagnosed with mild or moderate intellectual disability (i.e., mental retardation) according to criteria in the *Diagnostic and Statistical Manual of Mental Disorders,* Fourth Edition, Text Revision (*DSM–IV–TR*; American Psychiatric Association, 2000). Additional data were collected from individuals identified as intellectually gifted. The improved subtest floors and ceilings allow for better discrimination among individuals performing at the extreme ranges of cognitive ability, as well as an extended FSIQ score range of 40–160 (as compared to the WAIS–III FSIQ range of 45–155).

Item Bias

Contemporary methodologies for testing item bias were used for WAIS–IV item selection. Problematic items were deleted on the basis of formal expert review of items and empirical data from statistical and bias analyses. Experts in cross-cultural research and/or intelligence testing conducted formal reviews on three occasions. During the initial stages of the project, all WAIS–III subtests and items were reviewed by internal and external reviewers for potential bias, cultural obsolescence, content relevance, and clinical utility. During the tryout phase, and again during the standardization phase, content and bias experts reviewed the items and identified those that were potentially problematic.

Along with these reviews, empirical data from bias analyses were used to test hypotheses and assist in the item decision process. In order to ensure adequate sample sizes early in development, an oversample was collected during the tryout phase. Results from traditional Mantel-Haenszel bias analysis (Holland & Thayer, 1988) and item response theory (IRT) bias analyses (Hambleton, 1993) provided additional data on potentially problematic items.

Chapter 3

WAIS–IV Research Procedures, Standardization, and Norms Development

The 4-year research program leading to the publication of the WAIS–IV was an iterative process, with each stage of development leading to further refinements of the scale. This chapter reviews this process, beginning with the research procedures used to develop the scale and continuing with an overview of research stages and quality assurance procedures. The chapter concludes with a detailed examination of the standardization stage of the scale's development, including descriptions of the normative sample and norms development.

Research Guidelines

The *Standards for Educational and Psychological Testing* (*Standards*; American Educational Research Association, American Psychological Association, & National Council on Measurement in Education [AERA], 1999) served as a primary resource throughout the WAIS–IV research project and provided criteria for the "evaluation of tests, testing practices, and the effects of test use" (p. 2). Refer to the *Standards* for a comprehensive discussion of these and other issues related to test development and evaluation.

Major Research Stages

Several experimental editions of the WAIS–IV, based on a working blueprint of the scale, were developed prior to establishing the final test framework. Test development occurred in five general stages: conceptual development, pilot, national tryout, standardization, and final assembly and evaluation. The following sections provide brief descriptions of these stages, with a focus on research questions at each stage and the methods used to address these questions.

Conceptual Development Stage

The conceptual development stage was aimed at identifying revision goals and research questions, as well as delineating the method for achieving these objectives. Extensive literature reviews and consultation with customer service representatives from Pearson were conducted to provide an initial set of revision goals. Many additional sources of information provided invaluable guidance in the conceptualization of the WAIS–IV research program.

Market Research

Early in the development process, a telephone survey ($N = 174$) was conducted with WAIS–III users and with other professionals in adult and older adult assessment. The research team, advisory panel, and clinical measurement consultants reviewed the feedback from the telephone survey. Based on the cumulative findings, the working blueprint was established and a research version of the scale was developed for use in the pilot stage. Subsequent online and telephone surveys ($N = 130$ and 20, respectively) were conducted to provide customer perspectives on issues related to the final structure of the scale (e.g., subtest preference, subtest composition of composite scores).

Advisory Panel and Clinical Measurement Consultants

An advisory panel composed of nationally recognized experts in clinical psychology, clinical neuropsychology, and adult cognitive development was assembled to work with the research team throughout the project (see Appendix F for a list of advisory panel members). Clinical measurement consultants from Pearson also aided research team efforts. Following each major research stage (e.g., pilot, national tryout, and standardization), the working blueprint was revised based on psychometric results and feedback from the advisory panel, clinical measurement consultants, and examiners.

Semi-Structured Surveys of Experts and Examiners

Semi-structured surveys of other experts and examiners were conducted at all stages of data collection. The surveys allowed the experts and examiners to rate the research versions of the scale on such qualities as developmental appropriateness, clinical utility, and user-friendliness. Results from these surveys were summarized and discussed with advisory panel members and clinical measurement consultants. At all test development stages, modifications to the working blueprint and research versions of the scale were based on accumulated expert and examiner feedback, as well as qualitative analysis results.

Pilot Stage

The primary goal of the pilot stage was to produce a version of the scale for use in the subsequent national tryout stage. Multiple research questions were addressed through a pilot study ($N = 185$) and 10 mini-pilot studies ($N = 93, 32, 10, 92, 88, 31, 88, 35, 63,$ and 69, respectively). Each of these studies utilized a research version of the scale that included various subtest groupings retained from the WAIS–III and new, experimental subtests that were being considered for inclusion in the national tryout. This stage of development focused on such issues as item content and relevance, adequacy of subtest floors and ceilings, clarity of instructions to the examiner and examinee, identification of response processes, administration procedures, scoring criteria, item bias, and other relevant psychometric properties.

National Tryout Stage

The national tryout stage utilized a version of the scale with 18 subtests. Data were obtained from a stratified sample of 658 examinees who reflected key demographic variables in the national population. An analysis of data gathered by the U.S. Bureau of the Census (2005) provided the basis for stratification along the following variables: age, sex, race/ethnicity, self or parent education level, and geographic region. For each age group, the tryout sample closely approximated the census data for the five demographic variables.

Using this larger, more representative sample of individuals, research questions from the pilot stage were reexamined, and additional issues were addressed. Item order was refined based on more precise estimates of relative item difficulty, and exploratory and confirmatory factor analyses were conducted to determine the scale's underlying factor structure. Additional data were collected from a number of special groups (i.e., individuals identified as intellectually gifted, individuals with intellectual disability, individuals with traumatic brain injury, and individuals with probable Dementia of the Alzheimer's Type-Mild Severity) to provide additional evidence of adequacy of the subtest floors and ceilings, as well as the clinical utility of the scale. An oversample of 73 African American examinees and 96 Hispanic examinees was collected to allow for a statistical examination of item bias using IRT methods of analysis.

Standardization Stage

After reviewing the accumulated evidence from the pilot and national tryout studies, a standardization edition of the WAIS–IV was created. Additional research questions focused on the derivation of norms and the provision of reliability, validity, and clinical utility evidence for the final scale.

Data were obtained from a stratified sample of 2,200 examinees aged 16:0–90:11, as well as samples of individuals from 13 special groups. In order to provide evidence of the scale's validity, additional samples of examinees were administered the WAIS–IV and other measures (i.e., WAIS–III, WISC–IV, WMS–III, CMS, WIAT–II, Brown ADD, portions of D–KEFS, CVLT–II, and RBANS). Detailed demographic information on the normative sample is provided later in this chapter. Descriptions of the samples used in the concurrent validity and special group studies are provided in chapter 5.

Research team members, clinical measurement consultants, and the advisory panel again evaluated the psychometric results of the standardization studies along with reviews completed by experts and examiners. Based on the cumulative evidence from the entire research program, the final test framework was determined in order to assemble and evaluate the final, published version of the scale.

Final Assembly and Evaluation

Consistency of Item Sets, Instructions, and Stimulus Materials

To ensure that an adequate number of quality items remained after item selection, the WAIS–IV research editions included more items than were necessary for the final subtests. Items were evaluated throughout the development process and retained, modified, or deleted. Thus, the subtest item sets had already been evaluated on several occasions prior to the standardization of the scale. The final item selection decisions were based on data from the standardization samples and were primarily designed to eliminate redundant items or items that were either too easy or too difficult. An average of four items per subtest was dropped according to these criteria. Consistency with the standardization item order within subtests was maintained as much as possible. Items designated as start points on the standardization version were maintained as start points on the final version, with the exception of the Similarities subtest. The start point for the standardization version of Similarities was set at Item 1 to ensure an adequate number of responses was obtained to develop final scoring rules for the floor items. Item 4 was selected as the final start point on Similarities to reduce testing time, while ensuring that at least 97% of examinees in the normative sample passed the start point item.

All instructions to the examinee were maintained in identical form on the final version of the scale. No changes were made to stimulus materials.

In order to be sensitive to testing-time concerns for older adults, a smaller subset of WAIS–IV subtests (i.e., Block Design, Similarities, Digit Span, Matrix Reasoning, Vocabulary, Arithmetic, Symbol Search, and Visual Puzzles) was initially administered to examinees aged 65:0–90:11. However, in response to feedback from customers desiring additional flexibility for these ages, 227 examinees from the normative sample, aged 65:0–90:11, were subsequently administered four additional subtests (i.e., Information, Coding, Comprehension, and Picture Completion) in a second testing session to provide normative data for these subtests. Testing intervals ranged from 20–324 days with a mean of 115 days. Examinees with changes in health status or who no longer met inclusion criteria were not administered the additional subtests and were not included in the final normative sample. The mean subtest and composite scores of 122 examinees who were tested in two sessions were compared to the means from a matched control study with 200 iterations (with replacement). For each iteration, a matched control group that was tested on all subtests in a single session was randomly pulled from the normative sample. This iterative procedure was used to reduce the chance occurrence of mean differences due to sample variability. Average mean scores from the 200 iterative samples were compared to mean scores of the sample of examinees tested in two sessions. No significant differences in the mean subtest or composite scores for these groups were noted.

Consistency of Administration Order

Development of the final test framework included determination of subtest type (i.e., core or supplemental), which prompted a minor change to the subtest administration order. To ensure that the core subtests would come before the supplemental subtests in the final administration order, it was necessary to swap the standardization orders for the Information and Comprehension subtests in the final subtest order. A special study was conducted to examine the possible effects of the new testing order using a between-subjects design. The 15 subtests in the proposed final order were administered to 37 examinees aged 16–82. The subtest and composite scores of this group were compared to those of a matched control group of 37 examinees from the normative sample. The comparisons indicated no significant differences in the mean scores for these groups. Mean scores were slightly higher in the standardization sample for both subtests that changed order (Information and Comprehension), indicating no differential effect of administration sequence.

Quality Assurance Procedures

Qualifying Examiners

Examiners with extensive experience testing adults were recruited for all stages of data collection. Potential examiners completed a questionnaire by supplying information about their educational, professional, and assessment experience, as well as information about their certification and licensing status. Those selected as potential standardization examiners were very familiar with adult assessment practices, and most were certified or licensed professionals working in private or public facilities. Potential standardization examiners were provided training materials, including an interactive training CD that contained video components, a summary of common administration and scoring errors, and a training quiz. The training quiz required examiners to respond to questions about administration and scoring rules and to identify common administration and scoring errors. In response to any error on the training quiz, the training CD parameters required the examiner to review standardization materials to obtain accurate information and correct the error. Selected examiners scored 100% correct on the training quiz.

As an oversight measure, examiners were required to submit a review case prior to testing additional examinees. Every attempt was made to discuss administration and scoring errors on the review case with the examiner within 48 hours of its receipt. Subsequent cases were reviewed most often within 72 hours of receipt, and any errors resulting in the loss or inaccuracy of data were discussed with the examiner. A periodic newsletter was sent to all examiners, alerting them to potentially problematic areas.

Quality Assurance of Scoring and Data Entry

All scorers were required to have a bachelor's degree and to attend a training program led by members of the research team. To qualify as a scorer, candidates had to score at least 90% correct on a quiz that required them to identify scoring errors in a fictitious protocol. Due to the subjective nature of scoring verbal subtests, scorers were also evaluated on their ability to assign appropriate codes to verbatim responses. Each test protocol collected during the pilot, national tryout, and standardization stages was rescored and entered into a database by two qualified scorers working independently. Any discrepancies between the two scorers were resolved daily by a third scorer (resolver). The resolvers were selected based on their demonstration of exceptional scoring accuracy and previous scoring experience.

All scorers received feedback on scoring errors and additional training if needed. Over the course of data entry, the average agreement between scorers on the nonverbal subtests exceeded 98%, and the average agreement on the five subtests with verbatim responses (Similarities, Vocabulary, Information, Comprehension, and Picture Completion) exceeded 95%.

To prevent scoring drift, scorers did not discuss scoring rules with other scorers and directed any scoring questions to research team members. More importantly, *anchor protocols* were used to evaluate and correct scoring drift. Anchor protocols were actual protocols that had been scored by the research team. If two independent scorers made the same scoring errors on a protocol, comparison to the anchor score revealed the scoring drift. Scorers received feedback immediately to prevent repetition of the errors and to correct for scoring drift.

Other Quality Assurance Procedures

In addition to the scoring and data entry quality assurance procedures, several other procedures were employed to ensure data handling consistency. A computer program automatically checked the values entered by scorers for contradictory information. For example, a warning appeared if a value fell outside of a specified range. After all protocols were double-scored and discrepancies resolved, a data clean-up team performed additional checks for any remaining out-of-range values or contradictions in scoring information. Members of the research team also randomly selected and rescored multiple protocols and compared the results to the final data file.

Scoring Studies

Throughout the stages of test development, iterative scoring studies were performed on the Matrix Reasoning, Visual Puzzles, and Figure Weights subtests. Analyses of error responses by age and ability level, as well as distractor analyses, were performed to ensure the keyed responses represent the best choice for an item.

Separate scoring studies were conducted at the pilot, national tryout, and standardization stages to refine the scoring criteria of those subtests that require somewhat subjective evaluation of verbatim responses (i.e., Similarities, Vocabulary, Information, Comprehension, and Picture Completion). Each of these scoring studies was conducted using a similar procedure, and results across stages were consistent.

Trained scorers used a specified scoring system to code verbatim responses. The results were then subjected to psychometric analysis and clinical and bias expert review. When the final scoring study was completed, the research team made minor modifications to scoring criteria to eliminate any remaining areas of confusion, to combine responses that were similar in terms of content and point value, and to determine which responses should be retained as sample responses in the Administration and Scoring Manual.

Standardization

Locating and Testing the Samples

Trained recruiters, market research firms, and independent examiners used various approaches to identify individuals who met the specified inclusion criteria of the standardization samples and fit the sampling plan matrix. The trained recruiters visited community organization sites; staffed booths in shopping centers; distributed flyers in neighborhoods; offered self-referral via website, email, or Internet communities of shared interests; and encouraged referrals from other examinees. The market research firms were located in eight U.S. cities in the Northeast, Midwest, South, and West regions. Employees of these firms placed random telephone calls, published newspaper advertisements, and distributed flyers in senior centers and various community organizations. The independent examiners, who were located across the country, identified examinees in numerous ways (e.g., word-of-mouth, referrals from other examinees, posting and distributing flyers). Both examiners and examinees were paid an incentive for their participation in data collection.

Examinee candidates for the normative sample were screened for issues that could possibly affect cognitive test performance. Individuals with potentially confounding issues (e.g., history of stroke, current diagnosis of Major Depressive Disorder) were excluded from participation. Table 3.1 lists the criteria used to disqualify individuals from the normative sample. A representative proportion of individuals from the Intellectually Gifted and Intellectual Disability special group studies was included in the normative sample to accurately represent the population.

Table 3.1   Exclusionary Criteria for the Normative Sample

Primary language is not English

Primarily nonverbal or uncommunicative

Unable to understand instructions and participate fully in testing

Insufficient compliance with testing to ensure a valid assessment

Tested on any intelligence measure in the previous 6 months

Graduate-level training in psychology or familiarity with administration of intelligence tests

Family member or close friend of examiner

Identical sibling (e.g., twin) of another examinee in the sample

Uncorrected visual impairment

Uncorrected hearing loss

Upper extremity disability that would affect motor performance

Currently admitted to hospital or psychiatric facility

Currently taking medication that might impact cognitive test performance (e.g., anticonvulsants, antipsychotics, some antidepressants and anxiolytics)

Significant current or recent functional change related to cognitive status change

Currently receiving chemotherapy, or received chemotherapy in preceding 2 months

History of electroconvulsive therapy or radiation treatment of the central nervous system

Period of unconsciousness greater than 20 minutes related to medical condition

Previously or currently diagnosed with any physical condition or illness that might depress test performance, such as

    Stroke

    Epilepsy

    Brain tumor

    Traumatic brain injury

    Brain surgery

    Encephalitis

    Meningitis

    Attention-Deficit/Hyperactivity Disorder

    Psychotic Disorder

    Parkinson's disease

    Dementia

    Learning Disorder

    Mood Disorder

    Language Disorder

    Substance abuse or dependence

Consistent with the trend toward increased prescription medication use by adults in the U.S. (Cox, Mager, & Wisebart, 2008), many examinee candidates reported medication use that was noted by examiners and evaluated by the research team during early research stages. To reduce ambiguity and summarize previous evaluations of medications, a systematic approach to the evaluation of medication use was implemented during the standardization stage. Of specific interest were those medications with possible side effects that could affect cognitive test performance.

A compiled list of examinee medications reported during the early stages of research was submitted to a psychopharmacologist for further review and evaluation. Based on their potential effect on cognitive test performance, a classification system for the medications was provided at standardization, as well as a brief, self-report measure for the examinee's experience of side effects.

The classification system included three medication groups: excluded, provisionally acceptable, and acceptable. The excluded medications group consisted of medications that *frequently* produce side effects that could interfere with cognitive test performance (e.g., opiates, anticonvulsants, tricyclic antidepressants, and specific anxiolytics). Examinee candidates who had taken excluded medication(s) within 1 week of testing were excluded from participation. The provisionally acceptable medications group included medications that *sometimes* produce side effects that could interfere with cognitive test performance, particularly if taken within hours of testing (e.g., specific antidepressants and antihistamines). Examinee candidates who had taken provisionally acceptable medication(s) within 1 week of testing *and* reported medication-related side effects on the self-report measure were excluded from participation. The acceptable medications group included medications that *do not typically* produce side effects that could interfere with cognitive test performance (e.g., statins, over-the-counter pain relievers).

Description of the Sample

Normative information is based on a national sample representative of the U.S. English-speaking population of individuals aged 16:0–90:11. A stratified sampling plan ensured that the normative sample included representative proportions of individuals according to selected demographic variables. An analysis of data gathered in October 2005 by the U.S. Bureau of the Census provided the basis for stratification along the following variables: age, sex, race/ethnicity, self or parent education level, and geographic region. The following paragraphs present the characteristics of the normative sample.

Age. The normative sample included 2,200 examinees divided into 13 age groups: 16:0–17:11, 18:0–19:11, 20:0–24:11, 25:0–29:11, 30:0–34:11, 35:0–44:11, 45:0–54:11, 55:0–64:11, 65:0–69:11, 70:0–74:11, 75:0–79:11, 80:0–84:11, and 85:0–90:11. Each of the nine younger age groups was composed of 200 participants; each of the four older age groups was composed of 100 participants.

Sex. Except for the five older age groups (65:0–90:11), the normative sample consisted of an equal number of female and male examinees in each age group. The five older age groups included more women than men, in proportions consistent with census data.

Race/Ethnicity. For each age group in the normative sample, the proportions of Whites, African Americans, Hispanics, Asians, and other racial groups were based on the racial proportions of individuals within the corresponding age group of the U.S. population.

Education Level. The sample was stratified according to five education levels based on the number of years of school completed. The five education levels were defined as follows: ≤8 years, 9–11 years, 12 years (high school diploma or equivalent), 13–15 years (some college or associate's degree), and ≥16 years (college or graduate degree). For examinees aged 16–19, parent education was used. For this group, if the examinee reported information for only one parent or guardian, the educational level of that parent or guardian was assigned. However, if the examinee reported information for two parents, a parent and a guardian, or two guardians, the average of both individuals' educational levels was used, with partial levels rounded up to the next highest level.

Geographic Region. The United States was divided into the four major geographic regions specified by the census reports (see Figure 3.1): Northeast (NE), Midwest (MW), South (S), and West (W).

Figure 3.1   Normative Sampling Sites

Representativeness of the Sample

Table 3.2 presents detailed demographic information for the normative sample and the U.S. population according to age group, race/ethnicity, and education level. Table 3.3 shows the percentages of the normative sample and the U.S. population according to age group, sex, and education level. Table 3.4 provides the percentages of the normative sample and the U.S. population by age group, sex, and race/ethnicity, and Table 3.5 reports the percentages of the normative sample and the U.S. population by age group, race/ethnicity, and geographic region. These data indicate a close correspondence between the normative sample and the October 2005 U.S. census proportions. The percentages of the normative sample and the U.S. population according to education level, race/ethnicity, and geographic region are presented in Figure 3.2.

Table 3.2   Percentages of the Normative Sample and U.S. Population by Age Group, Race/Ethnicity, and Education Level

Age Group		White					African American					Hispanic					Asian					Other				
		≤8	9–11	12	13–15	≥16	≤8	9–11	12	13–15	≥16	≤8	9–11	12	13–15	≥16	≤8	9–11	12	13–15	≥16	≤8	9–11	12	13–15	≥16
16–17	U.S. Population	0.48	2.79	15.95	22.31	20.64	0.51	1.52	5.42	5.43	1.84	2.81	3.61	4.61	3.40	1.64	0.03	0.39	1.10	1.00	1.57	0.10	0.16	0.97	1.06	0.66
	Norm. Sample	1.00	2.50	18.00	21.50	19.50	—	1.00	4.50	5.50	2.00	3.50	3.00	4.00	4.00	2.00	—	1.00	0.50	1.00	1.50	—	—	1.00	1.50	1.50
18–19	U.S. Population	0.29	2.89	17.95	23.19	19.58	0.71	1.80	4.97	4.24	2.29	3.02	3.45	3.99	3.94	1.64	0.15	0.33	0.71	0.66	1.42	0.04	0.14	0.90	1.15	0.55
	Norm. Sample	—	3.00	18.50	23.50	20.50	—	1.00	6.00	4.50	2.00	4.00	3.00	3.50	3.50	1.50	—	1.00	0.50	—	1.00	—	1.50	0.50	1.50	0.50
20–24	U.S. Population	0.46	4.53	18.13	29.81	8.78	0.08	2.03	4.71	5.59	1.08	2.02	3.72	5.96	5.52	0.73	0.04	0.18	0.90	2.16	1.24	0.03	0.27	0.81	1.10	0.15
	Norm. Sample	—	4.50	18.00	29.50	8.50	1.00	2.50	4.50	6.00	1.00	1.50	3.00	6.50	6.00	1.00	—	0.50	1.00	2.00	1.00	—	—	0.50	1.00	0.50
25–29	U.S. Population	0.45	3.17	16.27	18.04	21.43	0.19	1.29	4.68	3.89	2.66	3.37	3.69	6.76	3.91	2.55	0.12	0.15	0.82	1.27	3.35	0.02	0.21	0.57	0.83	0.31
	Norm. Sample	0.50	3.00	16.00	18.00	21.50	0.50	1.50	4.00	4.00	2.50	3.00	4.00	7.50	3.50	3.50	—	—	0.50	1.50	3.00	—	—	1.00	1.00	—
30–34	U.S. Population	0.58	3.16	16.46	18.03	21.92	0.10	1.25	4.22	4.27	2.45	3.48	3.80	5.71	3.85	2.52	0.09	0.20	0.70	0.92	4.57	0.02	0.12	0.49	0.62	0.45
	Norm. Sample	1.00	3.00	16.50	18.00	21.50	—	2.00	3.50	5.00	3.50	1.50	3.00	6.50	4.50	2.00	0.50	0.50	0.50	—	5.00	0.50	0.50	0.50	—	0.50
35–44	U.S. Population	0.75	3.36	20.28	19.26	22.89	0.07	1.26	4.61	3.37	2.61	2.92	2.69	4.25	2.78	2.19	0.15	0.20	0.98	0.82	2.95	0.03	0.11	0.53	0.51	0.43
	Norm. Sample	1.00	4.00	20.50	19.00	23.00	—	1.00	4.50	4.00	3.00	3.00	2.50	4.50	3.00	2.00	—	—	0.50	0.50	2.50	—	—	0.50	0.50	0.50
45–54	U.S. Population	0.88	3.57	23.74	20.86	23.70	0.26	1.25	4.20	3.28	2.33	2.45	1.48	2.80	2.04	1.38	0.27	0.28	0.96	0.79	1.98	0.02	0.19	0.51	0.52	0.25
	Norm. Sample	1.50	3.50	23.50	19.50	23.50	—	1.50	5.00	3.50	2.00	2.50	1.50	2.00	2.50	2.00	—	—	1.00	1.00	2.00	—	0.50	0.50	1.00	—
55–64	U.S. Population	2.07	4.68	25.15	21.04	24.35	0.63	1.48	3.35	2.41	1.79	2.59	1.19	1.99	1.37	0.75	0.35	0.18	1.00	0.47	1.85	0.11	0.14	0.37	0.49	0.21
	Norm. Sample	2.00	4.00	25.50	21.00	24.00	0.50	1.50	3.00	2.50	1.50	3.00	1.50	2.50	2.00	1.50	—	—	0.50	—	2.00	—	0.50	0.50	0.50	—
65–69	U.S. Population	4.49	7.51	28.47	18.65	18.75	1.18	2.53	3.39	1.66	1.08	3.01	0.66	1.39	1.09	0.83	0.42	0.23	1.03	0.54	1.84	0.08	0.22	0.38	0.48	0.10
	Norm. Sample	3.50	7.00	29.50	19.50	19.50	2.50	3.00	3.50	1.50	1.00	3.00	1.00	1.00	1.00	1.00	—	0.50	0.50	0.50	1.50	—	—	0.50	0.50	—
70–74	U.S. Population	5.29	8.79	31.59	16.54	16.87	1.84	1.75	3.35	1.23	1.23	3.49	0.65	1.62	0.76	0.82	0.58	0.16	0.83	0.48	0.87	0.13	0.11	0.42	0.38	0.21
	Norm. Sample	5.00	8.00	33.00	17.00	16.00	2.00	1.00	4.00	1.00	2.00	4.00	2.00	1.00	1.00	2.00	—	—	—	—	—	—	—	—	—	—
75–79	U.S. Population	8.00	10.32	31.82	16.00	15.56	2.51	1.42	2.05	0.72	0.82	3.45	1.02	0.89	0.80	0.32	1.12	0.19	1.14	0.26	0.68	0.12	0.21	0.20	0.19	0.18
	Norm. Sample	8.00	11.00	33.00	15.00	16.00	3.00	1.00	1.00	2.00	1.00	3.00	1.00	2.00	1.00	—	1.00	—	—	—	—	—	—	—	—	—
80–84	U.S. Population	9.79	10.84	33.35	17.84	14.11	1.45	1.66	1.50	0.98	0.56	2.74	0.49	0.75	0.33	0.34	1.18	0.11	0.46	0.21	0.52	0.04	0.19	0.37	0.15	0.05
	Norm. Sample	11.00	12.00	32.00	18.00	14.00	1.00	1.00	2.00	1.00	2.00	2.00	—	1.00	1.00	—	—	—	1.00	—	—	1.00	—	—	—	—
85–90	U.S. Population	14.53	11.21	30.31	15.01	14.19	2.85	1.32	0.97	0.51	0.48	3.64	0.62	0.68	0.30	0.12	0.82	0.28	0.91	0.33	0.33	0.12	0.16	0.14	0.08	0.08
	Norm. Sample	13.00	13.00	32.00	15.00	14.00	6.00	1.00	1.00	1.00	—	2.00	—	1.00	1.00	—	1.00	—	—	—	—	1.00	—	—	—	—

Note. For examinees aged 16–19, education is based on parent education; for examinees aged 20–90, education is based on examinee education. U.S. Bureau of the Census (2005).

Table 3.3   Percentages of the Normative Sample and U.S. Population by Age Group, Sex, and Education Level

Age Group		Female					Male					Total				
		≤8	9–11	12	13–15	≥16	≤8	9–11	12	13–15	≥16	≤8	9–11	12	13–15	≥16
16–17	U.S. Population	2.14	4.04	14.26	17.18	12.37	1.79	4.44	13.78	16.02	13.97	3.93	8.48	28.04	33.20	26.35
	Normative Sample	3.50	4.50	14.50	15.00	12.50	1.00	3.00	13.50	18.50	14.00	4.50	7.50	28.00	33.50	26.50
18–19	U.S. Population	2.04	4.17	13.57	17.42	12.79	2.17	4.44	14.94	15.76	12.69	4.22	8.62	28.51	33.18	25.48
	Normative Sample	2.50	5.50	12.50	16.50	13.00	1.50	3.00	16.50	16.50	12.50	4.00	8.50	29.00	33.00	25.50
20–24	U.S. Population	0.96	4.57	13.85	23.45	7.17	1.67	6.15	16.65	20.73	4.80	2.63	10.72	30.50	44.18	11.97
	Normative Sample	1.50	4.50	13.50	23.50	7.00	1.00	6.00	17.00	21.00	5.00	2.50	10.50	30.50	44.50	12.00
25–29	U.S. Population	1.68	3.93	13.05	14.61	16.74	2.48	4.58	16.04	13.33	13.57	4.16	8.51	29.09	27.94	30.31
	Normative Sample	2.00	4.50	13.50	13.00	17.00	2.00	4.00	15.50	15.00	13.50	4.00	8.50	29.00	28.00	30.50
30–34	U.S. Population	1.85	3.93	12.65	14.47	17.09	2.43	4.60	14.92	13.24	14.81	4.28	8.53	27.58	27.71	31.91
	Normative Sample	3.00	2.50	12.50	15.00	17.00	0.50	6.50	15.00	12.50	15.50	3.50	9.00	27.50	27.50	32.50
35–44	U.S. Population	1.78	3.47	14.32	14.42	16.02	2.14	4.15	16.33	12.32	15.05	3.92	7.62	30.65	26.74	31.07
	Normative Sample	1.50	3.00	15.00	14.50	16.00	2.50	4.50	15.50	12.50	15.00	4.00	7.50	30.50	27.00	31.00
45–54	U.S. Population	1.86	3.14	15.94	14.33	14.72	2.03	3.63	16.27	13.16	14.91	3.89	6.77	32.22	27.49	29.63
	Normative Sample	2.00	3.00	15.50	14.50	15.00	2.00	4.00	16.50	13.00	14.50	4.00	7.00	32.00	27.50	29.50
55–64	U.S. Population	2.68	3.99	17.15	13.56	12.61	3.06	3.68	14.71	12.21	16.34	5.74	7.67	31.87	25.78	28.95
	Normative Sample	3.00	4.50	15.50	14.50	12.50	2.50	3.00	16.50	11.50	16.50	5.50	7.50	32.00	26.00	29.00
65–69	U.S. Population	4.91	6.05	19.84	11.96	10.24	4.26	5.09	14.82	10.46	12.37	9.17	11.14	34.66	22.42	22.61
	Normative Sample	7.00	5.50	20.50	10.50	9.50	2.00	5.50	14.00	12.00	13.50	9.00	11.00	34.50	22.50	23.00
70–74	U.S. Population	6.25	7.35	22.91	10.87	7.92	5.08	4.11	14.91	8.53	12.08	11.33	11.46	37.82	19.39	20.00
	Normative Sample	5.00	8.00	24.00	10.00	8.00	6.00	3.00	15.00	9.00	12.00	11.00	11.00	39.00	19.00	20.00
75–79	U.S. Population	8.18	7.21	23.18	10.54	7.84	7.02	5.96	12.93	7.42	9.72	15.20	13.17	36.11	17.97	17.56
	Normative Sample	8.00	7.00	26.00	10.00	6.00	7.00	6.00	10.00	8.00	12.00	15.00	13.00	36.00	18.00	18.00
80–84	U.S. Population	9.56	8.21	24.97	12.99	7.32	5.64	5.08	11.44	6.52	8.27	15.20	13.29	36.42	19.51	15.59
	Normative Sample	10.00	6.00	23.00	14.00	10.00	5.00	7.00	13.00	6.00	6.00	15.00	13.00	36.00	20.00	16.00
85–90	U.S. Population	14.73	9.29	23.29	10.57	8.64	7.23	4.29	9.72	5.67	6.56	21.96	13.58	33.01	16.24	15.21
	Normative Sample	17.00	9.00	24.00	9.00	8.00	5.00	5.00	9.00	7.00	7.00	22.00	14.00	33.00	16.00	15.00

Note. For examinees aged 16–19, education is based on parent education; for examinees aged 20–90, education is based on examinee education. U.S. Bureau of the Census (2005).

Table 3.4   Percentages of the Normative Sample and U.S. Population by Age Group, Sex, and Race/Ethnicity

Age Group		White	Female African American	Hispanic	Asian	Other	White	Male African American	Hispanic	Asian	Other	White	Total African American	Hispanic	Asian	Other
16–17	U.S. Population	30.79	7.59	8.09	2.03	1.50	31.39	7.12	7.98	2.04	1.46	62.18	14.71	16.07	4.08	2.95
	Normative Sample	30.00	5.00	9.00	3.50	2.50	32.50	8.00	7.50	0.50	1.50	62.50	13.00	16.50	4.00	4.00
18–19	U.S. Population	32.10	7.33	7.75	1.58	1.24	31.80	6.68	8.30	1.69	1.54	63.90	14.02	16.04	3.26	2.78
	Normative Sample	33.50	5.00	8.50	0.50	2.50	32.00	8.50	7.00	1.00	1.50	65.50	13.50	15.50	1.50	4.00
20–24	U.S. Population	31.05	7.10	8.39	2.18	1.28	30.65	6.38	9.56	2.33	1.08	61.71	13.48	17.95	4.51	2.36
	Normative Sample	30.50	7.00	9.00	2.50	1.00	30.00	8.00	9.00	2.00	1.00	60.50	15.00	18.00	4.50	2.00
25–29	U.S. Population	29.92	6.93	9.16	2.93	1.07	29.44	5.78	11.12	2.78	0.88	59.36	12.71	20.28	5.71	1.95
	Normative Sample	30.50	6.50	9.00	3.00	1.00	28.50	6.00	12.50	2.00	1.00	59.00	12.50	21.50	5.00	2.00
30–34	U.S. Population	30.21	6.73	8.95	3.28	0.84	29.96	5.55	10.41	3.21	0.87	60.16	12.28	19.36	6.49	1.70
	Normative Sample	29.00	8.00	8.50	3.50	1.00	31.00	6.00	9.00	3.00	1.00	60.00	14.00	17.50	6.50	2.00
35–44	U.S. Population	33.09	6.53	6.97	2.59	0.82	33.45	5.40	7.86	2.50	0.79	66.54	11.93	14.83	5.09	1.60
	Normative Sample	36.50	5.00	6.00	1.50	1.00	31.00	7.50	9.00	2.00	0.50	67.50	12.50	15.00	3.50	1.50
45–54	U.S. Population	35.97	6.08	4.95	2.25	0.76	36.79	5.24	5.20	2.03	0.73	72.76	11.32	10.15	4.28	1.49
	Normative Sample	37.00	5.50	4.50	2.00	1.00	34.50	6.50	6.00	2.00	1.00	71.50	12.00	10.50	4.00	2.00
55–64	U.S. Population	38.19	5.18	3.98	1.98	0.67	39.09	4.48	3.91	1.87	0.65	77.29	9.66	7.89	3.85	1.32
	Normative Sample	38.00	5.00	4.50	2.00	0.50	38.50	4.00	6.00	0.50	1.00	76.50	9.00	10.50	2.50	1.50
65–69	U.S. Population	40.66	5.60	4.05	2.06	0.63	37.21	4.25	2.93	1.99	0.62	77.87	9.85	6.97	4.05	1.26
	Normative Sample	42.00	6.00	4.50	0.50	—	37.00	5.50	2.50	2.00	—	79.00	11.50	7.00	2.50	—
70–74	U.S. Population	42.95	5.72	4.16	1.63	0.84	36.12	3.69	3.19	1.29	0.42	79.07	9.41	7.34	2.92	1.26
	Normative Sample	39.00	8.00	8.00	—	—	40.00	2.00	3.00	—	—	79.00	10.00	11.00	—	—
75–79	U.S. Population	46.49	4.51	3.46	2.07	0.42	35.20	3.02	3.03	1.33	0.47	81.69	7.53	6.48	3.40	0.90
	Normative Sample	49.00	3.00	4.00	1.00	—	34.00	6.00	3.00	—	—	83.00	9.00	7.00	1.00	—
80–84	U.S. Population	53.00	4.74	3.03	1.78	0.51	32.93	1.41	1.62	0.69	0.30	85.93	6.15	4.65	2.47	0.81
	Normative Sample	53.00	5.00	3.00	1.00	1.00	34.00	2.00	1.00	—	—	87.00	7.00	4.00	1.00	1.00
85–90	U.S. Population	57.12	4.26	3.13	1.56	0.45	28.13	1.88	2.22	1.11	0.13	85.25	6.13	5.35	2.68	0.58
	Normative Sample	59.00	5.00	3.00	—	—	28.00	3.00	—	1.00	1.00	87.00	8.00	3.00	1.00	1.00

Note. U.S. Bureau of the Census (2005).

Table 3.5   Percentages of the Normative Sample and U.S. Population by Age Group, Race/Ethnicity, and Geographic Region

Age Group		White				African American				Hispanic				Asian				Other			
		NE	MW	S	W	NE	MW	S	W	NE	MW	S	W	NE	MW	S	W	NE	MW	S	W
16–17	U.S. Population	12.29	17.99	20.52	11.38	2.83	3.08	7.93	0.87	2.63	1.41	5.36	6.67	1.04	0.43	0.61	1.99	0.18	0.67	0.78	1.32
	Norm. Sample	15.50	15.00	18.00	14.00	2.50	3.00	4.00	3.50	—	2.50	6.50	7.50	1.00	0.50	—	2.50	0.50	2.00	0.50	1.00
18–19	U.S. Population	14.68	19.61	18.74	10.87	2.63	2.27	7.99	1.12	2.14	1.24	5.71	6.95	0.51	0.43	0.66	1.67	0.19	0.56	0.80	1.23
	Norm. Sample	15.00	18.00	20.00	12.50	2.00	2.50	7.50	1.50	0.50	1.00	7.00	7.00	—	—	—	1.50	0.50	1.50	0.50	1.50
20–24	U.S. Population	11.79	18.28	20.17	11.47	2.24	2.50	7.59	1.14	2.44	1.50	6.25	7.76	0.86	0.60	0.85	2.19	0.20	0.55	0.64	0.96
	Norm. Sample	13.00	12.50	20.00	15.00	3.50	2.00	8.00	1.50	2.00	0.50	8.50	7.00	0.50	0.50	0.50	3.00	—	0.50	0.50	1.00
25–29	U.S. Population	10.71	16.23	19.66	12.75	2.08	2.25	7.18	1.20	2.68	2.08	6.93	8.59	1.01	0.90	1.11	2.70	0.11	0.31	0.72	0.81
	Norm. Sample	13.00	15.50	16.00	14.50	3.00	2.00	7.50	—	2.50	2.00	9.50	7.50	2.00	1.50	—	1.50	0.50	0.50	—	1.00
30–34	U.S. Population	11.69	15.49	21.51	11.47	1.93	2.15	7.39	0.81	2.21	2.02	6.57	8.56	1.22	1.21	1.37	2.69	0.13	0.31	0.53	0.74
	Norm. Sample	12.50	16.50	20.50	10.50	3.00	0.50	8.00	2.50	1.50	3.00	9.50	3.50	0.50	1.00	2.50	2.50	—	0.50	0.50	1.00
35–44	U.S. Population	13.84	17.39	22.47	12.84	2.11	2.13	6.45	1.25	2.24	1.19	5.53	5.86	1.03	0.62	1.16	2.29	0.14	0.27	0.53	0.67
	Norm. Sample	17.00	17.00	21.00	12.50	3.00	1.00	8.00	0.50	2.00	1.00	9.00	3.00	0.50	0.50	—	2.50	—	—	—	1.50
45–54	U.S. Population	14.50	19.83	24.55	13.87	1.88	1.97	6.42	1.06	1.44	0.69	3.94	4.08	0.93	0.46	0.72	2.16	0.13	0.33	0.52	0.52
	Norm. Sample	12.50	20.00	26.50	12.50	1.50	2.50	6.00	2.00	1.50	1.50	5.00	2.50	—	1.50	0.50	2.00	—	—	0.50	1.50
55–64	U.S. Population	15.59	19.02	27.16	15.52	1.87	1.84	5.16	0.79	1.10	0.57	2.70	3.51	0.76	0.30	0.64	2.15	0.10	0.21	0.54	0.46
	Norm. Sample	15.50	19.00	24.00	18.00	0.50	2.00	5.50	1.00	—	2.00	6.00	2.50	0.50	1.00	—	1.00	—	1.00	0.50	—
65–69	U.S. Population	15.22	19.40	27.29	15.95	2.05	1.71	5.17	0.92	1.34	0.31	2.71	2.61	1.24	0.37	0.43	2.02	0.14	0.25	0.51	0.36
	Norm. Sample	15.50	19.00	23.00	21.50	0.50	4.50	5.50	1.00	1.00	1.00	4.50	0.50	—	1.50	—	1.00	—	—	—	—
70–74	U.S. Population	16.79	19.19	27.26	15.83	1.68	1.61	5.05	1.06	0.71	0.38	3.45	2.79	0.68	0.21	0.30	1.74	0.13	0.29	0.42	0.41
	Norm. Sample	20.00	24.00	22.00	13.00	2.00	3.00	3.00	2.00	1.00	—	9.00	1.00	—	—	—	—	—	—	—	—
75–79	U.S. Population	17.57	20.23	28.06	15.82	1.30	1.24	4.03	0.96	0.90	0.26	2.71	2.62	0.73	0.32	0.18	2.17	0.03	0.21	0.51	0.15
	Norm. Sample	23.00	17.00	34.00	9.00	—	4.00	3.00	2.00	1.00	—	7.00	—	1.00	—	—	—	—	—	—	—
80–84	U.S. Population	19.44	22.18	28.61	15.69	0.87	1.66	3.05	0.57	0.53	0.12	2.16	1.84	0.55	0.11	0.39	1.42	0.07	0.14	0.30	0.30
	Norm. Sample	15.00	29.00	31.00	12.00	2.00	4.00	—	1.00	—	1.00	3.00	—	—	1.00	—	—	—	—	—	1.00
85–90	U.S. Population	19.15	22.75	26.43	16.92	0.75	0.93	4.10	0.36	0.88	0.15	3.01	1.32	0.82	0.06	0.16	1.63	0.04	0.08	0.06	0.40
	Norm. Sample	27.00	27.00	21.00	12.00	—	3.00	5.00	—	—	—	3.00	—	—	1.00	—	—	—	—	—	1.00

Note. NE = Northeast, MW = Midwest, S = South, W = West. U.S. Bureau of the Census (2005).

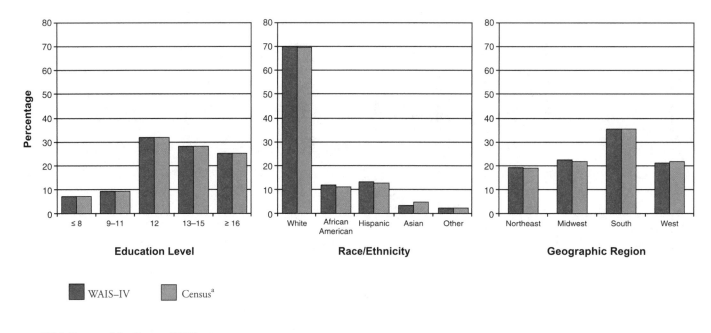

[a] U.S. Bureau of the Census (2005).

Figure 3.2   Demographic Characteristics of the Normative Sample Compared to the U.S. Population

Norms Development

This section summarizes the research methods used to develop the WAIS–IV normative information. The discussion begins with the procedures used to prepare the data for norming (e.g., the determination of subtest start points, discontinue rules, and time bonus points), and concludes with a focus on the research procedures used to derive the standard (subtest, process, and composite) scores.

Determining Start Points and Discontinue Rules

Start points and discontinue rules have been incorporated into the scale to avoid frustrating the examinee with overly easy or overly difficult items. In the standardization version of the scale, subtest items were ordered according to increasing difficulty as indicated by national tryout data. Standardization start points were set based on national tryout data to minimize the number of administered items as much as possible, while ensuring that at least 95% of subtest total raw scores and at least 98% of subtest scaled scores were unchanged following the application of the new start point. In the final version, start points for each subtest (with the exception of Similarities) were retained. All of the first start point items had pass rates of at least 97% in the overall normative sample, limiting the occurrence of reversal procedures and ensuring that the majority of examinees experienced success on the first items of administered subtests. The only exception was the Picture Completion start point item, which had an overall pass rate of 91%.

Standardization discontinue rules were set generously to allow the examinee to attempt all passable items, yet limit the number of items presented. Final adjustments to the discontinue rule for each subtest were made on the basis of empirical studies of the standardization data. The percentile ranks of examinees within an age group were compared before and after application of the reduced discontinue rule. The discontinue rule was set at the lowest number of consecutive scores of 0 that resulted in a rank-order correlation of .98 or higher. For example, the Similarities discontinue rule was five consecutive scores of 0 for standardization and was reduced to three consecutive scores of 0 for the final version of the scale. Following the reduction, 99% of the examinees' Similarities total raw scores remained at the same relative position within their age group.

Determining Time Bonuses

Preliminary analysis of standardization data for Block Design revealed that awarding bonus points for fast, accurate performance minimized ceiling effects and provided greater discrimination among high-ability examinees. The distributions of completion times for examinees that earned full credit on more difficult Block Design items were evaluated, and the time bonus structure was developed such that the number of bonus points awarded increased with shorter completion times.

Deriving Subtest Scaled Scores and Scaled Process Scores

The normative information was developed using the method of inferential norming (Wilkins, Rolfhus, Weiss, & Zhu, 2005). Various moments (means, standard deviations, and skewness) of each score were calculated for each of the 13 age groups of the normative sample. The moments were plotted across ages, and various polynomial regressions, ranging from linear to 4th degree polynomials, were fit to the moment data. Functions for each score moment were selected based on consistency with underlying theoretical expectations and the pattern of growth curves observed in the normative sample. For each subtest, the functions were used to derive estimates of the age group mid-point population moments. The estimated moments were then used to generate theoretical distributions for each of the reported normative age groups, yielding percentiles for each raw score. The progression of standard scores within and across age groups was then examined, and minor irregularities eliminated by smoothing. Due to their restricted range and limited amenability to norming procedures, the LDSF, LDSB, LDSS, and LLNS process scores are reported as raw scores and base rates and not as scaled scores. For this reason, these process scores do not appear in most tables in this manual.

The Administration and Scoring Manual presents scaled score equivalents of total raw scores for the subtests and four process scores, by age group, in Tables A.1 and C.1, respectively. With the exception of Letter–Number Sequencing, Figure Weights, and Cancellation, each subtest was normed for 13 age groups. Letter–Number Sequencing, Figure Weights, and Cancellation were normed for the nine younger age groups ages 16:0–69:11. The derived scaled scores range from 1 to 19, providing a range of 3 SDs on either side of the mean.

Deriving Reference-Group Subtest Scaled Scores

As with the WAIS–III, the WAIS–IV provides two sets of normative subtest scores. The first set of normative subtest scores, described in the previous section, is based on age-corrected subtest scaled scores. The second set of normative subtest scores, the reference-group subtest scaled scores, is based on the performance of all examinees in the normative sample aged 20:0–34:11 (the reference group). In terms of key demographic variables (sex, race/ethnicity, education level, and geographic region), the reference group is representative of the U.S. census proportions for this age range. The reference-group subtest scaled scores were derived using the procedure outlined above, but based on the performance of the reference group. The reference group was selected for comparability with the reference group norms reported in previous editions, and was not based on unique characteristics of group performance. The reference group norms, which are reported in Table A.2 in the Administration and Scoring Manual, are provided primarily for research purposes. See chapter 6 for a discussion of interpretive issues related to reference group norms.

Deriving Composite Scores

The composite scores (i.e., VCI, PRI, WMI, PSI, FSIQ, and GAI) are based on sums of age-corrected scaled scores. To construct the composite score tables, six sums of scaled scores (i.e., Verbal Comprehension, Perceptual Reasoning, Working Memory, Processing Speed, Full Scale, and General Ability) were calculated for each individual in the normative sample.

For each of the sampled age groups, the means and standard deviations of the Verbal Comprehension, Perceptual Reasoning, Working Memory, Processing Speed, and Full Scale sums of scaled scores are presented in Tables A.1–A.13. These data reveal a high degree of similarity from age to age within each of these scales. An analysis of variance revealed no statistically significant variation by age in the mean sum of scaled scores for each scale. Results of Bartlett's test for homogeneity of variance applied across the sampled age groups indicated that the variance of sums of scaled scores did not differ significantly by age. Moreover, examination of the distributions of the sums of scaled scores indicated that all of these sums were normally distributed. Consequently, the age groups were combined to construct the tables of composite score equivalents.

For each scale, the distribution of the sum of scaled scores was normalized and given a mean of 100 and an SD of 15. The appropriate composite score was then assigned to each sum of scaled scores. The resulting composite score distributions were smoothed visually to remove any irregularities, while attempting to keep the means and SDs of the scales close to 100 and 15, respectively. The normalization of the scale ensured that the composite score distributions would approximate the normal curve for the normative sample. Tables A.3–A.7 in the Administration and Scoring Manual present the composite score equivalents of sums of scaled scores for the Verbal Comprehension, Perceptual Reasoning, Working Memory, Processing Speed, and Full scales. Table C.1 in this manual presents the GAI equivalents of sums of scaled scores for the General Ability scale.

Chapter 4

Evidence of WAIS–IV Reliability

The statistical properties of the WAIS–IV determine the confidence practitioners can have in the accuracy and precision of obtained scores. Psychometric properties that are critical to score interpretation include reliability and stability coefficients, standard errors of measurement, confidence intervals, statistical significance of differences between scores (critical values), and frequency of score differences (base rates).

It is becoming well accepted among statisticians that there are serious limitations in the use of null hypothesis testing (e.g., Balluerka, Gómez, & Hidalgo, 2005; Cohen, 1990, 1994; Hubbard & Lindsay, 2008; Hunter, 1997; Kirk, 1996, 2001; Thompson, 1998). This has led to a call to report confidence intervals and effect size measures, rather than simply reporting statistical significance and p values (AERA, 2006). In this manual, confidence intervals and effect sizes are reported, along with statistical significance tests and p values, to inform judgments about reliability and validity.

Several conventions for reporting psychometric results were followed in this manual. All analyses use traditional values for significance level (alpha = .05). The term *standard difference* in this manual refers to Cohen's *d*. The reported values follow Cohen's suggestions for effect size interpretation (Cohen, 1988, 1992). Values for Cohen's *d* that range from .20 to .49 are reported as small effect sizes. Values that range from .50 to .79 are reported as moderate effect sizes, and values of .80 or greater are reported as large effect sizes.

This manual has adopted common conventions for statistical significance and effect size interpretation, but the actual values should always be considered. For example, although $p = .07$ is not statistically significant, it would be evaluated differently if the effect size was .90, rather than .10. Similarly, a p value of .04 is a significant result, but when paired with an effect size of .03, the effect is probably too small to be meaningful.

Cohen's suggestions were meant to be general guidelines; depending on the situation, the importance associated with a particular effect size might be very different from those suggested by these guidelines. In certain clinical situations, a small effect size might still represent an important finding. The reader is encouraged to evaluate the specifics of a given result when interpreting significance and effect size magnitudes.

Reliability and Errors of Measurement

The reliability of a test refers to the accuracy, consistency, and stability of test scores across situations (Anastasi & Urbina, 1997; Sattler, 2008a). Classical test theory posits that a test score is an approximation of an individual's hypothetical *true score*, that is, the score he or she would receive if the test were perfectly reliable. The difference between the hypothetical true score and the individual's obtained test score is *measurement error*. A reliable test has relatively small measurement error and produces consistent measurement results within one administration and on different occasions. The reliability of a test should always be considered when interpreting obtained test scores and differences between an individual's test scores on multiple occasions.

Evidence of Internal Consistency

Reliability coefficients were obtained utilizing the split-half and the Cronbach's coefficient alpha methods. The subtest's split-half reliability coefficient is the correlation between the total scores of the two half-tests corrected by the Spearman-Brown formula for the full subtest (Crocker & Algina, 1986; Li, Rosenthal, & Rubin, 1996). The alpha coefficient takes the variance of both the subtest total score and the item scores into account, and provides a reliability that is the average of all possible split-half reliabilities (Anastasi & Urbina, 1997; Cronbach, 1951; Sattler, 2008a).

Because Symbol Search, Coding, and Cancellation are Processing Speed subtests, the split-half coefficient is not a proper reliability estimate. Therefore, test-retest stability coefficients were used as the reliability estimates for these subtests. These stability coefficients were based on the scores of individuals who participated in the test-retest study described later in this chapter. The stability coefficient is the correlation between the scores on the first and second testings corrected for the normative sample's variability (Allen & Yen, 1979; Magnusson, 1967).

The composite score internal consistency reliability coefficients were calculated with the formula recommended by Guilford (1954) and Nunnally and Bernstein (1994). Table 4.1 presents the reliability coefficients of the subtest, process, and composite scores by age group. The average reliability coefficients were calculated using Fisher's z transformation (Silver & Dunlap, 1987; Strube, 1988).

Table 4.1　Reliability Coefficients of the Subtest, Process, and Composite Scores, by Age Group

Subtest/Process/ Composite Score	Age Group													Overall Average r_{xx}[a]
	16–17	18–19	20–24	25–29	30–34	35–44	45–54	55–64	65–69	70–74	75–79	80–84	85–90	
BD	.88	.87	.84	.90	.91	.89	.90	.88	.87	.89	.82	.80	.86	.87
SI	.81	.85	.85	.86	.87	.88	.88	.87	.88	.90	.86	.91	.91	.87
DS	.89	.92	.91	.94	.94	.94	.94	.92	.93	.94	.93	.92	.92	.93
MR	.88	.87	.88	.91	.91	.90	.90	.90	.91	.91	.94	.86	.92	.90
VC	.93	.93	.94	.93	.93	.94	.94	.94	.95	.95	.94	.94	.96	.94
AR	.89	.88	.84	.89	.90	.89	.91	.88	.89	.84	.90	.89	.86	.88
SS	.81	.81	.81	.81	.73	.73	.73	.81	.81	.86	.86	.86	.86	.81
VP	.90	.89	.90	.91	.90	.88	.92	.89	.92	.89	.89	.82	.78	.89
IN	.89	.91	.91	.91	.91	.92	.94	.95	.94	.94	.94	.94	.96	.93
CD	.85	.85	.85	.85	.84	.84	.84	.89	.89	.86	.86	.86	.86	.86
LN	.90	.90	.85	.88	.91	.86	.88	.87	.88	—	—	—	—	.88
FW	.90	.92	.88	.91	.92	.89	.91	.89	.90	—	—	—	—	.90
CO	.82	.87	.87	.88	.85	.89	.85	.87	.87	.82	.87	.87	.90	.87
CA	.81	.81	.81	.81	.71	.71	.71	.80	.80	—	—	—	—	.78
PCm	.80	.84	.82	.82	.86	.84	.83	.86	.85	.89	.86	.83	.82	.84
BDN	.87	.86	.81	.88	.89	.87	.87	.86	.85	.88	.82	.80	.86	.86
DSF	.77	.76	.80	.85	.77	.84	.83	.77	.79	.88	.81	.81	.78	.81
DSB	.79	.80	.80	.84	.84	.86	.86	.82	.78	.79	.80	.77	.82	.82
DSS	.73	.79	.82	.81	.80	.83	.82	.79	.81	.86	.86	.84	.92	.83
VCI	.94	.96	.96	.96	.96	.96	.97	.97	.97	.97	.96	.97	.98	.96
PRI	.95	.94	.94	.96	.96	.95	.96	.95	.95	.95	.94	.92	.93	.95
WMI	.93	.94	.92	.95	.95	.95	.95	.94	.94	.93	.95	.94	.93	.94
PSI	.88	.90	.90	.90	.87	.87	.87	.91	.91	.91	.92	.92	.92	.90
FSIQ	.97	.98	.98	.98	.98	.98	.98	.98	.98	.98	.98	.98	.98	.98

[a] Average reliability coefficients were calculated with Fisher's z transformation.

As the data in Table 4.1 indicate, for the overall normative sample, the average subtest reliability coefficients range from acceptable (Cancellation) to excellent (Digit Span, Matrix Reasoning, Vocabulary, Information, and Figure Weights). All remaining reliability coefficients are good. The reliability coefficients for the retained WAIS–III subtests are comparable or improved. The reliability coefficients for the two new Perceptual Reasoning subtests, Visual Puzzles and Figure Weights, are generally higher than the coefficients for the WAIS–III Perceptual Organization subtests. The WAIS–IV subtest reliabilities therefore maintain or improve upon the WAIS–III subtest reliabilities.

The reliability coefficients for WAIS–IV composite scores are excellent and are generally higher than those of the individual subtests that comprise the composite scores. This difference occurs because each subtest represents only a narrow portion of an individual's entire intellectual functioning, whereas the composite scores summarize the individual's performance on a broader sample of abilities. The high overall average reliability coefficients for the WAIS–IV composite scores are as expected. The average reliability coefficient for the PSI, although still in the excellent range, is slightly lower than the other composite scores; it is based on test-retest subtest reliabilities, which tend to be lower than split-half or alpha reliabilities. In addition, the WMI and the PSI composite reliabilities tend to be lower because only two subtests contribute to each composite. The composite score reliability coefficients are equal to (for VCI, WMI, and FSIQ) or higher than (for PRI and PSI) those of the WAIS–III.

Reliability information for special populations supports the instrument's generalizability. The evidence of internal consistency reliability from the special groups was obtained from examinees in the following groups: Intellectually Gifted, Intellectual Disability-Mild Severity, Intellectual Disability-Moderate Severity, Borderline Intellectual Functioning, Reading Disorder, Mathematics Disorder, Attention-Deficit/Hyperactivity Disorder (ADHD), Traumatic Brain Injury, Autistic Disorder, Asperger's Disorder, Major Depressive Disorder, Mild Cognitive Impairment, and Probable Dementia of the Alzheimer's Type-Mild Severity. Detailed demographic information for special groups is reported in chapter 5, and complete special group inclusion criteria descriptions appear in Appendix E.

Table 4.2 provides internal consistency reliability coefficients of the subtest and process scores for special groups. The reliability coefficients were calculated using the same methodology described for Table 4.1. The reliability coefficients for the three Processing Speed subtests (Symbol Search, Coding, and Cancellation) are not available for special groups, as these groups did not participate in the retest study.

As shown in the table, most of the special group subtest reliability coefficients are similar to or higher than those coefficients reported for the normative sample: This suggests that the WAIS–IV is a reliable tool for the assessment of individuals with intellectual giftedness and clinical diagnoses, as well as individuals who are more representative of the general population.

Table 4.2   Reliability Coefficients of the Subtest and Process Scores for Special Groups

Subtest/Process Score	GT		ID Mild		ID Mod		BIF		RD		MD		ADHD		TBI		AUT		ASP		DEP		MCI		ALZ		Average r_{xx}[a]
	N	r	N	r	N	r	N	r	N	r	N	r	N	r	N	r	N	r	N	r	N	r	N	r	N	r	
BD	34	.80	73	.91	31	.88	27	.89	34	.89	41	.90	44	.93	22	.96	16	.93	40	.90	41	.82	53	.81	43	.92	.90
SI	34	.88	73	.91	31	.94	27	.86	34	.95	41	.88	44	.85	22	.87	16	.86	40	.83	41	.88	53	.87	43	.92	.89
DS	34	.89	73	.87	31	.94	27	.93	34	.94	41	.90	44	.93	22	.98	16	.95	40	.94	41	.94	53	.93	44	.95	.94
MR	34	.74	73	.93	31	.96	27	.97	34	.93	41	.94	44	.91	22	.95	16	.97	40	.91	41	.88	53	.92	44	.90	.93
VC	34	.87	73	.91	31	.85	27	.92	34	.94	41	.97	44	.92	22	.96	16	.85	40	.91	41	.93	53	.94	43	.94	.92
AR	34	.87	73	.87	31	.86	27	.85	34	.91	41	.92	44	.91	22	.87	16	.86	40	.91	41	.84	53	.90	44	.94	.89
VP	34	.90	73	.93	31	.89	27	.97	34	.97	41	.94	44	.88	22	.95	16	.92	40	.94	41	.86	53	.88	43	.92	.93
IN	34	.91	73	.89	31	.67	27	.95	34	.96	41	.92	44	.92	22	.93	16	.92	40	.96	41	.94	40	.93	31	.95	.93
LN	34	.86	73	.94	31	.83	27	.87	34	.70	41	.83	44	.83	22	.90	16	.83	40	.87	33	.86	14	.94	—	—	.87
FW	34	.90	73	.90	31	.95	27	.95	34	.94	41	.96	44	.86	22	.92	16	.96	40	.91	33	.90	14	.91	—	—	.93
CO	33	.74	73	.89	30	.85	27	.87	34	.93	41	.89	44	.88	22	.88	16	.93	40	.91	36	.82	40	.90	31	.90	.88
PCm	34	.82	73	.94	31	.95	27	.95	34	.92	41	.90	44	.79	22	.89	16	.84	40	.81	36	.83	40	.88	24	.85	.89
BDN	34	.76	73	.92	31	.88	27	.85	34	.85	41	.90	44	.90	22	.95	16	.91	40	.86	41	.79	53	.82	43	.92	.88
DSF	34	.86	73	.91	31	.89	27	.94	34	.87	41	.90	44	.86	22	.84	16	.82	40	.86	41	.88	53	.78	44	.84	.87
DSB	34	.90	73	.92	31	.97	27	.94	34	.85	41	.91	44	.87	22	.78	16	.89	40	.82	41	.89	53	.88	44	.81	.89
DSS	34	.83	73	.84	31	.76	27	.91	34	.79	41	.85	44	.83	22	.89	16	.93	40	.78	41	.80	53	.93	44	.93	.86

Note. Symbol Search, Coding, and Cancellation are not reported because there were no test-retest data collected for special groups. Special group abbreviations are: GT = Intellectually Gifted; ID Mild = Intellectual Disability-Mild Severity; ID Mod = Intellectual Disability-Moderate Severity; BIF = Borderline Intellectual Functioning; RD = Reading Disorder; MD = Mathematics Disorder; ADHD = Attention-Deficit/Hyperactivity Disorder; TBI = Traumatic Brain Injury; AUT = Autistic Disorder; ASP = Asperger's Disorder; DEP = Major Depressive Disorder; MCI = Mild Cognitive Impairment; ALZ = Probable Dementia of the Alzheimer's Type-Mild Severity.

[a] Average reliability coefficients were calculated with Fisher's z transformation.

Standard Error of Measurement and Confidence Intervals

The standard error of measurement *(SEM)* provides an estimate of the amount of error in an individual's observed test score. Because the *SEM* is inversely related to the reliability, as reliability increases, the *SEM* decreases, and confidence in the observed test score precision increases. Measurement error is commonly expressed in terms of standard score units; that is, the *SEM* is the *SD* of the measurement error distribution. The *SEM* is calculated with the formula:

$$SEM = SD \sqrt{1 - r_{xx}}$$

where *SEM* represents the standard error of measurement, *SD* is the observed standard deviation of the scale, and r_{xx} is the reliability coefficient of the scale. Comparisons between the *SEM*s of the subtest scaled scores and the composite scores should not be made because they are based on different *SD*s. Because the *SD* is 3 for the subtest scaled scores and 15 for the composite scores, the *SEM*s of the subtest scaled scores usually appear smaller than those of the composite scores. However, the composite scores are generally more accurate measures than individual subtest scaled scores. The *SEM*s of the subtest, process, and composite scores are shown in Table 4.3 by age group.

Table 4.3   Standard Errors of Measurement of the Subtest, Process, and Composite Scores, by Age Group

Subtest/Process/ Composite Score	16–17	18–19	20–24	25–29	30–34	35–44	45–54	55–64	65–69	70–74	75–79	80–84	85–90	Overall Average SEM[a]
BD	1.04	1.08	1.20	0.95	0.90	0.99	0.95	1.04	1.08	0.99	1.27	1.34	1.12	1.08
SI	1.31	1.16	1.16	1.12	1.08	1.04	1.04	1.08	1.04	0.95	1.12	0.90	0.90	1.07
DS	0.99	0.85	0.90	0.73	0.73	0.73	0.73	0.85	0.79	0.73	0.79	0.85	0.85	0.81
MR	1.04	1.08	1.04	0.90	0.90	0.95	0.95	0.95	0.90	0.90	0.73	1.12	0.85	0.95
VC	0.79	0.79	0.73	0.79	0.79	0.73	0.73	0.73	0.67	0.67	0.73	0.73	0.60	0.73
AR	0.99	1.04	1.20	0.99	0.95	0.99	0.90	1.04	0.99	1.20	0.95	0.99	1.12	1.03
SS	1.31	1.31	1.31	1.31	1.56	1.56	1.56	1.31	1.31	1.12	1.12	1.12	1.12	1.32
VP	0.95	0.99	0.95	0.90	0.95	1.04	0.85	0.99	0.85	0.99	0.99	1.27	1.41	1.02
IN	0.99	0.90	0.90	0.90	0.90	0.85	0.73	0.67	0.73	0.73	0.73	0.73	0.60	0.80
CD	1.16	1.16	1.16	1.16	1.20	1.20	1.20	0.99	0.99	1.12	1.12	1.12	1.12	1.13
LN	0.95	0.95	1.16	1.04	0.90	1.12	1.04	1.08	1.04	—	—	—	—	1.03
FW	0.95	0.85	1.04	0.90	0.85	0.99	0.90	0.99	0.95	—	—	—	—	0.94
CO	1.27	1.08	1.08	1.04	1.16	0.99	1.16	1.08	1.08	1.27	1.08	1.08	0.95	1.11
CA	1.31	1.31	1.31	1.31	1.62	1.62	1.62	1.34	1.34	—	—	—	—	1.43
PCm	1.34	1.20	1.27	1.27	1.12	1.20	1.24	1.12	1.16	0.99	1.12	1.24	1.27	1.20
BDN	1.08	1.12	1.31	1.04	0.99	1.08	1.08	1.12	1.16	1.04	1.27	1.34	1.12	1.14
DSF	1.44	1.47	1.34	1.16	1.44	1.20	1.24	1.44	1.37	1.04	1.31	1.31	1.41	1.33
DSB	1.37	1.34	1.34	1.20	1.20	1.12	1.12	1.27	1.41	1.37	1.34	1.44	1.27	1.30
DSS	1.56	1.37	1.27	1.31	1.34	1.24	1.27	1.37	1.31	1.12	1.12	1.20	0.85	1.27
VCI	3.67	3.00	3.00	3.00	3.00	3.00	2.60	2.60	2.60	2.60	3.00	2.60	2.12	2.85
PRI	3.35	3.67	3.67	3.00	3.00	3.35	3.00	3.35	3.35	3.35	3.67	4.24	3.97	3.48
WMI	3.97	3.67	4.24	3.35	3.35	3.35	3.35	3.67	3.67	3.97	3.35	3.67	3.97	3.67
PSI	5.20	4.74	4.74	4.74	5.41	5.41	5.41	4.50	4.50	4.50	4.24	4.24	4.24	4.78
FSIQ	2.60	2.12	2.12	2.12	2.12	2.12	2.12	2.12	2.12	2.12	2.12	2.12	2.12	2.16

Note. The *SEM*s are reported in scaled-score units for the subtests and in composite-score units for the composite scores. The reliability coefficients shown in Table 4.1 and the population standard deviations (i.e., 3 for the subtests and 15 for the composite scores) were used to compute the *SEM*s.

[a] The average *SEM*s were calculated by averaging the squared *SEM*s for each age group and obtaining the square root of the result.

The *SEM* is used to calculate the confidence interval, or the band of scores around the observed score, in which the individual's true score is likely to fall. Confidence intervals express test score precision and serve as reminders that measurement error is inherent in all test scores and that observed test scores are only estimates of true ability.

Because the reliability coefficients for composite scores are very high and the *SEM*s are very similar across the age groups, the confidence intervals reported in Tables A.3–A.7 in the Administration and Scoring Manual and Table C.1 in this manual were calculated with the overall average reliability coefficients and overall average *SEM*s. Practitioners who wish to calculate confidence intervals for composite scores using the following equations can use either the overall average values for reliability estimates and *SEM*s, or values based on the examinee's age. The examples provided in this section utilize reliability coefficients and *SEM*s based on the examinee's age.

Confidence intervals can be used to report an individual's score as an interval that is likely to contain the individual's true score. For example, if an 18-year-old examinee obtained an FSIQ score of 106, the practitioner can be 95% confident that the individual's true FSIQ score falls in the range of 102–110 (because the 95% confidence interval is 106 ± 1.96 *SEM*, where the *SEM* is 2.12), and 90% confident that the individual's true FSIQ score is in the range of 103–109 (106 ± 1.65 *SEM*). Confidence intervals based on the *SEM* are calculated by the following formula:

$$p\% \text{ Confidence Interval} = \text{Observed Score} \pm Z_p(SEM)$$

where p is the confidence level, such as 90% or 95%, and Z_p is the Z value associated with the confidence level, which can be located in normal probability tables.

The confidence intervals provided in Tables A.3–A.7 in the Administration and Scoring Manual and Table C.1 of this manual were derived by a slightly different method. The 90% and 95% confidence intervals for the composite scores are based on the *estimated true score* and the *standard error of estimation* (*SEE*), according to the method proposed by Dudek (1979) and Glutting, McDermott, and Stanley (1987). The estimated true score is obtained by the formula:

$$\text{Estimated True Score} = 100 + r_{xx}(X-100)$$

where X is the observed composite score and r_{xx} is the reliability coefficient of the composite score. The *SEE* is derived by the formula proposed by Stanley (1971):

$$SEE = SD(r_{xx})\sqrt{1 - r_{xx}}$$

where *SEE* is the standard error of estimation, *SD* is the theoretical standard deviation of the composite score, and r_{xx} is the reliability coefficient of the related composite score. This method centers the confidence interval on the estimated true score rather than on the observed score, and in turn, results in an asymmetrical interval around the observed score. This asymmetry occurs because the estimated true score typically is closer to the mean of the scale than the observed score. A confidence interval based on the estimated true score and the *SEE* is a correction for true-score regression toward the mean. For example, if a 55-year-old examinee obtained an FSIQ score of 113, the examinee's estimated true score will be 112.7, the 95% confidence interval of the examinee's true FSIQ score will be 109–117 (because the 95% confidence interval is 112.7 ± 1.96 *SEE*, where the *SEE* is 2.08), and the 90% confidence interval of the examinee's true FSIQ score will be 109–116 (112.7 ± 1.65 *SEE*).

Because the composite score reliability estimates are relatively high, confidence intervals calculated with the *SEM* centered on the obtained score and those calculated with the *SEE* centered on the estimated true score will be the same or similar. Confidence intervals calculated by either method are interpreted in the same way.

Evidence of Test-Retest Stability

The evidence of test-retest stability for subtest, process, and composite scores was obtained by administering the WAIS–IV twice, with test-retest intervals ranging from 8–82 days and a mean interval of 22 days. Table 4.4 presents the demographic characteristics of the test-retest stability sample. The mean age of the sample is presented, followed by sex, race/ethnicity, education level, and geographic region data reported as percentages.

Table 4.4   Demographic Data for Test-Retest Stability and Interscorer Agreement Reliability Studies

	Test-Retest Stability	Interscorer Agreement Reliability
N	298	60
Age		
Mean	52.6	43.3
SD	23.6	23.5
Sex		
Female	55.4	50.0
Male	44.6	50.0
Race/Ethnicity		
White	72.2	60.0
African American	10.7	15.0
Hispanic	12.1	16.7
Asian	3.0	5.0
Other	2.0	3.3
Education		
≤8 years	9.1	8.3
9–11 years	12.7	10.0
12 years	31.5	30.0
13–15 years	23.5	26.7
≥16 years	23.2	25.0
Region		
Northeast	18.5	8.3
Midwest	21.5	28.3
South	28.5	38.4
West	31.5	25.0

Note. Except for sample size (*N*) and age, data are reported as percentages. For examinees aged 16–19, education was based on parent education; for examinees aged 20–90, education was based on examinee education.

The test-retest reliability was estimated for four age bands (16–29, 30–54, 55–69, and 70–90) using Pearson's product-moment correlation. The mean subtest, process, and composite scores and their standard deviations are presented in Table 4.5. The average stability coefficients for all ages were calculated using Fisher's z transformation. The table also reports the standard differences (i.e., effect sizes) between the first and second testings and the correlation coefficients corrected for the normative sample's variability (Allen & Yen, 1979; Magnusson, 1967). The standard difference was calculated using the mean score difference between the two testings divided by the pooled standard deviation (Cohen, 1988).

As the data in Table 4.5 indicate, the WAIS–IV scores possess adequate stability across time for all four age bands. The average corrected stability coefficient for Information is excellent (.90); the average corrected stability coefficients for Block Design, Similarities, Digit Span, Vocabulary, Arithmetic, Symbol Search, Coding, Letter–Number Sequencing, and Comprehension are good (in the .80s). Those of the other subtests and process scores are adequate (in the .70s). In addition, the average corrected stability coefficients for composites range from good to excellent (in the high .80s to middle .90s).

As the data also indicate, the mean retest scores for all subtests are higher than the scores from the first testing. In general, test-retest gains are less pronounced for the Verbal Comprehension and Working Memory subtests than the Perceptual Reasoning and Processing Speed subtests. These results are generally consistent with those reported for the WAIS–III.

Table 4.5   Stability Coefficients of the Subtest, Process, and Composite Scores

All Ages Subtest/Process/ Composite Score	First Testing		Second Testing		r_{12}[a]	Corrected r[b]	Standard Difference[c]
	Mean	SD	Mean	SD			
BD	10.2	2.9	11.0	2.8	.79	.80	.28
SI	9.9	2.8	10.4	2.8	.83	.87	.18
DS	10.0	2.9	10.6	3.0	.82	.83	.20
MR	10.1	3.1	10.5	3.1	.76	.74	.13
VC	9.9	3.0	10.0	3.0	.90	.89	.03
AR	9.9	2.8	10.4	2.9	.80	.83	.18
SS	10.1	2.9	11.0	3.3	.80	.81	.29
VP	10.0	2.8	10.9	3.0	.69	.74	.31
IN	9.8	3.0	10.5	3.2	.91	.90	.23
CD	10.0	2.7	10.6	2.8	.83	.86	.22
LN	10.1	2.7	10.5	3.1	.76	.80	.14
FW	10.0	3.0	10.8	3.2	.76	.77	.26
CO	10.0	3.0	10.2	2.9	.86	.86	.07
CA	10.2	2.8	10.8	3.0	.74	.78	.21
PCm	9.9	2.9	11.8	3.3	.74	.77	.61
BDN	10.3	2.9	11.0	2.8	.76	.78	.25
DSF	9.9	2.8	10.2	3.0	.74	.77	.10
DSB	10.2	2.9	10.7	3.1	.69	.71	.17
DSS	9.9	2.9	10.6	2.8	.70	.72	.25
VCI	99.3	14.4	101.8	15.0	.95	.96	.17
PRI	100.4	13.8	104.3	14.3	.85	.87	.28
WMI	99.5	14.0	102.6	14.7	.87	.88	.22
PSI	100.2	13.5	104.6	14.9	.84	.87	.31
FSIQ	99.7	13.8	104.0	15.0	.95	.96	.30

[a] Average stability coefficients across all ages were calculated with Fisher's z transformation.

[b] Correlations were corrected for the variability of the normative sample (Allen & Yen, 1979; Magnusson, 1967).

[c] The Standard Difference is the difference of the two test means divided by the square root of the pooled variance, computed using Cohen's (1996) Formula 10.4.

Table 4.5   Stability Coefficients of the Subtest, Process, and Composite Scores *(continued)*

Ages 16–29 Subtest/Process/ Composite Score	First Testing		Second Testing		r_{12}	Corrected r [a]	Standard Difference[b]
	Mean	SD	Mean	SD			
BD	10.1	3.0	11.3	2.9	.81	.81	.41
SI	10.5	3.2	10.9	3.0	.82	.80	.13
DS	10.1	2.8	10.7	2.9	.71	.75	.21
MR	10.5	3.2	10.7	3.0	.70	.66	.06
VC	10.3	3.1	10.5	3.2	.91	.90	.06
AR	10.0	2.9	10.5	2.9	.84	.85	.17
SS	10.4	3.3	11.6	3.4	.84	.81	.36
VP	9.9	2.6	11.0	3.0	.74	.80	.39
IN	10.0	2.9	10.7	3.1	.90	.91	.23
CD	9.8	2.8	10.3	2.8	.83	.85	.18
LN	10.1	2.5	10.8	3.4	.76	.83	.23
FW	10.4	3.0	11.4	3.4	.76	.76	.31
CO	10.2	3.2	10.2	2.9	.86	.84	.00
CA	9.7	2.9	10.8	3.3	.80	.81	.35
PCm	10.0	2.7	12.4	3.2	.74	.79	.81
BDN	10.3	2.7	11.3	2.4	.77	.81	.39
DSF	10.0	2.7	10.4	3.3	.67	.73	.13
DSB	10.4	2.5	11.2	3.0	.51	.66	.29
DSS	9.9	3.2	10.5	3.2	.65	.60	.19
VCI	101.4	14.9	103.6	15.4	.95	.95	.15
PRI	100.8	13.9	105.4	14.4	.84	.86	.33
WMI	100.5	14.7	103.2	14.5	.82	.83	.18
PSI	100.6	15.1	105.4	15.8	.87	.87	.31
FSIQ	101.0	13.8	105.4	14.9	.94	.95	.31

[a] Correlations were corrected for the variability of the normative sample (Allen & Yen, 1979; Magnusson, 1967).

[b] The Standard Difference is the difference of the two test means divided by the square root of the pooled variance, computed using Cohen's (1996) Formula 10.4.

Table 4.5   Stability Coefficients of the Subtest, Process, and Composite Scores *(continued)*

Ages 30–54 Subtest/Process/ Composite Score	First Testing		Second Testing				Standard
	Mean	SD	Mean	SD	r_{12}	Corrected r [a]	Difference[b]
BD	10.4	2.9	11.4	3.1	.80	.81	.33
SI	9.1	2.5	9.7	2.6	.85	.90	.24
DS	10.0	3.2	10.5	3.1	.81	.78	.16
MR	10.2	3.5	10.3	3.4	.85	.80	.03
VC	9.4	3.1	9.5	3.0	.90	.89	.03
AR	9.8	2.5	10.1	3.1	.76	.83	.11
SS	10.3	3.1	11.4	3.4	.75	.73	.34
VP	10.3	3.1	11.4	3.0	.70	.68	.36
IN	9.6	2.9	10.4	2.8	.86	.87	.28
CD	10.3	2.9	11.2	2.7	.83	.84	.32
LN	10.0	2.8	10.5	2.9	.81	.83	.18
FW	9.7	2.7	10.7	3.2	.77	.81	.34
CO	9.3	2.8	9.5	2.8	.89	.90	.07
CA	10.8	2.8	11.3	2.8	.67	.71	.18
PCm	10.1	3.0	12.4	3.3	.68	.68	.73
BDN	10.6	2.9	11.4	2.9	.70	.72	.28
DSF	10.1	3.0	10.2	3.0	.71	.71	.03
DSB	10.0	3.2	10.4	3.3	.73	.69	.12
DSS	10.2	3.0	10.5	2.7	.70	.70	.11
VCI	96.4	13.9	99.1	13.6	.95	.96	.20
PRI	101.2	15.4	105.7	15.9	.88	.87	.29
WMI	99.5	14.6	101.4	15.7	.84	.85	.13
PSI	102.0	13.7	107.3	14.7	.76	.80	.37
FSIQ	99.5	14.5	103.9	15.9	.96	.96	.29

[a] Correlations were corrected for the variability of the normative sample (Allen & Yen, 1979; Magnusson, 1967).

[b] The Standard Difference is the difference of the two test means divided by the square root of the pooled variance, computed using Cohen's (1996) Formula 10.4.

Table 4.5 Stability Coefficients of the Subtest, Process, and Composite Scores *(continued)*

Ages 55–69 Subtest/Process/ Composite Score	First Testing		Second Testing		r_{12}	Corrected r[a]	Standard Difference[b]
	Mean	SD	Mean	SD			
BD	10.5	3.1	11.1	2.9	.77	.75	.20
SI	10.2	2.5	10.9	2.5	.81	.87	.28
DS	10.0	2.9	10.8	3.1	.89	.90	.27
MR	9.9	3.0	10.7	3.3	.72	.72	.25
VC	10.3	3.2	10.5	3.0	.88	.86	.06
AR	9.6	2.9	10.4	2.7	.80	.81	.29
SS	10.0	2.9	11.1	3.2	.80	.81	.36
VP	10.4	2.9	10.8	3.0	.73	.75	.14
IN	10.5	3.1	11.4	3.4	.92	.91	.28
CD	10.1	2.7	10.7	3.1	.86	.89	.21
LN	10.0	2.8	10.1	2.8	.70	.74	.04
FW	9.7	3.2	10.3	2.9	.76	.73	.20
CO	10.4	2.9	10.4	2.9	.84	.85	.00
CA	10.1	2.6	10.3	2.7	.74	.80	.08
PCm	10.0	2.8	11.8	3.6	.78	.81	.56
BDN	10.3	3.3	11.1	3.3	.75	.70	.24
DSF	9.8	2.7	10.2	2.9	.76	.81	.14
DSB	10.3	3.0	11.1	3.2	.77	.77	.26
DSS	9.8	2.2	10.6	2.5	.71	.84	.34
VCI	101.5	14.3	104.8	14.9	.94	.95	.23
PRI	101.1	13.8	104.7	14.4	.87	.89	.26
WMI	98.7	13.7	103.0	14.1	.90	.92	.31
PSI	100.3	13.2	105.3	14.9	.89	.91	.36
FSIQ	100.6	14.5	105.5	15.4	.96	.96	.33

[a] Correlations were corrected for the variability of the normative sample (Allen & Yen, 1979; Magnusson, 1967).

[b] The Standard Difference is the difference of the two test means divided by the square root of the pooled variance, computed using Cohen's (1996) Formula 10.4.

Table 4.5   Stability Coefficients of the Subtest, Process, and Composite Scores *(continued)*

Ages 70–90 Subtest/Process/ Composite Score	First Testing		Second Testing		r_{12}	Corrected r [a]	Standard Difference [b]
	Mean	SD	Mean	SD			
BD	10.0	2.6	10.4	2.5	.79	.84	.16
SI	9.8	2.6	10.3	3.0	.84	.88	.18
DS	9.8	2.9	10.5	2.9	.84	.85	.24
MR	10.0	2.8	10.3	2.8	.73	.76	.11
VC	9.7	2.8	9.7	2.8	.91	.92	.00
AR	10.1	2.7	10.5	2.9	.80	.84	.14
SS	9.8	2.5	10.0	2.9	.80	.86	.07
VP	9.4	2.5	10.4	3.0	.57	.70	.36
IN	9.3	3.2	9.9	3.2	.93	.92	.19
CD	9.7	2.6	10.3	2.6	.81	.86	.23
CO	10.2	2.9	10.6	3.1	.85	.86	.13
PCm	9.4	3.0	10.6	2.9	.77	.77	.41
BDN	10.0	2.6	10.4	2.5	.80	.85	.16
DSF	9.9	2.9	10.0	2.9	.81	.82	.03
DSB	10.0	3.0	10.3	3.0	.71	.71	.10
DSS	9.6	3.1	10.7	2.8	.72	.70	.37
VCI	97.8	14.0	99.9	15.3	.95	.96	.14
PRI	98.7	12.4	101.9	12.7	.80	.86	.25
WMI	99.4	13.4	102.6	14.8	.89	.91	.23
PSI	98.5	12.0	101.2	13.8	.82	.88	.21
FSIQ	98.1	12.7	101.6	14.0	.94	.96	.26

[a] Correlations were corrected for the variability of the normative sample (Allen & Yen, 1979; Magnusson, 1967).

[b] The Standard Difference is the difference of the two test means divided by the square root of the pooled variance, computed using Cohen's (1996) Formula 10.4.

Evidence of Interscorer Agreement

All WAIS–IV protocols were double scored by two independent scorers, and evidence of inter-scorer agreement was obtained using the normative sample. Because most of the subtest scoring criteria are simple and objective, interscorer agreement was high, ranging from .98 to .99. For those subtests that require more judgment in scoring, special studies were conducted to evaluate interscorer agreement.

The subtests targeted for the special interscorer agreement studies were Similarities, Vocabulary, Information, and Comprehension. A sample of 60 cases was randomly selected from the norma-tive sample. Table 4.4 presents the demographic characteristics of the interscorer agreement sample. The mean age of the sample is presented, followed by percentages of sample representa-tion by sex, race/ethnicity, education level, and geographic region.

Three raters independently scored each of the test protocols in the selected sample. All raters were completing graduate-level clinical psychology programs. They had also completed at least a one-semester course in psychological assessment. None of the raters had any previous experience with the WAIS–IV scoring rules.

The interrater reliability coefficients were calculated according to appropriate intraclass correlation procedures (McGraw & Wong, 1996; Shrout & Fleiss, 1979). Total subtest scores were used in the analysis. Interscorer reliabilities were .93 for Similarities, .95 for Vocabulary, .97 for Information, and .91 for Comprehension. These results demonstrate that although these subtests require more judgment, they can be scored reliably, even by individuals with no prior experience with WAIS–IV scoring criteria.

Score Differences

The differences that occur between WAIS–IV scores from a single administration are an important consideration in interpreting the examinee's performance. The issue of score differences has two different aspects—the statistical significance of the difference and the base rate (frequency) of the difference in the population. These aspects are designed to address two questions: Is the difference real and not due to measurement error? Is the difference clinically meaningful?

Statistical Significance of Index Score Differences

A statistically significant difference between scores, for example between the VCI and PRI, refers to the likelihood that obtaining such a difference by chance is very low (e.g., $p < .05$) if the true difference between the scores is 0 (Matarazzo & Herman, 1985). The level of significance reflects the level of confidence the practitioner can have that the difference between the scores, called the difference score, is a true difference.

The difference between scores required for significance is computed from the standard error of measurement of the difference (SE_{diff}). This statistic provides an estimate for the standard deviation of the sampling distribution of the difference between the two obtained index scores. Multiplying the SE_{diff} by an appropriate z value yields the amount of difference required for statistical significance at any given level of confidence.

The differences between WAIS–IV index scores required for statistical significance (critical values) are presented in Table B.1 of the Administration and Scoring Manual. The critical values are provided for the .15 and .05 levels of significance, by age group and by overall normative sample. Although these differences vary slightly from age group to age group, average values for all of the age groups, which are given in the last two rows of the table, provide an acceptable approximation for many clinical situations. Table C.2 in this manual provides the differences required for statistical significance (critical values) for the optional comparison between the FSIQ and GAI scores.

Frequency of Index Score Differences

The prevalence or frequency of an observed score difference in the general population is also referred to as the *base rate*. Often the difference between an examinee's index scores (e.g., VCI and PRI) is significant in the statistical sense but is not infrequent. The statistical significance of differences between scores and the rarity of the difference are two different issues and consequently have different implications for test interpretation. For detailed discussion of the distinction between statistically and clinically meaningful differences between scores, refer to Groth-Marnat, 2003; Kaufman and Lichtenberger, 1999; Matarazzo and Herman, 1985; Payne and Jones, 1957; Sattler, 2008a; and Silverstein, 1981.

The frequencies of differences between index scores that occurred in the normative sample (base rates) are presented in Table B.2 of the Administration and Scoring Manual. Because the normative sample's index score discrepancies vary as a function of ability level and not age (Matarazzo & Herman, 1985; Sattler, 2008a; Wechsler, 1997a), the base rate data is presented in two general categories: by overall normative sample and by ability level. Within each category, the base rate data is provided by the direction of the difference, based on findings that showed the base rates of difference scores are not identical in both directions (Sattler, 2008a). For example, for individuals whose FSIQ is 79 points or less, 12.7% obtained PRI scores 15 or more points higher than their VCI scores, whereas only 6.3% obtained VCI scores 15 or more points higher than their PRI scores. Table C.3 in this manual provides similar base rate information for the optional evaluation of differences between an examinee's FSIQ and GAI scores.

Differences Between Subtest Scaled Scores

Very often an examinee's performance on a Wechsler intelligence scale varies across different subtests. An evaluation of subtest variability provides useful information for interpretation of index scores and helps the practitioner identify the individual's cognitive strengths and weaknesses. As with differences between index scores, the interpretation of differences between subtest scores should take into account the statistical significance of the observed difference and population base rate estimates. The common procedures for evaluating the variability across different subtests are comparison of scaled scores on a particular subtest pair, comparison of a single subtest scaled score to the average scaled score on a group of subtests, and scatter analysis. Examination of process score differences may be useful for evaluating the variability within a subtest (e.g., DSF vs. DSB) and the cognitive processes that contribute to performance (i.e., BD vs. BDN).

Statistical Significance of Differences Between Subtest Scaled Scores

The difference between scaled scores on a particular subtest pair (called pairwise comparison) may be of interest. When an index score is derived from two subtest scaled scores (i.e., the WMI and PSI), the practitioner can evaluate the significance and rarity of the difference between the subtest scaled scores to inform interpretation of the index score.

Table B.3 of the Administration and Scoring Manual presents minimum differences required for statistical significance at the .15 and .05 levels for every possible WAIS–IV subtest pair. The values for significance at the .15 level appear above the diagonal, and the values for significance at the .05 level appear below the diagonal. For example, a scaled score difference between Similarities and Vocabulary of 1.87 points or more is significant at the .15 level, and a difference of 2.54 points or more is significant at the .05 level.

The base rate data for differences between core subtests of the Working Memory (i.e., Digit Span and Arithmetic) and Processing Speed (i.e., Symbol Search and Coding) scales are reported in Table B.4 of the Administration and Scoring Manual. The table provides the base rate data by the direction of the difference. For example, about 1.5% of examinees from the normative sample obtained scaled scores for Coding that were 6 or more points higher than their scaled scores for Symbol Search, whereas about 2.0% obtained scaled scores for Symbol Search that were 6 or more points higher than their scaled scores for Coding.

Differences Between a Single Subtest Score and an Average of Subtest Scores

A common procedure for evaluating an individual's cognitive strengths and weaknesses involves comparing a single subtest scaled score to an average scaled score on a group of subtests. For instance, an examinee's Similarities scaled score may be compared to the mean scaled score of the three subtests that contribute to the VCI, or to the mean scaled score of the 10 subtests that contribute to the FSIQ. A single scaled score that is significantly greater than the examinee's own mean scaled score may reflect a relative strength, whereas one that is significantly less than the mean may indicate a relative weakness. The procedure for testing such differences for statistical significance was originally suggested by Davis (1959). Silverstein (1982) refined the procedure to account for the fact that several comparisons are being made simultaneously.

The interpretation of the difference between a single subtest score and the examinee's own mean score is an intra-individual comparison. Strengths and weaknesses identified in this way are strengths and weaknesses relative to the examinee's own ability level. A high subtest scaled score (i.e., well above 10) may still represent a relative weakness for an examinee of extremely high general ability. Conversely, a fairly low subtest scaled score may indicate a relative strength for an examinee of limited general ability.

The minimum differences between a single subtest scaled score and the mean scaled scores of various groups of subtests required for statistical significance at the .15 and .05 levels are provided in Table B.5 of the Administration and Scoring Manual. Using the table, if the difference between the Vocabulary scaled score and the mean scaled scores for the three Verbal Comprehension subtests is 1.29 points or more, it is significant at the .15 level, whereas a difference of 1.58 points or more is significant at the .05 level.

As with the differences between index scores, a difference between a single subtest scaled score and the mean of a group of subtest scaled scores may be statistically significant but not especially unusual in the population. If an examinee's scaled score on a single subtest, for example Similarities, is significantly less than his or her mean scaled score on the three Verbal Comprehension subtests, it does not necessarily indicate that the difference is clinically meaningful. For this purpose, the frequency of such a difference occurring in the normative sample can be very useful because it indicates whether the difference is rare or common in the general population.

Table B.5 also provides data on differences obtained by various percentages of the normative sample, which are the estimated base rates of differences in the general population. According to this table, a difference of 3.67 points or more between the Similarities subtest scaled score and the mean scaled score of the three Verbal Comprehension subtests occurred in ≤1% of the normative sample.

Intersubtest Scatter

Intersubtest scatter reflects the variability of an individual's scaled scores across the subtests (Matarazzo, Daniel, Prifitera, & Herman, 1988; Sattler, 2008a). Such variability has frequently been considered diagnostically significant. Although various scatter measures have been proposed (see Schinka, Vanderploeg, & Curtiss, 1997), the simple difference between the examinee's highest and lowest subtest scaled scores is the easiest to obtain and is the scatter index used in this manual.

Before interpreting the scatter exhibited in a particular test record, the practitioner should consider how common such a scatter is in the normative sample. The cumulative percentages of intersubtest scatter within various WAIS–IV composite scales are reported in Table B.6 of the Administration and Scoring Manual. For example, only 4.2% of the normative sample obtained a scatter of 11 or more points among the 10 core subtests contributing to the FSIQ score. A scatter of 9 or more points among the 10 subtests contributing to the FSIQ score was obtained by 16.7% of the same examinees.

Process Score Differences

The process-level discrepancy comparisons reflect the differences between scores for a subtest and its corresponding process score (i.e., BD and BDN), or differences between two process scores for a single subtest (e.g., DSF and DSB). These process-level discrepancy comparisons may be of particular clinical interest. For example, additional information on the contribution of speed to an examinee's Block Design performance may be obtained from comparing the BD and BDN scaled scores. Prior to interpretation, the practitioner should know whether such a difference is statistically significant and how frequently it occurs in the normative sample.

Table C.2 of the Administration and Scoring Manual presents minimum scaled score differences required for statistical significance at the .15 and .05 levels for various process-level discrepancy comparisons. The base rate data for the corresponding discrepancy comparisons are reported in Table C.3 of the Administration and Scoring Manual. Note that the tables provide the base rate data by the direction of the difference. For example, about 5.9% of examinees obtained Digit Span Forward scores that were 5 or more points higher than their Digit Span Backward scores, whereas about 5.5% obtained Digit Span Backward scores 5 or more points higher than their Digit Span Forward scores. The pairwise discrepancy comparisons among LDSF, LDSB, and LDSS utilize raw scores rather than scaled scores. Tables C.6–C.8 of the Administration and Scoring Manual present the base rate data for the LDSF, LDSB, and LDSS raw score discrepancy comparisons. See chapter 6 for additional information on process score interpretation.

Summary

This chapter has presented evidence for the reliability of scores derived from WAIS–IV administration. The referenced tables provide necessary data for reliable interpretation of differences between scores in a WAIS–IV profile. Seemingly large discrepancies between two scores, for example, may not necessarily be statistically significant, and some statistically significant differences may not be rare in the general population. The practitioner should keep in mind that measurement error contributes to part of observed score differences and that the errors in the differences between index scores (e.g., between VCI and PRI) will generally be smaller than the measurement errors in the differences between subtest scaled scores. This pattern occurs because the index scores are generally more reliable than the subtests. As always, when interpreting any score, the practitioner should integrate relevant information from a variety of sources, including the individual's presenting issues and referral question(s); educational background; medical, educational, and psychosocial history; and results from other administered instruments (e.g., measures of mental status, psychopathology, memory, and executive functioning).

Chapter 5

Evidence of WAIS–IV Validity

The validity of a test is the single most fundamental and important aspect of test development and evaluation (AERA, 1999; Angoff, 1988; Sattler, 2008a). Traditionally, researchers and test developers have referred to three major types of validity: content, criterion-related, and construct validity. A test was considered to have *content validity* if it adequately sampled relevant aspects of the construct being measured. A test was considered to have *criterion-related validity* if scores were shown to be related to specified external criteria, such as performance on some other measure or group membership. A test was characterized as having *construct validity* when the construct purported to be measured by the test was actually measured. Evidence of a test's construct validity can come from many different sources, including factor analysis, expert review, multitrait-mulitimethod studies, and clinical investigations.

Contemporary definitions of validity are more unitary in nature. As stated in the *Standards*, "evolving conceptualizations of . . . validity no longer speak of different types of validity but speak instead of different lines of validity evidence, all in service of providing information relevant to a specific intended interpretation of test scores" (AERA, 1999, p. 5). Validity refers to the degree to which evidence supports the interpretation of test scores for their intended purposes. As a result, the examination of a test's validity requires an evaluative judgment by the test user.

Although test developers are responsible for providing initial evidence of validity, the practitioner must evaluate whether the evidence supports the use of the test for the intended purpose. This does not mean that a test is valid only for the settings and purposes stated by test developers. A comprehensive evaluation of a scale's validity evidence also includes an examination of the relevant literature on previous versions of a scale, as well as the literature that results from the use of a newly revised measure for different purposes, in different settings, or with different populations. It is expected that future use of the WAIS–IV will lead to an expanding base of evidence for the scale's validity. Please refer to the *WAIS–III/WMS–III Technical Manual* (Wechsler, 1997a), *Clinical Use and Interpretation of the WAIS–III and WMS–III* (Tulsky et al., 2003), *Assessing Adult and Adolescent Intelligence,* 3rd Edition (Kaufman & Lichtenberger, 2006), and *Assessment of Children: Cognitive Foundations,* 5th Edition (Sattler, 2008a) for evidence supporting the validity of the WAIS–IV's predecessor, the WAIS–III.

This chapter provides evidence related to the validity of the WAIS–IV. Lines of evidence that support the scale's use as a measure of intellectual ability will be presented, including evidence based on the test content, response processes, internal structure, and relationships with other variables.

Evidence Based on Test Content

Examining relationships between a test's content and the construct it is intended to measure provides a major source of evidence about the validity of the test. Evidence of content validity is not based on statistics or empirical testing; rather, it is based on the degree to which the test items adequately represent and relate to the trait or function that is being measured. Test content also involves wording and format of items, as well as procedures for administering and scoring the test.

The goal of content revision in the WAIS–IV was to ensure that the items and subtests adequately sample the domains of intellectual functioning that the test is intended to measure. The items and subtests tap a broad range of cognitive processes, including verbal, analogical, sequential, and quantitative reasoning; concept formation; sequential and simultaneous processing; auditory comprehension; cognitive flexibility; working memory; perceptual organization; and psychomotor processing speed (Kaufman & Lichtenberger, 1999, 2006; Sattler, 2008a). Comprehensive literature and expert reviews were conducted to examine the content of the WAIS–III and to evaluate proposed new items and subtests designed to improve content coverage and relevance. See chapter 2 for a detailed discussion of WAIS–IV content and structure.

Evidence Based on Response Processes

For the WAIS–IV, validity evidence based on response processes should provide support that the individual engages the expected cognitive process when responding to subtest tasks. This type of evidence may be provided by theoretical sources or psychometric analysis.

Most of the WAIS–IV subtests have strong theoretical and empirical evidence of validity based on response processes. An extensive body of research on the response processes engaged during subtest performance supports the subtests retained from previous versions (Carroll, 1993; Kaufman & Lichtenberger, 1999, 2006; Sattler, 2008a). Extensive literature reviews, expert consultation, and empirical examinations were conducted for the new subtests to provide additional evidence of validity based on response processes. Details of the theoretical foundations of all subtests, including information on evoked response processes, are provided in chapter 2.

Additional evidence of validity was accumulated through empirical and qualitative examination of response processes during the scale's development. For example, response frequencies for multiple-choice items were examined to identify any responses that were commonly given in error. Frequently occurring incorrect responses were examined to determine their plausibility as acceptable answers. If this process revealed the possible existence of unintended, acceptable responses, changes were made to item content and items were reexamined in subsequent research stages.

Direct questioning can also be useful for revealing within-group differences in response processes, even on those subtests with long histories of use. For example, individuals were questioned about problem-solving strategies employed for Matrix Reasoning, Visual Puzzles, and Figure Weights. Appropriate adjustments were then made to the instructions and distractors on these subtests. As with all lines of validity evidence, it is expected that future research will provide additional evidence based on the response processes evoked by the items and subtests of the WAIS–IV.

Evidence Based on Internal Structure

An examination of a scale's internal structure "can indicate the degree to which the relationships among test items and test components conform to the construct on which the proposed test score interpretations are based" (AERA, 1999, p. 13). Research utilizing the Wechsler scales has provided strong evidence of validity based on the scales' internal structure (e.g., Wechsler, 1989, 1991, 1997a, 2002, 2003).

The nature of this evidence has evolved in line with advances in intelligence theory and assessment, as well as in the fields of neuropsychology and cognitive development. In a series of articles, Cohen (1952a, 1952b, 1957a, 1957b, 1959) presented and discussed factor analyses of the WB, the WAIS, and the WISC, which suggested the presence of a weaker third factor within the performance scale. The introduction of Symbol Search in the WISC–III was designed to clarify the third factor but instead revealed the presence of a fourth factor, Processing Speed. As a result, four optional WISC–III index scores were derived to represent more specific domains of cognitive functioning, in addition to the traditional VIQ, PIQ, and FSIQ scores. As the index scores gained acceptance and empirical support, evidence of their clinical utility became more apparent. The addition of Letter–Number Sequencing and Symbol Search to the WAIS–III further clarified the nature of the index scores: the Freedom from Distractibility Index was more appropriately labeled the Working Memory Index, and the Processing Speed Index was created. The WAIS–III therefore also provided four optional index scores to represent more specific domains of cognitive functioning, in addition to the traditional VIQ, PIQ, and FSIQ scores.

Three new subtests have been added to the WAIS–IV. The Visual Puzzles subtest was incorporated to replace Picture Arrangement and Object Assembly, providing an additional measure of Perceptual Reasoning. The Figure Weights subtest was incorporated to enhance the measure of fluid reasoning for ages 16–69. Cancellation was adapted from the WISC–IV and developed as a measure of processing speed for ages 16–69.

The interrelationships among items, subtests, and composite scores on the WAIS–IV were examined to provide evidence of validity based on the scale's internal structure. The internal consistency of item sets at the subtest level was examined and is reported in chapter 4.

Intercorrelation Studies

In their classic article, Campbell and Fiske (1959) presented a theoretical methodology for interpreting the patterns of correlations in a multitrait-multimethod matrix to provide evidence of *convergent validity* and *discriminant validity*. Their original methodology was based on the examination of correlational patterns in a matrix where relatively high correlations (convergent validity) are predicted for some variables and relatively low correlations (discriminant validity) are predicted for other variables. Data supporting a priori hypotheses about the pattern of the relationships provide evidence of construct validity.

Intercorrelations of Subtest, Process, and Composite Scores

Several a priori hypotheses were made regarding the intercorrelation studies. First, all scores would show some degree of correlation to one another, based on the assumption that all subtests measure a general intelligence factor (i.e., *g*). It was assumed that all subtests would have at least low to moderate correlations with each other.

Second, it was expected that subtests contributing to a specific index scale (i.e., Verbal Comprehension, Perceptual Reasoning, Working Memory, and Processing Speed) would have higher correlations with each other than with subtests comprising other scales. For example, the correlation between Similarities and Vocabulary (two Verbal Comprehension subtests) was expected to be higher than correlations between either of these subtests and any of the Perceptual Reasoning, Working Memory, or Processing Speed subtests (e.g., Block Design, Digit Span, or Symbol Search).

Third, evidence from previous studies indicates that some subtests are more related to g than other subtests. For example, Block Design, Similarities, Matrix Reasoning, Vocabulary, Arithmetic, Information, and Comprehension all have been shown to have high g loadings (Sattler, 2008a). Several predictions was made based on this evidence. It was expected that subtests with high g loadings, regardless of scale membership, would have relatively high correlations with each other. It was also expected that the correlation between two high g-loading subtests from the same scale (e.g., Verbal Comprehension) would be higher than the correlation between two high g-loading subtests from different scales (e.g., Verbal Comprehension and Perceptual Reasoning). Based on previous studies indicating patterns of split loading (Wechsler, 1997a), Picture Completion was expected to correlate with subtests on the Verbal Comprehension and Perceptual Reasoning scales, and Arithmetic was expected to correlate with subtests on the Verbal Comprehension and Working Memory scales. Fourth, it was expected that the correlations between subtests and their corresponding scaled process scores would be high, based on their shared item content.

Tables A.1 through A.13 report the intercorrelations of subtest, process, and composite scores for each of the 13 age groups. The average correlations for the age groups were computed using Fisher's z transformation. The average intercorrelations of the subtest, process, and composite scores are presented in Table 5.1. Each table includes the correlations of the subtests with the sums of scaled scores for each of the composites. The correlation between the sum of scaled scores for a composite and the scaled score for each contributing subtest was corrected by removing that subtest scaled score from the sum of the scaled scores to control for inflated correlations. The uncorrected coefficients appear below the diagonal and the corrected coefficients appear above the diagonal, in the shaded area.

Statistically, all intersubtest correlations are significant. The pattern of WAIS–IV intercorrelations is very similar to that found for the WAIS–III and other Wechsler intelligence tests in which most of the subtests have significant correlations with the other subtests (Wechsler, 1989, 1991, 1997a, 2002, 2003).

The subtests comprising the Verbal Comprehension scale correlate most highly with each other. Moderate to high correlations exist between the Verbal Comprehension subtests and all Perceptual Reasoning subtests, which were expected considering that subtests on both scales have high g loadings. Correlations between the Verbal Comprehension subtests and the Working Memory subtests range from moderate to high, with the highest correlations observed between Arithmetic and the Verbal Comprehension subtests. This is consistent with predictions based on previous split-loading patterns for this subtest. The correlations between the Verbal Comprehension subtests and Processing Speed subtests are generally lower than those observed between the Verbal Comprehension subtests and subtests from the Perceptual Reasoning and Working Memory scales.

The Perceptual Reasoning subtests generally correlate most highly with each other but exhibit correlations almost as high with the Verbal Comprehension subtests. Performance on Perceptual Reasoning subtests can in part be verbally mediated. Perceptual Reasoning subtests also show moderate to high correlations with Working Memory subtests. This suggests the probable role of working memory in fluid reasoning tasks. Figure Weights shows its highest correlation with Arithmetic, which is likely due to the quantitative nature of both tasks. Figure Weights also has a high correlation with Digit Span, a task that involves mental manipulation of numbers.

Working Memory subtests show high correlations with other Working Memory subtests and moderate to high correlations with Verbal Comprehension subtests. This is not surprising considering the auditory comprehension and verbal expression demands of subtests on both scales.

Processing Speed subtests are generally most highly related to other Processing Speed subtests. Moderate correlations with other subtests are also observed. For example, the moderate correlation between Block Design and Symbol Search may be related to the visualization and motor abilities that are required for both tasks. This is similar to the results found for the WAIS–III and the WISC–IV. Compared with Symbol Search and Coding, Cancellation has lower correlations with the subtests from the Verbal Comprehension and Perceptual Reasoning scales, suggesting a relatively lower *g* loading. However, consistent with Symbol Search and Coding, moderate correlations are observed between Cancellation and the subtests from the Working Memory scale, which is perhaps related to the attentional demands of these subtests.

As expected, the correlations between the subtests and their corresponding scaled process scores are high. Block Design and Block Design No Time Bonus share identical item content and therefore display a very high correlation. In contrast, Digit Span Forward, Digit Span Backward, and Digit Span Sequencing each contribute one-third of the items comprising Digit Span, and the correlations of those component tasks with Digit Span are relatively lower than that of Block Design and Block Design No Time Bonus. The intercorrelations of the component tasks of Digit Span are moderate to high, most likely due to shared method variance and similar content. The correlations of Arithmetic and Letter–Number Sequencing with Digit Span Forward, Digit Span Backward, and Digit Span Sequencing are also high, with the exception of the moderate correlation between Arithmetic and Digit Span Forward.

With minor exceptions, the same general pattern of intercorrelations also appears across the 13 age groups. These data generally support the expectation that subtests of similar functioning correlate more highly with each other than with subtests measuring different types of functioning, providing initial evidence of both convergent and discriminant validity of the WAIS–IV.

Table 5.1   Intercorrelations of Subtest, Process, and Composite Scores for All Ages

Subtest/Process/ Composite Score	BD	SI	DS	MR	VC	AR	SS	VP	IN	CD	LN	FW	CO	CA	PCm	BDN	DSF	DSB	DSS	VCI	PRI	WMI	PSI	FSIQ
BD																					.67			.66
SI	.49																			.74				.71
DS	.45	.48																				.60		.64
MR	.54	.51	.47																		.59			.67
VC	.45	.74	.50	.51																.81				.72
AR	.50	.54	.60	.52	.57																	.60		.70
SS	.41	.35	.40	.39	.34	.37																	.65	.54
VP	.64	.44	.40	.53	.42	.48	.38														.66			.62
IN	.44	.64	.43	.49	.73	.57	.34	.43												.73				.67
CD	.40	.41	.45	.45	.41	.43	.65	.37	.34														.65	.59
LN	.42	.45	.69	.45	.48	.56	.37	.41	.43	.38														
FW	.56	.53	.50	.57	.53	.61	.34	.58	.51	.36	.48													
CO	.44	.71	.48	.49	.74	.55	.32	.43	.66	.39	.47	.53												
CA	.34	.23	.34	.26	.24	.31	.46	.32	.22	.42	.30	.29	.21											
PCm	.49	.44	.39	.42	.39	.37	.41	.48	.41	.38	.37	.41	.40	.33										
BDN	.97	.47	.45	.54	.44	.48	.40	.61	.43	.40	.41	.54	.44	.33	.49									
DSF	.29	.35	.79	.29	.36	.43	.25	.24	.31	.29	.50	.34	.32	.23	.24	.30								
DSB	.37	.39	.83	.43	.43	.51	.31	.33	.36	.37	.59	.43	.39	.27	.32	.38	.53							
DSS	.42	.42	.79	.43	.42	.52	.40	.40	.37	.43	.59	.47	.43	.32	.37	.41	.42	.51						
VCI	.51	.88	.53	.56	.92	.63	.38	.48	.89	.43	.51	.59	.79	.26	.46	.50	.38	.44	.45					
PRI	.86	.57	.52	.82	.55	.59	.47	.86	.54	.48	.50	.68	.54	.36	.55	.84	.33	.45	.49	.61				
WMI	.53	.57	.90	.55	.60	.89	.43	.49	.56	.49	.70	.62	.57	.36	.43	.52	.68	.75	.73	.64	.62			
PSI	.45	.42	.47	.46	.41	.44	.91	.41	.37	.91	.41	.39	.39	.49	.43	.44	.30	.38	.46	.45	.52	.51		
FSIQ	.73	.77	.72	.75	.78	.77	.64	.70	.75	.68	.64	.71	.71	.44	.58	.71	.50	.60	.63	.85	.86	.83	.72	
Mean	10.0	10.0	10.0	10.1	10.0	10.0	10.0	10.0	10.0	10.0	10.0	10.1	10.0	10.0	10.0	10.1	10.0	10.1	10.0	30.1	30.1	20.1	20.0	100.3
SD	3.1	2.9	3.0	3.1	3.0	3.0	3.1	3.1	3.1	3.0	3.0	3.1	3.1	3.0	3.1	3.1	3.0	3.0	3.0	8.0	7.8	5.4	5.5	21.9

Note. Correlations for LN, FW, and CA are based only on examinees aged 16:0–69:11. Uncorrected coefficients appear below the diagonal, and corrected coefficients appear above the diagonal in the shaded area.

Confirmatory Factor-Analytic Studies

The factor model proposed for the WAIS–IV can be evaluated with structural equation modeling (Jöreskog & Sörbom, 1993). Confirmatory factor analysis is designed to replicate the factor structure specified by researchers a priori. In this sense, confirmatory factor analysis is different from an exploratory approach, because the grouping of subtests is made in advance rather than being generated by an algorithm. The specific relations between observed variables (e.g., subtests) and a latent variable (e.g., verbal comprehension ability) are specified in advance, and that model is tested to determine if the relations between observed and latent variables confirm the hypothesized structure.

Confirmatory factor analysis is preferred to exploratory factor analysis when an explicit theory of the factor structure is present, or there are competing models in the research literature (Stevens, 1996). Almost 70 years of research have been conducted on the Wechsler intelligence scales. Throughout this time, theoretical advances in intelligence theory and psychometric techniques have guided the scales' revisions. Subsequent research has subjected the WAIS and its successors to additional evaluations of the scales' structures (Blaha & Wallbrown, 1996; Leckliter, Matarazzo, & Silverstein, 1986). The addition of new subtests (e.g., Letter–Number Sequencing and Symbol Search) provided reliable and distinctive measures of new ability constructs (e.g., Working Memory and Processing Speed indexes), as demonstrated by factor-analytic results. The majority of research indicates that the WAIS–III measures four cognitive domains (for discussion, see Bowden, Weiss, Holdnack, & Lloyd, 2006; Dickinson, Iannone, & Gold, 2002; Taub, McGrew, & Witta, 2004; Wechsler, 1997a). In addition, the four-factor structure has demonstrated robustness across adaptions for English-speaking countries (e.g., Bowden, Lange, Weiss, & Saklofske, in press). However, some researchers have evaluated the fit of two and three-factor models and concluded that alternative models may have merit (Kaufman, Lichtenberger, & McLean, 2001; Ward, Ryan, & Axelrod, 2000).

The development of the WAIS–IV was predicated on the theoretical assumption that the scale provides an estimate of general cognitive ability (i.e., the FSIQ) that is measured by four cognitive domains (i.e., Verbal Comprehension, Perceptual Reasoning, Working Memory, and Processing Speed). Visual Puzzles and Figure Weights were designed to measure perceptual and fluid reasoning ability, respectively. The Cancellation subtest was designed to provide an additional measure of processing speed. Exploratory factor analysis was utilized in early phases of subtest development to evaluate the pattern of relationships between the new and retained subtests.

Based on previous research and results from early research phases, the test structure described in chapter 2 proposes the WAIS–IV factor structure as a second-order model, with four first-order factors (the Verbal Comprehension, Perceptual Reasoning, Working Memory, and Processing Speed factors) contributing to the second-order g factor (the Full Scale factor). A series of confirmatory factor analyses was conducted to evaluate the WAIS–IV factor structure. In particular, analyses were aimed at indicating the number and nature of the factors identified by the instrument and determining how well the WAIS–IV subtests measure the latent ability constructs. The proposed model was tested and compared to alternative models, using only core subtests in the first series of analyses, and again using the core and supplemental subtests in the second series of analyses.

Analysis of Core Subtests

Table 5.2 presents fit indexes for confirmatory factor analyses of the core subtests for the overall sample as well as for the following five age groups: 16–19, 20–34, 35-54, 55-69, and 70–90. For each of these samples, the following six structural models were tested and compared to a model with no common factors (Null Model). For Model 1, all subtests load directly on the g factor. Model 2 represents the historical two-factor model in which separate verbal and performance factors have causal links to the g factor. Model 3 represents the three-factor model in which the verbal factor, performance factor, and a combined working memory and processing speed factor have causal links to the g factor.

Models 4, 5, and 6 are variations on the basic four-factor model. In Model 4, the four index factors have causal links to the g factor and each subtest loads on only one factor. Model 5 is similar to Model 4, but it incorporates predicted loadings of the Arithmetic subtest on both the Verbal Comprehension and Working Memory factors. This pattern of split loadings has been noted in previous analyses of the Wechsler intelligence scales (Wechsler, 1997a, 2003). Model 6 is a first-order model, and does not, therefore, represent causal links to the g factor (i.e., only the four index factors are specified). In other respects, it is the same as Model 5. Model 6 is reported for comparability to WAIS–III results, and the factor intercorrelations that it reports provide additional validity evidence for the interpretability of the four index scores (see Arnau & Thompson [2000] for discussion about reporting first- and second-order confirmatory factor analysis results).

Details regarding the subtest composition of each model are provided below.

- Model 1 (One first-order factor)

  10 subtests on a general factor

- Model 2 (One second-order factor and two first-order factors)

  3 Verbal Comprehension subtests and 2 Working Memory subtests on the first factor

  3 Perceptual Reasoning subtests and 2 Processing Speed subtests on the second factor

- Model 3 (One second-order factor and three first-order factors)

  3 Verbal Comprehension subtests on the first factor

  3 Perceptual Reasoning subtests on the second factor

  2 Working Memory subtests and 2 Processing Speed subtests on the third factor

- Model 4 (One second-order factor and four first-order factors)

  3 Verbal Comprehension subtests on the first factor

  3 Perceptual Reasoning subtests on the second factor

  2 Working Memory subtests on the third factor

  2 Processing Speed subtests on the fourth factor

- Model 5 (One second-order factor and four first-order factors)

  Same as Model 4, but with Arithmetic allowed to load on both the Verbal Comprehension and Working Memory factors

- Model 6 (Four first-order factors)

  Same as Model 5, but with no second-order factor

Table 5.2   Goodness-of-Fit Statistics for Confirmatory Factor Analysis of Core Subtests

Model	Goodness-of-Fit Index					Improvement			
	χ^2	df	χ^2/df	AGFI	RMSEA	$\Delta\chi^2$	Δdf	TLI	CFI
Ages 16–90 (N = 2,200)									
Null Model	11235.87	45	249.69						
Model 1	2214.42	35	63.27	.74	.159	9021.45	10	.75	.83
Model 2	1439.83	31	46.45	.79	.139	774.59	4	.82	.88
Model 3	869.23	29	29.97	.86	.114	570.60	2	.88	.93
Model 4	323.15	27	11.97	.94	.069	546.08	2	.96	.97
Model 5	302.15	26	11.62	.94	.068	21.00	1	.96	.98
Model 6	287.60	28	10.27	.95	.063	—	—	.96	.98
Ages 16–19 (n = 400)									
Null Model	1734.37	45	38.54						
Model 1	364.52	35	10.41	.76	.148	1369.85	10	.75	.82
Model 2	269.46	31	8.69	.79	.135	95.06	4	.80	.87
Model 3	139.05	29	4.79	.88	.099	130.41	2	.90	.93
Model 4	57.09	27	2.11	.94	.051	81.96	2	.97	.98
Model 5	57.11	26	2.20	.94	.053	−.02	1	.97	.98
Model 6	51.22	28	1.83	.95	.044	—	—	.98	.99
Ages 20–34 (n = 600)									
Null Model	3156.13	45	70.14						
Model 1	672.68	35	19.22	.71	.163	2483.45	10	.74	.82
Model 2	474.16	31	15.30	.76	.148	198.52	4	.79	.87
Model 3	233.88	29	8.06	.86	.110	240.28	2	.90	.93
Model 4	98.77	27	3.66	.93	.066	135.11	2	.96	.98
Model 5	93.98	26	3.61	.94	.065	4.79	1	.96	.98
Model 6	89.25	28	3.19	.94	.060	—	—	.97	.98
Ages 35–54 (n = 400)									
Null Model	2167.27	45	48.16						
Model 1	502.69	35	14.36	.68	.177	1664.58	10	.72	.79
Model 2	340.68	31	10.99	.74	.156	162.01	4	.79	.86
Model 3	226.26	29	7.80	.81	.133	114.42	2	.86	.90
Model 4	105.91	27	3.92	.90	.087	120.35	2	.94	.96
Model 5	104.49	26	4.02	.90	.088	1.42	1	.94	.96
Model 6	103.63	28	3.70	.90	.082	—	—	.94	.96
Ages 55–69 (n = 400)									
Null Model	2262.38	45	50.28						
Model 1	431.47	35	12.33	.72	.155	1830.91	10	.77	.85
Model 2	225.38	31	7.27	.82	.122	206.09	4	.87	.92
Model 3	205.67	29	7.09	.82	.120	19.71	2	.88	.92
Model 4	113.69	27	4.21	.89	.087	91.98	2	.93	.96
Model 5	100.83	26	3.88	.90	.082	12.86	1	.94	.97
Model 6	89.33	28	3.19	.92	.071	—	—	.96	.97
Ages 70–90 (n = 400)									
Null Model	2186.26	45	48.58						
Model 1	426.61	35	12.19	.72	.156	1759.65	10	.76	.84
Model 2	271.58	31	8.76	.79	.134	155.03	4	.84	.90
Model 3	208.66	29	7.20	.82	.122	62.92	2	.87	.92
Model 4	95.52	27	3.54	.91	.077	113.14	2	.95	.97
Model 5	82.91	26	3.19	.92	.073	12.61	1	.95	.97
Model 6	82.65	28	2.95	.92	.068	—	—	.96	.98

Note. The chi-square values are weighted least squares from SAS® 9.1.

Most of the goodness-of-fit measures used to evaluate factor models are based on the chi-square statistic. The likelihood-ratio chi-square is a statistic used to test the null hypothesis that the matrix of subtest variances and covariances implied by the factor loadings and intercorrelations is the same as the observed variance-covariance matrix (Byrne, 2001; Schumacker & Lomax, 2004; Thompson, 2000). Therefore, if the data adequately fit the model, the null hypothesis is not rejected. The rescaled chi-square statistic (x^2/df) is also reported. Because of the sensitivity of the chi-square statistic to large sample sizes, evaluation of model fit using these test statistics alone is not recommended (Byrne; Schumacker & Lomax; Thompson).

Two additional model-fit statistics were used to determine the degree to which the sample and estimated variance-covariance matrices are equivalent. The adjusted goodness-of-fit index (AGFI; Jöreskog & Sörbom, 1993) is the proportion of the sample variance-covariance matrix explained by the estimated variance-covariance matrix, adjusted for the degrees of freedom used in the model (Schumacker & Lomax, 2004). Thompson (2000) noted that expectations for this statistic should be greater than .90 or .95. Steiger's (1990) root mean squared error of approximation (RMSEA) was chosen to explore model fit relative to a population covariance matrix. RMSEA is an estimate of how well the estimated variance-covariance matrix matches the population covariance matrix, adjusting for the degrees of freedom used in the fitted model. Browne and Cudeck (1993) and Cudeck (personal communication, 2002) suggest that a RMSEA value of .05 or less indicates a close model fit and that values up to .08 represent adequate model fit with reasonable errors of approximation in the population.

Two model comparison statistics were used to explore the degree to which the sample and estimated variance-covariance matrices are equivalent relative to a baseline model. The comparative fit index (CFI) evaluates how well the specified model reproduces the sample variance-covariance matrix as compared to a baseline model. Hu and Bentler (1999) recommend a CFI value of .95 or higher. The Tucker-Lewis non-normed fit index (TLI; Tucker & Lewis, 1973) measures the improved fit in a manner similar to the CFI, with an adjustment for the degrees of freedom used in the model.

The results shown in Table 5.2 confirm that the four-factor models (Models 4, 5, and 6) fit best for the total sample and for the five age groups. The fit for the one-, two-, and three-factor models was inadequate for all ages and for each of the five age groups. Comparison of the fit indexes for Models 4 and 5 indicates that there was a modest, but statistically significant, improvement of fit for Model 5, where Arithmetic is allowed to load on both the Verbal Comprehension and Working Memory factors.

Comparison of fit indexes for Models 5 and 6 indicates that the fit of the first-order model (Model 6) is slightly better than that of the corresponding second-order model. This is expected because the fit of a second-order model can never exceed the fit of the corresponding first-order model (Arnau & Thompson, 2000). Although the fit of Model 6 is slightly better than that of Model 5, Model 6 does not represent the presence of a second-order g factor, which is central to the Wechsler and other models of intelligence. The factor intercorrelations in Model 6 range from .52 (between Verbal Comprehension and Processing Speed) to .78 (between Perceptual Reasoning and Working Memory). Factor intercorrelations for the Processing Speed factor are lower (.52 to .66) than those among the other three factors (.71 to .78).

Because of its close correspondence to the predicted model, Model 5 was selected to represent the WAIS–IV test structure for the core subtests, and is depicted with factor loadings (for the total sample) in Figure 5.1.

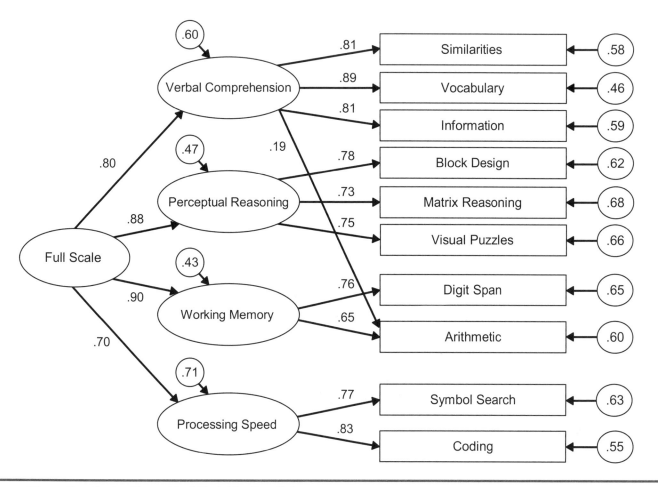

Figure 5.1   Four-Factor Hierarchical Model for Core Subtests

The analyses of Models 4, 5, and 6 suggested one additional model modification that would have substantially improved overall fit, namely, allowing the Block Design and Visual Puzzles subtests to have *correlated error*. Allowing error terms to correlate is a way of taking into account a common feature of two subtests that causes them to correlate more highly with each other than the factor model would predict. In the case of Block Design and Visual Puzzles, the common feature could plausibly be visualization, since Carroll (1993) identifies these types of tasks as paradigmatic measures of that ability. Allowing Block Design and Visual Puzzles to have correlated error resulted in reduced loadings for both subtests on the Perceptual Reasoning factor, as well as an increased loading of the Matrix Reasoning subtest on the Perceptual Reasoning factor; that is, it oriented the Perceptual Reasoning latent trait away from visualization ability and toward fluid reasoning ability. This modification also removed the residual correlations of Matrix Reasoning with *g* and the other three first-order factors that are found with Models 4, 5, and 6. Although the improvement in model fit was large (e.g., making this change to Model 5 would reduce chi-square from 302 to 198 with a loss of one degree of freedom), the decision was made not to incorporate this modification in the WAIS-IV factor model. Reducing the role of visualization ability in the definition of the Perceptual Reasoning latent trait would not represent accurately what the Perceptual Reasoning Index measures.

Analysis of Core and Supplemental Subtests

Table 5.3 presents results of a similar analysis of core and supplemental subtests for ages 16–69 as well as for the five age groups described previously. Because the availability of supplemental subtests differs for ages 16–69 and ages 70–90, the models tested for ages 70–90 did not include Letter–Number Sequencing, Figure Weights, and Cancellation. Details regarding the tested models are provided below, with ages 16–69 and 70–90 reported separately. Each model was compared to a model with no common factors (Null Model).

- Model 1 (One first-order factor)

   Ages 16–69

   15 subtests on a general factor

   Ages 70–90

   12 subtests on a general factor

- Model 2 (One second-order factor and two first-order factors)

   Ages 16–69

   4 Verbal Comprehension subtests and 3 Working Memory subtests on the first factor

   5 Perceptual Reasoning subtests and 3 Processing Speed subtests on the second factor

   Ages 70–90

   4 Verbal Comprehension subtests and 2 Working Memory subtests on the first factor

   4 Perceptual Reasoning subtests and 2 Processing Speed subtests on the second factor

- Model 3 (One second-order factor and three first-order factors)

   Ages 16–69

   4 Verbal Comprehension subtests on the first factor

   5 Perceptual Reasoning subtests on the second factor

   3 Working Memory subtests and 3 Processing Speed subtests on the third factor

   Ages 70–90

   4 Verbal Comprehension subtests on the first factor

   4 Perceptual Reasoning subtests on the second factor

   2 Working Memory subtests and 2 Processing Speed subtests on the third factor

- Model 4 (One second-order factor and four first-order factors)

    Ages 16–69

    4 Verbal Comprehension subtests on the first factor

    5 Perceptual Reasoning subtests on the second factor

    3 Working Memory subtests on the third factor

    3 Processing Speed subtests on the fourth factor

    Ages 70–90

    4 Verbal Comprehension subtests on the first factor

    4 Perceptual Reasoning subtests on the second factor

    2 Working Memory subtests on the third factor

    2 Processing Speed subtests on the fourth factor

- Model 5 (One second-order factor and four first-order factors)

    Ages 16–69

    Same as Model 4, but with Arithmetic allowed to load on both the Verbal Comprehension and Working Memory factors and Figure Weights allowed to load on both the Perceptual Reasoning and Working Memory factors

    Error allowed to correlate between Digit Span and Letter–Number Sequencing

    Ages 70–90

    Same as Model 4, but with Arithmetic allowed to load on both the Verbal Comprehension and Working Memory factors

- Model 6 (Four first-order factors)

    Ages 16–90

    Same as Model 5, but with no second-order factor

Table 5.3   Goodness-of-Fit Statistics for Confirmatory Factor Analysis of Core and Supplemental Subtests

Model	Goodness-of-Fit Index					Improvement			
	x^2	df	x^2/df	AGFI	RMSEA	Δx^2	Δdf	TLI	CFI
Ages 16–69 ($n = 1,800$)									
Null Model	15023.30	105	143.08						
Model 1	3897.96	90	43.31	.70	.135	11125.34	15	.70	.80
Model 2	2686.76	86	31.24	.77	.119	1211.20	4	.79	.85
Model 3	1544.03	84	18.38	.85	.093	1142.73	2	.88	.91
Model 4	828.46	82	10.10	.92	.068	715.57	2	.94	.95
Model 5	561.81	79	7.11	.94	.057	266.65	3	.96	.97
Model 6	530.38	81	6.55	.94	.054	—	—	.96	.97
Ages 16–19 ($n = 400$)									
Null Model	3015.14	105	28.72						
Model 1	805.96	90	8.96	.72	.129	2209.18	15	.71	.79
Model 2	653.95	86	7.60	.75	.120	152.01	4	.76	.83
Model 3	357.93	84	4.26	.85	.088	296.02	2	.88	.91
Model 4	234.78	82	2.86	.89	.069	123.15	2	.93	.95
Model 5	174.64	79	2.21	.92	.056	60.14	3	.96	.97
Model 6	166.50	81	2.06	.92	.052	—	—	.96	.97
Ages 20–34 ($n = 600$)									
Null Model	5296.40	105	50.44						
Model 1	1482.55	90	16.47	.67	.139	3813.85	15	.69	.80
Model 2	1057.37	86	12.30	.73	.124	425.18	4	.77	.85
Model 3	565.79	84	6.74	.84	.092	491.58	2	.88	.92
Model 4	304.33	82	3.71	.91	.065	261.46	2	.95	.96
Model 5	237.59	79	3.01	.92	.056	66.74	3	.96	.97
Model 6	231.39	81	2.86	.93	.054	—	—	.96	.97
Ages 35–54 ($n = 400$)									
Null Model	3450.39	105	32.86						
Model 1	1084.36	90	12.05	.65	.148	2366.03	15	.65	.76
Model 2	734.93	86	8.55	.72	.128	349.43	4	.76	.83
Model 3	499.08	84	5.94	.80	.105	235.85	2	.84	.89
Model 4	289.48	82	3.53	.87	.078	209.60	2	.92	.94
Model 5	207.69	79	2.63	.90	.063	81.79	3	.95	.96
Model 6	202.89	81	2.50	.91	.060	—	—	.95	.97
Ages 55–69 ($n = 400$)									
Null Model	3697.52	105	35.21						
Model 1	851.63	90	9.46	.70	.126	2845.89	15	.75	.84
Model 2	541.14	86	6.29	.79	.106	310.49	4	.85	.89
Model 3	404.49	84	4.82	.83	.092	136.65	2	.89	.92
Model 4	281.83	82	3.44	.87	.075	122.66	2	.93	.95
Model 5	217.44	79	2.75	.90	.065	64.39	3	.95	.96
Model 6	202.46	81	2.50	.91	.059	—	—	.96	.97
Ages 70–90 ($n = 400$)									
Null Model	2801.24	66	42.44						
Model 1	627.41	54	11.62	.70	.142	2173.83	12	.74	.84
Model 2	299.50	50	5.99	.83	.109	327.91	4	.88	.91
Model 3	243.99	48	5.08	.85	.099	55.51	2	.90	.93
Model 4	131.38	46	2.86	.91	.068	112.61	2	.96	.97
Model 5	113.83	45	2.53	.92	.063	17.55	1	.96	.97
Model 6	111.88	47	2.38	.93	.060	—	—	.97	.98

Note. The chi-square values are weighted least squares from SAS® 9.1.

Ages 16–69

Similar to predictions for analyses of the core subtests, it was predicted that the four-factor models would produce the best fit to the data relative to other models. The fit of Model 5 was predicted to be better than that of Model 4, which does not reflect the patterns of split-loadings or correlated errors noted in previous research. In addition to allowing Arithmetic to load on both the Verbal Comprehension and Working Memory factors, Model 5 permits Figure Weights to load on both the Perceptual Reasoning and Working Memory factors. This pattern of split-loadings was noted at preliminary research phases and was not surprising due to the inherent quantitative reasoning and working memory demands of this subtest. For successful completion of items, the examinee must retain the quantitative relationship(s) among shapes of different colors as the response options are evaluated. Model 5 also allows for covariance of the error terms for Digit Span and Letter–Number Sequencing to acknowledge the highly similar task demands of these subtests. This covariance has been noted in previous research (Arnau & Thompson, 2000; Wechsler, 1997a) and was likely due to the addition of the Sequencing task to Digit Span. Model 6 is identical to Model 5 but does not represent the second-order g factor. Although the simpler structure of Model 6 was expected to produce a superior fit to Model 5, Model 6 was not expected to be selected because of its inconsistency with previous research finding overwhelming support of the existence of a g factor (Carroll, 1993) and the theoretical foundations underlying the WAIS–IV development.

The results shown in Table 5.3 confirm that the one-, two-, and three-factor solutions fail to obtain an adequate fit, whereas all four-factor models (Models 4, 5, and 6) fit well for ages 16–69 and for the four age groups within that age range. Comparison of the fit indexes for Models 4 and 5 indicates that there is a substantial improvement of model fit when split-loadings are allowed for Arithmetic and Figure Weights, and when errors are allowed to covary for Digit Span and Letter–Number Sequencing.

As in the analysis of the core subtests, the slight improvement in model fit for Model 6 as compared to Model 5 is expected. Factor intercorrelations reported for Model 6 are similar to those found in the core subtest analyses, ranging from .50 (between Verbal Comprehension and Processing Speed) to .79 (between Perceptual Reasoning and Working Memory). The analysis results for Models 5 and 6 suggested only one noteworthy possible modification that would improve model fit. As in the analysis of the core subtests, this modification involved correlated error on Block Design and Visual Puzzles. For the reasons previously discussed, this change was not included in the factor structure for the expanded WAIS–IV battery.

Ages 70–90

Consistent with results for the younger age groups, the one-, two-, and three-factor models did not show acceptable fit to the data, whereas the four-factor models (Models 4, 5, and 6) fit well. Because the Figure Weights and Letter–Number Sequencing subtests are not administered at this age range, the only applicable modification to the four-factor model for ages 16–69 is the split loading of Arithmetic on the Verbal Comprehension and Working Memory factors. That modification, incorporated in Model 5, produced a statistically significant improvement in model fit over Model 4. The results for Model 5 did not indicate that additional model modifications would substantially improve model fit. As expected, Model 6 showed slightly better fit than Model 5, and factor intercorrelations ranged from .60 (between Verbal Comprehension and Processing Speed) to .79 (between Perceptual Reasoning and Working Memory).

To ensure representation of the second-order *g* factor, Model 5 was selected to represent the WAIS–IV test structure for the core and supplemental subtests and is depicted with factor loadings in Figures 5.2 and 5.3.

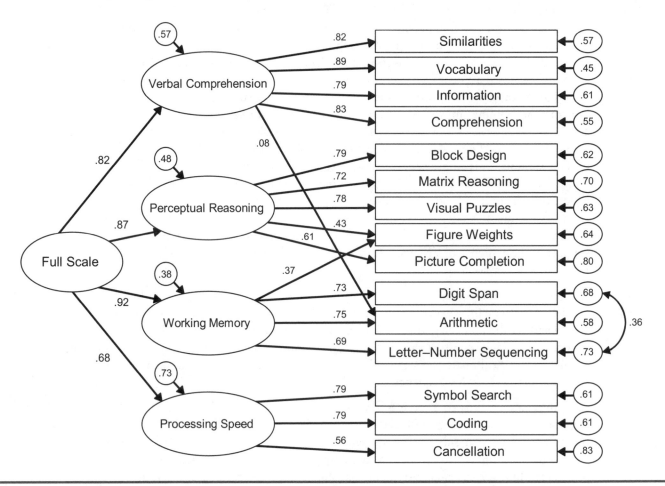

Figure 5.2   Four-Factor Hierarchical Model for Core and Supplemental Subtests, Ages 16–69

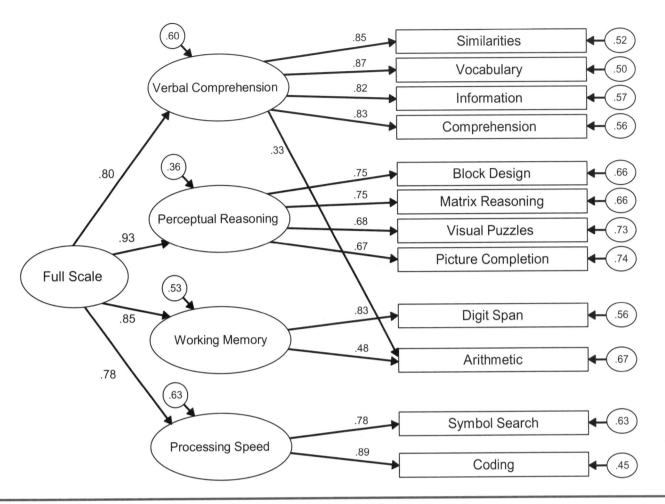

Figure 5.3   Four-Factor Hierarchical Model for Core and Supplemental Subtests, Ages 70–90

Evidence Based on Relationships With Other Variables

Examining relationships between test scores and related external variables provides additional evidence of a scale's validity. Frequently, this evidence is provided through an examination of the scale's relationship to other instruments designed to measure the same or similar constructs. In the development of the WAIS–IV, the instruments of interest included other measures of intellectual or cognitive ability, as well as measures of memory, achievement, ADHD symptoms, executive functioning, and neuropsychological status. Historically, this type of evidence has been referred to as concurrent validity, convergent and discriminant validity, predictive validity, and criterion-related validity. Regardless of the terminology, an examination of the relationship between test scores and other related variables provides important information regarding what a test measures and whether it behaves as expected when related to external variables.

The evidence of WAIS–IV validity described in this section is divided into two parts. The first section describes a series of studies that were conducted concurrently with the scale's standardization to examine the relationship between WAIS–IV test scores and other measures. Special group studies are described in the second section and provide evidence supporting the validity of WAIS–IV scores in special groups of individuals (e.g., Intellectual Giftedness, Intellectual Disability, Reading Disorder, and Probable Dementia of the Alzheimer's Type-Mild Severity).

Relationships to Other Measures

Cronbach and Meehl (1955) described validity evidence, supported by relation to other measures, as locating constructs within a nomological network of known variables. Campbell and Fiske (1959) also discussed the importance of comparing relations between closely related constructs (convergent validity) and between distantly related constructs (discriminant validity).

The relationships between the WAIS–IV and the following external measures were examined: WAIS–III, WISC–IV, WMS–III, CMS, WIAT–II, Brown ADD, D–KEFS, CVLT–II, and RBANS. Table 5.4 provides sample sizes and demographic data for each of the comparison studies. The mean age of each sample is presented, as well as percentages of sample representation by sex, race/ethnicity, education level, and geographic region. The WAIS–IV and the measures of intellectual ability were administered in counterbalanced order. For studies utilizing nonclinical samples, means, standard deviations, and correlation coefficients corrected for range restriction were calculated separately for the portion of the sample taking each administration sequence and then averaged. This method prevents practice effects from artificially lowering the correlation coefficients.

Table 5.4   Demographic Data for Validity Studies With Other Measures

| | WAIS–III | | | | | | | Brown ADD | D–KEFS | | | |
	Non-clinical	ID Mild	BIF	WISC–IV	WMS–III	CMS	WIAT–II	ADHD	Non-clinical	TBI	CVLT–II	RBANS
N	240	25	24	157	97	20	93	41	71	18	331	82
Age												
Mean	52.7	32.2	29.0	16.5	40.1	16.5	17.5	23.0	49.3	28.7	54.5	57.7
SD	24.5	13.1	15.7	0.3	17.5	0.3	0.8	3.7	24.3	7.9	22.7	20.4
Sex												
Female	62.1	36.0	62.5	45.9	54.6	45.0	48.4	39.0	66.2	22.2	53.2	54.9
Male	37.9	64.0	37.5	54.1	45.4	55.0	51.6	61.0	33.8	77.8	46.8	45.1
Race/Ethnicity												
White	66.6	84.0	87.4	71.3	66.0	75.0	63.5	75.6	63.4	44.4	69.8	73.2
African American	17.9	12.0	4.2	5.1	15.5	5.0	12.9	14.6	8.5	11.1	12.7	13.4
Hispanic	8.8	—	4.2	18.5	13.4	15.0	16.1	2.5	15.5	33.3	12.1	9.8
Asian	3.8	4.0	—	1.9	4.1	—	3.2	2.4	4.2	5.6	3.3	2.4
Other	2.9	—	4.2	3.2	1.0	5.0	4.3	4.9	8.4	5.6	2.1	1.2
Education												
≤8 years	5.8	4.0	4.2	3.2	6.2	—	4.3	2.4	9.9	—	8.5	7.3
9–11 years	9.6	16.0	20.8	5.7	6.2	10.0	7.5	12.2	18.3	11.1	10.6	15.9
12 years	32.1	64.0	54.1	24.8	33.0	35.0	28.0	17.1	21.1	38.9	32.3	25.6
13–15 years	27.9	8.0	16.7	31.9	29.9	15.0	32.2	43.9	22.5	22.2	26.3	24.4
≥16 years	24.6	8.0	4.2	34.4	24.7	40.0	28.0	24.4	28.2	27.8	22.3	26.8
Region												
Northeast	15.4	36.0	54.2	26.1	13.4	15.0	10.7	26.8	15.5	—	18.4	13.4
Midwest	31.3	20.0	33.3	19.1	25.8	10.0	19.4	14.6	29.6	11.1	24.8	24.4
South	29.6	44.0	12.5	27.4	27.8	35.0	24.7	48.8	25.3	66.7	36.3	36.6
West	23.7	—	—	27.4	33.0	40.0	45.2	9.8	29.6	22.2	20.5	25.6

Note. Unless otherwise noted, validity studies were conducted with nonclinical groups. Except for sample size (*N*) and age, data are reported as percentages. For examinees aged 16–19, education was based on parent education; for examinees aged 20–90, education was based on examinee education.

There are a number of possible influences on the validity coefficients and score differences between two instruments, many of which may also interact with one another. Some of these influences are: (1) time interval between tests; (2) developmental change or learning during the time interval; (3) structural differences between two measures; (4) regression to the mean from first to second testing; (5) reliability of each measure; (6) retention of test content from first administration; (7) differential procedural learning and practice; (8) motivation level of the individual; and (9) the Flynn effect (Flynn, 1984, 1987, 2007). These influences and their interactions with each other should be considered when interpreting the results of the comparison studies reported in this section (Bracken, 1992; Zhu & Tulsky, 2000). Many of these issues are discussed in detail in Bracken (1992) or Strauss, Spreen, and Hunter (2000). Methods have been proposed to estimate the relative contribution of these factors (McArdle & Woodcock, 1997).

Correlations With the WAIS–III

The WAIS–IV and the WAIS–III were administered to 240 examinees, aged 16–88, in counterbalanced order, with a testing interval of 6–163 days and a mean testing interval of 36 days. Table 5.5 presents the means, standard deviations, corrected and uncorrected correlations, and standard differences.

Table 5.5   Correlations Between the WAIS–IV and the WAIS–III

Subtest/ Composite Score	WAIS–IV			WAIS–III			r_{12}[b]	Corrected r_{12}[b]	Standard Difference[c]
	Mean[a]	SD[a]	n	Mean[a]	SD[a]	n			
BD	10.2	3.4	240	10.5	3.2	240	.80	.77	.09
SI	10.3	3.0	240	11.0	3.1	240	.75	.74	.23
DS	10.1	2.8	240	10.4	2.9	240	.74	.75	.11
MR	10.3	3.1	240	10.9	3.0	240	.70	.71	.20
VC	10.0	2.9	240	11.0	3.2	240	.86	.87	.33
AR	9.7	2.8	239	9.7	2.9	239	.77	.79	.00
SS	10.2	3.1	239	10.3	3.4	239	.71	.72	.03
VP	9.8	3.0	240						
IN	9.9	3.1	240	10.4	3.0	240	.89	.90	.16
CD[d]	9.8	3.0	240	10.0	3.4	240	.85	.85	.06
LN	10.3	2.8	152	10.5	3.1	152	.65	.70	.07
FW	9.5	2.8	152						
CO	10.1	2.9	240	10.5	3.1	240	.74	.74	.13
CA	9.4	2.6	152						
PCm	9.7	2.8	239	10.6	3.0	239	.64	.65	.31
VCI–VCI	100.1	14.9	240	104.4	15.5	240	.91	.91	.28
PRI–POI	100.3	15.5	240	103.7	15.3	240	.85	.84	.22
WMI–WMI	99.3	13.7	239	100.0	14.5	239	.86	.87	.05
PSI–PSI	100.1	14.9	239	100.8	17.2	239	.86	.86	.04
VCI–VIQ	100.1	14.9	240	102.8	15.0	240	.89	.89	.18
PRI–PIQ	100.3	15.5	240	102.5	15.7	240	.84	.83	.14
FSIQ–FSIQ	100.0	15.2	238	102.9	14.9	238	.94	.94	.19

Note. Correlations were computed separately for each order of administration in counterbalanced design and corrected for the variability of the WAIS–IV normative sample (Guilford & Fruchter, 1978).

[a] The values in the Mean and *SD* columns are the average of the means and *SD*s of the two administration orders.

[b] The weighted average across both administration orders was obtained with Fisher's *z* transformation.

[c] The Standard Difference is the difference of the two test means divided by the square root of the pooled variance, computed using Cohen's (1996) Formula 10.4.

[d] The WAIS–III Digit Symbol–Coding subtest is renamed Coding for the WAIS–IV.

The WAIS–IV mean composite scores ranged from 99.3 (WMI) to 100.3 (PRI). The WAIS–III mean composite scores were significantly higher than their corresponding WAIS–IV scores, based on a multivariate analysis of variance. With the exception of the small effect sizes found for the VCI–VCI and PRI–POI mean differences, effect sizes for composite mean differences were negligible. At the subtest level, small effect sizes were found for Similarities, Matrix Reasoning, Vocabulary, and Picture Completion.

The corrected correlation coefficients of composite scores for the two instruments ranged from .83 for PRI–PIQ to .94 for FSIQ–FSIQ. The WAIS–IV PRI includes more substantial changes in subtest content relative to its corresponding WAIS–III composite scores (i.e., the POI and PIQ) than the other WAIS–IV composite scores. For example, the PSI subtest composition (i.e., Symbol Search and Coding) was not changed in this revision, and the correlation between the two index scores was .86, near the limits of the PSI test-retest reliability. The FSIQ–FSIQ correlation was almost identical to that observed in the concurrent validity study with the WISC–IV (see Table 5.9). It is important to note that the correlation between the WAIS–IV VCI and the WAIS–III VCI (r = .91) is almost identical to the correlation between the WAIS–IV VCI and WAIS–III VIQ (r = .89). This relationship is commensurate with the correlation between the WAIS–R VIQ and WAIS–III VIQ (r = .94) reported during the last revision (Wechsler, 1997a). Although not as high as the correlations between the WAIS–IV and WAIS–III verbal composites, the correlation between the WAIS–IV PRI and the WAIS–III POI (r = .84) is almost identical to the correlation between the WAIS–IV PRI and WAIS–III PIQ (r = .83).

The corrected correlations between the common subtests of the two instruments ranged from .65 to .90. The lowest correlation was found for Picture Completion, which is consistent with the results reported in WAIS–III, where the correlation between the WAIS–III and the WAIS–R Picture Completion scores was .50. The correlational results suggest that the WAIS–IV measures similar constructs to those measured in the WAIS–III.

Expected WAIS–IV Composite Scores

Table 5.6 provides the ranges of expected WAIS–IV composite scores for WAIS–III composite scores. Ranges of expected WAIS–IV composite scores are presented separately for WAIS–III IQ and index scores, with the ranges of expected WAIS–IV composite scores for the WAIS–III IQ scores appearing in the top section of the table, and ranges of expected WAIS–IV composite scores for the WAIS–III index scores appearing in the bottom section. To determine the expected range of WAIS–IV composite scores for a given WAIS–III composite score, use the left column of the table to locate the value of the WAIS–III composite score of interest (e.g., VIQ) and read across to the column with the corresponding WAIS–IV composite score range (e.g., VCI). In many cases, the entire range of expected WAIS–IV scores is lower than the WAIS–III score. The ranges of the expected WAIS–IV composite scores associated with particular WAIS–III composite scores are relatively narrow near the middle of the score distribution (i.e., 100) and wider at the upper and lower score levels. In addition, the WAIS–IV PRI and WAIS–III PIQ and POI scores can be expected to differ more than the WAIS–IV VCI and the WAIS–III VIQ and VCI scores. The expected score ranges reported in Table 5.6 reflect 95% confidence intervals.

Table 5.6   Ranges of Expected WAIS–IV Composite Scores for Selected WAIS–III Scores

WAIS–III IQ Score	WAIS–IV Composite Score Range		
	VCI	PRI	FSIQ
55	50[a]–55	50[a]–56	50–54
70	65–69	65–70	65–69
85	81–84	81–84	81–83
100	96–98	97–99	96–98
115	111–113	111–114	111–113
130	126–129	126–130	126–128
145	140–145	140–146	140–144

WAIS–III Index Score	WAIS–IV Index Score Range				
	VCI	PRI	WMI	PSI	GAI
55	50[a]–53	50[a]–55	51–57	51–57	48–53
70	64–68	64–69	67–71	67–71	64–67
85	79–82	80–83	83–85	83–86	80–82
100	95–97	95–98	98–100	98–100	95–96
115	110–112	110–113	113–115	113–115	110–112
130	124–127	125–129	127–131	127–131	124–127
145	139–143	139–145	141–147	142–147	139–143

Note. Ranges are 95% confidence intervals based on mean equating (Angoff, 1984, Design II.B) of data for examinees administered both tests in counterbalanced order.

[a] The range is truncated due to minimum obtainable index scores.

Study With the Intellectual Disability-Mild Severity Group

The WAIS–IV and the WAIS–III were administered to 25 examinees with Intellectual Disability-Mild Severity, aged 16–56, with a testing interval of 14–57 days and a mean testing interval of 22 days. Although the data were collected in counterbalanced order, due to the small sample size, the means, standard deviations, and correlations were calculated using the combined sample from both orders rather than taking a weighted average across both administration orders. This methodology generally results in lower correlations than correlations computed separately for each administration sequence and then averaged.

Table 5.7 presents the means, standard deviations, correlations, and standard differences for this study.

Table 5.7   Correlations for the WAIS–IV/WAIS–III Validity Study With the Intellectual Disability-Mild Severity Group

Subtest/ Composite Score	WAIS–IV			WAIS–III			r_{12}	Standard Difference[a]
	Mean	SD	n	Mean	SD	n		
BD	3.9	2.1	25	4.5	1.7	25	.77	.31
SI	3.9	1.1	24	5.3	1.5	24	.72	1.06
DS	3.0	2.0	25	4.6	1.7	25	.80	.86
MR	3.6	1.9	25	4.8	1.6	25	.64	.68
VC	4.2	1.1	25	3.9	1.5	25	.73	.23
AR	3.8	1.5	25	2.7	1.4	25	.57	.76
SS	3.6	2.4	25	3.6	2.3	25	.79	.00
VP	4.5	1.9	25					
IN	4.2	0.9	25	4.6	1.2	25	.46	.38
CD[b]	3.3	2.0	25	3.7	1.4	25	.87	.23
LN	3.2	2.4	25	3.4	1.7	25	.77	.10
FW	3.8	1.3	25					
CO	3.3	1.1	24	3.4	0.9	24	.72	.10
CA	4.0	2.4	25					
PCm	5.0	2.7	25	5.0	1.9	25	.61	.00
VCI–VCI	66.1	4.9	24	69.6	6.8	24	.78	.59
PRI–POI	65.0	10.1	25	69.4	7.2	25	.86	.50
WMI–WMI	62.9	7.6	25	60.7	7.0	25	.76	.30
PSI–PSI	64.4	11.9	25	67.9	8.0	25	.89	.35
VCI–VIQ	66.1	4.9	24	65.2	5.2	24	.82	.18
PRI–PIQ	65.0	10.1	25	66.8	7.1	25	.86	.21
FSIQ–FSIQ	58.5	6.9	24	62.6	5.5	24	.86	.66

[a] The Standard Difference is the difference of the two test means divided by the square root of the pooled variance, computed using Cohen's (1996) Formula 10.4.

[b] The WAIS–III Digit Symbol–Coding subtest is renamed Coding for the WAIS–IV.

The WAIS–IV mean composite scores ranged from 58.5 (FSIQ) to 66.1 (VCI). The WAIS–III mean composite scores are higher than their corresponding WAIS–IV scores, with the exception of the WMI. The WAIS–III mean subtest scores are the same as or higher than their corresponding WAIS–IV mean subtest scores, with the exception of Vocabulary and Arithmetic. Small effect sizes were found for Block Design, Vocabulary, Information, and Coding. Moderate effect sizes were found for Matrix Reasoning and Arithmetic, and large effect sizes were found for Similarities and Digit Span. The relatively larger effect sizes for differences between WAIS–IV and WAIS–III subtests observed in the Intellectual Disability-Mild Severity group relative to the nonclinical sample are consistent with findings that the Flynn effect varies with ability level (Zhou & Zhu, 2007).

The correlation coefficients of composites for the two instruments ranged from .76 for WMI–WMI to .89 for PSI–PSI. The correlations between the common subtests of the two instruments ranged from .46 (Information) to .87 (Coding). With respect to decision consistency, all participants in this study had FSIQ scores of 75 points or lower on both the WAIS–IV and the WAIS–III. That is, both instruments classified all individuals in this study consistently. The correlational and decision consistency results suggest that among examinees with Intellectual Disability-Mild Severity, the WAIS–IV measures similar constructs to those measured in the WAIS–III.

Study With the Borderline Intellectual Functioning Group

The WAIS–IV and the WAIS–III were also administered to 24 examinees with Borderline Intellectual Functioning, aged 16–65, with a testing interval of 14–103 days and a mean testing interval of 27 days. As with the Intellectual Disability-Mild Severity study, the data were collected in counterbalanced order. Due to the small sample size however, the means, SDs, and correlations were calculated using the combined sample from both orders rather than taking a weighted average across both administration orders. Table 5.8 presents the means, standard deviations, correlations, and standard differences.

Table 5.8   Correlations for the WAIS–IV/WAIS–III Validity Study With the Borderline Intellectual Functioning Group

Subtest/ Composite Score	WAIS–IV			WAIS–III			r_{12}	Standard Difference[a]
	Mean	SD	n	Mean	SD	n		
BD	5.6	1.5	24	6.8	1.7	24	.48	.75
SI	6.5	1.5	24	7.0	1.7	24	.45	.31
DS	5.8	2.4	24	6.8	2.6	24	.86	.40
MR	5.5	2.2	24	6.3	2.2	24	.49	.36
VC	5.7	1.2	24	5.7	1.9	24	.77	.00
AR	5.1	1.3	24	4.6	2.1	24	.72	.29
SS	6.8	2.0	24	6.3	2.2	24	.37	.24
VP	6.2	1.9	24					
IN	6.1	2.2	24	6.2	1.9	24	.89	.05
CD[b]	5.8	2.4	24	5.7	1.9	24	.62	.05
LN	6.0	1.9	24	5.7	3.0	24	.66	.12
FW	5.2	1.6	24					
CO	5.9	1.6	24	5.5	1.7	24	.51	.24
CA	6.3	2.1	24					
PCm	6.5	2.7	24	7.0	2.3	24	.68	.20
VCI–VCI	78.2	7.4	24	79.3	8.3	24	.78	.14
PRI–POI	75.3	8.1	24	80.4	8.4	24	.63	.62
WMI–WMI	73.8	9.3	24	73.5	13.2	24	.89	.03
PSI–PSI	80.1	10.9	24	78.7	8.1	24	.50	.15
VCI–VIQ	78.2	7.4	24	75.7	8.4	24	.68	.32
PRI–PIQ	75.3	8.1	24	77.8	6.7	24	.65	.34
FSIQ–FSIQ	72.5	7.5	24	74.7	7.3	24	.82	.30

[a] The Standard Difference is the difference of the two test means divided by the square root of the pooled variance, computed using Cohen's (1996) Formula 10.4.

[b] The WAIS–III Digit Symbol–Coding subtest is renamed Coding for the WAIS–IV.

The WAIS–IV mean composite scores ranged from 72.5 (FSIQ) to 80.1 (PSI). The mean WAIS–III index scores were commensurate with the corresponding mean WAIS–IV composite scores. At the subtest level, small effect sizes were found for Similarities, Digit Span, Matrix Reasoning, Arithmetic, Symbol Search, Comprehension, and Picture Completion. A moderate effect size was observed for Block Design.

The correlation coefficients of composites for the two instruments ranged from .50 for PSI–PSI to .89 for WMI–WMI. The correlations between the common subtests of the two instruments ranged from .37 (Symbol Search) to .89 (Information).

With respect to decision consistency, 96% of these examinees with Borderline Intellectual Functioning had FSIQ scores 84 points or lower on both the WAIS–IV and the WAIS–III, and 4% of these individuals ($N = 1$) had FSIQ scores of above 84 points on both the WAIS–IV and the WAIS–III. That is, both instruments classified all individuals in this study consistently. The correlational and decision consistency results suggest that among examinees with Borderline Intellectual Functioning, the WAIS–IV measures similar constructs to those measured in the WAIS–III.

Correlations With the WISC–IV

The WAIS–IV and the WISC–IV were administered to 157 examinees, aged 16, in counterbalanced order, with a testing interval of 7–73 days and a mean testing interval of 17 days. Table 5.9 presents the means, standard deviations, uncorrected and corrected correlations, and standard differences.

Table 5.9 Correlations Between the WAIS–IV and the WISC–IV

Subtest/ Composite Score	WAIS–IV Mean[a]	SD[a]	n	WISC–IV Mean[a]	SD[a]	n	r_{12}[b]	Corrected r_{12}[b]	Standard Difference[c]
BD	11.0	2.8	157	10.8	2.8	157	.71	.72	.07
SI	10.5	2.8	155	10.8	2.7	155	.62	.66	.11
DS	10.0	2.6	155	10.4	3.2	155	.75	.77	.14
MR	10.1	2.8	154	11.1	2.7	154	.57	.62	.36
VC	9.7	2.8	156	10.4	2.6	156	.78	.82	.26
AR	10.3	2.9	157	10.9	3.0	157	.72	.74	.20
SS	10.4	2.7	151	10.3	2.5	151	.54	.61	.04
VP	10.2	2.7	156				.		
IN	10.4	2.9	157	10.7	2.8	157	.72	.75	.11
CD	10.0	2.5	157	9.9	2.9	157	.66	.72	.04
LN	10.1	2.8	157	10.2	2.5	157	.67	.68	.04
FW	10.3	3.0	157						
CO	9.7	2.5	156	10.5	2.2	156	.64	.74	.34
CA	9.8	2.5	147	9.3	3.0	147	.46	.51	.18
PCm	10.7	2.6	150	11.0	3.0	150	.57	.60	.11
VCI–VCI	101.0	13.3	154	102.7	12.3	154	.83	.88	.13
PRI–PRI	102.6	12.6	151	103.4	13.7	151	.72	.77	.06
WMI–WMI	100.9	13.5	155	101.1	14.7	155	.75	.78	.01
PSI–PSI	101.3	11.8	151	100.7	13.2	151	.68	.77	.05
FSIQ–FSIQ	102.5	12.2	141	103.7	12.7	141	.87	.91	.10

Note. Correlations were computed separately for each order of administration in counterbalanced design and corrected for the variability of the WAIS–IV normative sample (Guilford & Fruchter, 1978).

[a] The values in the Mean and *SD* columns are the average of the means and *SD*s of the two administration orders.

[b] The weighted average across both administration orders was obtained with Fisher's *z* transformation.

[c] The Standard Difference is the difference of the two test means divided by the square root of the pooled variance, computed using Cohen's (1996) Formula 10.4.

The WAIS–IV mean composite scores ranged from 100.9 (WMI) to 102.6 (PRI). The WAIS–IV mean FSIQ score was 102.5, whereas the WISC–IV mean FSIQ score was 103.7. Relative to the comparisons between the WAIS–IV and the WAIS–III composite scores, the WAIS–IV mean index scores were very similar to the WISC–IV mean index scores. This finding is consistent with the Flynn effect, in which norms collected at closer points in time (e.g., the WISC–IV and WAIS–IV norms) will be more consistent than norms collected at more distant points in time (e.g., the WAIS–IV and WAIS–III norms).

With the exception of the PSI, the means of WISC–IV composite scores were slightly higher than those of the corresponding WAIS–IV composite scores, based on a multivariate analysis of variance. Effect sizes for all differences between composites were negligible. At the subtest level, small effect sizes were found for Matrix Reasoning, Vocabulary, Arithmetic, and Comprehension. All other effect sizes at the subtest level were neglible.

The corrected correlation coefficients between the two instruments ranged from .77 (PRI–PRI and PSI–PSI) to .91 (FSIQ–FSIQ) for the composites and from .51 (Cancellation) to .82 (Vocabulary) for the common subtests of the two instruments. These results are consistent with those found between the WAIS–III and the WISC–IV (Wechsler, 2003). The magnitude of correlations suggests that the two instruments measure highly similar constructs.

Expected WAIS–IV Composite Scores

Table 5.10 provides the ranges of expected WAIS–IV composite scores for WISC–IV composite scores. The expected range of WAIS–IV scores (95% confidence intervals) contains the WISC–IV score in all cases. This indicates the WAIS–IV and the WISC–IV norms are highly consistent.

Table 5.10   Ranges of Expected WAIS–IV Composite Scores for WISC–IV Composite Scores

WISC–IV Composite Score	WAIS–IV Composite Score Range					
	VCI	PRI	WMI	PSI	GAI	FSIQ
55	50[a]–62	50[a]–62	50[a]–62	50[a]–63	44–61	45–62
70	62–75	63–75	64–75	65–76	62–74	63–75
85	79–87	80–88	81–89	82–89	79–87	80–88
100	95–101	96–102	97–103	98–103	95–101	96–102
115	110–117	111–117	111–118	113–119	110–116	111–117
130	123–134	125–134	125–135	126–135	123–133	124–134
145	136–150[a]	138–150[a]	138–150[a]	139–150[a]	136–150	137–151

Note. Ranges are 95% confidence intervals based on mean equating (Angoff, 1984, Design II.B) of data for examinees administered both tests in counterbalanced order.

[a] The range is truncated due to minimum obtainable index scores.

Correlations With the WMS–III

Understanding the relationship between intelligence and memory enables the clinician to better evaluate patterns of cognitive strengths and weaknesses. Moreover, it establishes the degree of relationship between intelligence and memory. If intelligence and memory are unrelated, then performance discrepancies may be common and may lack clinical meaningfulness. Studies between measures of intelligence and memory also provide evidence of divergent validity and establish that the tests, although related, measure different constructs.

Based on the pattern of correlations between the WAIS–III and the WMS–III, it was anticipated that the WAIS–IV composite scores would be moderately correlated with the WMS–III index scores; that is, most correlations would range from .30 to .69. Furthermore, the WMS–III auditory indexes were expected to correlate more highly with the VCI than with the PRI. A similar pattern for the WMS–III visual indexes was anticipated; that is, these indexes would correlate more highly with the PRI than with the VCI. Finally, the working memory indexes of the two scales were expected to correlate highly.

The WAIS–IV and the WMS–III were administered to 97 examinees aged 17–69, with a testing interval of 0–96 days and a mean testing interval of 25 days. Table 5.11 presents the means, standard deviations, and corrected correlations.

Table 5.11   Correlations Between the WAIS–IV and the WMS–III

WAIS–IV Subtest/Composite	WMS–III Index								WAIS–IV		
	Auditory Immediate	Visual Immediate	Immediate Memory	Auditory Delayed	Visual Delayed	Auditory Recognition Delayed	General Memory	Working Memory	Mean	SD	n
BD	.40	.26	.35	.31	.19	.22	.26	.45	10.1	2.7	97
SI	.47	.18	.39	.45	.17	.45	.42	.42	9.9	2.6	97
DS	.43	.18	.36	.34	.20	.30	.32	.57	10.1	2.6	97
MR	.44	.25	.40	.37	.26	.35	.39	.49	10.3	3.1	97
VC	.43	.13	.31	.42	.19	.43	.42	.36	10.0	2.7	97
AR	.50	.16	.36	.51	.18	.45	.44	.49	10.2	2.8	97
SS	.28	.23	.24	.28	.18	.43	.33	.31	10.0	2.5	96
VP	.30	.29	.31	.26	.35	.26	.31	.30	10.1	3.3	97
IN	.50	.18	.37	.45	.22	.37	.38	.39	9.9	3.0	97
CD	.27	.13	.20	.25	.14	.42	.33	.32	10.3	3.0	97
LN	.48	.19	.35	.41	.14	.49	.38	.63	10.1	2.4	97
FW	.39	.27	.36	.33	.29	.31	.33	.49	10.0	3.0	97
CO	.41	.14	.29	.37	.19	.40	.38	.38	9.9	2.8	97
CA	.07	.13	.08	.06	.10	.07	.08	.31	10.4	2.6	96
PCm	.36	.13	.26	.27	.22	.25	.27	.22	9.8	3.0	97
VCI	.54	.20	.41	.50	.22	.48	.46	.45	99.2	13.4	97
PRI	.45	.32	.42	.37	.33	.33	.39	.48	100.4	14.8	97
WMI	.53	.19	.42	.48	.21	.43	.44	.60	100.5	13.3	97
PSI	.30	.20	.25	.28	.18	.45	.37	.35	100.9	13.6	96
FSIQ	.63	.38	.59	.57	.34	.54	.59	.69	100.3	12.9	92
WMS–III											
Mean	107.7	103.3	107.1	108.9	103.9	107.2	108.5	104.6			
SD	14.3	13.9	14.7	14.2	14.2	15.4	13.9	15.5			
n	97	94	96	97	92	94	93	97			

Note. All correlations were corrected for the variability of the WAIS–IV normative sample (Guilford & Fruchter, 1978).

The WAIS–IV composite score means ranged from 99.2 for the VCI to 100.9 for the PSI. The WMS–III composite scores ranged from 103.3 for the Visual Immediate Index to 108.9 for the Auditory Delayed Index. The WMS–III composite score means were slightly elevated because all of the examinees in this study also participated in a counterbalanced validity study for WMS–IV. The majority of the examinees took the WMS–IV before the WMS–III and therefore, exhibited expected practice effects on the WMS–III scores.

The pattern of correlation coefficients between the VCI and PRI scales and the WMS–III auditory and visual indexes was as expected. The correlations between the VCI and the WMS–III auditory indexes and between the PRI and the WMS–III visual indexes were relatively higher than the other correlations. The high correlation between the WAIS–IV WMI and the WMS–III WMI (.60) was expected because they measure a similar construct. The correlations between the other WAIS–IV composites and the WMS–III WMI were in the moderate range, from .35 (PSI) to .69 (FSIQ). The PSI shared small to moderate correlations with all WMS–III indexes, with correlations ranging from .18 (Visual Delayed Index) to .45 (Auditory Recognition Delayed Index).

The pattern of correlations provides evidence of divergent validity, that is, that the two scales measure different constructs. Some modality-specific effects were observed: Verbal Comprehension subtests and the VCI correlated more highly with the auditory memory indexes than with visual memory indexes, and Perceptual Reasoning subtests and the PRI generally correlated more highly with the visual memory indexes than did the Verbal Comprehension subtests or the VCI. Overall, the WAIS–IV scores correlate more highly with the auditory memory indexes than with the visual memory indexes. Interestingly, Symbol Search, Coding, and the PSI did not display higher correlations with the visual memory indexes than with the auditory memory indexes; however, Cancellation was more highly correlated with the visual memory indexes than with the auditory memory indexes.

Clinically, impairment in general intellectual functioning would be expected to have an effect on memory measures, particularly working memory, general memory, immediate memory, and auditory immediate memory measures. If intellectual impairment affects performance on memory, the effects on visual memory tasks may be less observable. The results of this study support the association between intelligence and memory and the potential utility of comparison between intelligence and memory scores for determining weaknesses and impairment in memory relative to general ability level.

Correlations With the CMS

The WAIS–IV and the CMS were administered to 20 examinees, aged 16, with a testing interval of 3–30 days and a mean testing interval of 19 days. Table 5.12 presents the means, standard deviations, and corrected correlations at the subtest and composite levels.

Table 5.12   Correlations Between the WAIS–IV and the CMS

WAIS–IV Subtest/ Composite	CMS Index								WAIS–IV		
	Visual Immediate	Visual Delayed	Verbal Immediate	Verbal Delayed	General Memory	Attention/ Concentration	Learning	Delayed Recognition	Mean	SD	n
BD	.60	.50	.51	.49	.59	.67	.55	.37	10.8	2.9	20
SI	.24	.45	.45	.30	.40	.67	.51	.35	10.5	2.9	20
DS	.44	.53	.43	.46	.53	.76	.38	.34	10.4	2.9	20
MR	.79	.71	.21	.29	.47	.61	.62	.10	10.3	2.6	20
VC	.21	.36	.54	.42	.46	.83	.48	.36	10.1	2.9	20
AR	.46	.59	.26	.34	.43	.70	.36	.20	10.7	3.7	20
SS	.29	.63	.17	.21	.33	.45	.28	.06	11.0	2.9	20
VP	.31	.40	.46	.45	.49	.72	.42	.31	11.1	3.3	20
IN	.26	.34	.41	.37	.44	.51	.31	.45	10.8	3.2	20
CD	.13	.66	.26	.38	.41	.43	.17	.19	10.6	2.8	20
LN	.39	.33	.32	.30	.37	.76	.44	.17	10.8	3.1	20
FW	.60	.55	.41	.42	.51	.69	.72	.33	11.1	3.3	20
CO	.57	.66	.58	.51	.60	.72	.70	.51	9.8	2.0	20
CA	.44	.67	.41	.53	.59	.25	.01	.39	10.1	2.5	20
PCm	.10	.36	.25	.14	.23	.27	.59	.18	9.7	2.1	20
VCI	.27	.44	.52	.42	.50	.76	.49	.44	102.2	15.0	20
PRI	.64	.61	.48	.49	.61	.78	.61	.33	104.0	14.5	20
WMI	.47	.60	.36	.41	.50	.77	.38	.27	102.8	17.2	20
PSI	.23	.70	.22	.32	.40	.50	.26	.13	103.9	14.0	20
FSIQ	.50	.70	.51	.51	.63	.89	.56	.38	103.9	15.4	20
CMS											
Mean	95.9	92.7	103.0	98.9	97.0	104.8	100.3	100.6			
SD	13.5	14.7	30.1	29.0	29.4	15.4	13.1	28.4			
n	19	20	20	20	20	20	20	20			

Note. All correlations were corrected for the variability of the WAIS–IV normative sample (Guilford & Fruchter, 1978).

The WAIS–IV mean composite scores ranged from 102.2 for the VCI to 104.0 for the PRI. The mean CMS index scores ranged from 92.7 for Visual Delayed to 104.8 for Attention/Concentration.

The correlations between the WAIS–IV composites and the CMS indexes ranged from .13 (for PSI–Delayed Recognition) to .89 (for FSIQ–Attention/Concentration). The FSIQ demonstrated its highest correlation with Attention/Concentration (.89), and high correlations (.50–.70) were also observed with all other CMS indexes, except Delayed Recognition (.38). The VCI exhibited a similar pattern of correlations with the CMS indexes, although the values were generally moderate, and the highest values were for Attention/Concentration (.76) and Verbal Immediate (.52). The PRI correlations with CMS indexes were in the moderate to high range (.33–.78). The WMI correlations with CMS indexes were in the moderate to high range (.36–.77), except Delayed Recognition (.27). The PSI exhibited the lowest correlations with the CMS indexes; all correlations were in the small to moderate range with the exception of the Visual Delayed Index (.70) and the Attention/Concentration Index (.50). The CMS Attention/Concentration Index shares some of the highest correlations with the WAIS–IV subtests and composites.

The current results are consistent with the correlations between the WISC–IV and the CMS. For example, the correlation between the WISC–IV WMI and the Attention/Concentration Index was .74 (Wechsler, 2003), which is nearly identical to results in the current study with the WAIS–IV WMI (.77). The correlation between the WISC–IV PRI and the CMS Attention/Concentration Index was .55 (Wechsler, 2003). In this study, the correlation between the WAIS–IV PRI and the CMS Attention/Concentration Index was .78, suggesting that the WAIS–IV PRI may be more related to working memory than was the WISC–IV PRI.

Correlations With the WIAT–II

The WAIS–IV and the WIAT–II were administered to 93 examinees, aged 16–19. All examinees were enrolled in high school. Most examinees took the WAIS–IV first, with a testing interval of 0–60 days and a mean interval of 11 days. Table 5.13 presents the means, standard deviations, and correlation coefficients.

Table 5.13   Correlations Between the WAIS–IV and the WIAT–II

WAIS–IV Subtest/ Composite	WIAT–II Subtests									WIAT–II Composites					WAIS–IV		
	WR	NO	RC	SP	PD	MR	WE	LC	OE	Reading	Mathematics	Written Language	Oral Language	TA	Mean	SD	n
BD	.34	.56	.51	.28	.26	.63	.31	.49	.38	.46	.63	.32	.50	.56	10.3	3.0	93
SI	.53	.47	.70	.43	.28	.51	.37	.61	.49	.63	.52	.44	.64	.65	10.3	3.1	93
DS	.51	.56	.43	.44	.42	.56	.38	.29	.30	.54	.60	.45	.34	.56	9.8	2.6	93
MR	.48	.48	.45	.44	.26	.49	.51	.39	.40	.48	.52	.52	.46	.57	10.4	2.5	93
VC	.63	.58	.75	.58	.33	.56	.47	.76	.56	.71	.61	.58	.76	.76	10.3	2.8	93
AR	.54	.73	.57	.50	.51	.77	.48	.47	.50	.65	.80	.53	.57	.74	10.4	3.0	93
SS	.09	.28	.25	.19	.02	.38	.19	.22	.30	.17	.37	.21	.31	.31	9.7	2.6	93
VP	.40	.63	.48	.38	.31	.57	.50	.53	.56	.48	.64	.49	.64	.64	10.3	2.8	93
IN	.50	.52	.68	.43	.29	.50	.41	.70	.52	.62	.54	.46	.71	.67	10.5	2.7	93
CD	.28	.37	.27	.26	.12	.36	.42	.22	.24	.27	.40	.37	.27	.38	9.8	2.3	93
LN	.42	.38	.34	.39	.37	.39	.41	.35	.39	.47	.41	.44	.44	.51	10.0	2.8	93
FW	.46	.63	.47	.35	.27	.68	.49	.40	.52	.48	.70	.46	.54	.63	10.7	3.1	93
CO	.53	.48	.69	.42	.29	.54	.36	.64	.50	.62	.54	.44	.65	.64	9.9	3.0	93
CA	.18	.40	.22	.16	.08	.35	.16	.17	.11	.17	.40	.17	.16	.26	10.0	2.9	93
PCm	.23	.39	.42	.20	.17	.47	.14	.48	.31	.34	.47	.19	.46	.43	9.7	2.7	93
VCI	.63	.59	.80	.54	.33	.59	.47	.78	.59	.74	.63	.55	.80	.78	102.1	14.1	93
PRI	.48	.66	.58	.43	.33	.68	.52	.57	.53	.56	.72	.52	.64	.70	101.6	13.5	93
WMI	.57	.72	.55	.52	.51	.74	.48	.43	.45	.66	.78	.54	.51	.72	100.5	14.2	93
PSI	.22	.39	.31	.27	.08	.45	.35	.26	.33	.26	.46	.34	.35	.41	98.5	11.1	93
FSIQ	.65	.78	.77	.59	.42	.80	.60	.71	.64	.76	.84	.65	.79	.88	101.0	12.7	93
WIAT–II																	
Mean	102.1	100.4	109.1	102.2	100.3	101.6	101.9	101.7	106.3	103.6	101.0	102.1	104.2	102.6			
SD	12.3	16.1	16.5	12.1	12.9	14.7	13.8	13.6	15.2	14.0	16.4	13.7	15.1	14.6			
n	93	93	93	93	93	93	93	93	93	93	93	93	93	93			

Note. WIAT–II abbreviations are: WR = Word Reading, NO = Numerical Operations, RC = Reading Comprehension, SP = Spelling, PD = Pseudoword Decoding, MR = Math Reasoning, WE = Written Expression, LC = Listening Comprehension, OE = Oral Expression, TA = Total Achievement.

The WAIS–IV mean composite scores for this sample ranged from 98.5–102.1. The WIAT–II composite means ranged from 100.3–109.1. At the composite level, correlations ranged from .26 (for PSI–Reading) to .88 (for FSIQ–Total Achievement). The FSIQ exhibited the strongest relationship to Total Achievement (.88), whereas the PSI exhibited the lowest correlation (.41) with Total Achievement.

All WAIS–IV composites, with the exception of the PSI, correlated highly with WIAT–II Total Achievement. Beyond this, VCI correlated most highly with the Reading and Oral Language composites, and least with the Written Language composite. The PRI correlated most highly with the Mathematics composite. The WMI was most highly correlated with the Mathematics and Reading composites. The PSI was most highly correlated with the Mathematics composite. These correlations provide evidence of the convergent and discriminant relations between the WAIS–IV and WIAT–II composites.

At the subtest level, the pattern of correlations provides additional evidence of construct validity for the new subtest, Figure Weights. This subtest exhibited correlations ranging from low (.27 for Pseudoword Decoding) to high (.68 for Math Reasoning and .63 for Numerical Operations) across all WIAT–II subtests. Of all WIAT–II composites, Figure Weights correlated most highly with the Mathematics composite (.70).

Overall, the relations between the WAIS–IV and WIAT–II are similar to those reported between the WAIS–III and the WIAT–II (Wechsler, 2002a) and between the WISC–IV and WIAT–II (Wechsler, 2003). These results support the construct validity of the WAIS–IV, replicate findings from earlier research, and demonstrate that specific WAIS–IV subtests and composites relate differentially to specific domains of achievement. Tables B.1–B.11 and C.5–C.9 provide data for use in conducting ability-achievement comparisons with the WAIS–IV and WIAT–II. The use of these tables is discussed in chapter 6 and in Appendix C.

Correlations With the Brown ADD

The Brown ADD uses an executive functioning model to measure symptoms of attention-deficit disorders, such as organizing and activating for work (Activation), sustaining attention and concentration (Attention), sustaining energy and effort (Effort), managing affective interference (Affect), and utilizing working memory and accessing recall (Memory). The Brown ADD scores are scaled to T scores, with a mean of 50 and a standard deviation of 10, with higher scaled scores generally indicating more pronounced ADHD symptoms.

The WAIS–IV and the Brown ADD were administered to 41 examinees, aged 18–29, with diagnoses of ADHD, Combined Type, according to *DSM–IV–TR* criteria. The testing interval ranged from 0–104 days, with a mean testing interval of 8 days. Low inverse correlations were expected with most subtests. Prior results indicate that individuals with ADHD score relatively lower than nonclinical individuals on the WMI and the PSI (Barkley, Murphy, & Bush, 2001; Hinshaw, Carte, Sami, Treuting, & Zupan, 2002; Schweiger, Abramovitch, Doniger, & Simon, 2007; Willcutt et al., 2001). This suggests that, relative to other WAIS–IV subtest and composite scores, higher inverse correlations will be observed between the WAIS–IV Working Memory subtests, Processing Speed subtests, WMI, and PSI with the Brown ADD scores. Such a pattern may indicate these subtests and composites are somewhat sensitive to the severity of ADHD symptoms. Table 5.14 presents the means, standard deviations, and correlations at the subtest and composite levels.

Table 5.14   Correlations Between the WAIS–IV and the Brown ADD
for the Attention-Deficit/Hyperactivity Group

WAIS–IV Subtest/ Composite Score	Brown ADD Clusters					Brown ADD Total Score	WAIS–IV		
	Activation	Attention	Effort	Affect	Memory		Mean	SD	n
BD	.02	.05	.00	.02	.08	.04	10.1	3.0	41
SI	.05	−.01	−.18	−.05	.02	−.05	9.9	2.8	41
DS	−.01	−.10	−.15	.02	−.06	−.07	9.6	3.3	41
MR	.04	.01	−.04	.03	.11	.03	9.4	3.0	41
VC	.12	−.01	−.14	.00	.06	.00	10.4	3.1	41
AR	.01	−.03	−.16	−.14	−.18	−.13	8.6	2.6	41
SS	−.02	−.04	−.16	−.15	.07	−.06	9.4	3.1	41
VP	.05	−.12	−.12	−.13	.10	−.07	9.9	2.9	41
IN	.05	−.08	−.10	.02	.16	−.01	10.3	3.2	41
CD	.20	.03	.02	−.01	−.13	.02	8.5	2.5	41
LN	.11	−.04	−.28	−.12	−.11	−.09	9.7	3.0	41
FW	.04	.10	.04	−.14	.02	.04	9.8	2.6	41
CO	.23	.11	−.10	.12	.20	.13	10.3	3.1	41
CA	−.23	−.32	−.49	−.06	−.26	−.36	9.6	2.4	41
PCm	−.07	.00	.05	−.19	.11	−.04	10.2	2.7	41
VCI	.09	−.04	−.16	−.01	.09	−.02	100.7	15.0	41
PRI	.05	−.02	−.07	−.03	.12	.00	98.5	14.1	41
WMI	.00	−.09	−.18	−.06	−.13	−.11	94.6	14.3	41
PSI	.10	−.01	−.09	−.11	−.02	−.03	94.3	12.3	41
FSIQ	.08	−.04	−.15	−.05	.04	−.04	96.9	14.4	41
Brown ADD									
Mean	70.3	70.0	67.8	62.9	63.4	70.1			
SD	11.1	12.4	13.3	12.1	13.2	12.4			
n	41	41	41	41	41	41			

The WAIS–IV mean composite scores ranged from 94.3 for the PSI to 100.7 for the VCI. The Brown ADD scores ranged from 62.9 for Affect to 70.3 for Activation.

As predicted, low inverse correlations were observed between the WAIS–IV composites and Brown ADD scores, with few exceptions. The correlations ranged from -.18 (for WMI–Effort) to .12 (for PRI–Memory). The FSIQ demonstrated its highest correlation with Effort (-.15); all other correlations between the FSIQ and the Brown ADD scores were negligible. The VCI exhibited a similar pattern of correlations with the Brown ADD scores, showing its highest correlation with Effort (-.16). The PRI correlations with Brown ADD scores were negligible, with the exception of PRI–Memory (.12), which displayed a small positive correlation.

As expected, relative to the other WAIS–IV composites, the WMI was slightly more correlated with the Brown ADD scores: Small inverse correlations were observed between the WMI and three of the Brown ADD scores (i.e., Effort, Memory, and Brown ADD Total Score). Interestingly, the highest correlation for the WMI was not with Memory but with Effort. The Effort score is designed to measure inconsistent energy or insufficiently sustained effort. High scores sometimes are related to slowness in information processing, as well as inconsistent quality of work, and the Working Memory subtests require sustained effort for successful task performance. Inconsistent with predictions, the PSI exhibited negligible correlations with the Brown ADD scores, with the exception of a small inverse correlation with Affect (-.11) and a small correlation with Activation (.10). Cancellation displayed the highest and most consistent correlations with the Brown ADD scores, with the exception of Affect. Cancellation requires inhibitory control, and impulsivity is a hallmark feature of ADHD, Combined Type. Furthermore, a number of studies document that inhibitory control is impaired in ADHD (e.g., Schweiger et al., 2007; Young, Bramham, Tyson, & Morris, 2006). It is possible that the response inhibition component of Cancellation may result in some sensitivity to the severity of ADHD symptoms.

Correlations With the D–KEFS

The D–KEFS consists of nine tests that measure a wide spectrum of verbal and nonverbal executive functions. The WAIS–IV and two tests from the D–KEFS, Trail Making and Verbal Fluency, were administered to 71 examinees, aged 16–89, with a testing interval of 0–59 days and a mean testing interval of 8 days. The Trail Making completion time scores and the Trail Making Total Errors are scaled to a mean of 10 and a standard deviation of 3, with higher scaled scores indicating fewer errors and shorter completion times.

Several hypotheses were generated regarding the relations between the WAIS–IV and the D–KEFS scores. It was expected that the WAIS–IV subtest and index scores would show low to moderate correlations with the D–KEFS scores. Relative to other WAIS–IV subtest and index scores, higher correlations were expected between D–KEFS scores and scores for the Working Memory subtests, as well as the WMI. The Verbal Comprehension subtests and the VCI were expected to demonstrate higher correlations than the other WAIS–IV subtest and composite scores with the D–KEFS Letter Fluency and Category Fluency scores. Relative to the other WAIS–IV subtest and composite scores, the Processing Speed subtests and the PSI were expected to evidence higher correlations with the D–KEFS Trail Making completion time scores. Table 5.15 presents the means, standard deviations, and corrected correlations at the subtest and composite levels.

Table 5.15   Correlations Between the WAIS–IV and the D–KEFS

| WAIS–IV Subtest/ Composite Score | Trail Making | | | Verbal Fluency | | | | WAIS–IV | | |
	Number-Letter Switching— Completion Time	Combined Number Sequencing and Letter Sequencing— Total Completion Times	Total Errors (All Types)	Letter Fluency— Total Correct Response	Category Fluency— Total Correct Response	Category Switching— Total Correct Response	Category Switching— Total Switching Accuracy	Mean	SD	n
BD	.46	.22	.30	.12	.22	.38	.32	10.6	2.9	71
SI	.57	.40	.30	.57	.55	.44	.44	9.9	2.8	71
DS	.53	.38	.34	.27	.28	.39	.36	9.6	3.0	71
MR	.54	.39	.38	.25	.12	.20	.17	10.2	2.7	71
VC	.38	.26	.24	.50	.50	.28	.35	10.1	3.2	71
AR	.54	.45	.48	.47	.37	.34	.29	9.8	2.3	71
SS	.65	.59	.50	.40	.39	.49	.49	10.6	2.5	71
VP	.34	.31	.22	.24	.15	.31	.32	10.3	2.6	71
IN	.37	.24	.25	.41	.40	.25	.28	9.9	3.1	71
CD	.63	.46	.35	.32	.19	.42	.41	10.5	2.8	71
LN	.49	.44	.13	.26	.24	.36	.34	9.8	2.6	52
FW	.49	.34	.32	.36	.40	.56	.54	10.6	2.5	52
CO	.45	.34	.36	.59	.48	.44	.40	9.9	3.0	71
CA	.23	.15	.26	-.10	.01	.32	.28	10.3	3.0	52
PCm	.29	.09	.09	.04	.14	.33	.27	10.2	3.1	71
VCI	.49	.33	.30	.55	.53	.35	.39	99.5	15.2	71
PRI	.60	.41	.41	.27	.22	.40	.36	101.8	12.6	71
WMI	.63	.48	.47	.41	.37	.44	.40	98.2	12.9	71
PSI	.72	.58	.47	.40	.31	.51	.51	103.3	13.1	71
FSIQ	.77	.55	.53	.54	.50	.52	.52	100.7	13.1	71
D–KEFS										
Mean	10.4	11.0	10.9	10.3	10.3	10.6	10.4			
SD	3.2	3.4	2.3	3.4	3.0	3.6	3.4			
n	67	71	67	71	71	71	71			

Note. All correlations were corrected for the variability of the WAIS–IV normative sample (Guilford & Fruchter, 1978).

The WAIS–IV mean composite scores for this sample ranged from 98.2 (WMI) to 103.3 (PSI). Correlations between the WAIS–IV composite scores and the D–KEFS scores ranged from .22 (PRI with Category Fluency) to .77 (FSIQ with Trail Making Number-Letter Switching–Completion Time). Relative to most other WAIS–IV subtests and composites, the Verbal Comprehension subtests and the VCI demonstrated slightly higher correlations with the Letter Fluency and Category Fluency scores. This was particularly true for Similarities and Comprehension, which are tasks that involve generating novel responses that do not draw on overlearned information and are similar in that regard to Letter Fluency and Category Fluency. As expected, Symbol Search, Coding, and the PSI displayed some of the highest correlations with the D–KEFS Trail Making completion time scores, although the same pattern was not present for Cancellation.

Interestingly, Figure Weights showed higher correlations with the Verbal Fluency Category Switching scores than did any other WAIS–IV subtest or composite. Both Figure Weights and Verbal Fluency category switching require flexibility and the ability to relate multiple pieces of information simultaneously to perform the tasks successfully.

Study With the Traumatic Brain Injury Group

The WAIS–IV and the same two D–KEFS tests were also administered to 18 examinees, aged 19–44, who had experienced a moderate to severe traumatic brain injury (TBI). The testing interval ranged from 0–12 days, with a mean testing interval of 1 day. It was expected that a pattern of results would emerge that was similar to that observed for the nonclinical sample described above. However, relative to the nonclinical sample previously reported, the correlations between the Processing Speed subtests and the PSI with the D–KEFS scores were expected to be slightly higher because the PSI is sensitive to degree of impairment in TBI. Table 5.16 presents the means, standard deviations, and correlations at the subtest and composite levels.

Table 5.16 Correlations Between the WAIS–IV and the D–KEFS for the Traumatic Brain Injury Group

| WAIS–IV Subtest/ Composite Score | D–KEFS Score | | | | | | | WAIS–IV | | |
| | Trail Making | | | Verbal Fluency | | | | | | |
	Number-Letter Switching— Completion Time	Combined Number Sequencing and Letter Sequencing— Total Completion Times	Total Errors (All Types)	Letter Fluency— Total Correct Response	Category Fluency— Total Correct Response	Category Switching— Total Correct Response	Category Switching— Total Switching Accuracy	Mean	SD	n
BD	.67	.47	.45	.65	.45	.63	.65	8.3	3.4	18
SI	.46	.33	.45	.40	.21	.38	.39	8.5	2.9	18
DS	.63	.36	.45	.35	.05	.38	.39	8.0	3.0	18
MR	.63	.50	.61	.50	.29	.44	.47	7.7	3.3	18
VC	.64	.37	.61	.46	.35	.52	.47	9.1	3.1	18
AR	.69	.58	.38	.54	.27	.59	.57	7.6	3.3	18
SS	.83	.81	.50	.66	.59	.64	.69	6.2	2.8	18
VP	.58	.35	.53	.57	.40	.49	.55	8.1	3.5	18
IN	.80	.60	.59	.63	.56	.71	.66	9.2	3.0	18
CD	.84	.76	.39	.87	.72	.86	.84	6.5	4.3	18
LN	.71	.58	.65	.51	.42	.51	.47	8.5	3.4	18
FW	.62	.44	.63	.46	.38	.52	.39	8.1	2.8	18
CO	.49	.34	.47	.52	.28	.56	.54	7.9	3.0	18
CA	.62	.50	.29	.60	.58	.69	.66	6.8	4.5	18
PCm	.75	.64	.56	.62	.38	.53	.55	9.1	3.3	18
VCI	.68	.46	.60	.53	.39	.57	.54	93.8	15.4	18
PRI	.69	.49	.60	.63	.42	.58	.61	88.3	17.7	18
WMI	.70	.49	.44	.47	.17	.51	.51	87.4	17.0	18
PSI	.88	.83	.47	.83	.71	.82	.83	80.2	18.1	18
FSIQ	.82	.64	.58	.70	.49	.70	.71	85.7	17.7	18
D–KEFS										
Mean	6.9	6.5	10.4	8.3	6.7	6.5	7.4			
SD	4.6	5.0	3.1	4.2	3.2	4.0	3.4			
n	15	18	15	18	17	18	18			

The WAIS–IV mean composite scores for this sample ranged from 80.2 (PSI) to 93.8 (VCI). The correlations between the WAIS–IV composite scores and the D–KEFS scores ranged from .17 (WMI with D–KEFS Category Fluency–Total Correct Response) to .88 (PSI with Number-Letter Switching–Completion Time). As expected, the correlations between all Processing Speed subtests and the PSI with the D–KEFS scores were higher than those observed in the nonclinical sample. Symbol Search and Coding, in particular, showed high correlations with most D–KEFS scores. Interestingly, Cancellation displayed high correlations with the D–KEFS Category Switching scores, although the same was not true for the nonclinical sample. Cancellation shares some similarities with the Verbal Fluency Category Switching task, in that both require the examinee to accurately track and relate two associated categories of relevant information. In general, all correlations are higher than those observed in the nonclinical study; however, this may be due, in part, to the relatively smaller sample size in the clinical sample.

Correlations With the CVLT–II

The CVLT–II measures free recall, cued recall, and recognition of two word lists over several immediate- and delayed-memory trials. The WAIS–IV and the CVLT–II were administered to 331 examinees, aged 16–90, with a testing interval of 0–49 days and a mean testing interval of 5 days. It was expected that the WAIS–IV subtests and composites would show low to moderate correlations with most CVLT–II scores. However, low inverse correlations were expected between the WAIS–IV subtests and composites and the CVLT–II error scores. Table 5.17 presents the means, standard deviations, and corrected correlations at the subtest and composite levels.

Table 5.17   Correlations Between the WAIS–IV and the CVLT–II

WAIS–IV Subtest/ Composite Score	CVLT–II Score											WAIS–IV		
	Trials 1–5	Trial 1	Trial 5	Trial B	Short-Delay Free Recall	Short-Delay Cued Recall	Long-Delay Free Recall	Long-Delay Cued Recall	Free-Recall Intrusions	Cued-Recall Intrusions	Total Recognition Discriminability	Mean	SD	n
BD	.34	.21	.33	.20	.27	.33	.34	.31	−.07	−.21	.31	10.3	3.0	331
SI	.36	.24	.38	.19	.32	.40	.34	.36	−.10	−.24	.34	10.2	3.0	331
DS	.36	.29	.33	.22	.30	.33	.33	.33	−.06	−.16	.31	10.0	3.0	331
MR	.34	.21	.32	.21	.29	.28	.29	.29	−.07	−.18	.29	10.2	3.4	331
VC	.40	.27	.40	.24	.33	.39	.35	.36	−.15	−.25	.33	10.3	3.1	331
AR	.39	.28	.37	.27	.29	.36	.32	.35	−.08	−.18	.29	10.1	3.0	331
SS	.30	.19	.28	.19	.26	.26	.28	.27	.00	−.10	.25	10.1	3.0	331
VP	.32	.21	.33	.20	.28	.35	.31	.27	−.04	−.18	.29	10.1	3.0	331
IN	.30	.21	.33	.17	.31	.36	.31	.32	−.13	−.26	.29	10.1	3.1	331
CD	.39	.23	.38	.25	.31	.31	.32	.35	−.04	−.13	.30	10.0	2.9	329
LN	.36	.32	.31	.31	.30	.30	.30	.29	−.01	−.07	.23	10.3	3.3	234
FW	.50	.35	.46	.36	.41	.51	.50	.49	−.07	−.22	.42	10.1	3.0	234
CO	.34	.24	.36	.20	.30	.35	.31	.31	−.13	−.23	.30	10.4	3.1	331
CA	.34	.32	.30	.12	.25	.37	.31	.33	−.05	−.15	.33	10.2	3.1	234
PCm	.27	.15	.26	.14	.26	.29	.27	.27	−.08	−.13	.24	9.8	3.1	331
VCI	.38	.26	.40	.22	.35	.42	.37	.38	−.13	−.27	.35	100.7	15.7	331
PRI	.40	.25	.39	.24	.34	.38	.37	.35	−.08	−.22	.35	101.0	15.5	331
WMI	.40	.30	.38	.26	.31	.37	.35	.36	−.08	−.19	.32	99.9	15.4	331
PSI	.38	.24	.37	.24	.32	.32	.33	.35	−.03	−.13	.31	100.4	14.6	329
FSIQ	.48	.32	.47	.29	.40	.46	.44	.44	−.10	−.25	.41	100.7	15.4	329
CVLT–II														
Mean	50.9	−0.4	−0.1	−0.2	−0.1	−0.2	−0.1	−0.2	0.3	0.2	0.0			
SD	11.6	1.2	1.1	1.1	1.2	1.1	1.1	1.1	1.2	1.1	1.0			
n	331	331	331	331	331	331	331	331	331	331	331			

Note. All correlations were corrected for the variability of the WAIS–IV normative sample (Guilford & Fruchter, 1978).

The WAIS–IV mean composite scores for this sample ranged from 99.9 (WMI) to 101.0 (PRI). As expected, correlations between the WAIS–IV composite scores and the CVLT–II scores ranged from .22 (VCI with Trial B Correct) to .48 (FSIQ with Trials 1–5 Correct). Correlations between the WAIS–IV composite scores and the CVLT–II error scores were small or negligible, ranging from -.03 to -.27. Notably, the Figure Weights subtest demonstrated the three highest correlations with CVLT–II scores, whereas Matrix Reasoning, another measure of fluid reasoning, did not show the same pattern. It is likely that Figure Weights and the CVLT–II share similar response processes and task demands, such as chunking and reorganizing information.

Correlations With the RBANS

The RBANS provides index scores for Immediate Memory, Visuospatial/Constructional Abilities, Language, Attention, and Delayed Memory, as well as an RBANS Total Score. Based on results of a correlational study between the WAIS–R and the RBANS (Randolph, 1998) and some similarities in content, several hypotheses were generated. The FSIQ was expected to correlate most highly with the RBANS Total Score and to display moderate to large correlations with the RBANS index scores. The PRI and the Perceptual Reasoning subtests were expected to correlate more highly with Visuospatial/Constructional Abilities than with other RBANS index scores. The WMI and the Working Memory subtests were expected to correlate more highly with the RBANS Attention Index than with other RBANS index scores: A parallel version of the Digit Span subtest appears on the RBANS and contributes to the RBANS Attention Index. The WMI and the Working Memory subtests were also expected to correlate relatively highly with the Immediate Memory Index. Similar to the WMI and the Working Memory subtests, the PSI and the Processing Speed subtests were expected to correlate more highly with the RBANS Attention Index than with other RBANS index scores: A parallel version of the Coding subtest appears on the RBANS and contributes to the RBANS Attention Index.

The WAIS–IV and the RBANS were administered to 82 examinees, aged 20–89, with a testing interval of 0–46 days and a mean testing interval of 6 days. Table 5.18 presents the means, standard deviations, and corrected correlations at the subtest and composite levels.

Table 5.18 Correlations Between the WAIS–IV and the RBANS

WAIS–IV Subtest/ Composite Score	RBANS Score						WAIS–IV		
	Immediate Memory	Visuospatial/ Constructional	Language	Attention	Delayed Memory	Total Score	Mean	SD	n
BD	.41	.49	.43	.50	.26	.58	9.6	2.9	82
SI	.53	.43	.52	.37	.32	.58	9.8	2.9	82
DS	.33	.42	.27	.65	.22	.55	10.0	2.8	82
MR	.45	.52	.32	.53	.27	.59	9.9	2.9	82
VC	.44	.49	.34	.41	.22	.53	9.7	2.8	82
AR	.38	.35	.30	.48	.22	.50	9.8	3.3	82
SS	.24	.28	.35	.55	.29	.48	9.9	3.1	82
VP	.28	.51	.31	.44	.27	.51	9.6	2.8	82
IN	.37	.44	.22	.32	.24	.45	9.6	3.2	82
CD	.24	.32	.23	.56	.31	.47	10.7	3.2	82
LN	.21	.20	.26	.52	.10	.39	9.9	2.6	54
FW	.44	.21	.09	.36	.33	.44	10.0	2.8	54
CO	.50	.42	.41	.43	.39	.59	9.9	2.9	82
CA	.32	.15	.20	.37	.28	.41	10.0	3.5	54
PCm	.23	.36	.14	.45	.22	.40	10.0	2.8	82
VCI	.50	.51	.40	.42	.30	.59	98.0	14.7	82
PRI	.50	.66	.46	.64	.36	.72	98.2	13.3	82
WMI	.41	.43	.32	.62	.25	.58	99.5	15.2	82
PSI	.27	.34	.32	.63	.34	.54	101.6	15.3	82
FSIQ	.53	.61	.46	.69	.38	.75	98.9	14.5	82
RBANS									
Mean	95.0	85.2	96.2	97.9	89.5	90.2			
SD	15.7	14.9	12.5	19.2	13.6	14.3			
n	82	82	82	82	82	82			

Note. All correlations were corrected for the variability of the WAIS–IV normative sample (Guilford & Fruchter, 1978).

The WAIS–IV mean composite scores for this sample ranged from 98.0 (VCI) to 101.6 (PSI). The correlations between the FSIQ and the RBANS scores ranged from .38 (Delayed Memory) to .75 (RBANS Total Score). As anticipated, the FSIQ correlated most highly with the RBANS Total Score. Among the RBANS index scores, the VCI correlated most highly with the Visuospatial/Constructional Abilities Index. It is likely that both are highly related to *g*. As expected, the PRI correlated more highly with the Visuospatial/Constructional Abilities Index than with the other RBANS index scores. Perceptual Reasoning subtests displayed some of their highest correlations with the Visuospatial/Constructional Abilities Index with the exception of Figure Weights, which was more highly correlated with the Immediate Memory and Attention Index scores. This may reflect the working memory component inherent in fluid reasoning tasks, as some of the highest correlations for Matrix Reasoning were also with the Immediate Memory Index and the Attention Index. As expected, the WMI and the Working Memory subtests correlated more highly with the RBANS Attention Index than with other RBANS index scores, and the WMI correlated moderately with the Immediate Memory Index. Similar to the WMI and the Working Memory subtests, the PSI and the Processing Speed subtests correlated more highly with the RBANS Attention Index than with other RBANS index scores.

Special Group Studies

In addition to the studies comparing the WAIS–IV scores to the scores on external measures, additional evidence of validity, based on test-criterion relationships, is provided based on the results of special group studies. Evidence of a scale's clinical utility and specificity is crucial when its results are part of a comprehensive diagnostic assessment. Because the WAIS–IV is often used as part of a diagnostic assessment, several special group studies were conducted concurrently with the scale's standardization to examine the clinical utility of the instrument.

Independent examiners and researchers collected the data for the special group studies. Candidates for these studies were drawn from a variety of clinical settings and were accepted for participation in special group samples based on specified inclusion criteria (see Appendix E for specific inclusion criteria for each special group).

It is important to note the limitations of these studies. The samples were not randomly selected but were selected based on availability. Therefore, these studies may not be representative of the diagnostic category as a whole. Because data for each special group sample were collected in a variety of clinical settings, the diagnoses of individuals within the same special group might have been made on the basis of different criteria and procedures. In addition, the sample sizes for some of the studies are small and cover only a portion of the WAIS–IV age range. Finally, only group performance is reported. For these reasons, the data from these samples are presented as examples and are not intended to be fully representative of these diagnostic groups. The purpose of the studies is to provide evidence that the WAIS–IV can provide valid estimates of intellectual ability for individuals in these special groups. Scores on the WAIS–IV should never be used as the sole criteria for diagnostic or classification purposes.

The demographic characteristics of samples for the WAIS–IV special group studies are presented in Table 5.19. The mean age of each sample is presented followed by percentages of sample representation by sex, race/ethnicity, education level, and geographic region. All control groups were matched on these demographic variables. Tables 5.20–5.32 report the mean WAIS–IV performance of the special groups and their corresponding matched control group.

Table 5.19   Demographic Data for the Special Groups

| | | ID | | | | | | | | | | | |
	GT	Mild	Moderate	BIF	RD	MD	ADHD	TBI	AUT	ASP	DEP	MCI	ALZ
N	34	73	31	27	34	41	44	22	16	40	41	53	44
Age													
Mean	34.4	32.0	30.5	30.1	18.1	17.8	23.1	29.0	20.3	22.5	62.8	73.7	77.2
SD	14.6	13.6	13.8	15.9	1.6	1.9	3.8	7.2	4.4	6.6	8.7	7.3	7.8
Sex													
Female	38.2	54.8	38.7	63.0	50.0	53.7	36.4	27.3	6.3	22.5	73.2	47.2	75.0
Male	61.8	45.2	61.3	37.0	50.0	46.3	63.6	72.7	93.7	77.5	26.8	52.8	25.0
Race/Ethnicity													
White	79.4	83.6	90.3	81.5	73.5	73.2	77.3	45.5	87.5	82.5	70.7	94.3	88.6
African American	5.9	8.2	6.5	7.4	5.9	9.7	13.6	13.7	0.0	2.5	24.4	3.8	11.4
Hispanic	5.9	6.8	3.2	7.4	17.7	12.2	2.3	31.8	0.0	10.0	4.9	1.9	0.0
Asian	2.9	1.4	0.0	0.0	0.0	0.0	2.3	4.5	0.0	0.0	0.0	0.0	0.0
Other	5.9	0.0	0.0	3.7	2.9	4.9	4.5	4.5	12.5	5.0	0.0	0.0	0.0
Education													
≤8 years	0.0	12.3	6.4	3.7	5.9	0.0	2.3	0.0	0.0	2.5	7.3	9.4	4.5
9–11 years	0.0	6.9	12.9	25.9	23.5	4.9	13.6	13.7	0.0	0.0	0.0	3.8	2.3
12 years	5.9	64.4	58.1	48.2	26.5	31.7	15.9	31.8	25.0	32.5	26.8	28.3	25.0
13–15 years	35.3	8.2	12.9	18.5	29.4	39.0	45.5	31.8	37.5	30.0	34.2	18.9	27.3
≥16 years	58.8	8.2	9.7	3.7	14.7	24.4	22.7	22.7	37.5	35.0	31.7	39.6	40.9
Region													
Northeast	14.7	28.8	29.0	51.9	26.5	34.1	25.0	4.6	12.5	17.5	9.7	34.0	4.6
Midwest	29.4	24.7	19.4	29.6	2.9	4.9	13.6	13.6	18.7	15.0	22.0	17.0	13.6
South	50.0	43.8	41.9	18.5	61.8	51.2	50.0	63.6	62.5	60.0	51.2	39.6	50.0
West	5.9	2.7	9.7	0.0	8.8	9.8	11.4	18.2	6.3	7.5	17.1	9.4	31.8

Note. Except for sample size (*N*) and age, data are reported as percentages. For examinees aged 16–19, education was based on parent education; for examinees aged 20–90, education was based on examinee education.

Individuals Identified as Intellectually Gifted

Individuals identified as intellectually gifted demonstrate high performance capability in intellectual functioning, creative and productive thinking, leadership, performing or visual arts, and/or other specific ability areas (Marland, 1972; Sparrow & Gurland, 1998; Winner, 2000). Several studies have examined the performance of children identified as intellectually gifted on measures of cognitive ability (Sparrow & Gurland; Sweetland, Reina, & Tatti, 2006; Wechsler, 2002, 2003; Winner), whereas there is a relative paucity of analogous studies for adults. In general, results suggest that individuals identified as intellectually gifted obtain significantly higher verbal, nonverbal, and overall cognitive ability scores than do individuals in the general population. Although it is more common for gifted individuals to perform well on both the verbal and nonverbal subtests of the Wechsler intelligence scales, some gifted individuals may show unusually large discrepancies between their verbal and nonverbal scores (Mitchell, Grandy, & Lupo, 1986; Saccuzzo, Johnson, & Russell, 1992; Sparrow & Gurland; Winner).

Studies that focus on the identification of intellectual giftedness are complicated by several factors. First, different cognitive ability measures produce highly correlated, yet different, estimates of cognitive ability. Second, the criteria for identifying individuals as intellectually gifted vary from site to site, as well as from state to state. Third, the focus on intellectual giftedness has evolved over the past 60 years, such that not all intellectually gifted adults had the opportunity to be identified or to receive services as children. Many may have attended honors or advanced placement classes rather than received services for intellectual giftedness, as the latter may not have been available in their area or when they attended school. Finally, many adults do not have access to cognitive ability scores if they were tested as children.

Based on previous research, it was expected that the intellectually gifted group would have significantly higher mean scores than a matched control group for all WAIS–IV composite and subtest scores. The WAIS–IV was administered to 34 examinees, aged 17–64, who were identified as intellectually gifted. In order to qualify for this study, candidates were required to have scores on a standardized measure of cognitive ability that were at least 2 SDs above the mean, or to be a current member of Mensa *and* have received services for intellectual giftedness or the equivalent during primary and/or secondary education. Table 5.20 presents the means and standard deviations of the WAIS–IV subtest, process, and composite scores for the intellectually gifted group and for the matched control group.

Table 5.20   Mean Performance of Intellectually Gifted and Matched Control Groups

Subtest/ Process/ Composite Score	Intellectually Gifted		Matched Control		Group Mean Comparison				
	Mean	SD	Mean	SD	n	Difference	t value	p value	Standard Difference[a]
BD	13.4	2.5	10.5	3.2	34	−2.91	−4.16	<.01	−1.01
SI	14.3	2.5	10.8	2.7	34	−3.47	−5.35	<.01	−1.33
DS	14.7	2.9	11.2	3.0	34	−3.44	−4.45	<.01	−1.18
MR	13.6	2.0	11.2	2.6	34	−2.44	−4.82	<.01	−1.05
VC	15.2	2.2	11.2	2.7	34	−3.97	−8.30	<.01	−1.61
AR	13.7	2.7	10.8	2.8	34	−2.91	−4.56	<.01	−1.06
SS	11.9	2.3	10.3	3.5	34	−1.56	−2.19	.04	−.52
VP	13.2	2.3	9.9	3.3	34	−3.29	−4.59	<.01	−1.15
IN	14.6	2.2	11.5	2.9	34	−3.09	−5.67	<.01	−1.22
CD	12.7	3.1	10.5	3.0	34	−2.24	−3.66	<.01	−.74
LN	14.2	3.6	11.9	3.8	34	−2.29	−2.20	.03	−.62
FW	13.4	1.8	11.1	3.5	34	−2.32	−3.72	<.01	−.83
CO	14.4	1.8	11.4	3.3	33	−2.97	−4.53	<.01	−1.11
CA	11.6	2.8	10.7	3.1	34	−.85	−1.18	.24	−.29
PCm	12.5	2.2	10.6	3.1	34	−1.94	−2.91	<.01	−.72
BDN	13.4	1.9	10.8	3.3	34	−2.56	−3.88	<.01	−.94
DSF	13.3	2.7	11.4	3.1	34	−1.91	−2.55	.02	−.66
DSB	14.7	3.1	10.8	2.7	34	−3.91	−5.23	<.01	−1.34
DSS	12.9	2.6	11.0	3.1	34	−1.91	−2.76	<.01	−.67
VCI	127.2	10.7	106.2	13.2	34	−21.06	−8.68	<.01	−1.75
PRI	119.6	9.7	102.7	15.2	34	−16.85	−5.45	<.01	−1.33
WMI	123.3	12.2	105.5	14.2	34	−17.82	−5.18	<.01	−1.35
PSI	112.4	12.6	102.1	16.6	34	−10.38	−3.17	<.01	−.70
FSIQ	126.5	8.5	105.3	14.5	34	−21.15	−7.72	<.01	−1.78

[a] The Standard Difference is the difference of the two test means divided by the square root of the pooled variance, computed using Cohen's (1996) Formula 10.4.

As expected, composite scores for the intellectually gifted group were significantly higher than those obtained in the matched control group. The composite scores ranged from 112.4 (PSI) to 127.2 (VCI). Effect sizes for the mean composite score differences were large, with the exception of the PSI, which had a moderate effect size. The PSI was relatively lower than the other composites, and the lowest mean subtest scores for the intellectually gifted group occurred on the Cancellation and Symbol Search subtests. These results are consistent with previous research, which found that individuals identified as intellectually gifted had more variability and lower performance on subtests designed to measure processing speed relative to performance in other cognitive domains (Sparrow & Gurland, 1998; Watkins, Greenawalt, & Marcell, 2002; Wechsler, 2003). At the subtest level, the largest effect sizes for the mean scaled score differences were obtained for Vocabulary, Similarities, and Information.

Additional analysis indicates that 77% of individuals identified as intellectually gifted, based on history, had current FSIQ scores of 120 points or higher. In contrast, only 18% of individuals achieved these scores in the matched control group.

The higher scores obtained by individuals in the intellectually gifted group are consistent with their previous identification as intellectually gifted, as well as the results of previous comparison studies with child samples (Wechsler, 1991, 2002, 2003). The consistency of results between the WAIS–IV and previous Wechsler scales also suggests that the instruments are measuring similar constructs. These results provide strong evidence that the WAIS–IV provides scores that are useful in the assessment of intellectual giftedness. As previously mentioned, this study is limited to individuals who have been identified as intellectually gifted; therefore, the results should not be generalized to individuals who are gifted in other domains. Additional research is necessary to examine the intellectual functioning of individuals who are gifted in other areas.

Individuals With Mild or Moderate Intellectual Disability

According to criteria specified in the *DSM–IV–TR*, an individual diagnosed with mental retardation must demonstrate "significantly subaverage intellectual functioning" and significant impairment in adaptive functioning in at least two of the following areas: communication, self-care, home living, social/interpersonal skills, use of community resources, self-direction, functional academic skills, work, leisure, and health and safety.

The American Association on Intellectual and Developmental Disabilities (AAIDD; 2007) prefers the term *intellectual disability* to the previously used term *mental retardation*. According to the AAIDD, intellectual disability originates before the age of 18 and is characterized by significant limitations in both intellectual functioning and adaptive behavior expressed as conceptual, social, and practical skills (Schalock, Luckasson, & Shogren, 2007). In both the *DSM–IV–TR* and AAIDD definitions, significantly low performance on a test of general cognitive ability, such as the WAIS–IV, is a necessary but not sufficient criterion for the diagnosis of mental retardation or intellectual disability. Adaptive functioning must also be assessed. Both the *DSM–IV–TR* and the AAIDD criteria emphasize the need to consider a scale's standard error of measurement in interpreting scores, thus reemphasizing the requirement to consider multiple criteria and to exercise careful clinical judgment in identifying individuals with intellectual disability.

In the normal distribution of IQ scores, about 2.2% of individuals obtain scores at least 2 *SD*s below the mean (IQ ≤70). However, the prevalence of intellectual disability varies from study to study, ranging from 2.5% to 3.0% of the general population, because the diagnosis of intellectual disability must take into account both intellectual ability and adaptive functioning.

Many studies have been conducted to evaluate the performance of individuals with intellectual disability on previous versions of the Wechsler intelligence scales. The prevalence of large and unusual discrepancies between verbal and nonverbal composite scores has been shown to decrease with decreasing levels of ability (Slate, 1995; Spruill, 1996, 1998; Wechsler, 1997a, 2002, 2003). In addition, the standard deviations for composite and subtest scores have been shown to be smaller for individuals with intellectual disability than for individuals in the general population (Wechsler, 1981, 1997a). Thus, there appears to be less variability in performance at both the composite and subtest levels for adults with intellectual disability than for adults in the general population.

For the WAIS–IV study, it was expected that the mean composite scores of individuals with intellectual disability would be about 2 to 3 SDs lower than the means for individuals in the matched control group. It was also predicted that individuals with intellectual disability would have less variability (i.e., smaller SDs) among composite and subtest scores than the matched control group.

The WAIS–IV was administered to 104 noninstitutionalized examinees, aged 16–63, who were diagnosed with intellectual disability. The group was composed of individuals with either mild or moderate intellectual disability, with 73 participants in the mild severity subgroup and 31 participants in the moderate severity subgroup. Participants had existing scores on standardized measures of cognitive ability that were either 2–3 SDs below the mean (e.g., $55 \leq \text{FSIQ} \leq 70$) for the mild severity group or 3–4 SDs below the mean (e.g., $40 \leq \text{FSIQ} \leq 54$) for the moderate severity group. Tables 5.21 and 5.22 present the mean subtest, process, and composite scores for individuals with intellectual disability at both levels of severity and for their corresponding matched control groups.

Table 5.21   Mean Performance of Intellectual Disability-Mild Severity and Matched Control Groups

Subtest/ Process/ Composite Score	Intellectual Disability-Mild Severity		Matched Control		Group Mean Comparison				
	Mean	SD	Mean	SD	n	Difference	t value	p value	Standard Difference[a]
BD	4.0	1.9	9.9	2.8	73	5.85	14.59	<.01	2.48
SI	3.8	1.3	9.5	2.8	73	5.67	16.62	<.01	2.58
DS	2.8	1.9	9.7	2.6	73	6.92	21.20	<.01	3.06
MR	3.6	2.0	10.3	3.0	73	6.60	16.07	<.01	2.60
VC	4.1	1.1	9.4	3.0	73	5.23	15.50	<.01	2.34
AR	3.6	1.5	9.4	2.7	73	5.84	15.31	<.01	2.69
SS	3.5	2.4	10.3	3.0	73	6.77	14.65	<.01	2.47
VP	4.7	1.6	10.1	3.0	73	5.36	13.04	<.01	2.24
IN	4.3	1.3	9.4	2.7	73	5.16	15.74	<.01	2.40
CD	3.2	2.3	9.9	2.8	73	6.66	14.62	<.01	2.60
LN	3.1	2.4	9.8	2.3	73	6.73	17.43	<.01	2.91
FW	3.9	1.4	10.5	3.1	73	6.60	16.01	<.01	2.76
CO	3.4	1.3	9.5	3.1	73	6.04	16.45	<.01	2.56
CA	3.9	2.3	10.2	2.7	73	6.22	16.55	<.01	2.52
PCm	4.2	2.4	9.9	2.7	73	5.63	12.89	<.01	2.21
BDN	3.6	2.1	10.0	2.9	73	6.40	15.30	<.01	2.50
DSF	4.4	2.7	10.0	2.7	73	5.59	15.38	<.01	2.08
DSB	4.4	2.4	10.1	3.0	73	5.64	13.71	<.01	2.08
DSS	3.2	1.8	9.5	2.4	73	6.30	17.08	<.01	3.02
VCI	65.9	6.3	96.6	14.0	73	30.68	19.18	<.01	2.83
PRI	65.4	8.7	100.1	13.4	73	34.66	18.52	<.01	3.07
WMI	61.5	7.7	97.4	13.2	73	35.85	20.87	<.01	3.32
PSI	63.8	12.6	100.2	14.5	73	36.45	15.58	<.01	2.69
FSIQ	58.5	7.5	98.1	11.8	73	39.59	25.09	<.01	4.01

[a] The Standard Difference is the difference of the two test means divided by the square root of the pooled variance, computed using Cohen's (1996) Formula 10.4.

Table 5.22   Mean Performance of Intellectual Disability-Moderate Severity and Matched Control Groups

Subtest/ Process/ Composite Score	Intellectual Disability-Moderate Severity		Matched Control		Group Mean Comparison				
	Mean	SD	Mean	SD	n	Difference	t value	p value	Standard Difference[a]
BD	1.9	1.1	9.4	3.4	31	7.52	11.67	<.01	2.98
SI	2.0	1.1	9.5	2.8	31	7.42	13.99	<.01	3.50
DS	1.3	0.7	9.4	3.1	31	8.10	13.54	<.01	3.61
MR	2.0	1.2	9.4	3.1	31	7.35	12.40	<.01	3.16
VC	3.1	0.9	9.2	3.2	31	6.16	10.28	<.01	2.62
AR	1.9	1.3	9.7	2.8	31	7.77	14.23	<.01	3.58
SS	1.7	1.6	10.0	3.5	31	8.26	12.41	<.01	3.04
VP	3.4	1.3	9.7	3.1	31	6.32	10.97	<.01	2.66
IN	3.0	1.0	10.0	3.1	31	6.97	12.59	<.01	3.01
CD	1.6	1.1	9.7	3.2	31	8.06	13.22	<.01	3.43
LN	1.2	0.6	9.4	2.8	31	8.19	16.24	<.01	4.09
FW	2.9	1.6	9.9	3.2	31	7.06	12.70	<.01	2.84
CO	2.1	1.0	9.4	2.9	30	7.23	13.30	<.01	3.32
CA	2.0	1.8	10.1	3.2	31	8.06	12.15	<.01	3.11
PCm	2.7	1.8	9.4	3.3	31	6.77	11.82	<.01	2.55
BDN	1.5	0.8	9.4	3.6	31	7.94	12.62	<.01	3.03
DSF	2.3	1.6	9.7	3.1	31	7.39	11.45	<.01	3.00
DSB	2.1	2.3	9.3	2.8	31	7.16	10.01	<.01	2.81
DSS	1.7	0.9	9.7	3.1	31	8.00	14.79	<.01	3.54
VCI	56.8	4.8	97.4	15.3	31	40.61	14.91	<.01	3.58
PRI	55.0	5.1	96.7	15.9	31	41.68	14.60	<.01	3.54
WMI	53.1	4.6	97.1	14.9	31	44.03	15.44	<.01	4.00
PSI	53.8	7.3	98.9	16.7	31	45.10	13.74	<.01	3.50
FSIQ	48.2	4.7	96.9	15.6	31	48.71	17.96	<.01	4.24

[a] The Standard Difference is the difference of the two test means divided by the square root of the pooled variance, computed using Cohen's (1996) Formula 10.4.

For the mild severity subgroup, mean composite scores ranged from 58.5 (FSIQ) to 65.9 (VCI), and all were significantly lower than the corresponding means of the matched control group. As expected, the composite score means for individuals with moderate intellectual disability were even lower, ranging from 48.2 (FSIQ) to 56.8 (VCI). All effect sizes for the mean composite score differences were large.

The variability in performance at both levels of severity was small, with even less variability in the composite and subtest scores of the moderate severity subgroup than the mild severity subgroup. The SDs for composite scores ranged from 6.3 (VCI) to 12.6 (PSI) for the mild severity subgroup, and from 4.6 (WMI) to 7.3 (PSI) for the moderate severity subgroup. Both of these ranges are much smaller than that found in the general population (15). A similar pattern was noted for the standard deviations of the subtests.

At the subtest level, both subgroups scored significantly lower on all subtests than the corresponding matched control group. For the mild severity subgroup, the largest effect sizes for the mean scaled score differences were obtained for Digit Span, Letter–Number Sequencing, Figure Weights, Arithmetic, Matrix Reasoning, and Similarities. For the moderate severity subgroup, largest effect sizes for the mean subtest scaled score differences were obtained for Letter–Number Sequencing, Digit Span, Arithmetic, Similarities, Coding, and Comprehension. These relative weaknesses are consistent with results of studies that indicate poor performance of individuals with intellectual disability on those subtests related to verbal working memory (Baddeley & Jarrold, 2007; Conners, Rosenquist, Arnett, Moore, & Hume, 2008; Jarrold, Purser, & Brock, 2006; Van der Molen, Van Luit, Jongmans, & Van der Molen, 2007), and symbolic or visual-spatial reasoning (Caffrey & Fuchs, 2007; Fontana, 2004; Wechsler, 2003).

All individuals with Intellectual Disability-Mild Severity had FSIQ scores of 75 points or lower versus only 7% of individuals achieving these scores in the matched control group. Similarly, 97% of individuals with Intellectual Disability-Moderate Severity had FSIQ scores of 60 points or lower versus only 3% of individuals in the matched control group. The results for both subgroups provide strong evidence that the WAIS–IV can be used as a measure of cognitive ability as part of a comprehensive assessment for individuals with intellectual disability.

Individuals With Borderline Intellectual Functioning

According to the *DSM–IV–TR*, Borderline Intellectual Functioning is a diagnostic category that can be used when clinical attention is focused on subaverage intellectual functioning, but for those with an IQ range that is higher than the range for intellectual disability, typically, an IQ ranging from 71–84. At times, Intellectual Disability-Mild Severity can be diagnosed for individuals with IQ scores ranging from 71–75; however, the diagnosis of Intellectual Disability-Mild Severity requires the additional presence of adaptive functioning deficits.

For the WAIS–IV study, it was expected that the composite scores of individuals with Borderline Intellectual Functioning would be about 1 to 2 *SD*s lower than individuals in the matched control group. It was also predicted that adults with Borderline Intellectual Functioning would have less variability (i.e., smaller *SD*s) among composite and subtest scores than the matched control group.

The WAIS–IV was administered to a total of 27 noninstitutionalized individuals, aged 16–65, with Borderline Intellectual Functioning. Participants had existing scores on a standardized measure of cognitive ability that ranged from 71–84. Table 5.23 presents the means and standard deviations of the subtest, process, and composite scores for the Borderline Intellectual Functioning group and for the matched control group.

Table 5.23   Mean Performance of Borderline Intellectual Functioning and Matched Control Groups

Subtest/ Process/ Composite Score	Borderline Intellectual Functioning		Matched Control		Group Mean Comparison				
	Mean	SD	Mean	SD	n	Difference	t value	p value	Standard Difference[a]
BD	5.6	1.5	10.1	3.2	27	4.48	6.49	<.01	1.78
SI	6.3	1.6	9.8	3.0	27	3.48	5.06	<.01	1.44
DS	5.9	2.4	9.5	2.8	27	3.67	5.55	<.01	1.42
MR	5.6	2.2	10.0	2.8	27	4.41	5.75	<.01	1.76
VC	5.6	1.3	9.2	2.7	27	3.63	6.39	<.01	1.70
AR	5.1	1.3	9.3	3.3	27	4.19	6.03	<.01	1.67
SS	6.7	1.9	9.7	2.8	27	2.96	3.86	<.01	1.22
VP	6.3	1.8	9.9	3.1	27	3.59	4.41	<.01	1.41
IN	6.0	2.4	9.0	2.7	27	3.00	4.39	<.01	1.17
CD	6.2	2.7	9.2	2.4	27	3.07	4.60	<.01	1.22
LN	6.0	2.2	10.0	3.2	27	4.04	6.23	<.01	1.47
FW	5.4	1.6	9.3	3.4	27	3.96	4.86	<.01	1.49
CO	5.9	1.8	9.5	3.2	27	3.63	4.59	<.01	1.41
CA	6.7	2.5	8.9	2.9	27	2.15	3.79	<.01	.79
PCm	6.7	2.6	9.7	2.9	27	3.07	3.70	<.01	1.11
BDN	5.4	1.9	9.9	3.1	27	4.48	6.22	<.01	1.73
DSF	7.0	2.7	9.7	3.2	27	2.70	3.30	<.01	.91
DSB	6.8	2.5	9.9	2.5	27	3.07	4.83	<.01	1.24
DSS	6.1	1.8	9.4	2.4	27	3.37	6.19	<.01	1.57
VCI	77.3	8.5	96.2	14.5	27	18.89	5.85	<.01	1.59
PRI	75.8	7.8	99.7	15.5	27	23.89	6.10	<.01	1.95
WMI	74.2	9.3	96.6	15.2	27	22.37	6.80	<.01	1.78
PSI	80.9	11.1	96.9	12.4	27	15.96	4.67	<.01	1.36
FSIQ	72.7	7.2	96.9	14.1	27	24.22	7.27	<.01	2.16

[a] The Standard Difference is the difference of the two test means divided by the square root of the pooled variance, computed using Cohen's (1996) Formula 10.4.

Composite scores for the Borderline Intellectual Functioning group ranged from 72.7 (FSIQ) to 80.9 (PSI), and all means were significantly lower than the corresponding means of the matched control group. All effect sizes for the mean composite score differences were large.

The variability in performance of the Borderline Intellectual Functioning group was much smaller than that observed in the general population. The SDs for composite scores of the Borderline Intellectual Functioning group ranged from 7.2 (FSIQ) to 11.1 (PSI). These are comparable to individuals with Intellectual Disability-Mild Severity and are much smaller than that found in the general population (15). A similar pattern was noted for the SDs of the subtests.

At the subtest level, individuals with Borderline Intellectual Functioning scored significantly lower on all subtests than individuals in the matched control group. Largest effect sizes for the mean scaled score differences were obtained for Block Design, Matrix Reasoning, Vocabulary, and Arithmetic. Additional research is needed to determine if these patterns of subtest strengths and weaknesses are replicated in larger, more representative groups of individuals with Borderline Intellectual Functioning.

Of the individuals in the Borderline Intellectual Functioning group, 96% had FSIQ scores of 84 points or lower. By contrast, only 22% of individuals in the matched control group achieved these scores. The lower scores obtained by individuals in the Borderline Intellectual Functioning group are consistent with their previous scores. These results provide strong evidence that the WAIS–IV provides measures of cognitive ability that are useful as part of a comprehensive assessment for individuals with Borderline Intellectual Functioning.

Individuals With Learning Disorders

Criteria for the identification of individuals with learning disabilities may vary at the local, state, and national levels of the educational system. Diagnostic criteria from the *DSM–IV–TR* Learning Disorder categories were used as the primary inclusion criteria for an individual's participation in the corresponding WAIS–IV special group studies. According to the *DSM–IV–TR* criteria, individuals are diagnosed with Learning Disorders when performance on achievement tests is substantially below what is expected for their age, education, and intellectual ability. The individual's learning problems must significantly interfere with academic achievement or daily activities. All individuals identified according to *DSM–IV–TR* Learning Disorder criteria were also currently identified in their respective schools as having a learning disability (if they were school age and currently attending school).

Reading Disorder. The WAIS–IV was administered to 34 individuals, aged 16–24, who were identified with Reading Disorder, based on the ability-achievement discrepancy model defined in *DSM–IV–TR* diagnostic criteria. Table 5.24 presents the means and standard deviations of the WAIS–IV subtest, process, and composite scores for the Reading Disorder and matched control groups.

Table 5.24   Mean Performance of Reading Disorder and Matched Control Groups

Subtest/ Process/ Composite Score	Reading Disorder		Matched Control		Group Mean Comparison				
	Mean	SD	Mean	SD	n	Difference	t value	p value	Standard Difference[a]
BD	8.5	3.1	9.7	2.5	34	1.15	1.61	.12	.41
SI	8.6	2.9	9.8	3.4	34	1.24	1.75	.09	.39
DS	8.5	2.2	10.4	3.2	34	1.82	2.70	.01	.66
MR	8.4	2.6	9.4	2.8	34	.94	1.74	.09	.35
VC	7.5	2.5	9.9	3.6	34	2.41	4.13	<.01	.78
AR	7.5	1.7	10.1	3.4	34	2.59	4.17	<.01	.97
SS	9.9	2.9	9.5	2.4	34	−.35	−.54	.60	−.13
VP	8.5	2.8	9.7	2.6	34	1.15	1.92	.06	.42
IN	8.3	2.7	9.5	3.0	34	1.21	2.18	.04	.43
CD	8.2	2.1	9.4	2.4	34	1.24	2.09	.04	.56
LN	8.4	1.5	11.1	3.4	34	2.68	3.92	<.01	1.03
FW	8.8	3.1	10.9	4.2	34	2.12	2.67	.01	.58
CO	8.2	2.7	9.4	3.1	34	1.18	1.91	.06	.41
CA	8.5	2.6	9.7	2.7	34	1.21	1.96	.06	.46
PCm	9.2	2.9	9.7	3.2	34	.41	.55	.59	.14
BDN	8.6	3.1	9.7	2.6	34	1.15	1.63	.11	.40
DSF	7.8	2.5	10.4	3.5	34	2.56	3.32	<.01	.84
DSB	8.9	2.4	10.7	3.0	34	1.76	2.86	<.01	.64
DSS	9.6	2.4	10.1	3.0	34	.50	.74	.47	.19
VCI	89.5	13.3	98.6	16.2	34	9.06	3.19	<.01	.61
PRI	91.1	13.8	97.3	11.9	34	6.24	2.13	.04	.48
WMI	88.9	9.4	101.1	16.8	34	12.21	3.64	<.01	.90
PSI	94.5	12.0	97.1	11.7	34	2.59	.85	.40	.22
FSIQ	88.7	11.7	97.9	14.0	34	9.18	3.18	<.01	.71

[a] The Standard Difference is the difference of the two test means divided by the square root of the pooled variance, computed using Cohen's (1996) Formula 10.4.

When compared to a matched control group, individuals with Reading Disorder obtained lower mean scores for all composites, with large effect sizes for the WMI, moderate effect sizes for the VCI and the FSIQ, and small effect sizes for the PRI and the PSI. The WMI effect size is consistent with other results (Goldstein, Beers, Siegel, & Minshew, 2001; Wechsler, 1997a, 2003) and with contemporary research that indicates a relationship between reading achievement and difficulties with tasks requiring short-term or working memory (Gathercole, Hitch, Service, & Martin, 1997; Swanson & Howell, 2001).

At the subtest level, the largest effect sizes were noted for Letter–Number Sequencing, Arithmetic, and Vocabulary. The relatively low scores obtained by the Reading Disorder group on Arithmetic and Letter–Number Sequencing are further indication of the possible role of working memory in Reading Disorder. Lower scores on Vocabulary may reflect, in part, a cumulative deficiency in the general fund of information normally acquired through reading.

Mathematics Disorder. The WAIS–IV was administered to 41 individuals, aged 16–24, who were identified as having Mathematics Disorder, based on the discrepancy model defined in *DSM–IV–TR* diagnostic criteria. Table 5.25 presents the means and standard deviations of the WAIS–IV subtest, process, and composite scores for the Mathematics Disorder and matched control groups.

Table 5.25   Mean Performance of Mathematics Disorder and Matched Control Groups

Subtest/ Process/ Composite Score	Mathematics Disorder		Matched Control		Group Mean Comparison				
	Mean	SD	Mean	SD	n	Difference	t value	p value	Standard Difference[a]
BD	8.1	2.4	9.9	3.0	41	1.80	3.45	<.01	.67
SI	8.7	2.6	9.9	3.6	41	1.27	1.86	.07	.41
DS	7.8	2.2	9.7	2.7	41	1.88	3.17	<.01	.77
MR	7.7	2.7	9.6	2.8	41	1.90	3.42	<.01	.70
VC	8.3	2.3	9.6	3.0	41	1.32	2.45	.02	.49
AR	6.6	2.0	9.8	3.1	41	3.24	6.18	<.01	1.26
SS	9.5	3.0	9.3	2.2	41	−.17	−.34	.74	−.06
VP	7.5	2.1	9.2	2.9	41	1.73	3.23	<.01	.69
IN	8.3	2.3	9.3	2.9	41	1.00	1.84	.07	.39
CD	8.0	2.2	9.5	2.8	41	1.54	2.83	<.01	.61
LN	8.0	2.4	10.1	2.9	41	2.15	3.52	<.01	.81
FW	7.3	2.4	9.9	3.2	41	2.61	4.16	<.01	.93
CO	8.7	2.2	10.0	3.4	41	1.27	1.92	.06	.44
CA	8.4	2.4	9.0	2.5	41	.63	1.05	.30	.25
PCm	9.4	2.7	9.3	2.8	41	−.12	−.20	.84	−.04
BDN	8.3	2.8	9.8	2.6	41	1.44	2.82	<.01	.53
DSF	8.4	2.9	10.2	3.0	41	1.73	2.41	.02	.59
DSB	8.6	2.1	9.4	2.6	41	.88	1.72	.09	.37
DSS	7.4	2.4	9.9	3.2	41	2.41	3.58	<.01	.86
VCI	91.2	11.8	97.7	15.5	41	6.56	2.29	.03	.48
PRI	86.8	10.6	97.3	14.3	41	10.44	4.15	<.01	.83
WMI	84.1	10.9	98.7	14.6	41	14.63	5.07	<.01	1.14
PSI	93.2	12.6	96.8	11.3	41	3.56	1.51	.14	.30
FSIQ	86.2	10.0	96.8	12.7	41	10.59	4.45	<.01	.93

[a] The Standard Difference is the difference of the two test means divided by the square root of the pooled variance, computed using Cohen's (1996) Formula 10.4.

Mean scores for the Mathematics Disorder group were lower than mean scores for the matched control group for all composites. Large effect sizes were observed for the PRI, the WMI, and the FSIQ. The effect size for the mean WMI difference was the largest among the composite-level group comparisons. This is primarily due to differential performance on the Arithmetic subtest, which is highly correlated with measures of mathematics achievement.

At the subtest level, largest effect sizes were observed for group differences on Arithmetic, Figure Weights, and Letter–Number Sequencing. The validity study between the WAIS–IV and the WIAT–II reports high correlations between Arithmetic and Figure Weights and with the WIAT–II scores that involve mathematics achievement. The Letter–Number Sequencing effect size is larger than observed in prior studies (Wechsler, 2003). This difference may be due in part to the improved gradient and additional teaching for this subtest.

Together with the large effect size for group differences on the WMI, these findings are consistent with research suggesting an association between working memory difficulties and the occurrence of learning disabilities in mathematics (Bull & Scerif, 2001; Goldstein et al., 2001; Greiffenstein & Baker, 2002; Swanson & Jerman, 2006; Wechsler, 1997a, 2003).

Individuals With Attention-Deficit/Hyperactivity Disorder

The WAIS–IV was administered to 44 individuals, aged 18–31, who were identified as having ADHD according to *DSM–IV–TR* diagnostic criteria for ADHD, Combined Type. For the ADHD group, 18% of the individuals were taking medication for ADHD symptoms at the time of testing. Table 5.26 presents the means and standard deviations of the WAIS–IV subtest, process, and composite scores for the ADHD and matched control groups.

Table 5.26   Mean Performance of Attention-Deficit/Hyperactivity Disorder and Matched Control Groups

Subtest/ Process/ Composite Score	Attention-Deficit/ Hyperactivity Disorder		Matched Control		Group Mean Comparison				
	Mean	SD	Mean	SD	n	Difference	t value	p value	Standard Difference[a]
BD	10.1	3.1	10.9	3.3	44	.73	1.28	.21	.23
SI	9.9	2.7	10.4	3.6	44	.48	.83	.41	.15
DS	9.5	3.2	10.3	2.5	44	.75	1.33	.19	.26
MR	9.3	2.9	10.6	2.8	44	1.20	2.17	.04	.42
VC	10.4	3.0	10.8	3.1	44	.39	.75	.46	.13
AR	8.6	2.6	10.0	3.1	44	1.36	2.50	.02	.47
SS	9.4	3.1	10.1	2.8	44	.66	1.14	.26	.22
VP	9.9	2.9	10.5	2.6	44	.55	.99	.33	.20
IN	10.3	3.1	10.4	3.3	44	.02	.03	.97	.01
CD	8.4	2.4	10.1	3.1	44	1.68	3.38	<.01	.61
LN	9.7	2.9	10.6	1.7	44	.89	2.00	.05	.37
FW	9.8	2.5	11.0	2.4	44	1.14	2.53	.02	.46
CO	10.3	3.0	10.5	3.5	44	.23	.36	.72	.07
CA	9.7	2.5	10.2	3.3	44	.55	.88	.38	.19
PCm	10.4	2.8	10.6	2.7	44	.23	.47	.64	.08
BDN	10.6	2.9	10.6	2.7	44	.00	.00	1.00	.00
DSF	9.9	3.2	10.3	2.7	44	.36	.58	.56	.12
DSB	9.9	3.4	10.4	2.7	44	.45	.69	.49	.15
DSS	9.4	2.9	10.2	2.3	44	.80	1.73	.09	.30
VCI	100.9	14.5	102.8	17.6	44	1.93	.67	.51	.12
PRI	98.6	14.3	103.4	13.9	44	4.82	1.82	.08	.34
WMI	94.7	14.1	100.6	13.2	44	5.91	2.40	.02	.43
PSI	94.0	12.0	100.4	14.0	44	6.36	2.56	.01	.49
FSIQ	96.9	14.0	102.4	14.1	44	5.52	2.39	.02	.39

[a] The Standard Difference is the difference of the two test means divided by the square root of the pooled variance, computed using Cohen's (1996) Formula 10.4.

A negligible effect size was observed for group mean differences on the VCI, and small effect sizes were observed for group mean differences on the other composites. Although not as large as expected, the effect sizes for the PSI and WMI were larger than the VCI and PRI effect sizes. At the subtest level, the largest effect sizes for group mean scaled score differences occurred on the Coding and Arithmetic subtests. Effect sizes for Matrix Reasoning and Figure Weights were similar to the effect size observed on Arithmetic, likely reflecting the working memory demands that are inherent in these fluid reasoning tasks. These results are consistent with research indicating that individuals with ADHD typically achieve scores near the average range of intellectual functioning, but may score lower on measures of working memory and processing speed

(Barkley et al., 2001; Calhoun & Mayes, 2005; Dige & Wik, 2005; Gualtieri & Johnson, 2006; Marchetta, Hurks, Krabbendam, & Jolles, 2008; Mayes & Calhoun, 2007). Additional research is needed with separate samples of individuals with ADHD, Predominantly Inattentive Type, and ADHD, Predominantly Hyperactive/Impulsive Type, as well as investigations comparing the performance of medicated and unmedicated individuals.

Individuals With Traumatic Brain Injury

Traumatic brain injury (TBI) is a neurological condition of relatively high incidence in adolescence and early adulthood (Lucas & Addeo, 2006; Williamson, Scott, & Adams, 1996). TBI can be associated with numerous cognitive impairments (Dikmen, Reitan, & Temkin, 1983; Lezak et al., 2004). The actual functioning that becomes impaired depends on the site and the severity of the damage. The frontal lobes and anterior temporal lobes are particularly vulnerable to contusions, hemorrhages, and hematomas associated with acceleration and deceleration forces of closed head injury (Mattson & Levin, 1990). Frontal lobe damage is associated primarily with executive dysfunction; in severe injuries, the dysfunction can be quite debilitating because the individual experiences greatly impaired flexibility in problem solving or in adaptability (Lezak et al.).

TBI is highly variable in its long-term effects, with previous research suggesting its relationship to cognitive impairments in such areas as

language (Dikmen, Machamer, Winn, & Temkin, 1995; Green, Melo, Christensen, Ngo, Monette, & Bradbury, 2008),

attention (Gualtieri & Johnson, 2006; Mathias & Wheaton, 2007),

working memory (Crawford, Johnson, Mychalkiw, & Moore, 1997; Donders, Tulsky, & Zhu, 2001; Park, Moscovitch, & Robertson, 1999; Perbal, Couillet, Azouvi, & Pouthas, 2003),

processing speed (Axelrod, Fichtenberg, Liethen, Czarnota, & Stucky, 2001, 2002; Gualtieri & Johnson, 2006; Hiscock, Inch, & Gleason, 2002; Mathias & Wheaton, 2007; Perbal et al., 2003),

visual perception and processing (Donders et al., 2001; Green et al., 2008; Hiscock et al., 2002),

visual-spatial and visual-motor skills (Donders, 1997; Green et al., 2008; Verger et al., 2000), and

abstract reasoning (Dikmen et al., 1995; Green et al., 2008).

Conclusions drawn from previous TBI research are limited in part due to methodological inconsistencies, inadequate knowledge of premorbid intellectual functioning, and diffuse control functions of brain anatomy. The cognitive sequelae of TBI have been shown to vary with the area of injury, injury severity, and age at which the injury occurred (Duncan, Burgess, & Emslie, 1995; Lezak et al., 2004; Tremont, Mittenberg, & Miller, 1999; Verger et al., 2000).

The WAIS–IV was administered to a total of 22 individuals, aged 20–44, who were identified with a history of moderate or severe TBI. Only individuals who sustained a TBI within 6 to 18 months prior to the date of testing were included. Those with premorbid intelligence estimates or scores in the range expected for individuals with intellectual disability were excluded. The means and standard deviations of the WAIS–IV subtest, process, and composite scores are reported for the TBI and matched control groups in Table 5.27.

Table 5.27   Mean Performance of Traumatic Brain Injury and Matched Control Groups

Subtest/ Process/ Composite Score	Traumatic Brain Injury		Matched Control		Group Mean Comparison				
	Mean	SD	Mean	SD	n	Difference	t value	p value	Standard Difference[a]
BD	7.9	3.4	10.2	3.3	22	2.36	2.36	.03	.71
SI	8.2	3.2	9.5	3.0	22	1.27	1.63	.12	.41
DS	7.5	3.5	9.4	3.1	22	1.91	2.31	.03	.58
MR	7.1	3.3	9.7	2.9	22	2.59	3.22	<.01	.84
VC	8.9	3.2	10.2	3.4	22	1.27	1.84	.08	.38
AR	7.4	3.1	10.0	2.9	22	2.59	4.33	<.01	.87
SS	6.1	3.3	9.6	2.9	22	3.50	4.60	<.01	1.13
VP	7.9	3.2	10.6	2.7	22	2.68	3.35	<.01	.91
IN	8.8	3.1	10.9	3.6	22	2.05	2.49	.02	.61
CD	6.6	4.4	9.4	3.1	22	2.77	2.97	<.01	.73
LN	8.1	3.6	10.0	2.8	22	1.95	2.68	.01	.61
FW	7.8	2.8	10.6	3.1	22	2.73	4.10	<.01	.92
CO	7.7	2.9	9.5	4.4	22	1.82	1.88	.07	.49
CA	7.1	4.7	9.7	2.5	22	2.68	2.60	.02	.71
PCm	8.5	3.5	10.7	2.5	22	2.23	2.88	<.01	.74
BDN	7.9	3.8	10.5	3.1	22	2.55	2.31	.03	.73
DSF	8.0	3.8	9.2	3.0	22	1.23	1.25	.23	.36
DSB	8.6	2.9	9.4	2.4	22	.77	1.32	.20	.29
DSS	7.1	2.7	10.0	3.5	22	2.95	3.80	<.01	.95
VCI	92.1	16.5	100.8	17.3	22	8.73	2.26	.03	.52
PRI	86.1	17.4	100.7	13.6	22	14.64	3.64	<.01	.94
WMI	85.3	17.2	97.9	14.9	22	12.59	3.45	<.01	.78
PSI	80.5	19.9	97.6	15.1	22	17.09	4.01	<.01	.97
FSIQ	83.9	18.4	99.4	14.8	22	15.50	4.19	<.01	.93

[a] The Standard Difference is the difference of the two test means divided by the square root of the pooled variance, computed using Cohen's (1996) Formula 10.4.

Group mean differences resulted in large effect sizes for the PRI, PSI, and FSIQ, with the largest difference for the PSI. Effect sizes for the VCI and WMI group mean differences were moderate, with the WMI effect size almost reaching the cutoff for large effect sizes ($\geq.80$).

At the subtest level, the largest effect sizes occurred on Symbol Search, Figure Weights, Visual Puzzles, Arithmetic, and Matrix Reasoning. Moderate effect sizes were observed for Block Design, Digit Span, Information, Coding, Letter–Number Sequencing, Cancellation, and Picture Completion. Small effect sizes were observed for Similarities, Vocabulary, and Comprehension; the smallest effect size was obtained for Vocabulary. At the process score level, it is interesting to note the larger effect size for Digit Span Sequencing relative to Digit Span Forward and Digit Span Backward. This task appears to increase the sensitivity of Digit Span to TBI.

These results are consistent with the findings from previously described research and with study results suggesting that individuals with TBI have relatively preserved verbal ability (Lezak et al., 2004; Tremont et al., 1999).

Individuals With Autistic Disorder

Individuals diagnosed with Autistic Disorder are characterized by deficits in verbal and nonverbal communication and social interaction. They may also exhibit stereotyped movements, repetitive activities, and resistance to change (*DSM–IV–TR*).

The WAIS–IV was administered to 16 individuals, aged 16–28, who were identified with Autistic Disorder according to *DSM–IV–TR* criteria. Individuals diagnosed with Autistic Disorder were excluded from this study if they had existing IQ scores lower than 60. Males constituted most of the sample. This overrepresentation most likely reflects the combined effects of a higher prevalence rate for Autistic Disorder in males than females (four times higher) and the greater prevalence of intellectual disability in females with Autistic Disorder (*DSM–IV–TR*). Table 5.28 presents the means and standard deviations of the WAIS–IV subtest, process, and composite scores for the Autistic Disorder and matched control groups.

Table 5.28   Mean Performance of Autistic Disorder and Matched Control Groups

Subtest/ Process/ Composite Score	Autistic Disorder		Matched Control		Group Mean Comparison				
	Mean	SD	Mean	SD	n	Difference	t value	p value	Standard Difference[a]
BD	7.9	3.0	10.9	3.2	16	3.00	2.80	.01	.97
SI	6.1	2.1	9.8	2.3	16	3.69	4.41	<.01	1.71
DS	7.4	3.3	10.6	2.2	16	3.19	3.85	<.01	1.14
MR	8.6	3.5	11.1	3.8	16	2.50	2.15	.05	.68
VC	6.0	1.4	10.2	2.9	16	4.19	5.12	<.01	1.86
AR	7.6	2.7	10.9	1.8	16	3.31	4.51	<.01	1.46
SS	5.6	1.8	10.0	2.6	16	4.44	5.54	<.01	1.99
VP	8.3	3.4	10.4	2.8	16	2.19	1.88	.08	.70
IN	7.6	3.1	10.8	2.6	16	3.13	3.72	<.01	1.09
CD	5.1	2.3	9.3	2.9	16	4.19	5.96	<.01	1.62
LN	7.6	2.3	10.6	1.7	16	3.00	3.99	<.01	1.46
FW	7.9	2.9	10.5	2.2	16	2.63	2.82	.01	1.02
CO	5.7	1.8	10.3	3.0	16	4.56	4.90	<.01	1.86
CA	7.4	3.5	9.9	3.2	16	2.56	2.02	.06	.77
PCm	7.3	2.2	9.7	3.8	16	2.44	2.00	.06	.79
BDN	7.9	3.5	10.6	2.5	16	2.69	2.55	.02	.88
DSF	7.9	3.3	10.9	2.8	16	3.00	3.06	<.01	.99
DSB	8.7	3.4	10.3	2.6	16	1.63	1.75	.10	.54
DSS	7.1	3.4	10.8	3.2	16	3.63	3.18	<.01	1.10
VCI	80.9	9.7	101.1	12.0	16	20.19	5.23	<.01	1.85
PRI	89.7	16.8	104.5	15.9	16	14.81	2.56	.02	.91
WMI	85.7	15.0	103.9	9.4	16	18.19	4.55	<.01	1.45
PSI	75.1	9.2	97.9	13.6	16	22.81	6.39	<.01	1.96
FSIQ	79.8	10.8	102.5	12.4	16	22.69	5.69	<.01	1.95

[a] The Standard Difference is the difference of the two test means divided by the square root of the pooled variance, computed using Cohen's (1996) Formula 10.4.

Individuals in the Autistic Disorder group scored significantly lower than the matched control group on all composites. Effect sizes for all mean composite score differences were large. The largest effect sizes were obtained for the PSI, the FSIQ, and the VCI; the smallest effect size was observed for the PRI. This is consistent with research that indicates individuals with Autistic Disorder demonstrate lowered general intellectual functioning, especially on verbal and processing speed tasks, and obtain relatively higher scores on perceptual tasks (Goldstein et al., 2001; Goldstein, Minshew, Allen, & Seaton, 2002; Liss et al., 2001; Mayes & Calhoun, 2003).

The mean scaled score differences between the Autistic Disorder and matched control groups were large for most subtests. The largest effect sizes were observed on Symbol Search, Vocabulary, Comprehension, Similarities, and Coding. The highest mean subtest scaled scores for individuals in the Autistic Disorder group were obtained on Matrix Reasoning, Visual Puzzles, Block Design, and Figure Weights. These results are consistent with previous research that showed individuals with Autistic Disorder perform better on perceptual tasks, such as Block Design and Object Assembly relative to their performance on other subtests (Bölte & Poustka, 2004; Dennis, Lockyer, Lazenby, Donnelly, Wilkinson, & Schoonheyt, 1999; Goldstein et al., 2001; Siegel et al., 1996; Wechsler, 2003).

A wide variety of subtest performance patterns have been noted in other studies of individuals with Autistic Disorder (Goldstein et al., 2002; Minshew, Siegel, Goldstein, & Weldy, 1994; Siegel et al., 1996). Additional research is therefore needed to determine if these results are consistent in individuals with Autistic Disorder functioning at differing levels of overall cognitive ability, and are replicated in larger samples.

Individuals With Asperger's Disorder

Differential diagnosis of Autistic Disorder and Asperger's Disorder relies primarily on the levels of overall language ability and social interaction. Individuals diagnosed with Asperger's Disorder display less severe deficits in verbal ability and fewer delays in cognitive development related to learning skills and adaptive behaviors than those with Autistic Disorder (*DSM–IV–TR*; Gilchrist, Green, Cox, Burton, Rutter, & Le Couteur, 2001).

The WAIS–IV was administered to 40 individuals, aged 16–40, who were identified with Asperger's Disorder according to *DSM–IV–TR* criteria. The sample consisted of 22.5% females and 77.5% males. Individuals diagnosed with Asperger's Disorder were excluded from this study if they had existing general cognitive ability scores more than 2 *SD*s below the mean (i.e., FSIQ <70). Table 5.29 presents the means and standard deviations of the WAIS–IV subtest, process, and composite scores for the Asperger's Disorder and matched control groups.

Table 5.29   Mean Performance of Asperger's Disorder and Matched Control Groups

Subtest/ Process/ Composite Score	Asperger's Disorder		Matched Control		Group Mean Comparison				
	Mean	SD	Mean	SD	n	Difference	t value	p value	Standard Difference[a]
BD	10.2	3.2	10.4	3.1	40	.20	.31	.76	.06
SI	10.0	2.7	11.0	3.3	40	1.03	1.60	.12	.34
DS	9.2	3.0	11.0	2.9	40	1.88	3.16	<.01	.63
MR	10.0	2.6	10.8	3.1	40	.78	1.17	.25	.27
VC	10.9	3.3	10.9	3.6	40	−.03	−.03	.97	−.01
AR	9.5	3.5	10.9	3.1	40	1.40	2.30	.03	.43
SS	8.4	3.2	10.4	2.9	40	1.93	2.90	<.01	.63
VP	10.0	3.3	10.9	3.1	40	.93	1.46	.15	.29
IN	11.6	3.7	11.2	3.0	40	−.38	−.55	.59	−.11
CD	7.3	2.6	9.9	2.7	40	2.68	4.59	<.01	1.02
LN	9.6	3.3	11.2	3.3	40	1.60	2.13	.04	.48
FW	10.0	2.8	11.3	3.4	40	1.35	1.82	.08	.44
CO	9.3	3.2	11.2	3.4	40	1.95	2.60	.01	.59
CA	7.7	3.2	10.3	2.7	40	2.63	4.25	<.01	.89
PCm	9.5	2.7	10.9	2.7	40	1.48	2.82	<.01	.55
BDN	10.1	2.9	10.3	3.1	40	.23	.40	.69	.08
DSF	9.0	3.2	10.8	2.9	40	1.85	2.96	<.01	.60
DSB	9.7	2.8	11.1	2.9	40	1.40	2.36	.02	.49
DSS	9.2	2.7	11.1	3.1	40	1.93	2.96	<.01	.66
VCI	104.5	16.8	105.9	16.7	40	1.35	.37	.71	.08
PRI	100.0	14.4	103.7	15.5	40	3.70	1.26	.22	.25
WMI	96.0	16.1	105.1	14.9	40	9.13	3.19	<.01	.59
PSI	88.4	13.8	100.7	13.3	40	12.33	4.24	<.01	.91
FSIQ	97.5	14.1	104.9	15.4	40	7.35	2.47	.02	.50

[a] The Standard Difference is the difference of the two test means divided by the square root of the pooled variance, computed using Cohen's (1996) Formula 10.4.

The PSI group mean difference exhibited a large effect size, and the WMI and FSIQ group mean differences produced moderate effect sizes. The PRI group mean difference exhibited a small effect size, and the difference for the VCI was negligible. These data are consistent with results of previous investigations that found lower processing speed performance relative to other cognitive ability measures (Barnhill, Hagiwara, Myles, & Simpson, 2000; Cederlund & Gillberg, 2004; Koyama, Tachimori, Osada, Takeda, & Kurita, 2007) and preserved verbal ability (Ambery, Russel, Perry, Morris, & Murphy, 2006; Cederlund & Gillberg; Gilchrist et al., 2001; Koyama et al., 2007; Spek, Scholte, & van Berckelaer-Onnes, 2008) in individuals with Asperger's Disorder.

Group mean differences for Coding, Cancellation, and Symbol Search produced the largest effect sizes. This pattern of results is consistent with previous results noting lower performance on processing speed subtests for individuals with Asperger's Disorder (Barnhill et al., 2000; Cederlund & Gillberg, 2004; Gilchrist et al., 2001; Koyama et al., 2007; Nakahachi et al., 2006; Spek et al., 2008). The effect size for Digit Span is of the same magnitude as that of Symbol Search; however, deficits in working memory for individuals with Asperger's Disorder are less consistently observed in the literature (see Cederlund & Gillberg; Koyama et al.; Spek et al.). It is possible that the addition of the Sequencing task to Digit Span may have increased the sensitivity of this subtest to Asperger's Disorder relative to previous versions.

It is noteworthy that a moderate effect size was obtained for Comprehension and that this was larger than the negligible and small effect sizes observed for the other Verbal Comprehension subtests. Results from prior studies have found that, of the Verbal Comprehension subtests, individuals with Asperger's Disorder perform lowest on Comprehension (Barnhill et al., 2000; Cederlund & Gillberg, 2004; Koyama et al., 2007), with some notable exceptions (Spek et al., 2008). Individuals with Asperger's Disorder show impairment in social interactions, and Comprehension is thought to measure knowledge of conventional standards of behavior and social judgment. Additional research is needed to determine if this pattern of results is consistent in samples of individuals with Asperger's Disorder who are functioning at lower levels of overall cognitive ability and in larger samples of individuals with Asperger's Disorder.

Individuals With Major Depressive Disorder

According to the *DSM–IV–TR*, Major Depressive Disorder is characterized by depressed mood or loss of interest in most activities and other associated symptoms, such as weight changes, sleep problems, psychomotor agitation or retardation, fatigue or loss of energy, and difficulty thinking or concentrating. The WAIS–IV was administered to 41 individuals, aged 50–86, who were identified with Major Depressive Disorder according to *DSM–IV–TR* criteria. For the Major Depressive Disorder group, 78% were taking medication for depression at the time of testing. Table 5.30 presents the means and standard deviations of the WAIS–IV subtest, process, and composite scores for the Major Depressive Disorder and matched control groups.

Table 5.30   Mean Performance of Major Depressive Disorder and Matched Control Groups

Subtest/ Process/ Composite Score	Major Depressive Disorder		Matched Control		Group Mean Comparison				
	Mean	SD	Mean	SD	n	Difference	t value	p value	Standard Difference[a]
BD	9.4	2.7	9.7	2.8	41	.37	.73	.47	.13
SI	10.2	3.0	10.4	2.5	41	.24	.51	.62	.09
DS	10.3	3.1	9.8	2.4	41	−.49	−.81	.42	−.18
MR	10.4	3.1	9.9	3.0	41	−.44	−.89	.38	−.14
VC	10.6	3.1	10.5	3.2	41	−.10	−.17	.86	−.03
AR	9.6	2.5	9.6	3.2	41	.02	.05	.96	.01
SS	9.4	2.5	9.8	2.9	41	.34	.63	.53	.13
VP	9.2	3.2	10.0	3.2	41	.71	1.26	.21	.22
IN	10.4	2.8	9.9	3.4	36	−.44	−.77	.45	−.14
CD	9.0	3.2	10.2	2.9	36	1.19	2.06	.05	.39
LN	9.8	2.6	9.8	2.9	33	.06	.09	.93	.02
FW	9.2	2.8	10.2	3.0	33	1.06	1.92	.06	.37
CO	9.8	3.0	10.2	3.3	36	.39	.56	.58	.12
CA	9.6	2.6	10.4	2.5	33	.79	1.32	.19	.31
PCm	10.2	3.5	9.9	3.2	36	−.28	−.42	.68	−.08
BDN	9.3	2.9	9.4	2.8	41	.07	.13	.89	.02
DSF	10.8	3.6	9.9	2.2	41	−.90	−1.29	.20	−.30
DSB	10.0	3.1	9.7	2.8	41	−.37	−.58	.57	−.13
DSS	10.0	2.4	10.1	2.5	41	.12	.24	.81	.05
VCI	101.8	14.6	101.6	15.0	36	−.17	−.06	.95	−.01
PRI	97.8	14.5	99.1	15.1	41	1.27	.54	.59	.09
WMI	99.5	13.9	98.2	13.7	41	−1.27	−.50	.62	−.09
PSI	95.8	13.5	99.4	14.5	36	3.61	1.36	.18	.26
FSIQ	98.6	14.7	99.4	16.1	36	.83	.34	.73	.05

[a] The Standard Difference is the difference of the two test means divided by the square root of the pooled variance, computed using Cohen's (1996) Formula 10.4.

At the composite level, a small effect size was observed for the PSI. All other effect sizes for composite scores were negligible. These data are consistent with previous investigations that found lowered processing speed performance relative to performance on other types of cognitive ability measures in individuals with Major Depressive Disorder (Gorlyn, Keilp, Oquendo, Burke, Sackeim, & Mann, 2006; Iverson, Turner, & Green, 1999; Mandelli et al., 2006; Morasco, Gfeller, & Chibnall, 2006), and lowered processing speed performance in older adults with depression relative to a nonclinical sample of older adults (Feehan, Knight, & Partridge, 1991).

Small effect sizes were observed for group mean differences on Visual Puzzles, Coding, Figure Weights, and Cancellation. These results are consistent with those of previous studies that indicated individuals with Major Depressive Disorder consistently show lower performance on processing speed tasks relative to other types of cognitive tasks and compared to nonclinical individuals (Gorlyn et al., 2006; Gualtieri & Johnson, 2006; Iverson et al., 1999; Mandelli et al., 2006). Results from some prior studies (e.g., Naismith et al., 2003) report that, relative to nonclinical individuals, individuals with Major Depressive Disorder perform somewhat worse on timed subtests (as on Visual Puzzles and Figure Weights) than untimed subtests; however, this result has not been replicated consistently.

It should be noted that the age range of this sample did not include individuals below age 50. Additional research is needed to determine if this pattern of results is consistent in samples of younger individuals with Major Depressive Disorder and is replicated in larger samples.

Individuals With Mild Cognitive Impairment

Various criteria have been proposed for use in diagnosing mild cognitive impairment (MCI; Chertkow et al., 2008; Petersen, Stevens, Ganguli, Tangalos, Cummings, & DeKosky, 2001; Ritchie, Artero, & Touchon, 2001). Initial criteria specified that MCI must involve memory impairment (Petersen et al., 2001), but the criteria are no longer exclusive to memory impairment. General consensus is emerging that individuals with MCI exhibit objectively measured evidence of memory impairment *or* impairment in another cognitive domain, yet do not meet the criteria to be diagnosed with dementia. Individuals with MCI may have a history of decline from a previously normal level of cognitive functioning; preserved basic daily functioning; and if memory loss is present, there is no evidence of other medical, neurological, or psychiatric causes for the memory loss (for discussion, see Chertkow et al; Petersen, Smith, Waring, Ivnik, Tangalos, & Kokmen, 1999; Petersen et al.). In recent years, researchers have drawn further distinctions among subtypes of MCI (e.g., amnestic MCI-single or -multiple domain, nonam- nestic MCI-single or -multiple domain). For discussion, see Busse, Hensel, Gühne, Angermeyer, and Riedel-Heller, 2006, Chertkow et al., and Loewenstein et al., 2006.

Diagnostic issues and group heterogeneity have complicated MCI research (Luis, Loewenstein, Acevedo, Barker, & Duara, 2003; Palmer, Wang, Backman, Winblad, & Fratiglioni, 2002; Petersen et al., 2001; Ritchie et al., 2001). Certainly, these issues have resulted in varied findings with respect to cognitive functioning in MCI. For example, most studies show lower perfor- mance on measures of processing speed (Devanand et al., 2006; Gualtieri & Johnson, 2006; Nordlund, Rolstad, Klang, Lind, Hansen, & Wallin, 2007), but the results are less consistent for verbal (Doniger et al., 2006; Nordlund et al., 2007; Wylie, Ridderinkhof, Eckerle, & Manning, 2007), visuospatial (Bennett, Golob, Parker, & Starr, 2006; Doniger et al.; Nordlund et al.), and working memory abilities (Economou, Papageorgiou, & Karageorgiou, 2006; Nordlund et al.).

Studies indicate higher rates of progression to Alzheimer's disease in individuals with amnestic MCI relative to individuals without MCI (Boyle, Wilson, Aggarwal, Tang, & Bennett, 2006; Fischer et al., 2007; Ganguli, Dodge, Shen, & DeKosky, 2004; Visser, Kester, Jolles, & Verhey, 2006). Progression to other types of dementia is less well-researched or established (Fischer et al.; Luis et al., 2003). Early identification and intervention may enable clinicians to recommend appropriate medical interventions and aid families in long-term planning.

The WAIS–IV was administered to 53 individuals, aged 59–90, who were identified with MCI according to criteria established in the research literature (Chertkow et al., 2008; Petersen et al., 2001; Ritchie et al., 2001). No distinction was made among subtypes. Table 5.31 presents the means and standard deviations of the WAIS–IV subtest, process, and composite scores for the MCI and matched control groups.

Table 5.31 Mean Performance of Mild Cognitive Impairment and Matched Control Groups

Subtest/ Process/ Composite Score	Mild Cognitive Impairment		Matched Control		Group Mean Comparison				
	Mean	SD	Mean	SD	n	Difference	t value	p value	Standard Difference[a]
BD	8.9	2.5	10.6	3.0	53	1.62	2.96	<.01	.58
SI	9.9	2.6	10.9	3.0	53	1.02	2.22	.03	.36
DS	9.5	3.6	10.9	2.7	53	1.45	2.62	.01	.45
MR	9.5	3.0	10.9	2.9	53	1.42	2.43	.02	.48
VC	10.1	2.7	10.3	2.9	53	.23	.47	.64	.08
AR	9.4	3.1	10.8	2.6	53	1.42	2.74	<.01	.49
SS	9.0	3.5	10.0	2.3	53	.92	1.44	.16	.31
VP	8.6	2.6	9.9	3.1	53	1.34	2.26	.03	.47
IN	9.8	3.2	11.7	3.1	40	1.85	3.10	<.01	.59
CD	9.0	2.7	10.8	2.6	40	1.78	2.61	.01	.67
LN	8.0	2.9	10.4	2.1	14	2.43	2.08	.06	.96
FW	8.9	3.9	10.4	2.5	14	1.57	1.09	.30	.48
CO	9.2	3.0	11.1	2.6	40	1.90	3.88	<.01	.68
CA	7.9	4.1	9.6	2.4	14	1.64	1.08	.30	.48
PCm	8.5	3.2	10.6	2.7	40	2.18	3.23	<.01	.74
BDN	8.9	2.5	10.6	3.2	53	1.72	3.02	<.01	.60
DSF	10.2	3.1	10.3	2.9	53	.13	.24	.81	.04
DSB	9.5	3.3	10.9	3.0	53	1.42	2.53	.01	.45
DSS	8.9	4.1	10.9	2.4	53	2.08	2.98	<.01	.62
VCI	99.0	13.8	106.1	15.0	40	7.13	2.82	<.01	.49
PRI	93.9	13.1	102.4	14.7	53	8.43	2.96	<.01	.61
WMI	96.6	17.1	104.7	12.8	53	8.13	3.10	<.01	.54
PSI	94.9	15.7	102.2	11.9	40	7.33	2.04	.05	.53
FSIQ	94.8	14.5	104.8	13.4	40	10.00	3.36	<.01	.72

[a] The Standard Difference is the difference of the two test means divided by the square root of the pooled variance, computed using Cohen's (1996) Formula 10.4.

The MCI group included college-educated individuals in larger proportion than in the normative sample. At both the composite and subtest level, the MCI group means were similar to the means for the normative sample. Mean composite scores for the MCI group ranged from 93.9 (PRI) to 99.0 (VCI); however, all were significantly lower than the corresponding means of the matched control group. All effect sizes for the mean composite score differences were moderate, except VCI, which showed a small effect size. The largest effect size observed was for the FSIQ. At the subtest level, a large effect size was obtained for Letter–Number Sequencing, and moderate effect sizes were observed for Block Design, Information, Coding, Comprehension, and Picture Completion.

For this particular heterogeneous group of individuals with MCI, some early signs of decline are present; however, verbal ability is relatively preserved. The moderate effect sizes for Information and Comprehension were somewhat unexpected, but the MCI group means for Information and Comprehension are close to the mean for the normative sample. It is possible that these results are related to the strong performance of the matched control group on these two particular subtests rather than to a particular weakness in the MCI group. Additional research is needed to determine if these patterns of subtest strengths and weaknesses are replicated across subtypes of MCI and in larger samples of individuals with MCI.

Individuals With Probable Dementia of the Alzheimer's Type-Mild Severity

The National Institute of Neurological and Communicative Disorders and Stroke and the Alzheimer's Disease and Related Disorders Association (NINCDS-ADRDA) criteria for probable Alzheimer's disease specify that the individual must be experiencing dementia, deficits in two or more areas of cognition, progressive decline in memory and other cognitive functions, with no disturbance in consciousness and an absence of systemic disorders or brain disease that may account for the decline (McKhann, Drachman, Folstein, Katzman, Price, & Stadlan, 1984). The criteria were revised in 2007 to improve specificity relative to other dementias, facilitate testing of earlier interventions, distinguish from amnestic MCI, and acknowledge new biological markers for Alzheimer's disease that are now accessible due to scientific and technological advancements in imaging and molecular pathology (Dubois et al., 2007). The new criteria require episodic memory impairment for more than 6 months that is objectively documented with testing results. It further requires evidence of medial temporal lobe atrophy as evidenced with MRI, a cerebrospinal fluid biomarker, PET functional neuroimaging, or a proven Alzheimer's dementia autosomal mutation within the individual's immediate family (Dubois et al.)

Alzheimer's disease is the most common form of dementia among older adults (Zec, 1993). It is associated with diffuse cognitive deficits (Demakis, Sawyer, Fritz, & Sweet, 2001; Earnst et al., 2001; Golden, Bouvier, Selden, Mattis, Todd, & Golden, 2005; Giovannetti et al., 2001) and progressive deterioration of cognitive functions (Lezak et al., 2004). The primary purpose of intelligence testing of individuals with Alzheimer's disease is to obtain a baseline of premorbid cognitive ability for use in assessing the degree of deterioration in memory function.

The WAIS–IV was administered to 44 examinees, aged 58–90, who were identified with probable Dementia of the Alzheimer's Type-Mild Severity according to the 1984 NINCDS-ADRDA criteria for probable Alzheimer's disease (McKhann et al., 1984). The 1984 criteria were used because the 2007 criteria were not available when the sample was defined. Table 5.32 presents the means and standard deviations of the WAIS–IV subtest, process, and composite scores for the Probable Dementia of the Alzheimer's Type-Mild Severity and matched control groups.

Table 5.32   Mean Performance of Probable Dementia of the Alzheimer's Type-Mild Severity and
Matched Control Groups

Subtest/ Process/ Composite Score	Probable Dementia of the Alzheimer's Type-Mild Severity		Matched Control		Group Mean Comparison				
	Mean	SD	Mean	SD	n	Difference	t value	p value	Standard Difference[a]
BD	7.8	3.8	10.6	3.0	43	2.72	4.82	<.01	.79
SI	7.5	3.7	10.4	3.5	43	2.81	4.16	<.01	.78
DS	7.3	3.3	10.2	3.1	44	2.84	4.52	<.01	.89
MR	7.5	3.3	10.1	3.0	44	2.57	4.51	<.01	.82
VC	8.4	2.8	10.9	2.9	43	2.51	5.29	<.01	.88
AR	7.1	2.7	10.2	2.6	44	3.11	6.87	<.01	1.18
SS	5.3	3.0	10.2	3.0	44	4.89	7.76	<.01	1.64
VP	7.3	2.7	10.2	2.7	43	2.84	5.97	<.01	1.07
IN	6.5	2.9	10.8	3.0	31	4.35	7.98	<.01	1.47
CD	6.1	3.5	10.7	3.0	31	4.61	5.50	<.01	1.41
CO	7.8	3.1	11.2	3.5	31	3.45	4.30	<.01	1.05
PCm	6.7	3.3	9.0	2.7	24	2.38	3.77	<.01	.80
BDN	7.9	3.8	10.4	2.9	43	2.53	4.52	<.01	.75
DSF	8.8	2.8	10.3	3.3	44	1.55	2.69	.01	.51
DSB	7.8	2.8	10.1	2.6	44	2.27	4.17	<.01	.83
DSS	6.8	3.6	10.1	3.3	44	3.27	4.30	<.01	.95
VCI	86.2	15.5	103.0	16.9	31	16.84	5.80	<.01	1.04
PRI	85.8	17.0	101.5	13.9	43	15.72	6.14	<.01	1.01
WMI	84.3	15.7	100.9	13.8	44	16.66	6.49	<.01	1.12
PSI	76.6	15.2	102.6	15.4	31	26.06	6.62	<.01	1.70
FSIQ	81.2	16.6	102.0	16.8	30	20.87	6.15	<.01	1.25

[a] The Standard Difference is the difference of the two test means divided by the square root of the pooled variance, computed using Cohen's (1996) Formula 10.4.

Mean composite scores for the Probable Dementia of the Alzheimer's Type-Mild Severity group ranged from 76.6 (PSI) to 86.2 (VCI), and all were significantly lower than the corresponding means of the matched control group. All effect sizes for the mean composite score differences were large, with the largest effect size noted for the PSI.

At the subtest level, the Probable Dementia of the Alzheimer's Type-Mild Severity group scored significantly lower than the matched control group on all subtests. Largest effect sizes for the mean scaled score differences were obtained for Symbol Search, Information, Coding, and Arithmetic. At the process level, it is interesting to note that of the Digit Span process scores, the largest effect size was observed for Digit Span Sequencing. This is consistent with findings from prior research that has demonstrated the sensitivity of digit ordering tasks to probable Dementia of the Alzheimer's Type (MacDonald, Almor, Henderson, Kempler, & Andersen, 2001).

These results are also consistent with those of previous studies that indicated individuals with Alzheimer's disease show lower performance than nonclinical individuals on a wide variety of cognitive tasks involving verbal concept formation (Golden et al., 2005; Giovannetti et al., 2001; Kazui, Hashimoto, Hirono, & Mori, 2003; Lange & Chelune, 2006; Larrabee, Largen, & Levin, 1985), semantic memory (Golden et al.; Kazui et al., 2003), visuospatial ability (Golden et al.; Lange & Chelune), mathematical ability (Hirono et al., 1998), working memory (Earnst et al., 2001; Golden et al.; Hill, Storandt, & LaBarge, 1992; Hirono et al.), and processing speed (Demakis et al., 2001; Earnst et al.; Golden et al.; Hart, Kwentus, Wade, & Hamer, 1987). Additional research is needed to determine if these patterns of subtest strengths and weaknesses are replicated in samples of individuals diagnosed with probable Alzheimer's disease utilizing the revised 2007 criteria (Dubois et al., 2007).

Chapter 6

Interpretive Considerations

Results from the WAIS–IV provide important information regarding an examinee's cognitive functioning, but they should never be interpreted in isolation. Item responses and scores provide qualitative and quantitative information that is best interpreted in conjunction with a thorough history and careful clinical observations of an individual. Many additional sources of information are typically available to the practitioner: medical, educational, and psychosocial history; direct behavioral observations; previous test scores; qualitative aspects of test performance; and results from other relevant instruments given in a battery. In addition, the practitioner should evaluate results within the context of the referral question or purpose of the evaluation.

Many interpretation strategies, methods, and procedures that were developed and refined by experienced practitioners and researchers for previous Wechsler intelligence scales continue to be valid and useful (Groth-Marnat, 2003; Kaufman & Lichtenberger, 1999, 2006; Sattler, 2008a, 2008b). The practitioner must consider the changes in content that have occurred between versions when applying these interpretative guidelines.

A detailed, systematic, and complete method of protocol analysis is beyond the scope of this manual. However, basic interpretive considerations, including information on reporting scores and performing the basic profile analysis, are provided in the following sections. Based on their primary applicability to specific research or referral questions, interpretive information on the reference group norms and ability-achievement discrepancies appears at the end of the chapter.

Reporting and Describing Performance

The conversion of raw scores into standard scores enables practitioners to compare scores within a scale and between the scale and other related measures. The use of age-corrected standard scores enables the practitioner to compare each examinee's cognitive functioning with the cognitive functioning of examinees of similar age. Standard scores provide the most accurate description of test data. However, for individuals who are unfamiliar with test interpretation, standard scores may be difficult to understand in isolation. Other information, such as percentile ranks, confidence intervals, and descriptive classifications, is often used in conjunction with standard scores to describe an examinee's performance.

Standard Scores

Two types of age-corrected standard scores are provided in the WAIS–IV: scaled scores and composite scores. Scaled scores represent an examinee's performance relative to his or her same-age peers. They are typically derived from the total raw scores for each subtest and are scaled to a metric with a mean of 10 and a standard deviation (SD) of 3. A scaled score of 10 reflects the average performance of a given age group. Scores of 7 and 13 are 1 SD below and above the mean, respectively. Scaled scores of 4 and 16 are 2 SDs below and above the mean, respectively. The scaled process scores (i.e., BDN, DSF, DSB, and DSS) are derived in the same manner as the subtest scaled scores. Table 6.1 presents the relation of scaled scores to SDs from the mean and percentile rank equivalents.

Table 6.1   Relation of Scaled Scores to Standard Deviations From the Mean and Percentile Rank Equivalents

Scaled Score	Number of SDs From the Mean	Percentile Rank Equivalent[a]
19	+3	99.9
18	$+2\frac{2}{3}$	99.6
17	$+2\frac{1}{3}$	99
16	+2	98
15	$+1\frac{2}{3}$	95
14	$+1\frac{1}{3}$	91
13	+1	84
12	$+\frac{2}{3}$	75
11	$+\frac{1}{3}$	63
10	0 (Mean)	50
9	$-\frac{1}{3}$	37
8	$-\frac{2}{3}$	25
7	−1	16
6	$-1\frac{1}{3}$	9
5	$-1\frac{2}{3}$	5
4	−2	2
3	$-2\frac{1}{3}$	1
2	$-2\frac{2}{3}$	0.4
1	−3	0.1

[a] The percentile ranks are theoretical values for a normal distribution.

The composite scores (i.e., VCI, PRI, WMI, PSI, and FSIQ) are standard scores based on various sums of subtest scaled scores. The composite scores are scaled to a metric with a mean of 100 and an SD of 15. A score of 100 on any of the composites defines the average performance of examinees similar in age, and scores of 85 and 115 are 1 SD below and above the mean, respectively. Scores of 70 and 130 are 2 SDs below and above the mean, respectively. Approximately 68% of all examinees obtain composite scores between 85 and 115, about 96% score in the 70–130 range, and nearly all examinees (about 99.8%) obtain scores between 55 and 145 (3 SDs on either side of the mean). The relation of composite scores to SDs from the mean and the associated percentile rank equivalents are presented in Table 6.2.

Table 6.2   Relation of Composite Scores to Standard Deviations From the Mean and Percentile Rank Equivalents

Composite Score	Number of SDs From the Mean	Percentile Rank Equivalent[a]
145	+3	99.9
140	$+2\frac{2}{3}$	99.6
135	$+2\frac{1}{3}$	99
130	+2	98
125	$+1\frac{2}{3}$	95
120	$+1\frac{1}{3}$	91
115	+1	84
110	$+\frac{2}{3}$	75
105	$+\frac{1}{3}$	63
100	0 (Mean)	50
95	$-\frac{1}{3}$	37
90	$-\frac{2}{3}$	25
85	−1	16
80	$-1\frac{1}{3}$	9
75	$-1\frac{2}{3}$	5
70	−2	2
65	$-2\frac{1}{3}$	1
60	$-2\frac{2}{3}$	0.4
55	−3	0.1

[a] The percentile ranks are theoretical values for a normal distribution.

Percentile Ranks

Age-based percentile ranks are provided for the standard scores to indicate an examinee's standing relative to other examinees of the same age. Percentile ranks reflect points on a scale below which a given percentage of scores lie, based on the normative sample. Percentile ranks typically range from 1 to 99, with 50 as the mean and median. For example, examinees with a percentile rank of 15 perform as well as, or better than, 15% of other examinees the same age (or perform as low as, or lower than, 85% of other examinees the same age).

Although easy to understand and useful for explaining an examinee's performance relative to that of others, percentile ranks have various limitations. Percentile ranks do not have equal intervals. Percentile ranks in a normal distribution, such as the FSIQ, tend to cluster near the median (the 50th percentile). Consequently, for examinees who score within the average range, a change of 1 or 2 total raw score points may produce a large change in their percentile ranks. For those examinees with more extreme scores, a change of 1 or 2 total raw score points is not likely to produce a sizable change in their percentile ranks.

Standard Errors of Measurement and Confidence Intervals

Scores obtained on measures of cognitive ability are based on observational data and represent *estimates* of an examinee's *true* scores. They reflect an examinee's true abilities combined with some degree of measurement error. An examinee's true score is more accurately represented by establishing a confidence interval, a specified range of scores in which the true score is likely to lie. Confidence intervals provide another means of expressing score precision and serve as a reminder that measurement error is inherent in all test scores. Scores that are less reliable have a broader range while those that are more reliable have a narrower range. Practitioners are encouraged to report confidence intervals around the composite scores and to use this information to ensure greater accuracy when interpreting the test scores.

Tables A.3–A.7 in the Administration and Scoring Manual and Table C.1 in this manual provide confidence intervals of the composite scores using *SEE* and estimated true scores. The confidence intervals calculated with *SEM* are banded around the observed scores, whereas the confidence intervals calculated with *SEE* are banded around the estimated true scores corrected for regression toward the mean.

Descriptive Classifications

The composite scores are often described in qualitative terms according to the examinee's level of performance. Descriptive classifications provide qualitative terms that characterize the examinee's level of composite score performance relative to same age peers. Table 6.3 lists the descriptive classifications of the composite scores. Test results can be described in a manner similar to the following example:

> Relative to examinees of comparable age, this individual is currently functioning within the [*insert appropriate descriptive classification*] range of intelligence on a standardized measure of intellectual ability.

Table 6.3   Descriptive Classifications of Composite Score Ranges

Composite Score Range	Descriptive Classification	Percent Included	
		Theoretical Normal Curve	Actual Sample[a]
130 and above	Very Superior	2.5	2.3
120–129	Superior	7.2	6.8
110–119	High Average	16.6	17.1
90–109	Average	49.5	50.2
80–89	Low Average	15.6	15.0
70–79	Borderline	6.5	6.1
69 and below	Extremely Low	2.1	2.5

[a] The percentages shown are for the FSIQ and are based on the total normative sample ($N = 2,200$). The percentages obtained for the other composite scores are very similar.

Suggested Procedures for Basic Profile Analysis

An examinee's performance can be evaluated in terms of his or her patterns of scores on the composites and on the core and supplemental subtests. Profile analysis can occur from both an intra-individual and inter-individual perspective by comparing the examinee's score patterns across composites or subtests, or by comparing his or her score patterns to the appropriate normative reference group. These ability comparisons can help the practitioner identify potentially meaningful patterns of strengths and weaknesses, which is important in describing functional impairment and for designing and preparing treatment plans (Kaufman & Lichtenberger, 2006; Sattler, 2008a, 2008b).

Appropriate application of profile analysis begins with the generation of hypotheses that are based on the examinee's pattern of scores. These hypotheses are then either corroborated or refuted by other evaluation results, background information, or direct behavioral observations (Kaufman & Lichtenberger, 2006; Tulsky, Zhu, & Prifitera, 2000). Although the Record Form is designed to assist the practitioner with profile analysis, practitioners should always attempt to obtain as much collaborative data as possible, including information about the individual's developmental history; familial and cultural
background; medical, social, and educational history; and previous assessment results. The additional information should be considered in the interpretation of an examinee's performance and incorporated into reports of his or her test results.

The following section outlines the mechanics of basic profile analysis, but meaningful interpretation requires integration of these data with the full clinical picture by a knowledgeable practitioner. For more comprehensive texts on clinical interpretation of the Wechsler scales, see Kaufman and Lichtenberger, 1999, 2006; Sattler, 2008a, 2008b; and Tulsky et al., 2003.

Performing the Basic Profile Analysis

For the practitioner's convenience and to assist in report writing, the information in this section proceeds in sequence from the general to the specific, similar to the presentation order within a typical interpretive report. Information relevant to reporting and describing the composite scores is followed by more detailed information relevant to investigating the examinee's subtest- and process-level scores. However, when conceptualizing interpretation of the scores, evaluation of the examinee's performance at the subtest- and process-level informs the interpretation of performance at the composite level. For example, interpretation of the WMI should reflect the examinee's relative performance on the two contributing subtests: Digit Span and Arithmetic. When interpreting the examinee's test performance, the practitioner should thoroughly evaluate and consider all test-related data, including obtained scores, measurement error, and relevant behavioral observations from the testing session (Kaufman & Lichtenberger, 2006; Sattler, 2008a).

Step 1. Report and Describe the FSIQ

The FSIQ is the most reliable score and is traditionally the first score to be considered in profile interpretation. It is derived from the combined sums of scaled scores used to derive the VCI, PRI, WMI, and PSI. The FSIQ is usually considered the score that is most representative of general intellectual functioning (g).

As indicated on the Record Form, the FSIQ should be reported with the corresponding percentile rank and confidence interval. Note that the interpretation of the FSIQ depends on the combined information described above, as well as comparisons between index scores (e.g., VCI and PRI, PRI and WMI, PRI and PSI). The variability in subtest scaled scores *within* the composites should also be evaluated. (See Kaufman & Lichtenberger [2006], and Sattler [2008a] for additional details regarding consideration of subtest scatter in the interpretation of composite scores.)

The constructs measured by the VCI, PRI, WMI, and PSI contribute to general intelligence in important ways. Analysis of these four index scores is recommended as the primary level of clinical interpretation, especially in cases with considerable variability across the index and/or subtest scores.

Step 2. Report and Describe the VCI

The VCI is a measure of verbal concept formation, verbal reasoning, and knowledge acquired from one's environment (Kaufman & Lichtenberger, 2006). The subtests that contribute to the WAIS–IV VCI are the same subtests that contributed to the WAIS–III VCI, but are different from those that composed the WAIS–III VIQ. The WAIS–IV VCI does not include Arithmetic or Comprehension and can therefore be conceptualized as a more refined, purer measure of verbal reasoning and concept formation than the WAIS–III VIQ. Record the VCI on the Record Form with its corresponding percentile rank and confidence interval.

Step 3. Report and Describe the PRI

The PRI is a measure of perceptual and fluid reasoning, spatial processing, and visual-motor integration. Two core subtests, Block Design and Matrix Reasoning, were retained from the WAIS–III, and one new core subtest, Visual Puzzles, was added. Figure Weights, a new supplemental subtest for ages 16–69, was designed to measure quantitative and analogical reasoning. Picture Completion was also retained from the WAIS–III but has been transitioned from a core to a supplemental subtest.

To evaluate the relative contributions of accuracy and speed in the examinee's Block Design performance, the Block Design No Time Bonus (BDN) score was added as an optional process score. (See Step 10 for additional details on interpreting the BDN process score.)

Relative to the WAIS–III PIQ, the PRI has reduced emphasis on motor performance and processing speed, because the PRI does not include Picture Arrangement or Coding. With the introduction of Visual Puzzles and the transition of Picture Completion from a core to a supplemental subtest, greater emphasis is placed on analysis, synthesis, and nonverbal reasoning, and the emphasis on visual attention to detail is reduced relative to the WAIS–III POI. Record the PRI on the Record Form with its corresponding percentile rank and confidence interval.

Step 4. Report and Describe the WMI

The WMI provides a measure of the examinee's working memory abilities. Working memory tasks require the ability to temporarily retain information in memory, perform some mental operation on, or manipulation of, it and produce a result. Working memory involves attention, concentration, mental control, and reasoning. Contemporary research indicates that working memory is an essential component of other higher order cognitive processes (Buehner, Krumm, Ziegler, & Pluecken, 2006; Ribaupierre & Lecerf, 2006; Salthouse & Pink, 2008; Unsworth & Engle, 2007).

Two core Working Memory subtests, Digit Span and Arithmetic, are retained from the WAIS–III. With the addition of Digit Span Sequencing to Digit Span, the task demands of this subtest and Letter–Number Sequencing became more similar. As a result, Letter–Number Sequencing was transitioned from a core subtest to a supplemental subtest (for ages 16–69).

Separate process scores for Digit Span Forward, Backward, and Sequencing are available to represent the emphasis on different memory demands for each task (i.e., registration for Digit Span Forward, and mental manipulation for Digit Span Backward and Digit Span Sequencing). Process scores are also available to represent the longest span or sequence correctly completed in a single trial. (See Step 10 for additional details on interpreting the Digit Span and Letter–Number Sequencing process scores.) Relative to the WAIS–III, the addition of the Digit Span Sequencing task to the WAIS–IV Digit Span subtest increases the emphasis on mental manipulation in the WAIS–IV WMI. Record the WMI on the Record Form with the corresponding percentile rank and confidence interval.

Step 5. Report and Describe the PSI

Research indicates a significant correlation between processing speed and cognitive ability (Jenkinson, 1983; Jensen, 1982; Kail, 2000; Kail & Salthouse, 1994) and the sensitivity of processing speed measures to clinical conditions such as ADHD, learning disabilities, TBI, and dementia. Research suggests that declines in processing speed ability are associated with age-related declines in performance on other measures of cognitive ability (Lindenberger, Mayr, & Kliegl, 1993; Salthouse, 1996, 2000, Salthouse & Ferrer-Caja, 2003).

The PSI provides a measure of the examinee's ability to quickly and correctly scan, sequence, or discriminate simple visual information. This composite also measures short-term visual memory, attention, and visual-motor coordination (Groth-Marnat, 2003; Kaufman & Lichtenberger, 1999, 2006; Sattler, 2008a, 2008b). It is important to note that the subtests contributing to the PSI are not measures of simple reaction time or simple visual discrimination. A cognitive decision-making or learning component is involved in these tasks.

Symbol Search and Coding have been retained from the WAIS–III as the core processing speed subtests. All stimuli have been enlarged to reduce the need for discrimination of fine visual details. Cancellation is a new supplemental processing speed subtest for ages 16–69. As with all composite scores, more confident interpretation of the PSI can be made when scores on the contributing subtests are similar than when the scores are different. The practitioner should note any influence of motor functioning on the PSI score. Record the PSI on the Record Form with the corresponding percentile rank and confidence interval.

Step 6. Evaluate Index-Level Discrepancy Comparisons

In constructing the IQ scores for the *Wechsler–Bellevue Intelligence Scale* (1939), Wechsler emphasized the FSIQ score and described it as an average of the examinee's performance on all administered subtests (Wechsler, 1944). However, Wechsler noted that occasions arose when the verbal and performance scores must be evaluated separately, especially for examinees "with special disabilities who need special consideration" (Wechsler, 1944, p. 138). Although statistically significant, pairwise differences do occur in many clinical populations; similar magnitudes of score differences also may occur frequently in the normative sample (Kaufman & Lichtenberger, 2006; Matarazzo, 1990; Sattler, 2008a).

Practitioners should note that index scores are estimates of overall functioning in a particular cognitive domain or content area. As such, these scores should always be evaluated in the context of the contributing subtests. Extreme variability of subtest scaled scores that contribute to an index score represents a summary of diverse abilities. The practitioner should closely examine relative performance on the subtests that comprise the index when interpreting these scores. When significant and unusual differences are noted, interpretations of comparisons between the composite scores must take this variability in subtest performance into account (Sattler, 2008a).

The Record Form Analysis page provides a table to assist in the evaluation of pairwise discrepancies at the index and subtest levels of performance. The first step in performing a pairwise comparison is to determine if the absolute value of the score difference is statistically significant. Table B.1 of the Administration and Scoring Manual provides the minimum differences between index scores required for statistical significance (critical values) at the .15 and .05 levels by age group. When the absolute value of the obtained difference between two scores is equal to or larger than the critical value, the difference is considered a true difference rather than a difference due to measurement error or random fluctuation. If the index scores are *not* significantly different, this indicates that the examinee's ability levels in the two domains are fairly similar. If the index scores *are* significantly different, this indicates that the examinee's ability levels in the two domains differ. For all significant differences between index scores, the practitioner should then judge how rare the difference is in the general population.

Table B.2 of the Administration and Scoring Manual provides the cumulative frequency of discrepancies among the various index scores in the WAIS–IV normative sample (base rates). The frequency of occurrence in the normative sample provides a basis for estimating the rarity or commonness of an obtained score difference compared to the general population. Table B.2 provides base rate data by overall normative sample and by ability level. This is because data analyses revealed that the frequency of the index score discrepancies differs significantly across various levels of intellectual ability. For example, among individuals whose FSIQ scores were 120 points or higher, about 14.5% obtained VCI scores that are 15 or more points higher than their PRI scores. Among individuals whose FSIQ scores were 79 points or less, about 6.3% obtained such a discrepancy. Table B.2 also provides the base rate data separately for two directions of discrepancy (e.g., VCI < PRI and VCI > PRI). This is because the direction of the discrepancy influences interpretation and, given the same absolute value, the base rate for two directions may be quite different (Sattler, 2008a). For example, among individuals whose FSIQ scores were 79 points or less, about 6.3% obtained VCI scores that were 15 or more points higher than their PRI scores, while 12.7% obtained PRI scores that were 15 or more points higher than their VCI scores.

Practitioners frequently ask what level of occurrence (base rate) should be considered rare—15%, 10%, 5%, or 1%? Clinical judgment and factors such as the individual's cultural background and medical or physical condition should be considered when determining the rarity of a discrepancy score. Sattler (2008a) suggests that differences between scores that occur in less than 15% of the normative sample should be judged as unusual.

Step 7. Evaluate Strengths and Weaknesses

Most individuals have areas of relative cognitive strengths and weaknesses. It is, in fact, very uncommon for the average person to function at the same level in every ability area. Practitioners should have a clear reason for calculating a difference score, and that reason should be based on the individual's history, the referral question, behavioral observations, and other test results. It should also be remembered that a difference between two scores may be clinically meaningful for one individual, but not for another individual.

The hypothesis-testing model is proposed as a means of reducing the possible over-interpretation of discrepancies and specific profiles of cognitive strengths and weaknesses. The practitioner must consider a number of factors that affect subtest performance, which may or may not be clinically meaningful. Corroborating evidence should be provided to support the interpretation of performance, and additional testing may be warranted to refute or confirm a specific hypothesis. For example, an examinee who performs significantly worse on Block Design compared with Matrix Reasoning and Visual Puzzles may have difficulties with visual-motor skills or poor motor coordination. Any interpretation that identifies a particular cognitive weakness should include corroboration from within the test or from external sources. If the obtained data do not corroborate the original hypothesis, the data may point to a new set of hypotheses that can be evaluated through further assessment or other data collection techniques. Clinically relevant findings that do not corroborate the original hypothesis should be investigated completely before a final judgment is made.

Table B.5 of the Administration and Scoring Manual provides the minimum differences between a single subtest and the average of subtest scaled scores required for statistical significance (critical values) at the .15 and .05 levels. This table also provides the base rate data for differences between a single subtest and either the overall mean of subtests contributing to the FSIQ or the mean of the three subtests contributing to the VCI and the three subtests contributing to the PRI. Using this table, the practitioner can decide if the obtained score differences are statistically significant and if so, how rare they are in the normative sample. Note that the values reported in Table B.5 are based on means derived from administration of the core subtests. The values in this table may be used with caution to evaluate an examinee's strengths and weaknesses if an allowable subtest substitution(s) was made, but the possible introduction of additional measurement error should be evaluated and noted in the report.

The Record Form Analysis page provides a section for determining the examinee's strengths and weaknesses at the subtest level. The practitioner must choose whether to use the mean score of the 10 subtests used to derive the FSIQ or the mean scores of three Verbal Comprehension and three Perceptual Reasoning subtests separately. If the latter method is used, the mean score of the three Verbal Comprehension subtests is the basis against which each Verbal Comprehension subtest score is compared, and the mean score of the three Perceptual Reasoning subtests is the basis against which each Perceptual Reasoning subtest score is compared. *In general, if there is no significant discrepancy among the index scores, the mean of 10 core subtests should be used for the strength and weakness analysis* (see Kaufman & Lichtenberger, 2006). If separate Verbal Comprehension and Perceptual Reasoning mean scores are chosen as a basis for comparison, evaluation of the Working Memory and Processing Speed subtests as strengths or weaknesses is not possible. Although the Record Form requires the practitioner to choose a basis for comparison of scores (i.e., the overall mean or the Verbal Comprehension and Perceptual Reasoning means), the use of both methods is possible and further described in Sattler (2008a).

Step 8. Evaluate Subtest-Level Discrepancy Comparisons

In some situations, the practitioner may wish to compare two subtest scores. For example, comparison of performance on Digit Span and Arithmetic may inform interpretation of the WMI score (Kaufman & Lichtenberger, 2006) and provide useful information regarding the examinee's auditory rote memory and quantitative reasoning ability when facility with numbers is required (Sattler, 2008a). The Record Form provides space to perform the pairwise comparisons relevant to interpretation of the WMI and PSI: the Digit Span to Arithmetic comparison and the Symbol Search to Coding comparison. Table B.3 in the Administration and Scoring Manual provides the differences between *all* possible pairs of core and supplemental subtests required for significance at the .15 and .05 levels. Table B.4 provides the cumulative percentage of examinees in the normative sample (base rates) that obtained the same or greater discrepancy between subtest scaled scores for the Digit Span–Arithmetic and Symbol Search–Coding comparisons appearing on the Record Form.

Step 9. (Optional) Evaluate the Pattern of Scores Within Subtests

To further analyze an examinee's profile, the practitioner should consider the pattern of scores within a subtest. For example, the examinee who achieves a scaled score of 10 on a subtest by getting 20 items correct and then meeting the discontinue criterion is quite different from the examinee who gets the same number of items correct but does so with substantial item scatter (e.g., misses easy items but passes harder ones). The examinee with an uneven pattern of scores on several subtests may have certain problems related to attention or language that need to be further evaluated, or may be a very bright individual who is bored with the test. This type of intrasubtest evaluation represents a process approach to assessment. Additional details regarding a process-oriented approach to assessment are provided in the following section as part of the process analysis.

Step 10. (Optional) Perform the Process Analysis

The final step in a profile analysis is the qualitative analysis of individual responses. Unusual responses or response patterns can often be very revealing. It is also useful to examine the process by which an examinee arrived at a correct response or the reasons for an incorrect response. The process approach to interpretation advocated by Kaplan (1988; Kaplan, Fein, Morris, & Delis, 1991) was designed to help the practitioner determine the nature of errors that were committed on standard tests. Although each subtest of an intelligence scale is primarily designed to measure a specific cognitive process, other cognitive processes can also be invoked during task performance. A score of 0 points on an item may occur for various reasons. For example, examinees may fail a Block Design item because they did not perceive the design correctly, were not able to analyze the configuration of the design, or ran out of time.

The WAIS–IV process scores are designed to provide more detailed information on the cognitive abilities that contribute to an examinee's subtest performance. Process analysis can occur from an inter-individual perspective by comparing the examinee's process scores to those obtained by his or her same-age peers. Intra-individual process analysis is performed by evaluating process scores in relation to other obtained scores (i.e., subtest or process scores). The process analysis can assist the practitioner in evaluating specific information processing styles, which can be important when describing cognitive strengths and weaknesses, making diagnostic decisions, or generating remedial strategies as part of a treatment plan or educational program.

The Record Form Analysis page includes a section that is designed to assist the practitioner with basic process analysis of three subtests: Block Design, Digit Span, and Letter–Number Sequencing. The Total Raw Score to Scaled Score Conversion table and the Raw Score to Base Rate Conversion table are used to derive the process scores. These scores represent the examinee's performance as it compares to other examinees of the same age through scaled scores or base rates in the normative sample. In order to examine intra-individual patterns of information processing, several process-level discrepancy comparisons are also included on the Record Form.

Block Design

The Block Design No Time Bonus (BDN) process score is based on the examinee's performance on Block Design *without* additional time bonus points for rapid completion of items. The score's reduced emphasis on speed of performance may be particularly useful when an examinee's physical limitations, problem-solving strategies, or personality characteristics are believed to affect performance on timed tasks (Elliott, 1990). Like the subtest scaled scores, BDN is scaled to a metric with a mean of 10 and an *SD* of 3.

At the intra-individual level of process analysis, the discrepancy between the Block Design subtest scaled score and the BDN scaled process score may provide information on the relative contributions of speed and accuracy to performance on Block Design. Tables C.2 and C.3 of the Administration and Scoring Manual provide critical values and base rates in the normative sample for the difference scores. These data are used to determine the statistical significance of the difference score, and its frequency of occurrence in the normative sample. For most examinees, there is very little difference between these two scores. If the examinee's Block Design score is high, the discrepancy between Block Design and BDN should be interpreted with caution due to the limited upper range of the BDN score in some of the younger age groups.

Digit Span

The Digit Span Forward (DSF), Digit Span Backward (DSB), and Digit Span Sequencing (DSS) process scores are also scaled scores and are derived from the total raw scores for the corresponding Digit Span tasks. Although all of these tasks require storage and retrieval of information through immediate auditory recall, the Digit Span Backward task places additional demands on the examinee's working memory abilities and attention (de Jonge & de Jong, 1996; Sattler, 2008a; Wechsler, 1997a), as do tasks that are similar to Digit Span Sequencing (MacDonald et al., 2001; Werheid et al., 2002).

In some situations, an examinee exhibits variable performance across items (e.g., scores of 1 point and 0 points on trials within an item, and/or across items), rather than a more typical pattern of performance (e.g., correct responses on initial items, followed by occasional scores of 0 just prior to meeting the discontinue criterion). This type of variable response pattern may result in DSF, DSB, and DSS scores that are similar to those obtained by examinees with more typical response patterns, despite the difference in the individuals' performances. Three additional process scores were included to further evaluate performance on the three Digit Span tasks: Longest Digit Span Forward (LDSF), Longest Digit Span Backward (LDSB), and Longest Digit Span Sequencing (LDSS). These raw scores reflect the number of digits recalled on the last trial scored 1 point in the corresponding Digit Span task. Base rates in the normative sample are provided for the LDSF, LDSB, and LDSS raw scores, as well as for the pairwise discrepancies among the three scores, in Tables C.4 and C.6–C.8 of the Administration and Scoring Manual.

Letter–Number Sequencing

Similar to Digit Span, an examinee with variable performance across the trials and/or items of Letter–Number Sequencing can obtain a scaled score that is similar to that obtained by an examinee with a typical response pattern. For examinees with variable performance across items, the Longest Letter–Number Sequence (LLNS) score may provide additional information about the examinee's performance on the Letter–Number Sequencing subtest. The LLNS score is a raw score that reflects the number of numbers and letters recalled on the last trial scored 1 point. Base rates in the normative sample are provided in Table C.5 of the Administration and Scoring Manual.

Reference-Group Subtest Scaled Scores

The Record Form provides space on the Summary page to calculate scaled scores that are based on the performance of examinees aged 20:0–34:11 (i.e., the reference group). These are optional scores that cannot be used to derive composite scores. However, when research or clinical questions dictate comparisons of an individual's performance to that of a reference group, the reference-group subtest norms can be used. It is important to note that optimal subtest performance does not always occur within this age group, and reference-group subtest scaled scores should therefore be interpreted accordingly.

Although Wechsler was aware that the age of optimal performance varied by subtest, he viewed the age-corrected subtest scores as optional (Wechsler, 1955, 1981) and corrected scores at the composite level. Beginning with the WAIS–III, the correction took place at the subtest level. This approach evolved in response to research by Ryan, Paolo, and Brungardt (1990) and Ivnik et al. (1992) that involved the collection of normative data for the WAIS–R and WMS–R for individuals older than 74 years. Ryan et al. (1990) found that the mean Performance subtest score for ages 75–79 was approximately 1.5 SDs lower than the mean of the reference group, and even lower for ages 80 and older. Even for the Verbal subtests, the means ranged from .5 SD to 1 SD lower than the reference group mean. According to these data, older adults appeared significantly impaired or abnormal when their performance was compared to that of a younger reference group, although their subtest scores may actually have been average when compared to those of their same-age peers. To address this problem, Ivnik et al. deviated from the traditional method of reference group comparisons to calculate the performance of these older adults. Instead of using the reference-group subtest scores, each examinee's performance was compared to the performance of others of similar age using a method similar to that employed for the WISC–III. The subtest scaled scores were adjusted for normal aging differences.

Studies conducted using the WAIS–III normative sample data to compare age-adjusted and reference-group subtest norms provided additional insight into differential subtest performance across age groups. Kaufman (2000) examined education-adjusted subtest means for all age groups. He demonstrated that optimal performance on the Verbal Comprehension subtests occurred between ages 45 and 54, with Similarities subsequently declining somewhat more precipitously than the other Verbal Comprehension subtests after the age of 55. All Verbal Comprehension subtests showed a pattern of preserved ability over the age range relative to performance on subtests from other index scales. Performance on Processing Speed subtests showed the largest declines with age (beginning between ages 20 and 24), followed by Perceptual Organization subtests (beginning between ages 30 and 34). Subtests from the Working Memory scale displayed different patterns, with performance on Letter–Number Sequencing declining at an earlier age (beginning between ages 25 and 29) and more precipitously than performance on Digit Span or Arithmetic. Performance on all Working Memory subtests was found to decline after age 45. In summary, for Processing Speed and Perceptual Organization subtests, performance rapidly and steadily declined with age, whereas for the Verbal Comprehension and Working Memory subtests, the performance decline was relatively less precipitous and began in older age groups. Kaufman concluded that Verbal Comprehension and Working Memory subtest performance was less related to age than Perceptual Organization or Processing Speed subtest performance.

Ryan, Sattler, and Lopez (2000) found similar results when they examined the subtest scaled scores obtained for the same raw scores by age and by reference group as well as the minimum subtest total raw scores required to obtain scaled scores of 10 for each age group. The highest performing age groups varied widely according to index scale, with some variability across subtests within each index scale. For most of the Verbal Comprehension subtests, peak performance occurred between ages 45 and 54, with a small, gradual increase between ages 16 and 45, and a small, gradual decrease between ages 55 and 89. For most of the Perceptual Organization subtests, optimal performance occurred from ages 16 through 34 and declined thereafter. Arithmetic performance increased through ages 45–54, peaked at those ages, and then declined thereafter. Consistent performance was observed between ages 16 and 69 for Digit Span, and between ages 16 and 44 for Letter–Number Sequencing, and performance on both subtests declined thereafter. For Processing Speed subtests, performance remained relatively stable from ages 16 to 44 and declined precipitously after age 44.

The aforementioned results serve to illustrate why interpretive errors are common with the use of reference-group subtest norms. Such misinterpretations are due, in part, to the low subtest scaled scores that older examinees typically receive on Perceptual Reasoning and Processing Speed subtests when their scores are compared to the scores of a younger reference group. Compared to the scores of their same-age peers, the performance of these older examinees might be viewed and interpreted differently.

Ability-Achievement Discrepancy

There are a number of criticisms of the use of the ability-achievement discrepancy (AAD) model for determining learning disabilities (Shinn, 2007; Siegel, 1989, 2003). Some proponents of the response-to-intervention (RTI) model have criticized the use of intellectual assessment in psycho-educational evaluations (Shinn). Although components of RTI—early screening and intervention for at-risk individuals, in particular—are laudable, the model has not adequately established diagnostic criteria or provided a mechanism to determine the underlying neurocognitive processes of learning problems (Kavale, Holdnack, & Mostert, 2005). Critics assert that the problem with AAD is the failure of practitioners to consistently apply the criteria (Scruggs & Mastropieri, 2002; Shinn) or to consider the results of the psychological test data fully when making an eligibility determination (Berninger & O'Donnell, 2005; MacMillan & Forness, 1998).

Although several new models for evaluating learning disabilities have been proposed recently (Berninger, Dunn, & Alper, 2005; Berninger & O'Donnell, 2005; Hale & Fiorello, 2004), diagnostic markers generally have yet to be agreed upon and consistently applied in research, government policy, and clinical practice. Some progress has been made in this area, however. For example, pseudoword decoding and rapid automatized naming appear to predict early reading disorders. When applying the AAD model in the context of a referral for possible Reading Disorder, it is therefore good practice to conduct a thorough evaluation for other signs of specific reading problems, such as deficits in phonological processing (Miller et al., 2006; Stanovich, 1986; Stanovich & Siegel, 1994; Vukovic & Siegel, 2006) and/or rapid naming (Denckla & Rudel, 1976; Miller et al.).

An AAD is an indication that some problem exists, as achievement is not at a level commensurate with cognitive ability. Because individuals underachieve for many reasons, an AAD alone cannot be considered a diagnostic marker of a learning disability. The reasons for underachievement and diagnosis cannot be determined without further evaluation. Some individuals with learning disability do not demonstrate an AAD due to high levels of motivation, persistence, and compensatory strategies or support. Underachievement also may be related to the overall ability level of individuals in a particular school.

Proponents of the RTI model have argued that eligibility for special education services should be determined solely on the basis of the student's low achievement and failure to respond to empirically supported educational instruction, regardless of the results of cognitive evaluations (Fletcher, Coulter, Reschly, & Vaughn, 2004). Others have defended the role of cognitive assessment in the evaluation of individuals with brain-based learning disorders, while not necessarily advocating strict adherence to AAD as the only method for classification (Flanagan & Mascolo, 2005; Fletcher-Janzen & Reynolds, 2008; Hale, Naglieri, Kaufman, & Kavale, 2004; Kaufman & Lichtenberger, 2006; Scruggs & Mastropieri, 2002.)

The Individuals with Disabilities Education Improvement Act of 2004 (IDEA) does not require the presence of an AAD for the purposes of classification; however, a comprehensive evaluation is required and classification cannot be determined by a process of RTI alone (Berninger & Holdnack, 2008). The law introduces greater flexibility in the assessment process, requiring practitioners to consider how to best measure and diagnose learning disabilities. The absence of a requirement for the presence of an AAD does not obviate the need for assessment of general cognitive abilities. The focus, however, is on specific scores (e.g., Verbal Comprehension, Working Memory) applied independently in a differential diagnosis, yet integrated with findings from measures of academic functioning. Very specific guidelines have been established for integrating test results with an examinee's historical data for making diagnoses of learning disabilities (Berninger, O'Donnell, & Holdnack, 2008).

The changes to IDEA allow states to decide to continue the use of AADs as general screeners for nonspecific learning problems and classification. As a result, the scores utilized to identify individuals as learning disabled may vary considerably by state. It is important to know the local regulations when providing assessments that are to be used for eligibility determination. Good clinical practice indicates that the finding of such a discrepancy should be followed with additional assessment before a formal diagnosis or qualification is rendered. Academic progress within the educational intervention should be carefully monitored and more extensive assessment undertaken if gains are insufficient.

The progression toward utilizing a number of approaches to assess learning disabilities is evident in federal legislation. The final regulations of the IDEA (Assistance to States for the Education of Children With Disabilities and Preschool Grants for Children With Disabilities, 2006) indicate that local education agencies should ensure that a variety of assessment tools and strategies are used to gather relevant functional, developmental, and academic information that may assist in determining whether or not the individual has a learning disability. The final regulations further state that, in general, a local educational agency is *not required* to take into consideration whether an individual has a severe AAD in determination of a specific learning disability. Local education agencies may continue to use the AAD method if desired, but states cannot mandate that local education agencies employ this approach. State education agencies must allow determination of specific learning disability based on the individual's response to scientific, research-based interventions. States may also allow the use of other research-based procedures to determine specific learning disability.

There are two methods for comparing intellectual ability and academic achievement: the predicted-difference method and the simple-difference method. Although both methods are used, the predicted-difference method is generally preferred because the formula accounts for the reliabilities of and the correlations between the two measures. The predicted-difference method uses the ability score to predict an achievement score, and the predicted and observed achievement scores are compared. The simple-difference method compares the observed ability and achievement scores. In both methods, the practitioner must take into account the statistical significance and the base rate of the discrepancies. The *WIAT–II Examiner's Manual: Update 2005* (Harcourt Assessment, 2005) provides details related to the rationale for choosing these methods and the statistical procedures involved.

The FSIQ score should be used as the best estimate of intellectual ability unless there is some compelling reason to use the VCI, PRI, or GAI (e.g., visual or motor problems that may interfere with the validity of some subtests, working memory or processing speed issues related to some clinical conditions). Appendix B provides tables for AAD analysis, using the WAIS–IV FSIQ, VCI, and PRI and the WIAT–II subtest and composite scores. Appendix C provides tables for AAD analysis, using the WAIS–IV GAI and the WIAT–II subtest and composite scores. It is important to note that the data for evaluating ability-achievement discrepancies reported in these appendixes were based on the sample of examinees who were administered both the WAIS–IV and WIAT–II (see Table 5.4 for demographic details of this sample). All examinees in this sample were currently enrolled in high school and between the ages of 16:0 and 19:11. Data pertaining to the use of ability-achievement comparisons should, therefore, only be utilized for examinees with similar demographic characteristics.

Summary

Only knowledgeable, trained professionals should compare and interpret the various scores reported on the Record Form. "Psychological assessment is a clinical activity that employs test scores, but only as one of the sources from which an astute practitioner develops a well-integrated and comprehensive psychological portrait of the adult or child examined" (Wechsler, 1991, p. iii). The practitioner using tests as part of assessment activity is responsible for interpreting results and making diagnostic decisions.

Intercorrelation Tables

Table A.1 Intercorrelations of Subtest, Process, and Composite Scores for Ages 16:0–17:11

Subtest/Process/ Composite Score	BD	SI	DS	MR	VC	AR	SS	VP	IN	CD	LN	FW	CO	CA	PCm	BDN	DSF	DSB	DSS	VCI	PRI	WMI	PSI	FSIQ
BD																					.65			.67
SI	.45																			.62				.53
DS	.46	.33																				.63		.63
MR	.49	.31	.44																		.54			.58
VC	.45	.59	.44	.38																.70				.64
AR	.49	.35	.63	.48	.49																	.63		.65
SS	.32	.03	.28	.23	.17	.22																	.46	.35
VP	.64	.37	.43	.49	.43	.45	.25														.66			.64
IN	.41	.53	.40	.34	.64	.42	.22	.41												.66				.59
CD	.27	.19	.34	.32	.17	.35	.46	.28	.13														.46	.40
LN	.52	.38	.73	.35	.44	.60	.24	.42	.48	.26														
FW	.55	.40	.46	.49	.48	.56	.19	.50	.46	.29	.49													
CO	.44	.63	.36	.34	.66	.35	.13	.40	.54	.19	.37	.43												
CA	.35	.10	.46	.30	.26	.41	.36	.38	.29	.34	.40	.29	.11											
PCm	.49	.43	.42	.39	.37	.34	.26	.46	.38	.20	.44	.32	.42	.36										
BDN	.93	.45	.47	.48	.46	.46	.30	.60	.43	.26	.55	.53	.50	.31	.53									
DSF	.33	.26	.77	.31	.28	.42	.24	.29	.31	.20	.54	.26	.25	.33	.30	.35								
DSB	.40	.32	.83	.35	.39	.55	.18	.36	.34	.29	.64	.47	.29	.37	.33	.43	.50							
DSS	.41	.23	.76	.43	.38	.57	.26	.40	.31	.30	.54	.41	.33	.40	.38	.40	.41	.48						
VCI	.51	.84	.46	.40	.87	.49	.16	.47	.85	.19	.51	.52	.72	.25	.46	.53	.33	.41	.36		.56	.52	.21	.80
PRI	.86	.45	.53	.79	.51	.57	.32	.85	.46	.35	.52	.62	.47	.41	.53	.81	.37	.45	.50	.56		.61	.39	.87
WMI	.52	.38	.89	.51	.51	.91	.28	.49	.45	.38	.73	.57	.39	.48	.41	.51	.65	.76	.73	.52	.61		.39	.81
PSI	.34	.13	.36	.33	.20	.34	.85	.31	.21	.85	.29	.28	.18	.41	.27	.33	.26	.28	.33	.21	.39	.39		.57
FSIQ	.76	.64	.71	.68	.72	.74	.46	.72	.68	.51	.67	.67	.61	.48	.56	.74	.51	.60	.61	.80	.87	.81	.57	
Mean	9.7	10.1	9.7	10.0	9.7	10.1	9.6	9.7	10.0	9.6	9.9	10.2	9.7	9.5	9.6	9.7	9.7	9.9	9.9	29.7	29.5	19.8	19.2	98.2
SD	3.1	3.0	2.7	3.0	2.7	3.0	2.5	2.8	2.8	2.5	3.1	3.2	2.9	2.8	2.8	2.8	3.0	2.8	3.0	7.3	7.4	5.1	4.2	18.7

Note. Uncorrected coefficients appear below the diagonal, and corrected coefficients appear above the diagonal in the shaded area.

Table A.2   Intercorrelations of Subtest, Process, and Composite Scores for Ages 18:0–19:11

Subtest/Process/ Composite Score	BD	SI	DS	MR	VC	AR	SS	VP	IN	CD	LN	FW	CO	CA	PCm	BDN	DSF	DSB	DSS	VCI	PRI	WMI	PSI	FSIQ
BD																					.70			.64
SI	.41																			.74				.66
DS	.29	.34																				.57		.47
MR	.55	.42	.39																		.59			.64
VC	.47	.74	.36	.49																.79				.71
AR	.44	.46	.57	.47	.52																	.57		.69
SS	.39	.42	.26	.38	.37	.41																	.66	.57
VP	.67	.47	.22	.52	.51	.49	.38														.68			.64
IN	.53	.62	.32	.52	.68	.55	.43	.54												.70				.72
CD	.36	.37	.34	.37	.36	.49	.66	.32	.39														.66	.56
LN	.30	.30	.61	.34	.32	.42	.29	.25	.29	.18														
FW	.52	.54	.45	.53	.54	.60	.36	.60	.51	.35	.34													
CO	.48	.70	.39	.52	.74	.57	.34	.52	.66	.41	.38	.55												
CA	.40	.32	.42	.30	.33	.40	.48	.35	.38	.44	.24	.32	.32											
PCm	.45	.45	.32	.38	.38	.37	.32	.48	.46	.27	.23	.47	.49	.26										
BDN	.53	.39	.31	.54	.43	.43	.40	.60	.53	.38	.32	.50	.46	.42	.47									
DSF	.15	.29	.76	.21	.30	.38	.19	.10	.23	.29	.38	.25	.34	.31	.15	.19								
DSB	.25	.23	.83	.36	.26	.47	.14	.16	.22	.26	.52	.40	.29	.32	.32	.26	.50							
DSS	.33	.32	.78	.41	.32	.52	.33	.28	.34	.31	.56	.44	.34	.33	.33	.34	.36	.50						
VCI	.53	.89	.38	.54	.91	.58	.46	.57	.86	.42	.34	.59	.79	.39	.48	.51	.31	.27	.37					
PRI	.88	.51	.35	.80	.58	.55	.45	.86	.62	.41	.35	.65	.59	.41	.51	.83	.18	.30	.40	.64				
WMI	.42	.45	.89	.49	.50	.88	.38	.40	.49	.47	.58	.59	.54	.46	.39	.42	.65	.73	.73	.54	.51			
PSI	.41	.43	.33	.41	.41	.49	.91	.38	.45	.91	.26	.39	.41	.51	.32	.43	.26	.22	.36	.48	.47	.47		
FSIQ	.72	.74	.57	.72	.78	.76	.66	.72	.79	.66	.46	.70	.75	.54	.55	.70	.40	.44	.55	.87	.85	.75	.72	
Mean	10.3	10.3	10.1	10.0	10.3	9.8	10.1	10.2	10.1	9.9	10.1	10.3	10.2	9.9	9.9	10.0	10.1	10.4	10.1	30.7	30.4	19.9	19.9	101.0
SD	3.3	3.2	2.9	2.8	3.0	2.9	3.0	2.8	3.0	3.0	3.0	3.2	3.2	3.1	3.0	2.8	2.9	2.9	3.2	8.2	7.6	5.1	5.5	21.2

Note. Uncorrected coefficients appear below the diagonal, and corrected coefficients appear above the diagonal in the shaded area.

Table A.3   Intercorrelations of Subtest, Process, and Composite Scores for Ages 20:0–24:11

Subtest/Process/ Composite Score	BD	SI	DS	MR	VC	AR	SS	VP	IN	CD	LN	FW	CO	CA	PCm	BDN	DSF	DSB	DSS	VCI	PRI	WMI	PSI	FSIQ
BD																								.62
SI	.49																			.75				.72
DS	.42	.41																				.58		.61
MR	.47	.50	.47																		.50			.59
VC	.41	.74	.52	.49																.82				.75
AR	.49	.57	.58	.46	.64																	.58		.73
SS	.41	.37	.36	.27	.38	.42																	.64	.54
VP	.66	.52	.45	.43	.49	.49	.31														.64			.63
IN	.31	.66	.33	.48	.75	.56	.35	.42												.75				.64
CD	.34	.32	.42	.30	.32	.43	.64	.30	.25														.64	.51
LN	.40	.43	.65	.46	.52	.57	.26	.47	.44	.32														
FW	.52	.57	.52	.55	.57	.60	.32	.60	.52	.29	.57													
CO	.42	.71	.48	.52	.79	.61	.34	.51	.70	.36	.53	.61												
CA	.40	.22	.39	.21	.25	.37	.49	.41	.20	.52	.33	.26	.23											
PCm	.46	.34	.38	.30	.39	.32	.33	.43	.33	.26	.38	.37	.35	.36										
BDN	.93	.49	.42	.47	.40	.47	.39	.60	.31	.32	.38	.50	.42	.35	.44									
DSF	.35	.33	.80	.40	.38	.41	.25	.28	.26	.26	.47	.36	.38	.31	.31	.37								
DSB	.29	.30	.81	.33	.40	.44	.27	.33	.23	.32	.47	.41	.30	.30	.29	.27	.52							
DSS	.38	.37	.79	.39	.44	.51	.33	.46	.28	.38	.61	.49	.46	.30	.29	.37	.43	.47						
VCI	.45	.88	.47	.54	.92	.66	.41	.53	.89	.33	.51	.62	.82	.25	.39	.45	.36	.35	.41					
PRI	.87	.61	.54	.76	.56	.58	.40	.85	.49	.38	.53	.68	.58	.41	.48	.82	.41	.38	.50	.61				
WMI	.51	.55	.90	.52	.65	.88	.44	.52	.50	.48	.69	.63	.61	.43	.39	.50	.69	.71	.74	.63	.63			
PSI	.42	.38	.43	.31	.39	.47	.91	.34	.33	.90	.32	.34	.39	.56	.33	.40	.29	.33	.40	.41	.43	.51		
FSIQ	.70	.78	.69	.68	.81	.79	.64	.71	.72	.61	.63	.71	.76	.48	.50	.67	.52	.52	.61	.86	.84	.83	.69	
Mean	10.1	10.2	10.2	10.0	10.5	10.0	10.5	10.0	10.1	10.3	10.3	10.2	10.2	10.3	10.3	10.4	10.2	10.4	10.1	30.8	30.2	20.2	20.8	101.9
SD	3.0	3.0	3.0	2.8	3.2	2.7	3.2	2.9	3.1	3.0	2.9	2.8	3.0	3.1	3.0	2.9	3.1	2.9	3.2	8.3	7.1	5.1	5.7	21.3

Note. Uncorrected coefficients appear below the diagonal, and corrected coefficients appear above the diagonal in the shaded area.

Table A.4   Intercorrelations of Subtest, Process, and Composite Scores for Ages 25:0–29:11

Subtest/Process/Composite Score	BD	SI	DS	MR	VC	AR	SS	VP	IN	CD	LN	FW	CO	CA	PCm	BDN	DSF	DSB	DSS	VCI	PRI	WMI	PSI	FSIQ
BD	—																				.66			.67
SI	.48	—																		.76				.72
DS	.51	.55	—																			.62		.68
MR	.51	.51	.48	—																	.56			.63
VC	.47	.78	.53	.46	—															.84				.73
AR	.50	.55	.62	.48	.59	—																.62		.69
SS	.46	.37	.46	.36	.35	.37	—																.64	.55
VP	.65	.44	.42	.52	.42	.45	.40	—													.67			.61
IN	.40	.62	.39	.37	.72	.52	.23	.40	—											.71				.60
CD	.38	.37	.45	.39	.38	.39	.64	.29	.26	—													.64	.54
LN	.57	.54	.73	.49	.54	.64	.43	.48	.44	.36	—													
FW	.55	.50	.50	.56	.48	.52	.24	.54	.45	.33	.55	—												
CO	.46	.70	.52	.44	.75	.53	.32	.45	.54	.33	.50	.49	—											
CA	.34	.25	.30	.31	.18	.27	.51	.33	.21	.39	.28	.31	.16	—										
PCm	.51	.33	.35	.40	.30	.23	.37	.51	.32	.29	.36	.40	.36	.35	—									
BDN	.94	.49	.52	.52	.46	.49	.46	.63	.37	.38	.55	.53	.49	.34	.51	—								
DSF	.41	.45	.82	.37	.41	.53	.33	.31	.23	.33	.60	.34	.37	.18	.23	.42	—							
DSB	.42	.47	.86	.42	.48	.49	.37	.34	.38	.37	.63	.46	.44	.23	.27	.42	.57	—						
DSS	.45	.45	.80	.41	.43	.52	.52	.42	.34	.45	.57	.43	.49	.37	.33	.44	.52	.56	—					
VCI	.50	.89	.55	.50	.93	.62	.35	.47	.87	.38	.57	.53	.74	.24	.35	.49	.41	.50	.45	—				
PRI	.85	.57	.56	.82	.54	.57	.49	.85	.47	.42	.61	.66	.54	.39	.56	.83	.44	.47	.51	.58	—			
WMI	.56	.61	.91	.54	.62	.89	.47	.48	.50	.47	.76	.56	.58	.32	.32	.56	.76	.76	.74	.64	.63	—		
PSI	.46	.41	.51	.42	.41	.42	.90	.38	.27	.91	.43	.32	.36	.50	.36	.46	.36	.41	.53	.41	.50	.52	—	
FSIQ	.75	.78	.76	.72	.79	.76	.64	.69	.68	.63	.73	.65	.70	.43	.50	.73	.59	.64	.67	.84	.86	.84	.70	—
Mean	10.0	10.2	10.2	10.3	10.0	10.0	10.2	10.3	10.3	10.1	10.2	10.2	10.0	10.2	10.1	10.2	10.0	10.3	10.0	30.5	30.5	20.2	20.3	101.5
SD	3.2	3.0	3.3	3.4	3.0	3.0	2.9	3.0	2.9	3.0	2.9	2.9	3.3	3.0	3.0	3.1	3.3	3.4	2.9	8.0	8.1	5.6	5.4	22.1

Note. Uncorrected coefficients appear below the diagonal, and corrected coefficients appear above the diagonal in the shaded area.

Table A.5   Intercorrelations of Subtest, Process, and Composite Scores for Ages 30:0–34:11

Subtest/Process/ Composite Score	BD	SI	DS	MR	VC	AR	SS	VP	IN	CD	LN	FW	CO	CA	PCm	BDN	DSF	DSB	DSS	VCI	PRI	WMI	PSI	FSIQ
BD																					.68			.66
SI	.43																			.75				.65
DS	.49	.47																				.61		.70
MR	.54	.48	.58																		.62			.70
VC	.47	.70	.54	.52																.78				.72
AR	.56	.53	.61	.57	.57																	.61		.74
SS	.35	.33	.48	.37	.39	.41																	.64	.55
VP	.67	.43	.49	.58	.45	.58	.33														.71			.66
IN	.50	.70	.49	.54	.74	.59	.40	.48												.78				.72
CD	.36	.28	.50	.47	.40	.48	.64	.38	.35														.64	.58
LN	.47	.48	.75	.48	.55	.61	.47	.49	.55	.50														
FW	.55	.53	.56	.62	.56	.67	.42	.63	.58	.41	.54													
CO	.47	.76	.50	.56	.77	.54	.36	.49	.70	.40	.57	.58												
CA	.34	.12	.36	.27	.21	.29	.48	.34	.21	.43	.36	.30	.18											
PCm	.46	.37	.39	.41	.33	.39	.39	.46	.40	.26	.35	.38	.36	.36										
BDN	.52	.41	.49	.53	.45	.54	.34	.62	.50	.34	.46	.51	.45	.33	.47									
DSF	.33	.37	.82	.42	.43	.46	.38	.35	.37	.34	.55	.46	.38	.24	.27	.33								
DSB	.43	.42	.85	.53	.48	.55	.38	.39	.45	.42	.68	.49	.46	.33	.36	.45	.59							
DSS	.45	.41	.78	.48	.44	.52	.43	.46	.40	.50	.63	.48	.43	.35	.36	.44	.46	.50						
VCI	.52	.89	.56	.57	.90	.62	.42	.50	.91	.39	.58	.62	.83	.20	.41	.50	.43	.50	.46					
PRI	.86	.52	.61	.84	.56	.67	.41	.88	.59	.47	.56	.71	.59	.37	.52	.82	.43	.53	.54	.62				
WMI	.58	.56	.90	.64	.62	.90	.49	.59	.60	.55	.76	.69	.58	.36	.44	.57	.71	.78	.72	.66	.71			
PSI	.39	.34	.54	.47	.43	.49	.91	.39	.42	.90	.53	.46	.41	.50	.36	.38	.40	.44	.51	.44	.49	.57		
FSIQ	.73	.72	.77	.77	.78	.80	.64	.73	.78	.66	.72	.75	.75	.42	.52	.70	.58	.67	.66	.84	.87	.87	.72	
Mean	10.0	9.9	10.0	10.1	10.0	10.0	10.2	9.9	10.1	10.0	10.4	9.9	9.9	10.0	10.2	10.0	9.8	10.3	10.0	30.0	30.0	20.1	20.2	100.2
SD	3.1	2.9	3.1	3.3	2.9	3.1	3.3	3.2	3.1	3.0	3.5	3.1	3.0	3.0	3.2	3.2	2.9	2.9	3.0	8.0	8.2	5.6	5.7	22.8

Note. Uncorrected coefficients appear below the diagonal, and corrected coefficients appear above the diagonal in the shaded area.

Table A.6 Intercorrelations of Subtest, Process, and Composite Scores for Ages 35:0–44:11

Subtest/Process/Composite Score	BD	SI	DS	MR	VC	AR	SS	VP	IN	CD	LN	FW	CO	CA	PCm	BDN	DSF	DSB	DSS	VCI	PRI	WMI	PSI	FSIQ
BD																					.73			.64
SI	.51																			.74				.72
DS	.39	.51																				.63		.63
MR	.63	.56	.46																		.69			.70
VC	.44	.75	.50	.49																.83				.71
AR	.46	.55	.63	.51	.60																	.63		.71
SS	.34	.27	.41	.40	.27	.39																	.66	.50
VP	.69	.51	.39	.63	.43	.44	.34														.73			.64
IN	.39	.62	.43	.46	.73	.53	.17	.42												.72				.60
CD	.29	.36	.41	.40	.38	.48	.66	.31	.23														.66	.54
LN	.33	.44	.69	.42	.44	.54	.30	.36	.35	.25														
FW	.52	.51	.48	.55	.53	.57	.36	.56	.47	.33	.46													
CO	.47	.73	.45	.51	.75	.54	.25	.46	.64	.33	.44	.55												
CA	.25	.16	.22	.16	.12	.26	.33	.23	.17	.36	.11	.24	.17											
PCm	.50	.39	.32	.45	.32	.28	.42	.41	.24	.29	.34	.35	.28	.24										
BDN	.97	.50	.40	.62	.42	.45	.36	.67	.35	.31	.33	.51	.46	.24	.49									
DSF	.17	.38	.83	.23	.40	.49	.21	.15	.32	.26	.59	.34	.31	.14	.16	.19								
DSB	.33	.39	.86	.44	.37	.53	.39	.36	.35	.37	.58	.36	.35	.17	.28	.35	.61							
DSS	.43	.46	.76	.46	.48	.57	.40	.46	.41	.40	.61	.49	.43	.19	.34	.42	.43	.53						
VCI	.50	.88	.54	.56	.93	.63	.27	.51	.88	.36	.46	.56	.79	.17	.35	.47	.41	.41	.50					
PRI	.89	.60	.47	.86	.52	.54	.41	.88	.48	.38	.42	.62	.55	.24	.52	.86	.21	.43	.51	.59				
WMI	.47	.58	.91	.53	.61	.89	.44	.46	.53	.49	.69	.58	.54	.26	.33	.47	.74	.78	.74	.64	.56			
PSI	.35	.35	.45	.44	.36	.48	.91	.36	.22	.91	.30	.38	.32	.38	.39	.36	.26	.42	.44	.34	.44	.51		
FSIQ	.72	.77	.72	.77	.77	.78	.61	.72	.68	.64	.57	.68	.71	.32	.51	.70	.48	.62	.68	.83	.84	.83	.69	
Mean	9.9	9.8	10.1	10.0	9.9	10.0	10.0	10.1	9.9	10.0	10.1	10.0	9.8	10.4	10.0	10.1	10.2	10.0	9.9	29.6	29.9	20.0	20.1	99.6
SD	3.2	2.7	3.2	3.1	2.9	2.9	3.2	3.1	3.0	3.3	3.0	3.0	3.4	3.1	3.1	3.4	3.3	3.0	2.9	7.7	8.2	5.5	6.0	21.9

Note. Uncorrected coefficients appear below the diagonal, and corrected coefficients appear above the diagonal in the shaded area.

Table A.7   Intercorrelations of Subtest, Process, and Composite Scores for Ages 45:0–54:11

Subtest/Process/Composite Score	BD	SI	DS	MR	VC	AR	SS	VP	IN	CD	LN	FW	CO	CA	PCm	BDN	DSF	DSB	DSS	VCI	PRI	WMI	PSI	FSIQ
BD																					.68			.65
SI	.45																			.73				.71
DS	.39	.50																				.63		.61
MR	.51	.53	.45																		.55			.70
VC	.42	.75	.49	.56																.83				.70
AR	.52	.56	.63	.57	.31																	.63		.71
SS	.35	.31	.33	.39	.37	.34																	.64	.49
VP	.67	.47	.40	.50	.34	.48	.34														.67			.61
IN	.51	.62	.42	.55	.74	.60	.35	.35												.73				.69
CD	.38	.41	.38	.50	.42	.38	.64	.34	.35														.64	.57
LN	.34	.42	.70	.44	.45	.56	.31	.33	.41	.38														
FW	.63	.57	.52	.62	.48	.66	.28	.60	.53	.34	.44													
CO	.37	.72	.43	.52	.73	.48	.24	.39	.63	.39	.36	.47												
CA	.22	.15	.31	.27	.23	.19	.48	.20	.11	.42	.22	.14	.28											
PCm	.53	.34	.33	.35	.37	.30	.28	.51	.34	.39	.31	.42	.39	.33										
BDN	.97	.44	.38	.50	.43	.49	.35	.66	.50	.39	.30	.61	.38	.24	.55									
DSF	.27	.38	.81	.33	.41	.49	.29	.31	.36	.28	.51	.42	.28	.26	.28	.26								
DSB	.37	.44	.86	.43	.44	.57	.26	.36	.37	.36	.64	.44	.41	.25	.26	.35	.58							
DSS	.31	.41	.78	.36	.35	.51	.28	.32	.31	.32	.56	.43	.37	.26	.28	.32	.44	.52						
VCI	.52	.87	.52	.59	.93	.64	.34	.46	.89	.44	.48	.58	.77	.18	.39	.51	.43	.46	.39					
PRI	.85	.57	.49	.80	.51	.62	.43	.87	.59	.48	.44	.73	.51	.27	.55	.84	.36	.46	.39	.62				
WMI	.50	.58	.90	.57	.59	.91	.35	.49	.57	.42	.70	.65	.50	.27	.35	.48	.72	.79	.71	.64	.62			
PSI	.40	.40	.39	.49	.41	.38	.90	.37	.36	.91	.38	.34	.34	.47	.47	.41	.31	.35	.33	.43	.50	.43		
FSIQ	.72	.76	.69	.77	.77	.78	.60	.70	.76	.66	.60	.73	.67	.35	.55	.71	.55	.62	.55	.85	.87	.82	.70	
Mean	9.9	9.9	10.1	10.2	10.1	10.2	10.1	10.2	10.1	10.0	9.7	10.1	9.7	9.8	9.8	9.9	10.4	10.0	9.9	30.1	30.3	20.3	20.1	100.7
SD	3.1	2.7	3.2	3.4	3.2	3.4	3.2	3.4	3.2	3.2	2.8	3.2	3.0	2.9	3.4	3.3	3.1	3.1	2.9	8.1	8.3	6.0	5.8	23.1

Note. Uncorrected coefficients appear below the diagonal, and corrected coefficients appear above the diagonal in the shaded area.

Table A.8   Intercorrelations of Subtest, Process, and Composite Scores for Ages 55:0–64:11

Subtest/Process/Composite Score	BD	SI	DS	MR	VC	AR	SS	VP	IN	CD	LN	FW	CO	CA	PCm	BDN	DSF	DSB	DSS	VCI	PRI	WMI	PSI	FSIQ
BD																					.70			.65
SI	.43																			.76				.69
DS	.42	.48																				.55		.62
MR	.60	.44	.53																		.61			.68
VC	.40	.76	.52	.50																.83				.72
AR	.45	.59	.55	.48	.60																	.55		.67
SS	.48	.31	.40	.45	.30	.30																	.66	.55
VP	.61	.38	.26	.50	.43	.42	.43														.62			.59
IN	.39	.67	.48	.44	.77	.56	.34	.45												.77				.69
CD	.43	.40	.42	.52	.43	.43	.66	.37	.39														.66	.62
LN	.40	.48	.66	.55	.52	.53	.44	.37	.50	.53														
FW	.53	.52	.45	.57	.54	.57	.38	.56	.45	.38	.45													
CO	.41	.72	.48	.47	.77	.59	.26	.43	.66	.39	.48	.50												
CA	.35	.25	.24	.22	.22	.18	.52	.30	.17	.44	.33	.24	.25											
PCm	.52	.45	.33	.47	.46	.42	.43	.52	.50	.39	.40	.46	.49	.41										
BDN	.97	.39	.41	.59	.37	.43	.47	.58	.36	.44	.36	.52	.38	.33	.51									
DSF	.24	.28	.77	.27	.30	.31	.21	.07	.32	.22	.42	.20	.27	.13	.13	.20								
DSB	.40	.46	.81	.49	.46	.45	.37	.26	.38	.38	.58	.38	.44	.23	.29	.40	.42							
DSS	.41	.45	.81	.54	.52	.58	.39	.35	.48	.44	.62	.56	.45	.25	.37	.40	.44	.55						
VCI	.45	.88	.54	.51	.93	.64	.35	.47	.91	.45	.55	.55	.79	.23	.52	.41	.33	.47	.53					
PRI	.86	.49	.48	.83	.52	.53	.53	.84	.51	.52	.52	.66	.52	.34	.60	.83	.22	.45	.51	.56				
WMI	.49	.61	.86	.57	.64	.90	.39	.39	.60	.48	.67	.59	.61	.24	.43	.48	.60	.70	.78	.68	.58			
PSI	.50	.39	.45	.53	.40	.40	.91	.44	.40	.91	.53	.42	.35	.52	.45	.50	.23	.41	.46	.44	.58	.48		
FSIQ	.72	.75	.69	.76	.79	.74	.65	.68	.76	.70	.69	.69	.71	.40	.62	.69	.40	.61	.68	.85	.85	.82	.74	
Mean	10.0	10.0	9.9	10.0	10.1	10.0	9.9	9.8	10.3	10.0	9.6	10.1	10.1	10.4	9.9	9.9	10.0	9.8	10.1	30.4	29.8	19.9	19.9	100.0
SD	2.9	2.7	2.7	3.2	3.0	3.1	3.2	3.3	3.4	3.1	2.8	3.0	3.2	2.8	3.3	3.2	2.8	2.7	2.8	8.3	7.9	5.2	5.7	22.1

Note. Uncorrected coefficients appear below the diagonal, and corrected coefficients appear above the diagonal in the shaded area.

Table A.9 Intercorrelations of Subtest, Process, and Composite Scores for Ages 65:0–69:11

Subtest/Process/ Composite Score	BD	SI	DS	MR	VC	AR	SS	VP	IN	CD	LN	FW	CO	CA	PCm	BDN	DSF	DSB	DSS	VCI	PRI	WMI	PSI	FSIQ
BD																					.69			.72
SI	.60																			.73				.76
DS	.45	.55																				.60		.67
MR	.54	.56	.50																		.58			.70
VC	.56	.74	.57	.58																.81				.76
AR	.61	.67	.60	.61	.67																	.60		.79
SS	.48	.43	.48	.49	.40	.46																	.64	.60
VP	.66	.47	.47	.52	.49	.61	.46														.67			.67
IN	.55	.63	.46	.48	.73	.65	.35	.50												.73				.68
CD	.45	.53	.53	.50	.43	.49	.64	.41	.33														.64	.62
LN	.40	.53	.64	.47	.50	.52	.51	.48	.37	.55														
FW	.62	.61	.57	.62	.62	.70	.48	.61	.59	.52	.49													
CO	.51	.72	.53	.52	.71	.61	.37	.47	.64	.50	.56	.61												
CA	.38	.44	.36	.29	.34	.41	.44	.33	.27	.47	.40	.45	.37											
PCm	.57	.53	.48	.42	.52	.48	.45	.55	.51	.44	.46	.52	.53	.31										
BDN	.98	.58	.44	.55	.54	.59	.48	.64	.54	.45	.38	.60	.50	.37	.56									
DSF	.31	.40	.81	.38	.45	.39	.25	.32	.36	.36	.44	.41	.38	.20	.37	.30								
DSB	.35	.46	.87	.49	.51	.52	.45	.37	.40	.42	.54	.48	.46	.25	.38	.34	.65							
DSS	.45	.48	.77	.36	.44	.57	.49	.48	.35	.49	.58	.49	.45	.44	.45	.45	.37	.53						
VCI	.64	.87	.59	.60	.92	.74	.44	.55	.89	.47	.52	.68	.77	.39	.58	.62	.45	.51	.47		.70	.74	.50	.88
PRI	.86	.64	.56	.81	.64	.72	.57	.87	.60	.53	.53	.73	.59	.40	.60	.85	.40	.48	.51	.70		.72	.61	.90
WMI	.60	.68	.89	.62	.69	.90	.52	.60	.62	.57	.65	.71	.63	.43	.54	.58	.66	.77	.75	.74	.72		.60	.88
PSI	.52	.53	.56	.55	.45	.52	.91	.48	.37	.90	.59	.55	.48	.50	.49	.51	.33	.48	.54	.50	.61	.60		.76
FSIQ	.78	.81	.74	.76	.81	.84	.68	.74	.75	.69	.65	.78	.73	.49	.65	.76	.53	.63	.64	.88	.90	.88	.76	
Mean	10.2	10.0	10.1	10.1	10.2	10.0	10.0	10.4	10.0	10.0	9.9	9.9	10.4	9.7	9.9	10.0	10.0	10.0	10.1	30.1	30.7	20.1	20.0	100.9
SD	3.1	2.8	3.0	3.1	3.2	3.2	3.1	3.4	3.3	3.1	3.3	3.2	3.1	3.0	3.1	3.2	2.8	2.8	3.0	8.2	8.1	5.6	5.6	23.8

Note. Uncorrected coefficients appear below the diagonal, and corrected coefficients appear above the diagonal in the shaded area.

Table A.10 Intercorrelations of Subtest, Process, and Composite Scores for Ages 70:0–74:11

Subtest/Process/Composite Score	BD	SI	DS	MR	VC	AR	SS	VP	IN	CD	CO	PCm	BDN	DSF	DSB	DSS	VCI	PRI	WMI	PSI	FSIQ
BD																		.69			.70
SI	.56																.72				.68
DS	.52	.45																	.60		.65
MR	.60	.55	.45															.59			.69
VC	.36	.71	.50	.49													.78				.63
AR	.56	.46	.60	.53	.47														.60		.69
SS	.35	.12	.28	.27	.15	.29														.61	.37
VP	.57	.35	.36	.45	.17	.37	.17											.57			.46
IN	.40	.63	.46	.45	.70	.61	.20	.40									.72				.65
CD	.43	.39	.44	.49	.42	.40	.61	.27	.65											.61	.61
CO	.30	.66	.41	.39	.70	.47	.15	.27	.34	.34											
PCm	.56	.47	.42	.46	.30	.43	.41	.10	.34	.46	.25										
BDN	.98	.54	.53	.61	.35	.55	.32	.60	.38	.41	.29	.55									
DSF	.37	.31	.78	.28	.32	.49	.12	.29	.29	.24	.21	.22	.38								
DSB	.42	.40	.83	.37	.47	.46	.15	.30	.40	.37	.37	.33	.43	.57							
DSS	.46	.37	.78	.41	.41	.45	.37	.29	.39	.42	.39	.42	.46	.35	.49						
VCI	.50	.88	.53	.56	.90	.58	.17	.30	.88	.46	.75	.42	.48	.35	.48	.44					
PRI	.87	.58	.53	.81	.40	.58	.31	.82	.44	.47	.31	.62	.88	.38	.43	.46	.54				
WMI	.60	.51	.91	.55	.54	.88	.32	.41	.59	.47	.49	.47	.60	.72	.74	.70	.62	.62			
PSI	.44	.29	.40	.42	.32	.38	.89	.24	.34	.90	.28	.49	.41	.20	.29	.44	.36	.44	.44		
FSIQ	.77	.75	.73	.76	.71	.76	.48	.58	.73	.69	.59	.63	.76	.51	.60	.63	.83	.84	.83	.66	
Mean	9.9	10.1	9.8	9.6	9.9	10.0	9.5	9.7	9.7	9.9	10.5	9.9	9.8	9.8	9.6	9.9	29.7	29.2	19.8	19.4	98.0
SD	3.1	2.9	3.2	3.0	2.9	2.8	2.8	3.3	3.1	2.9	2.8	3.3	3.2	3.2	2.8	3.2	7.9	7.8	5.3	5.1	20.8

Note. Uncorrected coefficients appear below the diagonal, and corrected coefficients appear above the diagonal in the shaded area.

Table A.11 Intercorrelations of Subtest, Process, and Composite Scores for Ages 75:0–79:11

Subtest/Process/Composite Score	BD	SI	DS	MR	VC	AR	SS	VP	IN	CD	CO	PCm	BDN	DSF	DSB	DSS	VCI	PRI	WMI	PSI	FSIQ
BD																		.60			.65
SI	.49																.77				.74
DS	.48	.51																	.64		.66
MR	.47	.51	.39															.56			.64
VC	.51	.78	.52	.49													.83				.76
AR	.47	.54	.64	.50	.57														.64		.66
SS	.46	.50	.44	.43	.47	.31														.74	.63
VP	.59	.40	.51	.53	.47	.48	.44											.66			.62
IN	.41	.65	.42	.50	.72	.61	.43	.37									.73				.68
CD	.46	.54	.53	.47	.55	.36	.74	.42	.47											.74	.68
CO	.52	.69	.48	.51	.61	.60	.42	.48	.63	.45											
PCm	.40	.60	.48	.43	.56	.49	.39	.41	.58	.52	.57										
BDN	.98	.49	.49	.47	.51	.46	.42	.60	.37	.42	.49	.38									
DSF	.29	.32	.76	.11	.42	.44	.23	.38	.29	.30	.25	.30	.30								
DSB	.35	.36	.81	.42	.38	.57	.29	.37	.31	.40	.40	.36	.37	.49							
DSS	.48	.50	.80	.39	.43	.51	.48	.45	.35	.52	.46	.45	.47	.35	.53						
VCI	.52	.90	.54	.55	.93	.64	.52	.46	.88	.58	.72	.64	.51	.38	.39	.47					
PRI	.81	.56	.55	.82	.59	.58	.53	.86	.52	.54	.60	.50	.81	.31	.46	.53	.62				
WMI	.52	.58	.92	.49	.60	.89	.42	.55	.56	.50	.60	.53	.52	.67	.77	.73	.65	.63			
PSI	.49	.56	.52	.49	.55	.36	.93	.46	.48	.94	.47	.49	.45	.29	.37	.54	.59	.58	.49		
FSIQ	.72	.79	.74	.72	.81	.73	.71	.70	.75	.76	.72	.65	.70	.48	.57	.66	.87	.86	.81	.79	
Mean	10.4	10.3	10.4	10.4	9.9	10.0	10.0	9.8	10.0	9.8	10.4	10.3	10.2	9.9	10.4	10.2	30.2	30.6	20.4	19.8	101.0
SD	2.8	2.8	3.1	3.1	2.8	2.8	3.1	3.1	2.8	3.3	3.0	3.0	2.8	3.0	3.1	3.6	7.6	7.4	5.3	5.9	22.0

Note. Uncorrected coefficients appear below the diagonal, and corrected coefficients appear above the diagonal in the shaded area.

Table A.12   Intercorrelations of Subtest, Process, and Composite Scores for Ages 80:0–84:11

Subtest/Process/Composite Score	BD	SI	DS	MR	VC	AR	SS	VP	IN	CD	CO	PCm	BDN	DSF	DSB	DSS	VCI	PRI	WMI	PSI	FSIQ
BD																		.61			.59
SI	.41																.77				.73
DS	.44	.49																	.50		.59
MR	.50	.60	.42															.58			.72
VC	.44	.75	.44	.61													.82		.50		.73
AR	.46	.55	.50	.60	.53																.67
SS	.33	.42	.42	.43	.39	.34														.74	.59
VP	.56	.40	.27	.53	.38	.47	.47											.63			.58
IN	.45	.69	.46	.58	.75	.60	.42	.46									.77				.74
CD	.40	.46	.50	.46	.43	.39	.74	.45	.42											.74	.65
CO	.35	.75	.49	.46	.76	.54	.39	.33	.70	.42											
PCm	.46	.42	.34	.46	.28	.39	.51	.52	.39	.47	.23										
BDN	.99	.39	.44	.49	.42	.45	.34	.55	.44	.40	.34	.47									
DSF	.38	.30	.80	.20	.26	.34	.24	.08	.35	.38	.30	.18	.38								
DSB	.42	.39	.76	.50	.39	.46	.37	.26	.31	.46	.34	.34	.39	.43							
DSS	.33	.50	.83	.37	.41	.40	.39	.28	.46	.41	.51	.33	.34	.50	.50						
VCI	.47	.90	.51	.66	.91	.62	.45	.44	.90	.50	.81	.40	.46	.34	.40	.51					
PRI	.82	.57	.45	.82	.58	.62	.50	.84	.59	.53	.46	.58	.81	.26	.48	.39	.64				
WMI	.52	.60	.88	.59	.55	.85	.44	.42	.61	.52	.59	.42	.51	.67	.71	.72	.65	.51			
PSI	.39	.47	.49	.47	.44	.39	.94	.49	.47	.93	.43	.52	.39	.33	.44	.43	.51	.55	.51		
FSIQ	.67	.80	.68	.78	.79	.74	.68	.66	.81	.72	.72	.57	.66	.45	.59	.60	.88	.85	.81	.75	
Mean	10.4	9.9	10.1	10.1	9.8	10.1	10.4	9.8	9.6	10.2	10.0	10.0	10.5	9.9	10.3	10.1	29.4	30.2	20.2	20.6	100.4
SD	2.5	3.3	2.9	2.8	2.9	2.6	2.9	2.6	3.2	2.8	3.1	3.1	2.6	3.2	2.8	3.0	8.5	6.6	4.8	5.3	21.0

Note. Uncorrected coefficients appear below the diagonal, and corrected coefficients appear above the diagonal in the shaded area.

Table A.13   Intercorrelations of Subtest, Process, and Composite Scores for Ages 85:0–90:11

Subtest/Process/Composite Score	BD	SI	DS	MR	VC	AR	SS	VP	IN	CD	CO	PCm	BDN	DSF	DSB	DSS	VCI	PRI	WMI	PSI	FSIQ
BD																		.67			.69
SI	.58																.77				.80
DS	.51	.60																	.60		.71
MR	.59	.64	.53															.66			.73
VC	.46	.75	.55	.58													.81				.75
AR	.44	.57	.60	.46	.62														.60		.67
SS	.56	.54	.58	.54	.48	.50														.70	.70
VP	.62	.50	.53	.60	.43	.42	.55											.68			.66
IN	.47	.69	.51	.57	.74	.61	.48	.40									.76				.70
CD	.64	.63	.58	.61	.56	.47	.70	.60	.42											.70	.70
CO	.54	.75	.63	.56	.79	.61	.53	.46	.79	.52											.75
PCm	.48	.51	.50	.51	.47	.38	.54	.48	.52	.54	.55										
BDN	.99	.57	.51	.57	.46	.45	.56	.63	.46	.63	.53	.47									
DSF	.20	.41	.72	.19	.32	.38	.31	.21	.27	.27	.37	.18	.21								
DSB	.41	.44	.77	.45	.48	.51	.42	.41	.47	.39	.53	.40	.41	.42							
DSS	.49	.50	.84	.50	.44	.50	.54	.56	.39	.59	.52	.51	.47	.41	.45						
VCI	.56	.90	.61	.66	.91	.66	.55	.49	.90	.60	.86	.55	.55	.37	.51	.49					
PRI	.87	.67	.61	.86	.58	.51	.64	.84	.57	.72	.61	.57	.86	.23	.50	.60	.67				
WMI	.54	.66	.90	.55	.65	.89	.61	.53	.62	.59	.69	.49	.54	.62	.72	.75	.71	.63			
PSI	.65	.63	.63	.62	.56	.53	.94	.62	.49	.91	.57	.58	.64	.32	.44	.61	.62	.73	.65		
FSIQ	.76	.85	.77	.79	.80	.73	.77	.71	.77	.80	.80	.64	.75	.42	.61	.68	.89	.88	.84	.85	
Mean	10.2	9.9	9.8	10.1	9.7	10.0	9.8	10.1	9.9	9.9	9.9	9.5	10.3	9.6	10.2	9.9	29.5	30.4	19.8	19.7	99.3
SD	3.1	3.4	2.9	3.0	3.0	2.8	3.3	2.4	3.3	2.8	3.2	3.3	2.8	2.8	3.3	3.5	8.7	7.3	5.1	5.6	23.3

Note. Uncorrected coefficients appear below the diagonal, and corrected coefficients appear above the diagonal in the shaded area.

WIAT–II Tables

Table B.1   WIAT–II Subtest and Composite Scores Predicted From WAIS–IV FSIQ Scores

WAIS–IV FSIQ	WR	NO	RC	SP	PD	MR	WE	LC	OE	RD	MA	WL	OL	TA	WAIS–IV FSIQ
	subtest									composite					

WAIS–IV FSIQ	WR	NO	RC	SP	PD	MR	WE	LC	OE	RD	MA	WL	OL	TA	WAIS–IV FSIQ
40	61	53	54	65	75	52	64	57	62	54	50	61	53	47	40
41	62	54	55	65	75	53	65	58	62	55	50	62	53	48	41
42	62	55	55	66	76	54	65	59	63	56	51	62	54	49	42
43	63	56	56	66	76	54	66	60	64	57	52	63	55	50	43
44	64	56	57	67	76	55	66	60	64	57	53	64	56	51	44
45	64	57	58	68	77	56	67	61	65	58	54	64	57	52	45
46	65	58	58	68	77	57	68	62	65	59	55	65	57	52	46
47	66	59	59	69	78	58	68	62	66	60	55	66	58	53	47
48	66	59	60	69	78	58	69	63	67	60	56	66	59	54	48
49	67	60	61	70	79	59	69	64	67	61	57	67	60	55	49
50	68	61	62	71	79	60	70	65	68	62	58	68	61	56	50
51	68	62	62	71	79	61	71	65	69	63	59	68	61	57	51
52	69	63	63	72	80	62	71	66	69	64	60	69	62	58	52
53	69	63	64	72	80	62	72	67	70	64	61	69	63	59	53
54	70	64	65	73	81	63	72	67	71	65	61	70	64	60	54
55	71	65	65	73	81	64	73	68	71	66	62	71	64	60	55
56	71	66	66	74	82	65	74	69	72	67	63	71	65	61	56
57	72	66	67	75	82	66	74	69	72	67	64	72	66	62	57
58	73	67	68	75	82	66	75	70	73	68	65	73	67	63	58
59	73	68	68	76	83	67	75	71	74	69	66	73	68	64	59
60	74	69	69	76	83	68	76	72	74	70	66	74	68	65	60
61	75	70	70	77	84	69	77	72	75	70	67	75	69	66	61
62	75	70	71	78	84	70	77	73	76	71	68	75	70	67	62
63	76	71	72	78	84	70	78	74	76	72	69	76	71	67	63
64	77	72	72	79	85	71	78	74	77	73	70	77	72	68	64
65	77	73	73	79	85	72	79	75	78	73	71	77	72	69	65
66	78	73	74	80	86	73	80	76	78	74	71	78	73	70	66
67	79	74	75	81	86	74	80	77	79	75	72	79	74	71	67
68	79	75	75	81	87	74	81	77	80	76	73	79	75	72	68
69	80	76	76	82	87	75	81	78	80	76	74	80	76	73	69
70	81	77	77	82	87	76	82	79	81	77	75	81	76	74	70
71	81	77	78	83	88	77	83	79	81	78	76	81	77	74	71
72	82	78	78	83	88	78	83	80	82	79	76	82	78	75	72
73	82	79	79	84	89	78	84	81	83	79	77	82	79	76	73
74	83	80	80	85	89	79	84	82	83	80	78	83	79	77	74
75	84	81	81	85	90	80	85	82	84	81	79	84	80	78	75
76	84	81	82	86	90	81	86	83	85	82	80	84	81	79	76
77	85	82	82	86	90	82	86	84	85	83	81	85	82	80	77
78	86	83	83	87	91	82	87	84	86	83	82	86	83	81	78
79	86	84	84	88	91	83	87	85	87	84	82	86	83	82	79
80	87	84	85	88	92	84	88	86	87	85	83	87	84	82	80
81	88	85	85	89	92	85	89	87	88	86	84	88	85	83	81
82	88	86	86	89	92	86	89	87	88	86	85	88	86	84	82
83	89	87	87	90	93	86	90	88	89	87	86	89	87	85	83
84	90	88	88	91	93	87	90	89	90	88	87	90	87	86	84
85	90	88	88	91	94	88	91	89	90	89	87	90	88	87	85
86	91	89	89	92	94	89	92	90	91	89	88	91	89	88	86
87	92	90	90	92	95	90	92	91	92	90	89	92	90	89	87
88	92	91	91	93	95	90	93	91	92	91	90	92	91	89	88
89	93	91	92	94	95	91	93	92	93	92	91	93	91	90	89
90	94	92	92	94	96	92	94	93	94	92	92	94	92	91	90
91	94	93	93	95	96	93	95	94	94	93	92	94	93	92	91
92	95	94	94	95	97	94	95	94	95	94	93	95	94	93	92
93	95	95	95	96	97	94	96	95	96	95	94	95	94	94	93
94	96	95	95	96	97	95	96	96	96	95	95	96	95	95	94
95	97	96	96	97	98	96	97	96	97	96	96	97	96	96	95
96	97	97	97	98	98	97	98	97	97	97	97	97	97	96	96
97	98	98	98	98	99	98	98	98	98	98	97	98	98	97	97
98	99	98	98	99	99	98	99	99	99	98	98	99	98	98	98
99	99	99	99	99	100	99	99	99	99	99	99	99	99	99	99
100	100	100	100	100	100	100	100	100	100	100	100	100	100	100	100

Note. WIAT–II abbreviations are: WR = Word Reading, NO = Numerical Operations, RC = Reading Comprehension, SP = Spelling, PD = Pseudoword Decoding, MR = Math Reasoning, WE = Written Expression, LC = Listening Comprehension, OE = Oral Expression, RD = Reading, MA = Mathematics, WL = Written Language, OL = Oral Language, TA = Total Achievement.

Table B.1   WIAT–II Subtest and Composite Scores Predicted From WAIS–IV FSIQ Scores *(continued)*

WAIS–IV FSIQ	WR	NO	RC	SP	PD	MR	WE	LC	OE	RD	MA	WL	OL	TA	WAIS–IV FSIQ
	Subtest Scores									**Composite Scores**					
101	101	101	101	101	100	101	101	101	101	101	101	101	101	101	101
102	101	102	102	101	101	102	101	101	101	102	102	101	102	102	102
103	102	102	102	102	101	102	102	102	102	102	103	102	102	103	103
104	103	103	103	102	102	103	102	103	103	103	103	103	103	104	104
105	103	104	104	103	102	104	103	104	103	104	104	103	104	104	105
106	104	105	105	104	103	105	104	104	104	105	105	104	105	105	106
107	105	105	105	104	103	106	104	105	104	105	106	105	106	106	107
108	105	106	106	105	103	106	105	106	105	106	107	105	106	107	108
109	106	107	107	105	104	107	105	106	106	107	108	106	107	108	109
110	107	108	108	106	104	108	106	107	106	108	108	107	108	109	110
111	107	109	108	106	105	109	107	108	107	108	109	107	109	110	111
112	108	109	109	107	105	110	107	109	108	109	110	108	109	111	112
113	108	110	110	108	105	110	108	109	108	110	111	108	110	111	113
114	109	111	111	108	106	111	108	110	109	111	112	109	111	112	114
115	110	112	112	109	106	112	109	111	110	111	113	110	112	113	115
116	110	112	112	109	107	113	110	111	110	112	113	110	113	114	116
117	111	113	113	110	107	114	110	112	111	113	114	111	113	115	117
118	112	114	114	111	108	114	111	113	112	114	115	112	114	116	118
119	112	115	115	111	108	115	111	113	112	114	116	112	115	117	119
120	113	116	115	112	108	116	112	114	113	115	117	113	116	118	120
121	114	116	116	112	109	117	113	115	113	116	118	114	117	118	121
122	114	117	117	113	109	118	113	116	114	117	118	114	117	119	122
123	115	118	118	114	110	118	114	116	115	117	119	115	118	120	123
124	116	119	118	114	110	119	114	117	115	118	120	116	119	121	124
125	116	120	119	115	111	120	115	118	116	119	121	116	120	122	125
126	117	120	120	115	111	121	116	118	117	120	122	117	121	123	126
127	118	121	121	116	111	122	116	119	117	121	123	118	121	124	127
128	118	122	122	117	112	122	117	120	118	121	124	118	122	125	128
129	119	123	122	117	112	123	117	121	119	122	124	119	123	126	129
130	120	123	123	118	113	124	118	121	119	123	125	120	124	126	130
131	120	124	124	118	113	125	119	122	120	124	126	120	124	127	131
132	121	125	125	119	113	126	119	123	120	124	127	121	125	128	132
133	121	126	125	119	114	126	120	123	121	125	128	121	126	129	133
134	122	127	126	120	114	127	120	124	122	126	129	122	127	130	134
135	123	127	127	121	115	128	121	125	122	127	129	123	128	131	135
136	123	128	128	121	115	129	122	126	123	127	130	123	128	132	136
137	124	129	128	122	116	130	122	126	124	128	131	124	129	133	137
138	125	130	129	122	116	130	123	127	124	129	132	125	130	133	138
139	125	130	130	123	116	131	123	128	125	130	133	125	131	134	139
140	126	131	131	124	117	132	124	128	126	130	134	126	132	135	140
141	127	132	132	124	117	133	125	129	126	131	134	127	132	136	141
142	127	133	132	125	118	134	125	130	127	132	135	127	133	137	142
143	128	134	133	125	118	134	126	131	128	133	136	128	134	138	143
144	129	134	134	126	118	135	126	131	128	133	137	129	135	139	144
145	129	135	135	127	119	136	127	132	129	134	138	129	136	140	145
146	130	136	135	127	119	137	128	133	129	135	139	130	136	140	146
147	131	137	136	128	120	138	128	133	130	136	139	131	137	141	147
148	131	137	137	128	120	138	129	134	131	136	140	131	138	142	148
149	132	138	138	129	121	139	129	135	131	137	141	132	139	143	149
150	133	139	139	130	121	140	130	136	132	138	142	133	140	144	150
151	133	140	139	130	121	141	131	136	133	139	143	133	140	145	151
152	134	141	140	131	122	142	131	137	133	140	144	134	141	146	152
153	134	141	141	131	122	142	132	138	134	140	145	134	142	147	153
154	135	142	142	132	123	143	132	138	135	141	145	135	143	148	154
155	136	143	142	132	123	144	133	139	135	142	146	136	143	148	155
156	136	144	143	133	124	145	134	140	136	143	147	136	144	149	156
157	137	144	144	134	124	146	134	140	136	143	148	137	145	150	157
158	138	145	145	134	124	146	135	141	137	144	149	138	146	151	158
159	138	146	145	135	125	147	135	142	138	145	150	138	147	152	159
160	139	147	146	135	125	148	136	143	138	146	150	139	147	153	160

Note. WIAT–II abbreviations are: WR = Word Reading, NO = Numerical Operations, RC = Reading Comprehension, SP = Spelling, PD = Pseudoword Decoding, MR = Math Reasoning, WE = Written Expression, LC = Listening Comprehension, OE = Oral Expression, RD = Reading, MA = Mathematics, WL = Written Language, OL = Oral Language, TA = Total Achievement.

Table B.2   WIAT–II Subtest and Composite Scores Predicted From WAIS–IV VCI Scores

WAIS–IV VCI	WIAT–II Subtest Scores									WIAT–II Composite Scores					WAIS–IV VCI
	WR	NO	RC	SP	PD	MR	WE	LC	OE	RD	MA	WL	OL	TA	
50	69	71	60	73	84	71	77	61	71	63	69	73	60	61	50
51	69	71	61	74	84	71	77	62	71	64	69	73	61	62	51
52	70	72	62	74	84	72	77	63	72	64	70	74	62	63	52
53	70	72	62	75	84	72	78	63	72	65	70	74	62	63	53
54	71	73	63	75	85	73	78	64	73	66	71	75	63	64	54
55	72	73	64	76	85	73	79	65	73	67	72	75	64	65	55
56	72	74	65	76	85	74	79	66	74	67	72	76	65	66	56
57	73	75	66	77	86	75	80	66	75	68	73	76	66	66	57
58	74	75	66	77	86	75	80	67	75	69	74	77	66	67	58
59	74	76	67	78	86	76	81	68	76	70	74	77	67	68	59
60	75	76	68	78	87	76	81	69	76	70	75	78	68	69	60
61	75	77	69	79	87	77	82	70	77	71	75	79	69	70	61
62	76	78	70	79	87	78	82	70	78	72	76	79	70	70	62
63	77	78	70	80	88	78	83	71	78	73	77	80	70	71	63
64	77	79	71	81	88	79	83	72	79	73	77	80	71	72	64
65	78	79	72	81	88	79	84	73	79	74	78	81	72	73	65
66	79	80	73	82	89	80	84	73	80	75	79	81	73	73	66
67	79	81	74	82	89	81	84	74	81	76	79	82	74	74	67
68	80	81	74	83	89	81	85	75	81	76	80	82	74	75	68
69	80	82	75	83	90	82	85	76	82	77	80	83	75	76	69
70	81	82	76	84	90	82	86	77	82	78	81	84	76	77	70
71	82	83	77	84	90	83	86	77	83	79	82	84	77	77	71
72	82	83	78	85	91	83	87	78	83	79	82	85	78	78	72
73	83	84	78	85	91	84	87	79	84	80	83	85	78	79	73
74	84	85	79	86	91	85	88	80	85	81	84	86	79	80	74
75	84	85	80	87	92	85	88	81	85	82	84	86	80	81	75
76	85	86	81	87	92	86	89	81	86	82	85	87	81	81	76
77	86	86	82	88	92	86	89	82	86	83	86	87	82	82	77
78	86	87	82	88	93	87	90	83	87	84	86	88	82	83	78
79	87	88	83	89	93	88	90	84	88	84	87	88	83	84	79
80	87	88	84	89	93	88	91	84	88	85	87	89	84	84	80
81	88	89	85	90	94	89	91	85	89	86	88	90	85	85	81
82	89	89	86	90	94	89	92	86	89	87	89	90	86	86	82
83	89	90	86	91	94	90	92	87	90	87	89	91	86	87	83
84	90	91	87	91	95	91	92	88	91	88	90	91	87	88	84
85	91	91	88	92	95	91	93	88	91	89	91	92	88	88	85
86	91	92	89	92	95	92	93	89	92	90	91	92	89	89	86
87	92	92	90	93	96	92	94	90	92	90	92	93	90	90	87
88	92	93	90	94	96	93	94	91	93	91	92	93	90	91	88
89	93	94	91	94	96	94	95	91	94	92	93	94	91	91	89
90	94	94	92	95	97	94	95	92	94	93	94	95	92	92	90
91	94	95	93	95	97	95	96	93	95	93	94	95	93	93	91
92	95	95	94	96	97	95	96	94	95	94	95	96	94	94	92
93	96	96	94	96	98	96	97	95	96	95	96	96	94	95	93
94	96	96	95	97	98	96	97	95	96	96	96	97	95	95	94
95	97	97	96	97	98	97	98	96	97	96	97	97	96	96	95
96	97	98	97	98	99	98	98	97	98	97	97	98	97	97	96
97	98	98	98	98	99	98	99	98	98	98	98	98	98	98	97
98	99	99	98	99	99	99	99	98	99	99	99	99	98	98	98
99	99	99	99	99	100	99	100	99	99	99	99	99	99	99	99
100	100	100	100	100	100	100	100	100	100	100	100	100	100	100	100

Note. WIAT–II abbreviations are: WR = Word Reading, NO = Numerical Operations, RC = Reading Comprehension, SP = Spelling, PD = Pseudoword Decoding, MR = Math Reasoning, WE = Written Expression, LC = Listening Comprehension, OE = Oral Expression, RD = Reading, MA = Mathematics, WL = Written Language, OL = Oral Language, TA = Total Achievement.

Table B.2 WIAT–II Subtest and Composite Scores Predicted From WAIS–IV VCI Scores *(continued)*

WAIS–IV VCI	WIAT–II														WAIS–IV VCI
	Subtest Scores									Composite Scores					
	WR	NO	RC	SP	PD	MR	WE	LC	OE	RD	MA	WL	OL	TA	
101	101	101	101	101	100	101	100	101	101	101	101	101	101	101	101
102	101	101	102	101	101	101	101	102	101	101	101	101	102	102	102
103	102	102	102	102	101	102	101	102	102	102	102	102	102	102	103
104	103	102	103	102	101	102	102	103	102	103	103	102	103	103	104
105	103	103	104	103	102	103	102	104	103	104	103	103	104	104	105
106	104	104	105	103	102	104	103	105	104	104	104	103	105	105	106
107	104	104	106	104	102	104	103	105	104	105	104	104	106	105	107
108	105	105	106	104	103	105	104	106	105	106	105	104	106	106	108
109	106	105	107	105	103	105	104	107	105	107	106	105	107	107	109
110	106	106	108	105	103	106	105	108	106	107	106	106	108	108	110
111	107	106	109	106	104	106	105	109	106	108	107	106	109	109	111
112	108	107	110	106	104	107	106	109	107	109	108	107	110	109	112
113	108	108	110	107	104	108	106	110	108	110	108	107	110	110	113
114	109	108	111	108	105	108	107	111	108	110	109	108	111	111	114
115	109	109	112	108	105	109	107	112	109	111	109	108	112	112	115
116	110	109	113	109	105	109	108	112	109	112	110	109	113	112	116
117	111	110	114	109	106	110	108	113	110	113	111	109	114	113	117
118	111	111	114	110	106	111	108	114	111	113	111	110	114	114	118
119	112	111	115	110	106	111	109	115	111	114	112	110	115	115	119
120	113	112	116	111	107	112	109	116	112	115	113	111	116	116	120
121	113	112	117	111	107	112	110	116	112	116	113	112	117	116	121
122	114	113	118	112	107	113	110	117	113	116	114	112	118	117	122
123	114	114	118	112	108	114	111	118	114	117	114	113	118	118	123
124	115	114	119	113	108	114	111	119	114	118	115	113	119	119	124
125	116	115	120	114	108	115	112	120	115	119	116	114	120	120	125
126	116	115	121	114	109	115	112	120	115	119	116	114	121	120	126
127	117	116	122	115	109	116	113	121	116	120	117	115	122	121	127
128	118	117	122	115	109	117	113	122	117	121	118	115	122	122	128
129	118	117	123	116	110	117	114	123	117	121	118	116	123	123	129
130	119	118	124	116	110	118	114	123	118	122	119	117	124	123	130
131	120	118	125	117	110	118	115	124	118	123	120	117	125	124	131
132	120	119	126	117	111	119	115	125	119	124	120	118	126	125	132
133	121	119	126	118	111	119	116	126	119	124	121	118	126	126	133
134	121	120	127	118	111	120	116	127	120	125	121	119	127	127	134
135	122	121	128	119	112	121	116	127	121	126	122	119	128	127	135
136	123	121	129	119	112	121	117	128	121	127	123	120	129	128	136
137	123	122	130	120	112	122	117	129	122	127	123	120	130	129	137
138	124	122	130	121	113	122	118	130	122	128	124	121	130	130	138
139	125	123	131	121	113	123	118	130	123	129	125	121	131	130	139
140	125	124	132	122	113	124	119	131	124	130	125	122	132	131	140
141	126	124	133	122	114	124	119	132	124	130	126	123	133	132	141
142	126	125	134	123	114	125	120	133	125	131	126	123	134	133	142
143	127	125	134	123	114	125	120	134	125	132	127	124	134	134	143
144	128	126	135	124	115	126	121	134	126	133	128	124	135	134	144
145	128	127	136	124	115	127	121	135	127	133	128	125	136	135	145
146	129	127	137	125	115	127	122	136	127	134	129	125	137	136	146
147	130	128	138	125	116	128	122	137	128	135	130	126	138	137	147
148	130	128	138	126	116	128	123	137	128	136	130	126	138	137	148
149	131	129	139	126	116	129	123	138	129	136	131	127	139	138	149
150	132	130	140	127	117	130	124	139	130	137	132	128	140	139	150

Note. WIAT–II abbreviations are: WR = Word Reading, NO = Numerical Operations, RC = Reading Comprehension, SP = Spelling, PD = Pseudoword Decoding, MR = Math Reasoning, WE = Written Expression, LC = Listening Comprehension, OE = Oral Expression, RD = Reading, MA = Mathematics, WL = Written Language, OL = Oral Language, TA = Total Achievement.

Table B.3   WIAT–II Subtest and Composite Scores Predicted From WAIS–IV PRI Scores

WAIS–IV PRI	WR	NO	RC	SP	PD	MR	WE	LC	OE	RD	MA	WL	OL	TA	WAIS–IV PRI
50	76	67	71	79	84	66	74	72	74	72	64	74	68	65	50
51	76	68	72	79	84	67	75	72	74	73	65	75	69	66	51
52	77	68	72	79	84	67	75	73	75	73	65	75	69	66	52
53	77	69	73	80	84	68	76	73	75	74	66	76	70	67	53
54	78	70	73	80	85	69	76	74	76	74	67	76	71	68	54
55	78	70	74	81	85	69	77	74	76	75	68	77	71	69	55
56	79	71	74	81	85	70	77	75	77	75	68	77	72	69	56
57	79	72	75	82	86	71	78	75	77	76	69	78	72	70	57
58	80	72	76	82	86	71	78	76	78	76	70	78	73	71	58
59	80	73	76	82	86	72	79	77	78	77	70	79	74	71	59
60	81	74	77	83	87	73	79	77	79	78	71	79	74	72	60
61	81	74	77	83	87	73	80	78	79	78	72	80	75	73	61
62	82	75	78	84	87	74	80	78	80	79	73	80	76	73	62
63	82	76	79	84	88	75	81	79	80	79	73	81	76	74	63
64	83	76	79	85	88	76	81	79	81	80	74	81	77	75	64
65	83	77	80	85	88	76	82	80	81	80	75	82	78	76	65
66	84	78	80	85	89	77	82	81	82	81	76	82	78	76	66
67	84	78	81	86	89	78	83	81	83	82	76	83	79	77	67
68	85	79	81	86	89	78	83	82	83	82	77	83	80	78	68
69	85	80	82	87	90	79	84	82	84	83	78	84	80	78	69
70	86	80	83	87	90	80	84	83	84	83	78	84	81	79	70
71	86	81	83	88	90	80	85	83	85	84	79	85	81	80	71
72	87	82	84	88	91	81	85	84	85	84	80	85	82	80	72
73	87	82	84	88	91	82	86	85	86	85	81	86	83	81	73
74	88	83	85	89	91	82	86	85	86	85	81	86	83	82	74
75	88	84	86	89	92	83	87	86	87	86	82	87	84	83	75
76	88	84	86	90	92	84	88	86	87	87	83	88	85	83	76
77	89	85	87	90	92	84	88	87	88	87	83	88	85	84	77
78	89	85	87	91	93	85	89	87	88	88	84	89	86	85	78
79	90	86	88	91	93	86	89	88	89	88	85	89	87	85	79
80	90	87	88	91	93	86	90	89	89	89	86	90	87	86	80
81	91	87	89	92	94	87	90	89	90	89	86	90	88	87	81
82	91	88	90	92	94	88	91	90	90	90	87	91	88	87	82
83	92	89	90	93	94	88	91	90	91	90	88	91	89	88	83
84	92	89	91	93	95	89	92	91	92	91	88	92	90	89	84
85	93	90	91	94	95	90	92	91	92	92	89	92	90	90	85
86	93	91	92	94	95	90	93	92	93	92	90	93	91	90	86
87	94	91	92	94	96	91	93	93	93	93	91	93	92	91	87
88	94	92	93	95	96	92	94	93	94	93	91	94	92	92	88
89	95	93	94	95	96	93	94	94	94	94	92	94	93	92	89
90	95	93	94	96	97	93	95	94	95	94	93	95	94	93	90
91	96	94	95	96	97	94	95	95	95	95	94	95	94	94	91
92	96	95	95	97	97	95	96	95	96	96	94	96	95	94	92
93	97	95	96	97	98	95	96	96	96	96	95	96	96	95	93
94	97	96	97	97	98	96	97	97	97	97	96	97	96	96	94
95	98	97	97	98	98	97	97	97	97	97	96	97	97	97	95
96	98	97	98	98	99	97	98	98	98	98	97	98	97	97	96
97	99	98	98	99	99	98	98	98	98	98	98	98	98	98	97
98	99	99	99	99	99	99	99	99	99	99	99	99	99	99	98
99	100	99	99	100	100	99	99	99	99	99	99	99	99	99	99
100	100	100	100	100	100	100	100	100	100	100	100	100	100	100	100

Note. WIAT–II abbreviations are: WR = Word Reading, NO = Numerical Operations, RC = Reading Comprehension, SP = Spelling, PD = Pseudoword Decoding, MR = Math Reasoning, WE = Written Expression, LC = Listening Comprehension, OE = Oral Expression, RD = Reading, MA = Mathematics, WL = Written Language, OL = Oral Language, TA = Total Achievement.

Table B.3   WIAT–II Subtest and Composite Scores Predicted From WAIS–IV PRI Scores *(continued)*

WAIS–IV PRI	WR	NO	RC	SP	PD	MR	WE	LC	OE	RD	MA	WL	OL	TA	WAIS–IV PRI
			Subtest Scores									Composite Scores			
101	100	101	101	100	100	101	101	101	101	101	101	101	101	101	101
102	101	101	101	101	101	101	101	101	101	101	101	101	101	101	102
103	101	102	102	101	101	102	102	102	102	102	102	102	102	102	103
104	102	103	102	102	101	103	102	102	102	102	103	102	103	103	104
105	102	103	103	102	102	103	103	103	103	103	104	103	103	104	105
106	103	104	103	103	102	104	103	103	103	103	104	103	104	104	106
107	103	105	104	103	102	105	104	104	104	104	105	104	104	105	107
108	104	105	105	103	103	105	104	105	104	104	106	104	105	106	108
109	104	106	105	104	103	106	105	105	105	105	106	105	106	106	109
110	105	107	106	104	103	107	105	106	105	106	107	105	106	107	110
111	105	107	106	105	104	107	106	106	106	106	108	106	107	108	111
112	106	108	107	105	104	108	106	107	106	107	109	106	108	108	112
113	106	109	108	106	104	109	107	107	107	107	109	107	108	109	113
114	107	109	108	106	105	110	107	108	107	108	110	107	109	110	114
115	107	110	109	106	105	110	108	109	108	108	111	108	110	111	115
116	108	111	109	107	105	111	108	109	108	109	112	108	110	111	116
117	108	111	110	107	106	112	109	110	109	110	112	109	111	112	117
118	109	112	110	108	106	112	109	110	110	110	113	109	112	113	118
119	109	113	111	108	106	113	110	111	110	111	114	110	112	113	119
120	110	113	112	109	107	114	110	111	111	111	114	110	113	114	120
121	110	114	112	109	107	114	111	112	111	112	115	111	113	115	121
122	111	115	113	109	107	115	111	113	112	112	116	111	114	115	122
123	111	115	113	110	108	116	112	113	112	113	117	112	115	116	123
124	112	116	114	110	108	116	112	114	113	113	117	112	115	117	124
125	112	117	115	111	108	117	113	114	113	114	118	113	116	118	125
126	112	117	115	111	109	118	114	115	114	115	119	114	117	118	126
127	113	118	116	112	109	118	114	115	114	115	119	114	117	119	127
128	113	118	116	112	109	119	115	116	115	116	120	115	118	120	128
129	114	119	117	112	110	120	115	117	115	116	121	115	119	120	129
130	114	120	117	113	110	120	116	117	116	117	122	116	119	121	130
131	115	120	118	113	110	121	116	118	116	117	122	116	120	122	131
132	115	121	119	114	111	122	117	118	117	118	123	117	120	122	132
133	116	122	119	114	111	122	117	119	117	118	124	117	121	123	133
134	116	122	120	115	111	123	118	119	118	119	124	118	122	124	134
135	117	123	120	115	112	124	118	120	119	120	125	118	122	125	135
136	117	124	121	115	112	124	119	121	119	120	126	119	123	125	136
137	118	124	121	116	112	125	119	121	120	121	127	119	124	126	137
138	118	125	122	116	113	126	120	122	120	121	127	120	124	127	138
139	119	126	123	117	113	127	120	122	121	122	128	120	125	127	139
140	119	126	123	117	113	127	121	123	121	122	129	121	126	128	140
141	120	127	124	118	114	128	121	123	122	123	130	121	126	129	141
142	120	128	124	118	114	129	122	124	122	124	130	122	127	129	142
143	121	128	125	118	114	129	122	125	123	124	131	122	128	130	143
144	121	129	126	119	115	130	123	125	123	125	132	123	128	131	144
145	122	130	126	119	115	131	123	126	124	125	132	123	129	132	145
146	122	130	127	120	115	131	124	126	124	126	133	124	129	132	146
147	123	131	127	120	116	132	124	127	125	126	134	124	130	133	147
148	123	132	128	121	116	133	125	127	125	127	135	125	131	134	148
149	124	132	128	121	116	133	125	128	126	127	135	125	131	134	149
150	124	133	129	122	117	134	126	129	127	128	136	126	132	135	150

Note. WIAT–II abbreviations are: WR = Word Reading, NO = Numerical Operations, RC = Reading Comprehension, SP = Spelling, PD = Pseudoword Decoding, MR = Math Reasoning, WE = Written Expression, LC = Listening Comprehension, OE = Oral Expression, RD = Reading, MA = Mathematics, WL = Written Language, OL = Oral Language, TA = Total Achievement.

Table B.4   Differences Between Predicted and Obtained WIAT–II Subtest and Composite Scores Required for Statistical Significance (Critical Values): Predicted-Difference Method Using WAIS–IV FSIQ, VCI, and PRI for Ages 16:0–19:11

Subtest/Composite	Significance Level	FSIQ	VCI	PRI
Word Reading	.05	7.11	7.77	7.29
	.01	9.36	10.23	9.60
Numerical Operations	.05	7.90	8.18	8.41
	.01	10.40	10.77	11.07
Reading Comprehension	.05	7.88	8.92	8.15
	.01	10.37	11.74	10.73
Spelling	.05	8.67	9.04	8.78
	.01	11.41	11.90	11.56
Pseudoword Decoding	.05	5.38	5.54	5.54
	.01	7.09	7.29	7.29
Math Reasoning	.05	8.46	8.69	8.97
	.01	11.14	11.44	11.81
Written Expression	.05	10.89	11.04	11.14
	.01	14.33	14.53	14.66
Listening Comprehension	.05	13.48	14.11	13.67
	.01	17.74	18.58	18.00
Oral Expression	.05	11.69	12.03	11.91
	.01	15.39	15.83	15.67
Reading	.05	5.22	6.40	5.55
	.01	6.87	8.42	7.31
Mathematics	.05	6.17	6.56	6.95
	.01	8.13	8.64	9.15
Written Language	.05	7.69	8.06	7.97
	.01	10.13	10.61	10.49
Oral Language	.05	10.70	11.46	11.02
	.01	14.09	15.09	14.51
Total Achievement	.05	5.54	6.60	6.20
	.01	7.29	8.69	8.16

Table B.5   Differences Between Predicted and Obtained WIAT–II Subtest and Composite Scores for Various Percentages of the Theoretical Normal Distribution (Base Rates): Predicted-Difference Method Using WAIS–IV FSIQ

Subtest/Composite	Percentage of Theoretical Normal Distribution (Base Rates)								
	25%	20%	15%	10%	5%	4%	3%	2%	1%
Word Reading	8	10	12	15	19	20	22	24	27
Numerical Operations	7	8	10	13	16	17	18	20	22
Reading Comprehension	7	9	10	13	16	17	19	20	23
Spelling	9	11	13	16	20	22	23	25	29
Pseudoword Decoding	10	12	15	18	23	24	26	28	32
Math Reasoning	7	8	10	12	15	16	17	19	21
Written Expression	9	11	13	16	20	22	23	25	28
Listening Comprehension	8	9	11	14	18	19	20	22	25
Oral Expression	8	10	12	15	19	21	22	24	27
Reading	7	9	11	13	17	18	19	21	23
Mathematics	6	7	9	11	14	15	16	17	19
Written Language	8	10	12	15	19	20	22	24	27
Oral Language	7	8	10	12	16	17	18	19	22
Total Achievement	5	6	8	10	12	13	14	15	17

Table B.6   Differences Between Predicted and Obtained WIAT–II Subtest and Composite Scores for Various Percentages of the Theoretical Normal Distribution (Base Rates): Predicted-Difference Method Using WAIS–IV VCI

Subtest/Composite	Percentage of Theoretical Normal Distribution (Base Rates)								
	25%	20%	15%	10%	5%	4%	3%	2%	1%
Word Reading	8	10	13	15	20	21	22	24	28
Numerical Operations	9	11	13	16	20	22	23	25	29
Reading Comprehension	7	8	10	12	15	16	17	19	21
Spelling	9	11	14	17	21	23	24	26	30
Pseudoword Decoding	10	12	15	19	24	25	27	30	33
Math Reasoning	9	11	13	16	20	22	23	25	29
Written Expression	9	12	14	17	22	24	25	28	31
Listening Comprehension	7	8	10	13	16	17	18	20	22
Oral Expression	9	11	13	16	20	22	23	25	29
Reading	7	9	11	13	17	18	19	21	24
Mathematics	8	10	13	15	20	21	22	24	28
Written Language	9	11	13	17	21	22	24	26	30
Oral Language	7	8	10	12	15	16	17	19	21
Total Achievement	7	8	10	13	16	17	18	20	22

Table B.7   Differences Between Predicted and Obtained WIAT–II Subtest and Composite Scores for Various Percentages of the Theoretical Normal Distribution (Base Rates): Predicted-Difference Method Using WAIS–IV PRI

Subtest/Composite	Percentage of Theoretical Normal Distribution (Base Rates)								
	25%	20%	15%	10%	5%	4%	3%	2%	1%
Word Reading	9	12	14	17	22	24	25	28	31
Numerical Operations	8	10	12	15	19	20	22	24	27
Reading Comprehension	9	11	13	16	21	22	23	26	29
Spelling	10	12	15	18	23	24	26	28	32
Pseudoword Decoding	10	12	15	19	24	25	27	30	33
Math Reasoning	8	10	12	15	19	20	21	23	26
Written Expression	9	11	14	17	22	23	25	27	30
Listening Comprehension	9	11	13	16	21	22	24	26	29
Oral Expression	9	11	14	17	21	23	24	27	30
Reading	9	11	13	16	21	22	24	26	29
Mathematics	8	9	11	14	18	19	20	22	25
Written Language	9	11	14	17	22	23	25	27	30
Oral Language	8	10	12	15	19	21	22	24	27
Total Achievement	8	10	12	14	18	19	21	23	25

Table B.8   Differences Between WAIS–IV FSIQ, VCI, and PRI Scores and WIAT–II Subtest and Composite Scores Required for Statistical Significance (Critical Values): Simple-Difference Method for Ages 16:0–19:11

Subtest/Composite	Significance Level	FSIQ	VCI	PRI
Word Reading	.05	7.78	9.30	9.30
	.01	10.24	12.24	12.24
Numerical Operations	.05	8.32	9.75	9.75
	.01	10.95	12.84	12.84
Reading Comprehension	.05	8.32	9.75	9.75
	.01	10.95	12.84	12.84
Spelling	.05	9.30	10.60	10.60
	.01	12.24	13.95	13.95
Pseudoword Decoding	.05	6.57	8.32	8.32
	.01	8.65	10.95	10.95
Math Reasoning	.05	8.82	10.18	10.18
	.01	11.61	13.41	13.41
Written Expression	.05	11.39	12.47	12.47
	.01	14.99	16.42	16.42
Listening Comprehension	.05	13.79	14.70	14.70
	.01	18.15	19.35	19.35
Oral Expression	.05	12.12	13.15	13.15
	.01	15.96	17.31	17.31
Reading	.05	5.88	7.78	7.78
	.01	7.74	10.24	10.24
Mathematics	.05	6.57	8.32	8.32
	.01	8.65	10.95	10.95
Written Language	.05	8.32	9.75	9.75
	.01	10.95	12.84	12.84
Oral Language	.05	11.00	12.12	12.12
	.01	14.48	15.96	15.96
Total Achievement	.05	5.88	7.78	7.78
	.01	7.74	10.24	10.24

Table B.9   Differences Between WAIS–IV FSIQ Scores and WIAT–II Subtest and Composite Scores for Various Percentages of the Theoretical Normal Distribution (Base Rates): Simple-Difference Method

Subtest/Composite	Percentage of Theoretical Normal Distribution (Base Rates)								
	25%	20%	15%	10%	5%	4%	3%	2%	1%
Word Reading	9	11	14	17	21	22	24	26	30
Numerical Operations	7	9	11	13	17	18	19	21	24
Reading Comprehension	7	9	11	14	17	18	20	21	24
Spelling	10	12	15	18	23	24	26	28	32
Pseudoword Decoding	11	14	17	21	27	29	31	34	38
Math Reasoning	7	8	10	13	16	17	18	20	23
Written Expression	10	12	14	18	23	24	26	28	32
Listening Comprehension	8	10	12	15	19	20	22	24	27
Oral Expression	9	11	14	17	21	23	24	27	30
Reading	8	9	11	14	18	19	20	22	25
Mathematics	6	8	9	11	14	15	16	18	20
Written Language	9	11	14	17	21	22	24	26	30
Oral Language	7	9	11	13	16	18	19	20	23
Total Achievement	5	7	8	10	13	13	14	16	18

Note. Percentages represent the theoretical proportion of WIAT–II scores lower than WAIS–IV FSIQ scores by the specified amount or more.

Table B.10   Differences Between WAIS–IV VCI Scores and WIAT–II Subtest and Composite Scores for Various Percentages of the Theoretical Normal Distribution (Base Rates): Simple-Difference Method

Subtest/Composite	Percentage of Theoretical Normal Distribution (Base Rates)								
	25%	20%	15%	10%	5%	4%	3%	2%	1%
Word Reading	9	11	14	17	22	23	25	27	31
Numerical Operations	10	12	15	18	23	24	26	28	32
Reading Comprehension	7	8	10	13	16	17	18	20	23
Spelling	10	13	15	19	24	26	28	30	34
Pseudoword Decoding	12	15	18	23	29	31	33	36	41
Math Reasoning	10	12	15	18	23	24	26	28	32
Written Expression	11	13	17	20	26	28	30	32	36
Listening Comprehension	7	9	11	13	17	18	19	21	24
Oral Expression	10	12	15	18	23	24	26	28	32
Reading	8	10	12	14	18	19	21	23	26
Mathematics	9	11	14	17	22	23	25	27	31
Written Language	10	12	15	19	24	25	27	30	34
Oral Language	7	8	10	13	16	17	18	20	23
Total Achievement	7	9	11	13	17	18	19	21	24

Note. Percentages represent the theoretical proportion of WIAT–II scores lower than WAIS–IV VCI scores by the specified amount or more.

Table B.11   Differences Between WAIS–IV PRI Scores and WIAT–II Subtest and Composite Scores for Various Percentages of the Theoretical Normal Distribution (Base Rates): Simple-Difference Method

Subtest/Composite	Percentage of Theoretical Normal Distribution (Base Rates)								
	25%	20%	15%	10%	5%	4%	3%	2%	1%
Word Reading	11	13	16	20	26	27	29	32	36
Numerical Operations	9	11	13	16	21	22	24	26	29
Reading Comprehension	10	12	15	18	23	25	26	29	32
Spelling	11	14	17	21	27	29	31	33	38
Pseudoword Decoding	12	15	18	23	29	31	33	36	41
Math Reasoning	9	11	13	16	20	22	23	25	28
Written Expression	10	13	16	19	25	26	28	31	35
Listening Comprehension	10	12	15	18	23	25	27	29	33
Oral Expression	10	13	16	19	24	26	28	30	34
Reading	10	12	15	19	24	25	27	29	33
Mathematics	8	10	12	15	19	20	22	24	27
Written Language	10	13	16	19	25	26	28	31	35
Oral Language	9	11	14	17	21	23	24	27	30
Total Achievement	8	10	13	15	20	21	22	24	28

Note. Percentages represent the theoretical proportion of WIAT–II scores lower than WAIS–IV PRI scores by the specified amount or more.

Derivation and Use of the GAI

Overview

The GAI is a composite score that is based on the three Verbal Comprehension subtests and the three Perceptual Reasoning subtests that contribute to the VCI and PRI. The GAI does not include the Working Memory or Processing Speed subtests that contribute to the FSIQ.

Evolution of the GAI

The introduction of four index scores in the WAIS–III gave practitioners the flexibility to select the composite scores that best described verbal and perceptual ability, based on the outcome of the assessment. When necessary to aid in interpretation, the practitioner could describe verbal abilities, using the VCI in place of the VIQ, and describe perceptual abilities, using the POI in place of the PIQ. This flexibility was particularly useful when the VIQ was considered less descriptive of verbal ability than the VCI because Arithmetic—a Working Memory subtest—was discrepant from the Verbal Comprehension subtests at a level that was unusual in the normative sample, and when the PIQ was considered less descriptive of perceptual ability than the POI because Coding—a Processing Speed subtest—was discrepant from the Perceptual Organization subtests at a level that was unusual in the normative sample.

The WAIS–IV, however, no longer utilizes the dual IQ and index score structure. Instead, the WAIS–IV provides an FSIQ and a four-index framework similar to that of the WISC–IV. The framework is based on contemporary intelligence theory and is supported by clinical research and factor-analytic results. The elimination of the VIQ and PIQ reduces concerns about the influence of working memory and processing speed when summarizing verbal comprehension and perceptual reasoning abilities, respectively. The WAIS–IV FSIQ, however, includes (to a greater extent than the WAIS–III FSIQ) the influence of working memory and processing speed to reflect research that suggests both are important factors that contribute to overall intellectual functioning (Engle, Tuholski, Laughlin, & Conway, 1999; Fry & Hale, 1996; Süß, Oberauer, Wittmann, Wilhelm, & Schulze, 2002; Vigil-Colet & Codorniu-Raga, 2002). Recent research continues to confirm the importance of working memory and processing speed to cognitive ability and to refine knowledge about the nature of these relations (Colom, Rebollo, Palacios, Juan-Espinosa, & Kyllonen, 2004; Mackintosh & Bennett, 2003; Schweizer & Moosbrugger, 2004).

The FSIQ is used most frequently to describe an underlying, global aspect of general intelligence, or *g*. As used in clinical practice, the FSIQ serves a number of purposes. It can function as a summary of performance across a number of specific cognitive ability domains (i.e., Verbal Comprehension, Perceptual Reasoning, Working Memory, and Processing Speed). It is used for contextual comparisons with other measures in neuropsychological evaluations; in conjunction with other information as part of a diagnostic evaluation in clinics and hospital settings; to make decisions about services to be provided by local, state, or federal agencies (e.g., Social Security disability evaluations); to inform level of care and placement in residential settings; and to determine eligibility for special education services in public school settings.

The FSIQ is an aggregate score that summarizes performance across multiple cognitive abilities in a single number. When unusual variability is observed within the index scores or subtests that comprise the FSIQ, clinical interpretation should characterize this diversity of abilities.

The GAI was first developed for use with the WISC–III by Prifitera, Weiss, and Saklofske (1998). It provided a summary score to measure general cognitive ability based on the sum of scaled scores for all subtests that contributed to the traditional 10-subtest FSIQ, with the exception of Arithmetic and Coding. The eight remaining subtests were those used to compute the WISC–III VCI and POI. The GAI was recommended as a useful composite to estimate overall ability if a great deal of variability existed within VIQ and/or PIQ due to low scores on Arithmetic and/or Coding (Prifitera et al., 1998).

Subsequently, the WAIS–III GAI was developed (Tulsky, Saklofske, Wilkins, & Weiss, 2001). It included the subtests that contributed to the WAIS–III VCI and POI: Matrix Reasoning, Block Design, Vocabulary, Similarities, Information, and Picture Completion. The WISC–IV GAI similarly includes the subtests that contribute to the VCI and the PRI: Block Design, Similarities, Picture Concepts, Vocabulary, Matrix Reasoning, and Comprehension (Raiford, Weiss, Rolfhus, & Coalson, 2005; Saklofske, Prifitera, Weiss, Rolfhus, & Zhu, 2005).

Introduction to the WAIS–IV GAI

As with the WAIS–III GAI and the WISC–IV GAI, the WAIS–IV GAI provides the practitioner with a summary score that is less sensitive than the FSIQ to the influence of working memory and processing speed. For examinees with neuropsychological problems, such as ADHD, TBI, or dementia, difficulties with working memory and processing speed may result in lower FSIQ scores than examinees without neuropsychological problems (Raiford et al., 2005; Wechsler, 1997a, 2003). The GAI is less sensitive when working memory performance is discrepant from verbal comprehension performance, and/or when processing speed performance is discrepant from perceptual reasoning performance, at an unusual level. It can be compared to the FSIQ to assess the effects of working memory and processing speed on the expression of cognitive ability. For examinees with intact neuropsychological functioning, the GAI may provide a comparable approximation of overall intellectual ability, as represented by the FSIQ (Saklofske et al., 2005; Tulsky et al., 2001).

In general, the FSIQ is considered the most valid measure of overall cognitive ability. Working memory and processing speed are vital to the comprehensive evaluation of cognitive ability, and excluding measures of these abilities from a summary score reduces its breadth of construct coverage. In the presence of neuropsychological deficits, however, performance on the Working Memory and Processing Speed subtests that contribute to the FSIQ is more likely to be impaired than performance on the Verbal Comprehension and Perceptual Reasoning subtests. In these situations, impaired performance on the Working Memory and Processing Speed subtests may mask actual differences between general cognitive ability (represented by the FSIQ) and other cognitive functions (e.g., memory). The GAI was developed specifically to help practitioners with the identification of relative strengths and weaknesses that are based on comparisons between ability and other cognitive functions. The GAI does not replace the FSIQ, but it should be reported and interpreted along with the FSIQ and all index scores, including the WMI and PSI 3.

When to Use the GAI

The impact of neuropsychological problems related to working memory and/or processing speed deficiencies is evident in Table C.4, which shows that FSIQ < GAI discrepancies were obtained by more than 65% of the examinees in the following WAIS–IV special group samples: Intellectual Disability-Mild Severity, Intellectual Disability-Moderate Severity, Borderline Intellectual Functioning, ADHD, TBI, Autistic Disorder, Asperger's Disorder, and Probable Dementia of the Alzheimer's Type-Mild Severity. In these situations, the reduction in the FSIQ related to working memory and/or processing speed difficulties may complicate contextual interpretation of performance on other tests, such as measures of memory, executive function, or achievement. When assessing an examinee who presents with potential neuropsychological issues, the GAI may be useful to clarify interpretation. For example, if the referral question involves memory impairment, the GAI may be less sensitive to age-related cognitive decline than the FSIQ. The forthcoming *WMS–IV Technical and Interpretive Manual* (Wechsler, in press) will provide information regarding the use of ability-memory comparisons using the GAI.

The use of the WISC–IV GAI in educational settings has been discussed in Raiford et al., 2005. The WAIS–IV GAI may be used similarly to the WISC–IV GAI, as permitted by local and state education agencies. Tables C.5–C.9 are provided for use in ability-achievement discrepancy comparisons between the WAIS–IV GAI and the WIAT–II.

For other examinees with working memory and/or processing speed difficulties, it also may be clinically informative to evaluate the reduced impact of these abilities on an estimate of general cognitive ability by comparing the FSIQ and the GAI. This comparison may inform rehabilitation programs and/or educational intervention planning. More information about interpretation of such comparisons is available in Saklofske, Weiss, Raiford, and Prifitera (2006).

The practitioner may wish to consider using the GAI in a number of clinical situations, not limited to, but including the following:

- a significant and unusual discrepancy exists between VCI and WMI,

- a significant and unusual discrepancy exists between PRI and PSI,

- a significant and unusual discrepancy exists between WMI and PSI, or

- a significant and unusual subtest discrepancy between subtests within WMI and/or PSI.

To evaluate index score discrepancies, refer to chapter 2 and Tables B.1 and B.2 in the Administration and Scoring Manual. The Analysis page of the Record Form provides space for pairwise discrepancy comparisons in the Discrepancy Comparison table. A statistically significant difference between index scores, however, may not indicate that there is a clinically significant difference: The frequency of occurrence in the normative sample (base rate), not just the critical value, should be considered. Use Table B.2 to obtain the base rate for a given discrepancy. Sattler (2008a) suggests that any statistically significant difference is potentially meaningful and that differences between scores that occur in less than 15% of the normative sample should be judged as unusual. Tables B.3 and B.4 provide critical values and base rate information for the subtest-level pairwise comparisons related to the WMI and PSI (i.e., Digit Span–Arithmetic and Symbol Search–Coding).

Deriving and Analyzing the GAI

The GAI is derived using a similar procedure to that described for the FSIQ in chapter 2 of the Administration and Scoring Manual. The following steps are provided as a guide for deriving the GAI and comparing it to the FSIQ to obtain more information about an examinee's cognitive ability.

Step 1. Obtain the General Ability Sum of Scaled Scores

Calculate the General Ability sum of scaled scores, which is the sum of scaled scores for three Verbal Comprehension subtests, typically Similarities, Vocabulary, and Information, and three Perceptual Reasoning subtests, typically Block Design, Matrix Reasoning, and Visual Puzzles. Record the General Ability sum of scaled scores.

Limiting Substitution and Proration on the GAI

The normative information for the GAI is based on core subtests. Substitution of supplemental subtests and the use of prorated sums of scaled scores may introduce additional measurement error into composite scores. Restricting the use of substitution and proration limits possible sources of measurement error. The following restrictions apply to the use of subtest substitution and proration in isolation and in combination when deriving the GAI.

■   No more than two substitutions are allowed for the GAI, and, if two are necessary, they must come from different index scales (i.e., the Verbal Comprehension and Perceptual Reasoning index scales).

■   If both substitution and proration are required to derive the GAI, one substitution and one prorated sum of scaled scores are allowed, but they must occur on different index scales. For example, the GAI could be derived from a prorated sum of scaled scores for the VCI and the sum of scaled scores for the PRI with one substitution (e.g., Figure Weights was substituted for Block Design).

Invalidating the GAI

If an examinee obtains a total raw score of 0 (zero) on a subtest, that score does not indicate that the examinee entirely lacks the ability measured by the subtest. It indicates rather that the examinee's ability cannot be determined by the particular set of subtest items. For example, an examinee may score 0 points on Vocabulary but still know the names of some objects or the meanings of some easier words. If an examinee obtains total raw scores of 0 on two of the three subtests that contribute to the VCI, including potential substitutions, the GAI cannot be derived. Similarly, if an examinee obtains 0 points on two of the three subtests that contribute to the PRI, including potential substitutions, the GAI cannot be derived.

Step 2. Determine the GAI Score

Locate the General Ability sum of scaled scores in the shaded columns of Table C.1. Read across the row to determine the GAI score, as well as its corresponding percentile rank and confidence interval. Record the GAI score, the percentile rank, and the confidence interval (90% or 95%).

Table C.1   GAI Equivalents of Sums of Scaled Scores

Sum of Scaled Scores	GAI	Percentile Rank	Confidence Level 90%	Confidence Level 95%	Sum of Scaled Scores	GAI	Percentile Rank	Confidence Level 90%	Confidence Level 95%
6	40	<0.1	38–46	37–47	61	101	53	97–105	96–106
7	41	<0.1	39–47	38–48	62	101	53	97–105	96–106
8	42	<0.1	40–48	39–49	63	102	55	98–106	97–107
9	44	<0.1	42–50	41–51	64	103	58	99–107	98–108
10	45	<0.1	43–51	42–52	65	104	61	100–108	99–109
11	46	<0.1	43–52	43–53	66	105	63	101–109	100–110
12	48	<0.1	45–54	45–54	67	106	66	102–110	101–111
13	49	<0.1	46–55	46–55	68	107	68	103–111	102–112
14	50	<0.1	47–56	47–56	69	108	70	104–112	103–113
15	52	0.1	49–58	49–58	70	110	75	106–114	105–115
16	53	0.1	50–59	49–59	71	111	77	107–115	106–116
17	54	0.1	51–60	50–60	72	112	79	107–116	107–117
18	55	0.1	52–60	51–61	73	113	81	108–117	108–118
19	56	0.2	53–61	52–62	74	114	82	109–118	109–119
20	57	0.2	54–62	53–63	75	115	84	110–119	110–119
21	58	0.3	55–63	54–64	76	117	87	112–121	112–121
22	59	0.3	56–64	55–65	77	118	88	113–122	113–122
23	60	0.4	57–65	56–66	78	120	91	115–124	114–124
24	61	0.5	58–66	57–67	79	121	92	116–125	115–125
25	63	1	60–68	59–69	80	122	93	117–125	116–126
26	64	1	61–69	60–70	81	123	94	118–126	117–127
27	65	1	62–70	61–71	82	124	95	119–127	118–128
28	67	1	64–72	63–73	83	125	95	120–128	119–129
29	68	2	65–73	64–74	84	126	96	121–129	120–130
30	69	2	66–74	65–75	85	127	96	122–130	121–131
31	70	2	67–75	66–76	86	128	97	123–131	122–132
32	71	3	68–76	67–77	87	130	98	125–133	124–134
33	72	3	69–77	68–78	88	131	98	126–134	125–135
34	73	4	70–78	69–79	89	132	98	127–135	126–136
35	74	4	71–79	70–80	90	133	99	128–136	127–137
36	75	5	72–80	71–81	91	135	99	130–138	129–139
37	76	5	73–81	72–82	92	136	99	131–139	130–140
38	77	6	74–82	73–83	93	137	99	132–140	131–141
39	78	7	75–83	74–84	94	139	99.5	134–142	133–143
40	79	8	75–84	75–85	95	141	99.7	136–144	135–145
41	80	9	76–85	76–86	96	142	99.7	137–145	136–146
42	80	9	76–85	76–86	97	144	99.8	139–147	138–148
43	81	10	77–86	77–87	98	145	99.9	140–148	139–149
44	82	12	78–87	78–87	99	147	99.9	141–150	141–151
45	83	13	79–88	79–88	100	148	99.9	142–151	142–151
46	84	14	80–89	80–89	101	150	>99.9	144–153	144–153
47	86	18	82–91	81–91	102	151	>99.9	145–154	145–154
48	87	19	83–92	82–92	103	153	>99.9	147–156	146–156
49	88	21	84–93	83–93	104	154	>99.9	148–157	147–157
50	89	23	85–93	84–94	105	156	>99.9	150–158	149–159
51	91	27	87–95	86–96	106	157	>99.9	151–159	150–160
52	92	30	88–96	87–97	107	159	>99.9	153–161	152–162
53	93	32	89–97	88–98	108	160	>99.9	154–162	153–163
54	94	34	90–98	89–99	109	160	>99.9	154–162	153–163
55	95	37	91–99	90–100	110	160	>99.9	154–162	153–163
56	96	39	92–100	91–101	111	160	>99.9	154–162	153–163
57	97	42	93–101	92–102	112	160	>99.9	154–162	153–163
58	98	45	94–102	93–103	113	160	>99.9	154–162	153–163
59	99	47	95–103	94–104	114	160	>99.9	154–162	153–163
60	100	50	96–104	95–105					

Step 3. Perform the FSIQ–GAI Discrepancy Comparison

To perform the FSIQ–GAI discrepancy comparison, calculate the difference between the FSIQ and the GAI by subtracting the GAI score from the FSIQ score, remembering to note if the resulting value is positive or negative. Record this value. Table C.2 provides the required differences between the FSIQ and the GAI to attain statistical significance (critical values) at the .15 and .05 levels for each age group. Using Table C.2, find the examinee's age group and the desired level of significance. Read across the row to the appropriate column to determine the critical value, and record this value. Determine whether or not the absolute value of the examinee's difference score equals or exceeds the corresponding critical value. The absolute value of the examinee's difference score must equal or exceed that critical value to be statistically significant.

Table C.2   Differences Between the FSIQ and the GAI Required for Statistical Significance (Critical Values), by Age Group and Overall Normative Sample

Age Group	Level of Significance	Critical Value
16–17	.15	5.72
	.05	7.78
18–19	.15	4.83
	.05	6.58
20–24	.15	4.83
	.05	6.58
25–29	.15	4.83
	.05	6.58
30–34	.15	4.83
	.05	6.58
35–44	.15	4.83
	.05	6.58
45–54	.15	4.32
	.05	5.88
55–64	.15	4.83
	.05	6.58
65–69	.15	4.32
	.05	5.88
70–74	.15	4.83
	.05	6.58
75–79	.15	4.83
	.05	6.58
80–84	.15	4.83
	.05	6.58
85–90	.15	4.83
	.05	6.58
All Ages	.15	4.83
	.05	6.58

Note. Differences required for statistical significance are based on the standard errors of measurement of each composite score for each age group and calculated with the following formula:

$$\text{Critical Value of Difference Score} = Z\sqrt{SEM_a^2 + SEM_b^2}$$

where Z is the normal curve value associated with the desired two-tailed significance level and SEM_a and SEM_b are the standard errors of measurement for the two index scores.

Table C.3 provides the percentage of examinees in the WAIS–IV normative sample that obtained the same or greater discrepancy between the FSIQ and the GAI (base rate). The values reported in Table C.3 are provided for the overall normative sample and by ability level, and are separated into "-" and "+" columns, based on the direction of the difference. Locate the absolute value of the examinee's difference score in the Amount of Discrepancy column to the extreme left or right, and read across the row to the column that corresponds to the direction of the difference score (e.g., FSIQ < GAI) either by the overall sample or by ability level. Record this value.

Table C.3   Cumulative Percentages of Normative Sample (Base Rates) Obtaining Various FSIQ–GAI Discrepancies, by Overall Sample and GAI Ability Level

Amount of Discrepancy	Overall Sample		GAI ≤ 79		80 ≤ GAI ≤ 89		90 ≤ GAI ≤ 109		110 ≤ GAI ≤ 119		GAI ≥ 120		Amount of Discrepancy
	FSIQ<GAI (−)	FSIQ>GAI (+)	FSIQ<GAI (−)	FSIQ>GAI (+)	FSIQ<GAI (−)	FSIQ>GAI (+)	FSIQ<GAI (−)	FSIQ>GAI (+)	FSIQ<GAI (−)	FSIQ>GAI (+)	FSIQ<GAI (−)	FSIQ>GAI (+)	
≥40	0.0	0.0	0.0	0.0	0.0	0.0	0.0	0.0	0.0	0.0	0.0	0.0	≥40
39	0.0	0.0	0.0	0.0	0.0	0.0	0.0	0.0	0.0	0.0	0.0	0.0	39
38	0.0	0.0	0.0	0.0	0.0	0.0	0.0	0.0	0.0	0.0	0.0	0.0	38
37	0.0	0.0	0.0	0.0	0.0	0.0	0.0	0.0	0.0	0.0	0.0	0.0	37
36	0.0	0.0	0.0	0.0	0.0	0.0	0.0	0.0	0.0	0.0	0.0	0.0	36
35	0.0	0.0	0.0	0.0	0.0	0.0	0.0	0.0	0.0	0.0	0.0	0.0	35
34	0.0	0.0	0.0	0.0	0.0	0.0	0.0	0.0	0.0	0.0	0.0	0.0	34
33	0.0	0.0	0.0	0.0	0.0	0.0	0.0	0.0	0.0	0.0	0.0	0.0	33
32	0.0	0.0	0.0	0.0	0.0	0.0	0.0	0.0	0.0	0.0	0.0	0.0	32
31	0.0	0.0	0.0	0.0	0.0	0.0	0.0	0.0	0.0	0.0	0.0	0.0	31
30	0.0	0.0	0.0	0.0	0.0	0.0	0.0	0.0	0.0	0.0	0.0	0.0	30
29	0.0	0.0	0.0	0.0	0.0	0.0	0.0	0.0	0.0	0.0	0.0	0.0	29
28	0.0	0.0	0.0	0.0	0.0	0.0	0.0	0.0	0.0	0.0	0.0	0.0	28
27	0.0	0.0	0.0	0.0	0.0	0.0	0.0	0.0	0.0	0.0	0.0	0.0	27
26	0.0	0.0	0.0	0.0	0.0	0.0	0.0	0.0	0.0	0.0	0.0	0.0	26
25	0.0	0.0	0.0	0.0	0.0	0.0	0.0	0.0	0.0	0.0	0.0	0.0	25
24	0.0	0.0	0.0	0.0	0.0	0.0	0.0	0.0	0.0	0.0	0.0	0.0	24
23	0.0	0.0	0.0	0.0	0.0	0.0	0.0	0.0	0.0	0.0	0.0	0.0	23
22	0.0	0.0	0.0	0.0	0.0	0.0	0.0	0.0	0.0	0.0	0.0	0.0	22
21	0.0	0.0	0.0	0.0	0.0	0.0	0.0	0.0	0.0	0.0	0.0	0.0	21
20	0.0	0.0	0.0	0.0	0.0	0.0	0.0	0.0	0.0	0.0	0.0	0.0	20
19	0.0	0.0	0.0	0.0	0.0	0.0	0.0	0.0	0.0	0.0	0.0	0.0	19
18	0.0	0.0	0.0	0.0	0.0	0.0	0.0	0.0	0.0	0.0	0.0	0.0	18
17	0.0	0.0	0.0	0.0	0.0	0.0	0.0	0.0	0.0	0.0	0.4	0.0	17
16	0.0	0.0	0.0	0.0	0.0	0.0	0.0	0.0	0.0	0.0	0.4	0.0	16
15	0.0	0.1	0.0	0.0	0.0	0.0	0.0	0.1	0.0	0.3	0.4	0.0	15
14	0.2	0.2	0.0	0.0	0.0	0.0	0.0	0.2	0.0	0.9	1.6	0.0	14
13	0.4	0.4	0.0	1.0	0.0	0.0	0.1	0.4	0.0	0.9	3.2	0.0	13
12	0.7	0.7	0.0	1.5	0.0	0.6	0.5	0.5	0.6	1.5	3.6	0.0	12
11	1.5	1.3	0.0	2.1	0.0	1.5	1.0	1.2	1.9	1.9	6.0	0.0	11
10	2.3	2.2	1.0	2.6	0.3	2.1	1.6	2.1	3.7	2.5	7.1	2.0	10
9	3.6	3.4	1.0	3.1	0.9	4.0	2.7	3.4	5.6	3.4	10.7	2.8	9
8	5.7	5.2	1.5	4.6	1.5	7.1	4.0	5.3	8.6	3.7	17.9	4.8	8
7	8.1	8.0	4.1	6.7	2.8	10.1	6.4	8.5	10.8	5.6	22.2	7.1	7
6	12.4	11.6	7.7	8.8	5.2	14.1	10.2	12.6	15.4	9.9	31.0	8.7	6
5	17.6	17.4	14.4	12.9	10.1	23.3	13.9	19.6	21.0	11.7	41.7	11.1	5
4	23.8	23.3	21.1	21.6	13.2	31.6	19.7	25.4	28.7	16.7	50.8	13.5	4
3	30.3	30.1	28.9	27.8	18.7	38.0	25.3	33.8	38.0	21.6	58.3	16.3	3
2	37.6	38.4	37.6	36.1	24.2	47.2	33.2	42.5	44.4	31.5	65.5	19.4	2
1	44.9	46.3	49.5	41.2	32.5	55.8	40.0	51.5	51.5	39.2	69.8	24.2	1
Mean	4.2	4.1	3.4	4.1	3.4	4.2	4.0	4.0	4.5	3.9	5.6	4.5	Mean
SD	2.7	2.7	2.1	2.8	2.2	2.6	2.6	2.6	2.8	3.0	3.2	2.9	SD
Median	4.0	4.0	3.0	4.0	3.0	4.0	3.0	3.0	4.0	3.0	5.0	4.0	Median

In some situations, practitioners may wish to determine how unusual the same or greater FSIQ–GAI discrepancy was in a particular special group sample. Table C.4 provides cumulative percentages (base rates) of obtained FSIQ-GAI discrepancies for the 13 special group samples described in chapter 5.

To determine how rare or common the examinee's difference score is relative to a special group of interest, use Table C.4 and locate the absolute value of the examinee's difference score in the Amount of Discrepancy column to the extreme left or right. Read across the row to the column that corresponds to the special group of interest and the direction of the difference score (e.g., FSIQ < GAI). Record this value, remembering to note that this particular base rate pertains to a special group sample rather than to the normative sample.

Table C.4   Cumulative Percentages of Various Special Group Samples (Base Rates) Obtaining Various FSIQ–GAI Score Discrepancies

Amount of Discrepancy	Clinical Group														Amount of Discrepancy
	GT		ID Mild		ID Moderate		BIF		RD		MD		ADHD		
	FSIQ<GAI (-)	FSIQ>GAI (+)	FSIQ<GAI (-)	FSIQ>GAI (+)	FSIQ<GAI (-)	FSIQ>GAI (+)	FSIQ<GAI (-)	FSIQ>GAI (+)	FSIQ<GAI (-)	FSIQ>GAI (+)	FSIQ<GAI (-)	FSIQ>GAI (+)	FSIQ<GAI (-)	FSIQ>GAI (+)	
≥40	0.0	0.0	0.0	0.0	0.0	0.0	0.0	0.0	0.0	0.0	0.0	0.0	0.0	0.0	≥40
39	0.0	0.0	0.0	0.0	0.0	0.0	0.0	0.0	0.0	0.0	0.0	0.0	0.0	0.0	39
38	0.0	0.0	0.0	0.0	0.0	0.0	0.0	0.0	0.0	0.0	0.0	0.0	0.0	0.0	38
37	0.0	0.0	0.0	0.0	0.0	0.0	0.0	0.0	0.0	0.0	0.0	0.0	0.0	0.0	37
36	0.0	0.0	0.0	0.0	0.0	0.0	0.0	0.0	0.0	0.0	0.0	0.0	0.0	0.0	36
35	0.0	0.0	0.0	0.0	0.0	0.0	0.0	0.0	0.0	0.0	0.0	0.0	0.0	0.0	35
34	0.0	0.0	0.0	0.0	0.0	0.0	0.0	0.0	0.0	0.0	0.0	0.0	0.0	0.0	34
33	0.0	0.0	0.0	0.0	0.0	0.0	0.0	0.0	0.0	0.0	0.0	0.0	0.0	0.0	33
32	0.0	0.0	0.0	0.0	0.0	0.0	0.0	0.0	0.0	0.0	0.0	0.0	0.0	0.0	32
31	0.0	0.0	0.0	0.0	0.0	0.0	0.0	0.0	0.0	0.0	0.0	0.0	0.0	0.0	31
30	0.0	0.0	0.0	0.0	0.0	0.0	0.0	0.0	0.0	0.0	0.0	0.0	0.0	0.0	30
29	0.0	0.0	0.0	0.0	0.0	0.0	0.0	0.0	0.0	0.0	0.0	0.0	0.0	0.0	29
28	0.0	0.0	0.0	0.0	0.0	0.0	0.0	0.0	0.0	0.0	0.0	0.0	0.0	0.0	28
27	0.0	0.0	0.0	0.0	0.0	0.0	0.0	0.0	0.0	0.0	0.0	0.0	0.0	0.0	27
26	0.0	0.0	0.0	0.0	0.0	0.0	0.0	0.0	0.0	0.0	0.0	0.0	0.0	0.0	26
25	0.0	0.0	0.0	0.0	0.0	0.0	0.0	0.0	0.0	0.0	0.0	0.0	0.0	0.0	25
24	0.0	0.0	0.0	0.0	0.0	0.0	0.0	0.0	0.0	0.0	0.0	0.0	0.0	0.0	24
23	2.9	2.9	0.0	0.0	0.0	0.0	0.0	0.0	0.0	0.0	0.0	0.0	0.0	0.0	23
22	2.9	2.9	0.0	0.0	0.0	0.0	0.0	0.0	0.0	0.0	0.0	0.0	0.0	0.0	22
21	2.9	2.9	1.4	0.0	0.0	0.0	0.0	0.0	5.9	2.9	2.4	0.0	4.5	0.0	21
20	5.9	2.9	4.1	0.0	0.0	0.0	0.0	0.0	5.9	2.9	2.4	0.0	9.1	0.0	20
19	5.9	5.9	4.1	0.0	0.0	0.0	3.7	0.0	5.9	2.9	7.3	0.0	9.1	0.0	19
18	5.9	8.8	6.8	0.0	0.0	0.0	7.4	0.0	5.9	2.9	9.8	2.4	13.6	0.0	18
17	8.8	8.8	15.1	0.0	3.2	0.0	14.8	3.7	11.8	2.9	14.6	2.4	22.7	0.0	17
16	17.6	11.8	27.4	0.0	25.8	0.0	18.5	7.4	11.8	8.8	14.6	7.3	27.3	2.3	16
15	26.5	14.7	53.4	0.0	38.7	0.0	22.2	7.4	20.6	8.8	22.0	9.8	31.8	4.5	15
14	26.5	20.6	58.9	1.4	58.1	0.0	25.9	11.1	23.5	14.7	26.8	12.2	43.2	6.8	14
13	29.4	26.5	67.1	4.1	67.7	3.2	29.6	11.1	26.5	20.6	39.0	19.5	47.7	9.1	13
12	35.3	35.3	79.5	8.2	83.9	3.2	48.1	18.5	29.4	32.4	48.8	24.4	54.5	9.1	12
11	52.9	38.2	86.3	8.2	90.3	6.5	66.7	22.2	38.2	52.9	53.7	29.3	65.9	18.2	11
Mean	4.2	4.8	4.7	2.7	4.1	2.0	3.6	3.7	5.2	2.9	4.5	3.7	5.1	2.8	Mean
SD	3.5	3.4	2.3	0.8	1.7	1.4	2.7	2.4	4.2	2.6	2.8	2.2	3.5	2.1	SD
Median	4.0	4.0	5.0	2.5	4.0	2.0	2.0	3.0	5.0	2.0	3.5	3.0	4.0	2.0	Median

Note. GT = Intellectually Gifted, ID Mild = Intellectual Disability-Mild Severity, ID Mod = Intellectual Disability-Moderate Severity, BIF = Borderline Intellectual Functioning, RD = Reading Disorder,

Table C.4   Cumulative Percentages of Various Special Group Samples (Base Rates) Obtaining Various FSIQ–GAI Score Discrepancies *(continued)*

Clinical Group

Amount of Discrepancy	TBI FSIQ<GAI (−)	TBI FSIQ>GAI (+)	AUT FSIQ<GAI (−)	AUT FSIQ>GAI (+)	ASP FSIQ<GAI (−)	ASP FSIQ>GAI (+)	DEP FSIQ<GAI (−)	DEP FSIQ>GAI (+)	MCI FSIQ<GAI (−)	MCI FSIQ>GAI (+)	ALZ FSIQ<GAI (−)	ALZ FSIQ>GAI (+)
≥40	0.0	0.0	0.0	0.0	0.0	0.0	0.0	0.0	0.0	0.0	0.0	0.0
39	0.0	0.0	0.0	0.0	0.0	0.0	0.0	0.0	0.0	0.0	0.0	0.0
38	0.0	0.0	0.0	0.0	0.0	0.0	0.0	0.0	0.0	0.0	0.0	0.0
37	0.0	0.0	0.0	0.0	0.0	0.0	0.0	0.0	0.0	0.0	0.0	0.0
36	0.0	0.0	0.0	0.0	0.0	0.0	0.0	0.0	0.0	0.0	0.0	0.0
35	0.0	0.0	0.0	0.0	0.0	0.0	0.0	0.0	0.0	0.0	0.0	0.0
34	0.0	0.0	0.0	0.0	0.0	0.0	0.0	0.0	0.0	0.0	0.0	0.0
33	0.0	0.0	0.0	0.0	0.0	0.0	0.0	0.0	0.0	0.0	0.0	0.0
32	0.0	0.0	0.0	0.0	0.0	0.0	0.0	0.0	0.0	0.0	0.0	0.0
31	0.0	0.0	0.0	0.0	0.0	0.0	0.0	0.0	0.0	0.0	0.0	0.0
30	0.0	0.0	0.0	0.0	0.0	0.0	0.0	0.0	0.0	0.0	0.0	0.0
29	0.0	0.0	0.0	0.0	0.0	0.0	0.0	0.0	0.0	0.0	0.0	0.0
28	0.0	0.0	0.0	0.0	0.0	0.0	0.0	0.0	0.0	0.0	0.0	0.0
27	0.0	0.0	0.0	0.0	0.0	0.0	0.0	0.0	0.0	0.0	0.0	0.0
26	0.0	0.0	0.0	0.0	0.0	0.0	0.0	0.0	0.0	0.0	0.0	0.0
25	0.0	0.0	0.0	0.0	0.0	0.0	0.0	0.0	0.0	0.0	0.0	0.0
24	0.0	0.0	0.0	0.0	0.0	0.0	0.0	0.0	0.0	0.0	0.0	0.0
23	0.0	0.0	0.0	0.0	0.0	0.0	0.0	0.0	0.0	0.0	0.0	0.0
22	0.0	0.0	0.0	0.0	0.0	0.0	0.0	0.0	0.0	0.0	0.0	0.0
21	0.0	0.0	0.0	0.0	0.0	0.0	0.0	0.0	0.0	0.0	0.0	0.0
20	0.0	0.0	0.0	0.0	0.0	0.0	0.0	0.0	0.0	0.0	0.0	0.0
19	0.0	0.0	0.0	0.0	0.0	0.0	0.0	0.0	0.0	0.0	0.0	0.0
18	0.0	0.0	0.0	0.0	5.0	0.0	0.0	0.0	0.0	0.0	0.0	0.0
17	0.0	0.0	0.0	0.0	5.0	0.0	0.0	0.0	0.0	0.0	0.0	0.0
16	0.0	0.0	0.0	0.0	5.0	0.0	0.0	0.0	0.0	0.0	0.0	0.0
15	0.0	0.0	6.3	0.0	5.0	0.0	0.0	0.0	0.0	0.0	0.0	0.0
14	0.0	0.0	6.3	0.0	5.0	0.0	0.0	0.0	0.0	0.0	0.0	0.0
13	0.0	0.0	6.3	0.0	5.0	0.0	2.8	0.0	0.0	0.0	0.0	0.0
12	0.0	0.0	6.3	0.0	7.5	0.0	2.8	0.0	0.0	0.0	0.0	0.0
11	4.5	0.0	6.3	0.0	12.5	0.0	2.8	0.0	0.0	2.5	3.3	0.0
10	4.5	0.0	6.3	0.0	15.0	0.0	5.6	0.0	2.5	5.0	6.7	0.0
9	13.6	0.0	6.3	0.0	22.5	0.0	8.3	0.0	2.5	5.0	6.7	0.0
8	22.7	0.0	12.5	0.0	32.5	0.0	8.3	0.0	5.0	5.0	6.7	0.0
7	27.3	0.0	31.3	0.0	42.5	2.5	11.1	2.8	12.5	7.5	16.7	0.0
6	36.4	0.0	37.5	0.0	47.5	2.5	13.9	2.8	15.0	7.5	40.0	0.0
5	45.5	0.0	37.5	0.0	55.0	2.5	16.7	13.9	25.0	10.0	56.7	0.0
4	50.0	4.5	50.0	6.3	55.0	2.5	27.8	16.7	25.0	15.0	60.0	0.0
3	59.1	9.1	62.5	12.5	65.0	10.0	36.1	22.2	27.5	17.5	70.0	0.0
2	72.7	18.2	68.8	12.5	75.0	10.0	50.0	25.0	32.5	32.5	80.0	0.0
1	81.8	18.2	75.0	12.5	82.5	15.0	55.6	36.1	50.0	35.0	96.7	3.3
Mean	5.1	2.8	5.6	3.5	6.6	3.2	4.4	3.3	4.0	4.0	4.6	1.0
SD	3.1	1.0	3.7	0.7	4.3	2.6	3.2	2.0	2.9	3.1	2.6	—
Median	5.0	2.5	5.0	3.5	7.0	3.0	3.5	3.0	4.0	2.5	5.0	1.0

Note. TBI = Traumatic Brain Injury, AUT = Autistic Disorder, ASP = Asperger's Disorder, DEP = Major Depressive Disorder, MCI = Mild Cognitive Impairment, ALZ = Probable Dementia of the Alzheimer's Type–Mild Severity.

Basic Interpretation of the GAI

Interpretation of the GAI is optional and is designed to complement the 10-step procedure for interpretation of an examinee's WAIS–IV performance that is outlined in chapter 6 Refer to chapter 6 for relevant information about standard scores, percentile ranks, standard error of measurement and confidence intervals, and descriptive classifications. This information is applicable to interpretation of the GAI, as well as the other composite scores.

Evaluate the GAI

The GAI should always be evaluated in the context of the other composite and subtest scores. Significant and unusual discrepancies between the VCI and PRI suggest that the GAI represents a summary of diverse abilities, as does extreme variability among the contributing subtest scores.

Evaluate the FSIQ–GAI Discrepancy

The first step in performing a pairwise comparison is aimed at determining whether the absolute value of the score difference is significant. When the absolute value of the obtained difference between the FSIQ and the GAI is equal to or larger than the critical value, the difference is considered a true difference rather than a difference due to measurement error or random fluctuation. If the two scores are not significantly different, this implies that reducing the influence of working memory and processing speed on the estimate of overall ability resulted in little or no difference.

If comparison of the FSIQ and the GAI indicates a significant difference, the practitioner should then judge how rare the difference is in the normative sample. This base rate provides a basis for estimating how rare or common an examinee's obtained difference score is compared to the general population.

The practitioner may wish to determine how rare or common the examinee's difference score is relative to a WAIS–IV special group sample. This base rate provides a basis for estimating how rare or common an examinee's obtained score difference is compared to the special group sample. It is important to note that the special group studies may not be representative of all individuals from these categories, and this information should be interpreted accordingly (e.g., with attention to the diagnostic criteria listed in Appendix E, as well as demographic characteristics of these samples reported in chapter 5). Furthermore, the small sample size of some clinical groups may elevate the cumulative percentages (base rates).

Ability-Achievement Discrepancy Using the GAI

The evaluation of ability-achievement discrepancies may be used as part of the learning disability determination process. The WAIS–IV provides two methods for comparing intellectual ability and academic achievement: the predicted-difference method and the simple-difference method. Although both methods are used, the predicted-difference method is generally preferred because the formula accounts for the reliabilities of and the correlations between the two measures. Use of the predicted-difference method requires that the ability and achievement measures were co-normed on the same national sample. The predicted-difference method uses the ability score to predict an achievement score, and then compares the predicted and observed achievement scores. The simple-difference method merely compares the observed ability and achievement scores. The *WIAT–II Examiner's Manual: Update 2005* (Harcourt Assessment, 2005) provides additional details related to the rationale for choosing these methods and the statistical procedures involved.

It is important to note that the data for evaluating ability-achievement discrepancies reported in this appendix were based on the sample of examinees who were administered both the WAIS–IV and WIAT–II (see Table 5.4 for demographic details of this sample). All examinees in this sample were currently enrolled in high school and were ages 16:0–19:11. Data pertaining to the use of ability-achievement comparisons should, therefore, only be utilized for examinees with similar demographic characteristics.

Predicted-Difference Method

Table C.5 provides WIAT–II subtest and composite scores predicted from WAIS–IV GAI scores. Locate the GAI score in the extreme left or right column, and read across the row to obtain the examinee's predicted WIAT–II subtest and composite scores. Record the predicted scores. For each subtest or composite, subtract the examinee's predicted score from the obtained score to obtain the difference score. Record these difference scores.

Table C.5   WIAT–II Subtest and Composite Scores Predicted From WAIS–IV GAI Scores

WAIS–IV GAI	WIAT–II														WAIS–IV GAI
	Subtest Scores									Composite Scores					
	WR	NO	RC	SP	PD	MR	WE	LC	OE	RD	MA	WL	OL	TA	
40	63	59	53	68	78	58	67	54	62	56	55	64	51	50	40
41	63	59	54	68	78	59	68	55	63	56	56	65	52	51	41
42	64	60	55	69	79	59	68	56	63	57	57	65	53	52	42
43	65	61	56	69	79	60	69	57	64	58	57	66	54	53	43
44	65	61	56	70	79	61	69	57	65	59	58	66	55	54	44
45	66	62	57	70	80	62	70	58	65	59	59	67	55	54	45
46	67	63	58	71	80	62	70	59	66	60	60	68	56	55	46
47	67	63	59	71	80	63	71	60	67	61	60	68	57	56	47
48	68	64	59	72	81	64	71	60	67	62	61	69	58	57	48
49	68	65	60	72	81	64	72	61	68	62	62	69	59	58	49
50	69	66	61	73	82	65	73	62	69	63	63	70	60	59	50
51	70	66	62	74	82	66	73	63	69	64	63	71	60	59	51
52	70	67	63	74	82	66	74	64	70	64	64	71	61	60	52
53	71	68	63	75	83	67	74	64	70	65	65	72	62	61	53
54	71	68	64	75	83	68	75	65	71	66	66	72	63	62	54
55	72	69	65	76	83	69	75	66	72	67	66	73	64	63	55
56	73	70	66	76	84	69	76	67	72	67	67	74	64	63	56
57	73	70	66	77	84	70	76	67	73	68	68	74	65	64	57
58	74	71	67	77	84	71	77	68	74	69	69	75	66	65	58
59	75	72	68	78	85	71	77	69	74	70	69	75	67	66	59
60	75	72	69	78	85	72	78	70	75	70	70	76	68	67	60
61	76	73	70	79	86	73	79	70	75	71	71	77	68	68	61
62	76	74	70	79	86	73	79	71	76	72	72	77	69	68	62
63	77	74	71	80	86	74	80	72	77	73	72	78	70	69	63
64	78	75	72	81	87	75	80	73	77	73	73	78	71	70	64
65	78	76	73	81	87	76	81	73	78	74	74	79	72	71	65
66	79	77	73	82	87	76	81	74	79	75	75	80	72	72	66
67	80	77	74	82	88	77	82	75	79	76	75	80	73	73	67
68	80	78	75	83	88	78	82	76	80	76	76	81	74	73	68
69	81	79	76	83	89	78	83	76	80	77	77	81	75	74	69
70	81	79	77	84	89	79	84	77	81	78	78	82	76	75	70
71	82	80	77	84	89	80	84	78	82	79	78	83	77	76	71
72	83	81	78	85	90	80	85	79	82	79	79	83	77	77	72
73	83	81	79	85	90	81	85	79	83	80	80	84	78	78	73
74	84	82	80	86	90	82	86	80	84	81	81	84	79	78	74
75	85	83	81	87	91	83	86	81	84	82	81	85	80	79	75
76	85	83	81	87	91	83	87	82	85	82	82	86	81	80	76
77	86	84	82	88	91	84	87	83	86	83	83	86	81	81	77
78	86	85	83	88	92	85	88	83	86	84	84	87	82	82	78
79	87	86	84	89	92	85	88	84	87	84	84	87	83	83	79
80	88	86	84	89	93	86	89	85	87	85	85	88	84	83	80
81	88	87	85	90	93	87	90	86	88	86	86	89	85	84	81
82	89	88	86	90	93	87	90	86	89	87	87	89	85	85	82
83	89	88	87	91	94	88	91	87	89	87	87	90	86	86	83
84	90	89	88	91	94	89	91	88	90	88	88	90	87	87	84
85	91	90	88	92	94	90	92	89	91	89	89	91	88	88	85
86	91	90	89	92	95	90	92	89	91	90	90	92	89	88	86
87	92	91	90	93	95	91	93	90	92	90	90	92	89	89	87
88	93	92	91	94	96	92	93	91	92	91	91	93	90	90	88
89	93	92	91	94	96	92	94	92	93	92	92	93	91	91	89
90	94	93	92	95	96	93	95	92	94	93	93	94	92	92	90
91	94	94	93	95	97	94	95	93	94	93	93	95	93	93	91
92	95	94	94	96	97	94	96	94	95	94	94	95	94	93	92
93	96	95	95	96	97	95	96	95	96	95	95	96	94	94	93
94	96	96	95	97	98	96	97	95	96	96	96	96	95	95	94
95	97	97	96	97	98	97	97	96	97	96	96	97	96	96	95
96	98	97	97	98	99	97	98	97	97	97	97	98	97	97	96
97	98	98	98	98	99	98	98	98	98	98	98	98	98	98	97
98	99	99	98	99	99	99	99	98	99	99	99	99	98	98	98
99	99	99	99	99	100	99	99	99	99	99	99	99	99	99	99
100	100	100	100	100	100	100	100	100	100	100	100	100	100	100	100

Note. WIAT–II abbreviations are: WR = Word Reading, NO = Numerical Operations, RC = Reading Comprehension, SP = Spelling, PD = Pseudoword Decoding, MR = Math Reasoning, WE = Written Expression, LC = Listening Comprehension, OE = Oral Expression, RD = Reading, MA = Mathematics, WL = Written Language, OL = Oral Language, TA = Total Achievement.

Table C.5   WIAT–II Subtest and Composite Scores Predicted From WAIS–IV GAI Scores *(continued)*

WAIS–IV GAI	WIAT–II Subtest Scores									WIAT–II Composite Scores					WAIS–IV GAI
	WR	NO	RC	SP	PD	MR	WE	LC	OE	RD	MA	WL	OL	TA	
101	101	101	101	101	100	101	101	101	101	101	101	101	101	101	101
102	101	101	102	101	101	101	101	102	101	101	102	101	102	102	102
103	102	102	102	102	101	102	102	102	102	102	102	102	102	102	103
104	102	103	103	102	101	103	102	103	103	103	103	102	103	103	104
105	103	103	104	103	102	104	103	104	103	104	104	103	104	104	105
106	104	104	105	103	102	104	103	105	104	104	105	104	105	105	106
107	104	105	105	104	103	105	104	105	104	105	105	104	106	106	107
108	105	106	106	104	103	106	104	106	105	106	106	105	106	107	108
109	106	106	107	105	103	106	105	107	106	107	107	105	107	107	109
110	106	107	108	105	104	107	106	108	106	107	108	106	108	108	110
111	107	108	109	106	104	108	106	108	107	108	108	107	109	109	111
112	107	108	109	106	104	108	107	109	108	109	109	107	110	110	112
113	108	109	110	107	105	109	107	110	108	110	110	108	111	111	113
114	109	110	111	108	105	110	108	111	109	110	111	108	111	112	114
115	109	110	112	108	106	111	108	111	109	111	111	109	112	112	115
116	110	111	112	109	106	111	109	112	110	112	112	110	113	113	116
117	111	112	113	109	106	112	109	113	111	113	113	110	114	114	117
118	111	112	114	110	107	113	110	114	111	113	114	111	115	115	118
119	112	113	115	110	107	113	110	114	112	114	114	111	115	116	119
120	112	114	116	111	107	114	111	115	113	115	115	112	116	117	120
121	113	114	116	111	108	115	112	116	113	116	116	113	117	117	121
122	114	115	117	112	108	115	112	117	114	116	117	113	118	118	122
123	114	116	118	112	109	116	113	117	114	117	117	114	119	119	123
124	115	117	119	113	109	117	113	118	115	118	118	114	119	120	124
125	116	117	120	114	109	118	114	119	116	119	119	115	120	121	125
126	116	118	120	114	110	118	114	120	116	119	120	116	121	122	126
127	117	119	121	115	110	119	115	121	117	120	120	116	122	122	127
128	117	119	122	115	110	120	115	121	118	121	121	117	123	123	128
129	118	120	123	116	111	120	116	122	118	121	122	117	123	124	129
130	119	121	123	116	111	121	117	123	119	122	123	118	124	125	130
131	119	121	124	117	111	122	117	124	120	123	123	119	125	126	131
132	120	122	125	117	112	122	118	124	120	124	124	119	126	127	132
133	120	123	126	118	112	123	118	125	121	124	125	120	127	127	133
134	121	123	127	118	113	124	119	126	121	125	126	120	128	128	134
135	122	124	127	119	113	125	119	127	122	126	126	121	128	129	135
136	122	125	128	119	113	125	120	127	123	127	127	122	129	130	136
137	123	126	129	120	114	126	120	128	123	127	128	122	130	131	137
138	124	126	130	121	114	127	121	129	124	128	129	123	131	132	138
139	124	127	130	121	114	127	121	130	125	129	129	123	132	132	139
140	125	128	131	122	115	128	122	130	125	130	130	124	132	133	140
141	125	128	132	122	115	129	123	131	126	130	131	125	133	134	141
142	126	129	133	123	116	129	123	132	126	131	132	125	134	135	142
143	127	130	134	123	116	130	124	133	127	132	132	126	135	136	143
144	127	130	134	124	116	131	124	133	128	133	133	126	136	137	144
145	128	131	135	124	117	132	125	134	128	133	134	127	136	137	145
146	129	132	136	125	117	132	125	135	129	134	135	128	137	138	146
147	129	132	137	125	117	133	126	136	130	135	135	128	138	139	147
148	130	133	137	126	118	134	126	136	130	136	136	129	139	140	148
149	130	134	138	126	118	134	127	137	131	136	137	129	140	141	149
150	131	135	139	127	119	135	128	138	132	137	138	130	141	142	150
151	132	135	140	128	119	136	128	139	132	138	138	131	141	142	151
152	132	136	141	128	119	136	129	140	133	138	139	131	142	143	152
153	133	137	141	129	120	137	129	140	133	139	140	132	143	144	153
154	133	137	142	129	120	138	130	141	134	140	141	132	144	145	154
155	134	138	143	130	120	139	130	142	135	141	141	133	145	146	155
156	135	139	144	130	121	139	131	143	135	141	142	134	145	146	156
157	135	139	144	131	121	140	131	143	136	142	143	134	146	147	157
158	136	140	145	131	121	141	132	144	137	143	144	135	147	148	158
159	137	141	146	132	122	141	132	145	137	144	144	135	148	149	159
160	137	141	147	132	122	142	133	146	138	144	145	136	149	150	160

Note. WIAT–II abbreviations are: WR = Word Reading, NO = Numerical Operations, RC = Reading Comprehension, SP = Spelling, PD = Pseudoword Decoding, MR = Math Reasoning, WE = Written Expression, LC = Listening Comprehension, OE = Oral Expression, RD = Reading, MA = Mathematics, WL = Written Language, OL = Oral Language, TA = Total Achievement.

The practitioner must take into account the statistical significance and the base rate of the difference scores. Table C.6 provides the required differences between the predicted and obtained WIAT–II subtest and composite scores (critical values) at the .05 and .01 levels of significance. For each subtest or composite, read across the row that corresponds to the selected significance level to determine the critical value, and record it. The absolute value of the examinee's difference score must equal or exceed that critical value to be statistically significant. Determine whether the absolute value of the examinee's difference score equals or exceeds the corresponding critical value.

Table C.6   Differences Between Predicted and Obtained WIAT–II Subtest and Composite Scores Required for Statistical Significance (Critical Values): Predicted-Difference Method Using WAIS–IV GAI for Ages 16:0–19:11

Subtest/Composite	Significance Level	Critical Value
Word Reading	.05	7.29
	.01	9.60
Numerical Operations	.05	8.01
	.01	10.55
Reading Comprehension	.05	8.22
	.01	10.83
Spelling	.05	8.76
	.01	11.53
Pseudoword Decoding	.05	5.43
	.01	7.15
Math Reasoning	.05	8.56
	.01	11.26
Written Expression	.05	10.96
	.01	14.43
Listening Comprehension	.05	13.71
	.01	18.04
Oral Expression	.05	11.83
	.01	15.57
Reading	.05	5.61
	.01	7.39
Mathematics	.05	6.37
	.01	8.38
Written Language	.05	7.82
	.01	10.30
Oral Language	.05	10.99
	.01	14.46
Total Achievement	.05	5.93
	.01	7.80

If comparison of the predicted and obtained WIAT–II subtest or composite score indicates a significant difference, the practitioner should then judge how rare the difference is in the general population. Table C.7 provides differences between predicted and obtained WIAT–II scores for various percentages of the theoretical normal distribution (base rate). Locate the subtest or composite of interest in the left column, and read across the row to locate the examinee's difference score. If the examinee's difference score is equal to the difference score for an indicated percentage of the theoretical normal distribution, record that percentage (i.e., 1%, 2%, 3%, 4%, 5%, 10%, 15%, 20%, or 25%) as the base rate. If the examinee's difference score does not equal any of the difference scores for the indicated percentages (i.e., the examinee's difference score falls between two difference scores in the table), the base rate is reported as a range. For example, the base rate for a difference score of 26 between the GAI-predicted Word Reading score and the obtained Word Reading score is reported as 1%–2% (i.e., only 1%–2% of the theoretical normal distribution would be expected to obtain differences of 26 points between the predicted and obtained Word Reading scores).

Table C.7   Differences Between Predicted and Obtained WIAT–II Subtest and Composite Scores for Various Percentages of the Theoretical Normal Distribution (Base Rates): Predicted-Difference Method Using WAIS–IV GAI

Subtest/Composite	Percentage of Theoretical Normal Distribution (Base Rate)								
	25%	20%	15%	10%	5%	4%	3%	2%	1%
Word Reading	8	10	13	16	20	21	23	25	28
Numerical Operations	8	10	12	14	18	20	21	23	26
Reading Comprehension	7	8	10	13	16	17	18	20	22
Spelling	9	11	14	17	21	23	24	26	30
Pseudoword Decoding	10	12	15	18	23	25	27	29	33
Math Reasoning	8	10	12	14	18	19	21	23	25
Written Expression	9	11	13	17	21	22	24	26	30
Listening Comprehension	7	9	11	13	17	18	19	21	23
Oral Expression	8	10	13	15	20	21	22	24	28
Reading	7	9	11	13	17	18	19	21	24
Mathematics	7	9	11	13	17	18	19	21	24
Written Language	9	11	13	16	20	22	23	25	28
Oral Language	6	8	10	12	15	16	17	19	21
Total Achievement	6	8	9	11	14	15	16	18	20

Simple-Difference Method

Table C.8 provides the required differences between the obtained WAIS–IV GAI score and the obtained WIAT–II subtest and composite scores (critical values) at the .05 and .01 levels of significance. For each subtest or composite, read across the row that corresponds to the selected significance level to determine the critical value, and record it. The absolute value of the examinee's difference score must equal or exceed that critical value to be statistically significant. Determine whether the absolute value of the examinee's difference score equals or exceeds the corresponding critical value.

Table C.8   Differences Between WAIS–IV GAI Scores and WIAT–II Subtest and Composite Scores Required for Statistical Significance (Critical Values): Simple-Difference Method for Ages 16:0–19:11

Subtest/Composite	Significance Level	Critical Value
Word Reading	.05	8.32
	.01	10.95
Numerical Operations	.05	8.82
	.01	11.61
Reading Comprehension	.05	8.82
	.01	11.61
Spelling	.05	9.75
	.01	12.84
Pseudoword Decoding	.05	7.20
	.01	9.48
Math Reasoning	.05	9.30
	.01	12.24
Written Expression	.05	11.76
	.01	15.48
Listening Comprehension	.05	14.10
	.01	18.56
Oral Expression	.05	12.47
	.01	16.42
Reading	.05	6.57
	.01	8.65
Mathematics	.05	7.20
	.01	9.48
Written Language	.05	8.82
	.01	11.61
Oral Language	.05	11.39
	.01	14.99
Total Achievement	.05	6.57
	.01	8.65

If comparison of the WAIS–IV GAI score and the WIAT–II subtest or composite score indicates a significant difference, the practitioner should then judge how rare the difference is in the general population. Table C.9 provides differences between obtained WAIS–IV GAI and WIAT–II subtest and composite scores for various percentages of the theoretical normal distribution (base rates). Locate the subtest or composite of interest in the left column, and read across the row to locate the examinee's difference score. If the examinee's difference score is equal to the difference score for an indicated percentage of the theoretical normal distribution, record that percentage (i.e., 1%, 2%, 3%, 4%, 5%, 10%, 15%, 20%, or 25%) as the base rate. If the examinee's difference score does not equal any of the difference scores for the indicated percentages (i.e., the examinee's difference score falls between two difference scores in the table), the base rate is reported as a range. For example, the base rate for a difference score of 26 between the obtained WAIS–IV GAI and the obtained Word Reading score is reported as 2%–3% (i.e., 2%–3% of the theoretical normal distribution would be expected to obtain differences of 26 points between the obtained WAIS–IV GAI and the obtained Word Reading score).

Table C.9   Differences Between WAIS–IV GAI Scores and WIAT–II Subtest and Composite Scores
for Various Percentages of the Theoretical Normal Distribution (Base Rates):
Simple-Difference Method

Subtest/Composite	Percentage of Theoretical Normal Distribution (Base Rate)								
	25%	20%	15%	10%	5%	4%	3%	2%	1%
Word Reading	9	12	14	17	22	23	25	27	31
Numerical Operations	8	10	13	16	20	21	23	25	28
Reading Comprehension	7	9	11	13	17	18	19	21	24
Spelling	10	13	15	19	24	26	28	30	34
Pseudoword Decoding	12	15	18	22	28	30	32	35	40
Math Reasoning	8	10	13	15	20	21	22	24	28
Written Expression	10	12	15	19	24	25	27	30	34
Listening Comprehension	8	9	11	14	18	19	20	22	25
Oral Expression	9	11	14	17	22	23	25	27	31
Reading	8	10	12	14	18	19	21	23	26
Mathematics	8	9	11	14	18	19	20	22	25
Written Language	10	12	14	18	23	24	26	28	32
Oral Language	7	8	10	12	16	17	18	19	22
Total Achievement	6	8	10	12	15	16	17	18	21

Note. Percentages represent the theoretical proportion of WIAT–II scores lower than WAIS–IV GAI scores by the specified
amount or more.

Guidelines for the Use of Sign Language Interpreters and Cued Speech Transliterators

It is critically important to understand what constitutes interpreting and what constitutes transliterating. *Interpreting* is the receiving of a communicative act in one language and delivering it in another language, and/or a different sensory modality in a dynamic fashion (e.g., to and from Mexican Sign Language and spoken English). *Transliterating* is the receiving of one language and delivering it in a different modality, as is used in Cued Speech (e.g., spoken Spanish to and from Cued Spanish).

As a practitioner, you need to remain aware that both interpreting and transliterating are complex processes that necessitate high degrees of technical, linguistic, memory, and cognitive abilities. Both fields are highly specialized and represented by well-trained and experienced professionals. A person who simply knows both a native sign language or Cued Speech and English is not necessarily a qualified interpreter or transliterator. Only qualified professionals should be utilized in a psychological assessment that includes the WAIS–IV.

The primary role of an interpreter or transliterator, regardless of specialty or place of employment, is to facilitate all communication between persons. In addition to knowing and following a professional code of ethics, a professional sign language interpreter or Cued Speech transliterator must be able to adjust to a variety of situations, a broad range of individual preferences, and the interpretation needs for both the examiner and the examinee. Some examinees may use American Sign Language (ASL), a language with its own grammar and structure that is distinct from English, and others may prefer a form of signing that more closely follows the grammar and structure of spoken English. Some situations may require two or more interpreters or transliterators working simultaneously to satisfy the communication needs and preferences of a linguistically diverse audience. There may even be some occasions when an interpreter may be a deaf individual or a person fluent in a language other than English or ASL.

The use of an interpreter or transliterator inserts a complex variable, and potential source of error, into the assessment process. The presence of another person in the room may affect the examinee's performance and the rapport between the practitioner and examinee. For this reason, the interpreter or transliterator should be sufficiently skilled and flexible to adapt to the examinee's primary mode(s) of communication, as well as trained in and knowledgeable about the psychological assessment process. The use of professional interpreters or transliterators untrained in psychological assessment may unnecessarily alter the communication of directions and responses, the difficulty level of items, and the application of scoring criteria. Whenever an interpreter or transliterator must be used, it is recommended that you ensure that he or she is qualified (e.g., Registry of Interpreters for the Deaf [RID] certified).

Regardless of experience and qualifications, discourse via a trained interpreter may also fundamentally modify the validity and reliability of obtained results. The interpretation of some items from English into a three-dimensional, visual-spatial language may also significantly alter the functioning of the item and subtest. The use of different communication modalities by the examiner (e.g., spoken English) and interpreter or transliterator (e.g., Cued Speech) results in multiple presentations of an item in different modalities. Examiners should follow the administration guidelines contained in chapter 1 of the WAIS–IV Administration and Scoring Manual. Examiners should also be aware that interpreters and transliterators may request clarification of administration instructions to facilitate the communication process; this communication clarification could also affect the examinee's performance on those subtests that are timed or are limited to a single presentation of the items (e.g., Digit Span). As with any accommodation, the use of an interpreter or transliterator should be noted in the assessment report and considered when interpreting results from the WAIS–IV.

General guidelines for use of sign language interpreters and Cued Speech transliterators in psychological assessments are described below. When working with an interpreter or transliterator, you can increase the quality of the communication process and overall clinical rapport by implementing some of these suggestions.

- Conduct a pre-assessment session to orient the interpreter or transliterator to the goals of the assessment session and the instruments being administered. Discuss any issues related to the interpreting or transliterating process, including professional issues of confidentiality and dual relationships. These issues must also be addressed with the examinee (if appropriate) and the examinee's parents (if he or she is a minor) because prior relationships and contacts often exist among interpreters, the examinee, and the examinee's family.

- Remain in charge of and responsible for the session. As the practitioner, you should be the person introducing yourself and the interpreter or transliterator. Never assume that the examinee or the examinee's family members understand the role of the interpreter or transliterator. Explain your role and the role of the interpreter or transliterator to the examinee (if appropriate) and/or the examinee's family members.

- Determine the best physical locations for all parties to take during the assessment. It is recommended that the interpreter or transliterator sit slightly behind and to one side of you in order to maintain a rapport with the examinee and visually-based communication. This position also establishes clear roles and boundaries and allows for ease of access to the WAIS–IV materials when demonstrating a task.

- Permit time for the examinee to become familiar with the interpreter or transliterator and the communication process before beginning administration. Examinees may not be familiar with or know how best to utilize the services of an interpreter or transliterator. This time will also allow the interpreter/transliterator to become more familiar with the examinee's communication and language skills.

- Always attempt to face and make eye contact with the examinee. Address direct questions and comments to the examinee, not to the interpreter or transliterator. Avoid saying, "Ask him..." or "Tell her...."

- Remain cognizant that an examinee may use an interpreter or transliterator for receiving information, but may prefer to respond orally for herself or himself. If the examinee's speech is unclear, the interpreter or transliterator should be able to clarify.

- Know that the interpreter or transliterator can only provide information about the examinee's language and communication. Clinical or personal information or opinions about the examinee should not be solicited from or offered by the interpreter or transliterator.

- Expect that the interpreter or transliterator may occasionally interrupt to ask for an explanation or clarification of terms in order to provide an accurate interpretation.

- Be aware that some instructions, questions, and/or subtest items may function differently when communicated via a different language and/or modality and require greater or fewer words or signs to communicate it effectively.

- Be aware that facial expressions and body movements contribute significantly, linguistically and grammatically, to a deaf person's communication in all sign languages. This may impact your ability to accurately judge an examinee's emotional affect and engagement.

- Recognize that interpreters and transliterators have an ethical responsibility to interpret all that is said and heard in the presence of all individuals. The interpreter or transliterator should not omit anything that is said during the assessment, whether the comment was meant as an aside or unrelated to the testing process. If you do not wish for the examinee to know something (e.g., telephone conversation, side remarks, or comments), do not speak it during the course of the assessment.

- Be aware that the interpreter or transliterator is responsible only to interpret and is never responsible to supervise or evaluate the examinee.

- Conduct a post-assessment session with the interpreter or transliterator to sort out communication issues and possible therapeutic concerns that may have surfaced. This may also facilitate more valid and reliable interpretation of assessment results.

Considerations for Examinees Using Assistive Listening Devices

When assessing deaf or hard of hearing examinees who use assistive listening devices (ALDs), confirm the functioning of an examinee's ALD(s) immediately before the assessment. Some types of lighting systems and other electronic devices can emit frequencies and sounds that can be received by individuals using ALDs. It is highly recommended that the assessment be conducted in a well-lit room with no ambient noise and without visual distractions. ALDs amplify all sounds equally and may not screen out interfering background noise, which can cause ambient noises to significantly increase the difficulties of hearing and comprehending the practitioner.

It is also suggested that, whenever possible and appropriate, you use a room equipped with an appropriate amplification system; confirm that your microphone is turned on and that the examinee's ALD is switched to the proper channel. Microphones should be turned off and removed when the testing session is completed.

It is highly recommended that the seating and materials arrangement enable the examinee to have a clear view of your face. Subtest directions and items should be articulated clearly without exaggeration in intensity or altered rate of speed. When appropriate and allowed, you should confirm that the task instructions were comprehended by the examinee. Note that any and all accommodations and alterations from the standard administration procedures (e.g., use of an interpreter, translation of items, prompts) and alternate responses to individual items should be documented on the Record Form and in the interpretative report along with the credentials of the interpreter/transliterator.

Inclusion Criteria for Participation in Special Group Studies

General Inclusion Criteria for Special Groups

Examinees were eligible for inclusion if they met all of the following criteria:

- primary language is English;

- not primarily nonverbal or uncommunicative;

- normal hearing and vision (with aid);

- normal fine- and gross-motor ability (with the exception of mild motor impairment occurring in groups such as the Intellectual Disability and the Probable Dementia of the Alzheimer's Type-Mild Severity groups);

- no physical conditions, illnesses, or impairments that could affect cognitive functioning or test performance (with the exception of conditions or impairments associated with a specific special group);

- no diagnosis of a Pervasive Developmental Disorder (with the exception of the Autistic Disorder and Asperger's Disorder groups *only*) or of Intellectual Disability (with the exception of the Intellectual Disability subgroups);

- no diagnosis of a psychiatric disorder (e.g., Language Disorders, Psychotic Disorders, Mood Disorders, Substance Disorders [within a year prior to testing date]) other than that defined by the special group criteria;

- not currently admitted to a hospital, inpatient treatment, or psychiatric facility (with the exception of specified treatment settings that are pertinent to a given condition of interest [e.g., state schools or placements for Intellectual Disability subgroups or Autistic Disorder]);

- no diagnosis of a neurological condition (e.g., seizure disorder, epilepsy, encephalitis, brain surgery, brain tumor, Parkinson's, dementia, stroke) other than the condition of interest or as allowed for a given special group (e.g., seizure disorder in remission allowed for Intellectual Disability subgroups if controlled for at least 5 years);

- no history of a period of unconsciousness lasting 20 or more minutes (with the exception of the TBI group);

- no chemotherapy in the last 2 months;

- no history of electroconvulsive therapy or radiation to the central nervous system;

- not currently taking medication that might impact test performance, except as appropriate to treat condition of interest (e.g., cholinesterase inhibitor for mild cognitive impairment) or associated conditions (e.g., antidepressant to treat depression secondary to TBI);

- meets the criteria for one clinical group *only* (with the exception of dual diagnoses such as ADHD secondary to Intellectual Disability or Autistic Disorder, Major Depressive Disorder secondary to TBI); and

- has not completed the WAIS–III or any other measure of cognitive ability in the 6 months prior to testing date.

Specific Inclusion Criteria for Special Groups

Intellectually Gifted

Participation criteria included:

- age 16–64

AND

- scores ≥2*SD*s above the mean on a standardized, individually administered measure of cognitive ability (e.g., IQ ≥130).

OR

- Mensa membership *and* received services for intellectual giftedness or the equivalent during primary and/or secondary education.

Intellectual Disability

Participation criteria included:

- age 16–64

AND

- meets *DSM–IV–TR* criteria for Mental Retardation (Intellectual Disability), Mild or Moderate Severity.

OR

- scores on a standardized, individually administered measure of cognitive ability between 2 and 4 *SD*s below the mean (e.g., IQ of 40–70) were obtained before age 18; and

- meets criteria for deficits or impairments in adaptive functioning in at least two of the areas identified by *DSM–IV–TR* (i.e., communication, self-care, home living, social/interpersonal skills, use of community resources, self-direction, functional academic skills, work, leisure, health and safety).

Borderline Intellectual Functioning

Participation criteria included:

- age 16–65

AND

- meets *DSM–IV–TR* criteria for Borderline Intellectual Functioning.

OR

- scores on a standardized, individually administered measure of cognitive ability between 1 and 2 *SD*s below the mean (e.g., IQ of 71–84).

Learning Disorder

Participation criteria included:

- age 16–24;

- existing scores ≥80 on a standardized, individually administered measure of cognitive ability;

- meets *DSM–IV–TR* criteria for *only one* category of learning disorder listed below (i.e., only reading or only mathematics);

- significant interference with academic achievement or activities of daily living requiring the specific skill (reading or mathematics);

AND

- discrepancy of ≥15 points between ability and achievement (reading or mathematics) scores on standardized measures of achievement and cognitive ability in one of the following areas:

  ▶ reading only.

  ▶ mathematics only.

OR

- meets specific school district or facility criteria for learning disability in one of the following areas:

  ▶ reading only.

  ▶ mathematics only.

Attention-Deficit/Hyperactivity Disorder

Participation criteria included:

- age 18–34;

- the examinee has an estimated general cognitive ability in at least the average range;

AND

- meets *DSM–IV–TR* criteria for ADHD-Combined Type.

OR

- diagnosed by a physician or psychiatrist as having ADHD-Combined Type.

Traumatic Brain Injury

Participation criteria included:

- age 20–40;

- premorbid or estimated premorbid IQ is >70 (i.e., did not fall in the intellectual disability range prior to injury);

- diagnosed with moderate or severe TBI;

- at least 6 and no more than 18 months have elapsed between the date on which the TBI occurred and the test date;

- initial *Glasgow Coma Scale* (see Jennett, 2002) scores (or scores on another acute head injury scale) at admission fall in the moderate (e.g., 9–12) to severe (e.g., 3–8) range;

- duration of impaired consciousness at the time of injury was *at least* 1 hour;

- no diagnosis of a psychiatric disorder *prior* to the TBI;

- no diagnosis of a neurological condition (e.g., seizure disorder, stroke, brain surgery, multiple sclerosis, Parkinson's disease, Huntington's disease, or dementia) *prior* to the TBI;

- if diagnosed with seizure disorder, diagnosis must have been made subsequent to the TBI;

- injury is not due to a brain tumor, or other medical illness or condition (e.g., bacterial infection, meningitis, encephalitis); and

- no experience of posttraumatic amnesia at the time of testing.

Autistic Disorder

Participation criteria included:

- age 16–40;

- scores ≥60 on a standardized, individually administered measure of cognitive ability;

- meets *DSM–IV–TR* criteria for a current diagnosis of Autistic Disorder made by a qualified mental health professional; and

- adequate language skills to complete testing.

Asperger's Disorder

Participation criteria included:

- age 16–40;

- scores ≥70 on a standardized, individually administered measure of cognitive ability;

- meets *DSM–IV–TR* criteria for a current diagnosis of Asperger's Disorder; and

- no clinically significant delays in language, cognitive development, curiosity about the environment, self-help skills, and adaptive behavior (other than social interaction).

Major Depressive Disorder

Participation criteria included:

- age 55–90;

- meets *DSM–IV–TR* criteria for a current diagnosis of Major Depressive Disorder made by a qualified mental health professional;

- if taking antidepressant medication, qualifies for an active diagnosis of Major Depressive Disorder (i.e., not in remission); and

- no psychotic symptoms experienced as part of Major Depressive Disorder diagnosis for at least 6 weeks prior to testing.

Mild Cognitive Impairment

Participation criteria included:

- age 55–90;

- meets the following American Academy of Neurology diagnostic criteria for a diagnosis of mild cognitive impairment:

  - ▶ objective evidence of cognitive impairment in memory or another cognitive domain (e.g., language, perception), as indicated on a standardized, individually administered assessment;

  - ▶ may have history of decline from previously normal level of cognitive functioning;

  - ▶ may have preserved basic daily functioning;

  - ▶ if memory loss is present, there is no evidence of other obvious medical, neurological, or psychiatric causes for the memory loss;

  - ▶ does not meet criteria for any type of dementia; and

  - ▶ cognitive complaints are not consistent with normal aging; and

- not currently admitted to a medical hospital or psychiatric facility; however, admittance to a nursing home, assisted living center, or adult residential/day care/independent living facility is acceptable.

Probable Dementia of the Alzheimer's Type-Mild Severity

Participation criteria included:

- age 55–90;

- meets the NINCDS–ADRDA diagnostic criteria (McKhann et al., 1984) for a diagnosis of probable Alzheimer's disease that is in the *mild* stage of decline;

- shows objective evidence of dementia established by clinical examination and documented by a standardized, individually administered measure of dementia;

- displays deficits in two or more areas of cognitive function, such as language (e.g., aphasia), motor skills (e.g., apraxia), and perception (e.g., agnosia);

- exhibits progressive decline in memory or other cognitive functions;

- does not experience disturbances in consciousness or delirium;

- not experiencing systemic or other brain disease that could account for progressive deficits in memory or cognition. Symptoms are not due to a stroke, cerebral vascular accident, traumatic brain injury, or other neurological condition;

- score of ≤18 on the *Beck Depression Inventory—II* (BDI–II; Beck, Steer, & Brown, 1996) or a score of <15 on the Long Form of the *Geriatric Depression Scale* (Yesavage et al., 1982-1983) or the equivalent score on a similar depression inventory within 1 month of testing;

- score of 18–23 on the mini mental status exam; and

- not currently admitted to a medical hospital or psychiatric facility; however, admittance to a nursing home, assisted living center, or adult residential/day care/independent living facility is acceptable.

Advisory Panel, Reviewers and Consultants, Examiners, and Participating Clinics, Schools, and Organizations

Advisory Panel

Gordon J. Chelune, PhD, Center for Alzheimer's Care, Imaging and Research, University of Utah School of Medicine, Salt Lake City, Utah

C. Munro Cullum, PhD, University of Texas Southwestern Medical Center at Dallas, Dallas, Texas

Gerald Goldstein, PhD, VA Pittsburgh Healthcare System, Pittsburgh, Pennsylvania

Jacques Grégoire, PhD, Université Catholique de Louvain, Louvain-la-Neuve, Belgium

Joel Kramer, PsyD, University of California, San Francisco, Memory and Aging Center, San Francisco, California

Glenn J. Larrabee, PhD, Private practice, Sarasota, Florida

Jennifer J. Manly, PhD, Gertrude H. Sergievsky Center and the Taub Institute for Research on Alzheimer's Disease and the Aging Brain, Columbia University, New York, New York

Scott R. Millis, PhD, Department of Physical Medicine & Rehabilitation, Wayne State University School of Medicine, Detroit, Michigan

Donald H. Saklofske, PhD, Division of Applied Psychology, University of Calgary, Canada

Timothy A. Salthouse, PhD, Department of Psychology, University of Virginia, Charlottesville, Virginia

Reviewers and Consultants

Barbara Byrne, PhD

Craig Frisby, PhD

Steven Hardy-Braz, PhD

Vernon Neppe, MD, PhD

Martha Storandt, PhD

Lisa Suzuki, PhD

Bruce Thompson, PhD

Arthur Weider, PhD

Examiners

Melonee Adalikwu

Lisa Suzanne Adams

Hey Mi Ahn

Marjorie Aitken*

Greg Allen

Melissa Allison

Nancy Alspach*

Christine J. Aman

Kristin Ambrose

Alison Amshoff

JeNene M. Anderson

Donna E. Anderson

Emily Anderson

Laura Andrews

Glena L. Andrews

Barry Ardolf

Kristin Arnold

Stephanie Ann Asbeck

Beatriz Ashley

Verlann Atchley

Elizabeth Rose Avant

Nanci Avitable

Reid Axman

Jonathan Babin

Stacy Back

Tracy Bailey

Laura Bailey

Sheila M. Bailey

Sarah W. Baker

Coleen Baker Cuda

Heidi Baldassare

Andrea Balibay

Sheila A. Balog

Phyllis H. Banks

Jaime L. Barclay

Kathryn Barker

Mary Jo Bates

Sheryle G. Beatty

Bonnie Behee Semler

Gayle M. Bell

Teresa Belluscio

Jana C. Bennett

Lindsey Keller Berjansky

Kathy K. Bessom

Maria Bianco

Eleni Binioris

Molly Birkett

Kimberly Bischofberger

Herbert G. W. Bischoff

Barbara Bisio

Brittany Blackmon

Jessica Blalock

Teosha Blaylock

Sandra Renee Blocker

Daniel Blonigen

Erika Annell Blusewicz

Sara Bobenmoyer*

Helen Boehm-Morelli*

Khristy Bogney

Morella Bombardini

Courtney Nicole Bordelon

Kimberly Borkenhagen

Donna Borynack

Michelle Boswell

Kimberly Boutin

Melanie M. Bowen

Amy R. Boyd

Sandy Boyer

Jamie Brass

Alison W. Brett

Robert B. Breyer

Barbara Briggs

Cheryl Brischetto*

Catherine Brock*

Lisa M. Brockhuizen

Lorraine Brokaw

Kathy E. Brooks

Rita Brown

Catherine Brown

Mealika Brown

April A. Brownell

Joanne Brunetti

Carey Bruns

Brandon Bryan

Jennifer Budd

Katherine Buhrke

Brett Buican

Gwyn O. Burd

Wendi Burton

Amy Butler

Christopher Cadle

Myra Cain Dingle

Mary Lisa Callan

Bonnie B. Campbell

Chelsea Cangeleri

Nancy R. Canterbury

Mary Lou Cantrell

Nichole Capps

Sandra J. Carr

Dixie W. Carter

Ginger Casas

Vanessa Casillas

Amy Cassata

Tim Caufield

Carrie Champ Morera

Usha Chandrasekhar

Jill Chappell Zylker

Marni Choice Hermosillo

April Christy

Jorethia L. Chuck

Tiffany Civers

John Clabaugh

Susi Clark

Tammy Claypool

Shawna Clock

Renia E. B. Cobb

Stacie Coburn

Laura A. Cohen

Lori Y. Coleman

John Conway

Jenifer Cooper

Kellie Cooper

Tim Copeland

Alicia Rae Copestick

Barbara Corff

Gina Cortesi

Ayiesha Cottrell

Marylou Coutts

Dinah Covert

Tracey Cowan

Karen L. Coy

Nicole Crandall

Michael Crane

Kevin Crippen

Gladys L. Croom

B.J. Crossley

Rita Crump Weatherford

Ivette Cruz

JoAnn Cuellar

Tiffany Cummings

Rhonda Cunningham

Erica Cupuro

Melissa A. Cyders

Cindy J. D'Alberto

Lawrence D'Alberto

Amanda Dake

Patrick Dallas

Kimberly Daum

Anne Davidge

Teresa DaVigo

Melissa Davis

Kesha L. Davis

Larissa Dawkins

Jill Day

Carey Day

Terri Dean

Claire Dean

LeAnna DeAngelo

Mandy Dedrick

Chris Delap

Deborah A. Delker*

Nadia Delshad

Annie Deming

Susan Deneen

Carmen Deneen

Ellen M. Diana

Laura Diaz

Lucia Diaz Romero

Jennifer Dick

Lisa Dickison

John Doak

Lesli Doan

Robert Doss

Galen Downing

Teressa Drogue

Kristine Dukleth

Colleen Ryan Dupuis

Constance Dwinal

Jane Dycus

Kathye Easley

Melissa K. Eddy

Lisette Edgar

Beulah Eldridge

Joyce Elliot*

Monica Ellis

Ron Elniff

James English

Susan Erichson

Rose Marie Esparza

Trese Evans

Shauna C. Evans

Stephanie Evans

Kelly A. Faust

Kevin Favor

Hunter Todd Feaster

Yvette Feis

Marialid Feliciano

Craig Ferch

Linea Ferguson

Milton E. Findley

Joanne Finn

Karen Fischer Perkins

Cathy Fisher

Rita R. Flanagan

Esther Elaine Fleenor

Nancy D. Floodberg

Lesley Paige Flores

Dennis E. Ford

Maria Fragnito

Julie Franzese

Krista Freece

Christine L. French

Audra Frey

Tina Friedman

Michael J. Fuhrman

Annette Fulton Urbas

Lana Suzanne Fust

Theresa A. Gabler

Susan Galati

Jennifer Gale

Erik Gallemore

Eduardo Gambini Suarez

Cheryl Gamble

Debra Garrett

Rebecca Garza

Becky Gasca

Louise A. Gauthier

John Gawel

Tamra Gear

Andrea Gelske

Cassandra M. Germain

Michael Gilbride

William Gillen

Crystal Girgenti

Donna M. Glover

Lisa Goldstein

Jorge Javier Gontier

Mary V. Gooch

Vera Goodman

James F. Gormally

Jamira R. Grana

Karen Graves

Cornelia A. Green

Yvette Grier

Jennifer Grimes*

Derek Grimmell*

Debbie Groff

Kerry Grohman

Kathy Guebara

Linda Guttman

George B. Haarman

Joni Hale

Hayden Haller

Mark Hamel

Ann Hamer

Debra K. Hamilton

Sue M. Hamm

Robin Hanks

Rita Hanneman

Chisa Harris

Tamara Hart

Amy Lewallen Hartley

Sarah Hasker

Angie M. Hatlestad

Jennifer L. Haynes

Stacey L. Head

Alan Heath

Nichole Hebert

Carla Hedeen

Jennifer P. Hervey

Rebecca Hester

Karen D. Hewell

Susan Higgins

Diana Hill

Carol Hill

Thomas F. Hill

Candi Hill

Carol Hinman

Kelly Hird

Alexander D. Hirsch

Carrie L. Hlousek

Matthew Hocking

Helen Hoffman

Mira Hoffman

Caitlin K. Holley

Angela Hollis

Paige Holman

Julia Hood

V. Scott Hooper

Catalina Hooper

Tara Hopson

Yael Horowitz

Stephanie Horton

America Hottle

Pamela S. Howard

Jim Huckaby

Stephen M. Huggins

Mary Hundley

Man Hung

Sharyn Hunt

Crystal Hunter

Debra B. Huss

Amy Ibbetson

Teresa Imholte

Joanna Jablonski

Altran Jaime

Denise Janak

Dejan Jancevski

David G. Jansen

Lisa Jarvis Durham

Lorraine Jensen*

Stephanie Jensen

Aric Jensen

Carol Jernigan

Leslie H. Jernigan

Aubrey M. Johnson

Tonya Johnson

Samoan Johnson

Marcela Johnston

Tara H. Jones

Mary Margaret Jones

Blake Jones

Karen Jordan

Joan Joyce*

Kristin A. Juergens

Sarah Kachmaryk

Janet M. Kamer

Ann E. Kane

Kim Kazimour

Michael M. Keil

Brian Kelly

Megan M. Kelly

Mary Kennedy

Robert J. Kennerley

James G. Kessler

Beth Killary

Elaine S. King*

Shawna Kirby

Danielle Kirsch

Diana E. Kisielew Miner

Lora Klacik

Amy Knowles

Anita Kohler Ragusa

Kay Konz

Donna M. Kostik

Vasilike Kostouros

Tom Kot

Laura A. Krause

Cynthia Kreutzer

Doug Krug

Abbey Kruper

Lisa Kuhn

Jody Kyllo

Michelle La Spata

Kristi Lee Lackey

Tamela J. Ladner

Denise LaGrand

Yin Lam

Matthew E. Lambert

Evelyn M. LaMont

Geoffrey Lane

Dana LaPointe O'Sullivan

Allison Larsen

Tracy Larson

Stephanie Lee

Jamie Lemke

Dedra Lemon

Alice LeMond

Lisa Leon

Paul Leppanen

Allison Lerman

Michelle Lesinski

Laura Letzinger

Archie S. Lewis

Mary M. Lewis

Quinne Leyden

Lorraine Licata

Robin Liedtke

Yvette Lightbourn-Elias

Amber M. Lindeman Eldredge

Ross E. Linscott

Gregory Littlejohn

Marilyn Llanes

Kathryn A. Lockwood

Angie Loethen

Karen J. Lonski

Annabelle Lopez

Lindsay Lounder

James Loveland

Nina Lozier

Kristina J. Luna

Karen Lundin

Dawn Magers

Pamela Mahan

Michael K. Mahoney

Sandra D. Mahoney

Marilyn Maldonado

Tara Malec

Nafisa Mandani

Karen L. Mandel

Molly Marchman

Gladys Charlene Marcum

Donna Marland

Lauren Marshall

Ginger Martin

Antoinette Martin

Margaret A. Martin

Julia Martinez

Margaret Martinez

Laura Marullo

Elizabeth Mason*

Tania M. Massimino

Tiffany K. Mathis

Tamika Matthews

Melissa J. Matthews

Terry H. Mattingly

James McCray

Betty McCurdy

Dana McDonald

Donna McInnis

Shondalyn Lucky McIntyre

Gail McLean

Kristina McMenamy

Michael McMillan

Julia J. McNabb

Davina McNaney

Donna McPeek

Kimberly A. Mecca

Heidi Meck

Heather Meek

Ramona Mellott

Marissa I. Mendoza*

Melissa Merchant

Lynda Michelson*

Rachel Michelson Grippin

April Miller

Stacia Mitchell

Michelle D. Mitchell

Loraine M. Mitter

Jerry L. Molaison

James R. Moneypenny

Jennifer Montgomery

Sheryl A. Montgomery

Daniel Moore

Jamie Moore

Lisa Silva Moore

Laura C. Moore

Claudia Moreno

Angela R. Moses

Linda Mowry

Evelyn Mueller Elliott

Diana Lee Muller

Kathleen L. Munsell

Deborah T. Murphy

Patrick Murphy

Jeannie M. Napier

Tess Neal

Jessica Neubauer

Bridget Neumann

Carol Newberry

Becky Newman

Thuy Nguyen

Cassandra Nguyen

Melanie Norwood

Esther Nzewi

Deborah O'Banion

Carmen O'Brien

Kristin O'Donnell

Cheryl O'Heir

Patricia O'Neal

Susan Oberdorf

Ryan Oetting

Sonya Oliver

Cynthia Olson

Tracy L. Otto

Marguerite Overstreet

Amy B. Palmer

Vivian Pan

Rashmi Pandey

Diana Panizzon

Charity Pankratz

Alycia Muto Patierno

James H. Payne

Dody Pelts

Laura Pence

DeVonna Permann

Jenelle Perno

Ginette Perrin

Rachel Dawn Petersen

Nearl Phillips

James Piacopolos

Donna Picone

Shannon Piercey

Michele Pisarz

Alexander G. Pla

Jessica Plewinski*

Gloria Polk

Goldie Portnoy

Antoine Powell*

Shelley Preston

Cristine Sosa Price

Jennifer A. Prine

Antonio Puente

Katrina Raia

Veronica Rallis

Deborah Rangel-Friedman

Gerri C. Rankin

Amy Rasmussen

Jennifer Rawley

Phillip M. Reams

Rhonda Redmond

Hope C. Reed

Denise Reeves

Lydia D. Reid

Elizabeth Richards

Wanda Lee Rieman

Shannon Riggs

Doris Irine Riley

Jennifer Ring

Melanie Rivera

Ana Rivera

Robyn Rix

Abbey R. Roach

Sarah Robbins*

Larmia Robbins Brinson

Bronwyn Roberts

D. Jennifer Robertson

Jennifer L. Robertson

Alina Robinson*

Melinda Robinson

Floyd Robison

Lucas Rockwood

Julia Rodriguez

Danielle Rodriguez

Chrissy Rodriguez

Anaeli Rodriguez Goldstein

Delores F. Rogers

Nicole Rogers

Emily Rogers

Heather R. Romero

Amber Romriell

Sally Rosenwasser*

Erin Roush

Lori Ruffier*

Megan Ruiter

Jane D. Russell

Aaron D. Russell

Mona Ryan

Steve Saladin

Jennifer Salava

Michelle I. Saldivar

Joann Salerno

Natasha Sammons

Juanetta Sample

Stacy Daniel Sampson

Kristin Samuelson

G. Nohl Sandall

Alaina S. Sanderson Lopez

Lorina Santiago

Rachel Satter

Caryln L. Saunders

Suzanne J. Savoca Fletcher

Dave H. Schaumann

Lindsey Schipper

Kristi Schippers

Andrew Schlegelmilch

Kathie Schlemper

Shawn M. Schnabel

Janice Schneider

Jennifer J. Schnitzer**

Sara Schultz Mullins

Krista Schwenk

Donna Scranton

Deborah Seiferman

Jamey M.G. Self

Rachel Seligson

Debby Sexton

Anne Shandera

Kristi Sharbono

Darlene Shaw

Amy Shelley

Vanessa C. Short

Dayna Sikora

Gary Silbiger

Lisa A. Simms*

James Simonds

Susan Sinicki

Sarah D. Smith

Carlos Allen Smith

Alison Smith

Laurie Sodetani

Maria Elena Soto Rodriguez

Tara J. Southward

Steve Sparks

Jennifer Speckman

Georgianne Speliopoulos

Katrina Spottsville

Penny L. Sprecher

LaAngel St. Julian

Virginia A. Stanick

Jacalyn Stanley

Nancy Starewicz

Joan Steele

Amy Stefanovic*

Barbra Stein

Janna Stein*

Wendy Stephens Grube

Willie G. Stevens

Darrell Stiffey

Jeffry Stine

Robert M. Storer

Susan L. Stroh*

Lori Strunk

Cilla Stultz

Bettina Suarez

Jill Sullivan

Kristen Sullwold

Ronald R. Summerhill

Chris Sumner

Michelle Sussman

Jana Swedo

Rachel Swopes

Andrea Syrek

Shuen Hwee Rowena Tan

Alexandra S. Taylor

Michelle Tayrose

Kent Terry

Marilyn Thatcher

Sheree Thomas

Susan Thomas

Andrea Thomas Ingram

Verlinda Thompson

Tracy Thompson

David Toback

Katherine H. Todd

Mark S. Tomes

Christy Tomisek

Heather Towell

Debora J. Trainor

Annette M. Trantanella

Gary Troia

Patricia Tsui

Frances Tung

Midge Ulrich

Nancy Ann Uzoaru

Gloria Valley

Sherra D. Vance

Rachel Vanthomma

Kelly VanWyck Smith

Cynthia Vasquez

Emily E. Vaughn

Brenda Vavricek

Marilyn Veincentotzs

Nicole R. Villemarette Pittman

Barbara Vines

Cynthia Vines

Randy Vinzant

Marie Volbrecht

Denise Volker

Andrew C. Voluse

Juanita Waites

Tracey Walenta

Brenda Leigh Walker

Brenda Walker Moore

Donna Wallace

Jennifer Ward

Noel Warffuel

Ashly A. Warner

Nicole Warnygora

Jennifer Warzecha

Donna J. Washington

Tamara Waters Wheeler

Sara Wayntraub

Leah Nicole Webb

Jennifer Weeks

Fredric Weiner

Lauren Weiner

Garen Lee Ann Weitman

Shelley Welby

Anthony Wells

Alice Weng

Christina Weyer Jamora

Heather L. Whalen

Jennifer Whitman

Martin Wiese

Brenda J. Wilburn

Vanessa Wilkinson

Brenee K. Williams

Janell Dawn Williams

Meca R. Williams

Ira Williamson

Jacquelyn Williamson

Deborah J. Wilson

Heather L. Winslow

Janina Winston Roberts

Susan Witkowski

Sara Wohlgemuth

Shirley Wolfe*

Vivian V. Wolfe

Sharna L. Wood

Nancy Means Wood

Barri Woodfork

Mary Diltz Woolsey

Weston Wyble

Julia Beatrice Wynn

Steven Yalkowsky

Yuko Yamato

Christopher Yanusas

J. Robert Yohman

Alicia Young

Lisa J. Young

Tristan T. Young

Judy M. Zarit

Daniel M. Zimet

Meghan Chance Zito

Donna M. Zook

Participating Clinics, Schools, and Organizations

American Legion Auxillary

Associated Neurologists, PC

Atlantic Psychiatric Services

Behavior Management Systems, Inc.

Belleville Area Special Services Cooperative

Benita Family Center

Brighton Gardens

Bulverde Senior Center

Clinic for Adult Attention Problems

Colorado Neuropsychological & Behavioral Center, LLC

Communication Nation

Cornerstone Wellness Center

Crossroads Psychological Associates

Decide/Decide

Diamante Psychological Services

Doelger Senior Center

Duke University Medical Center

DYS Development Group

Ebony Marketing Research, Inc.

Escapees Care, Inc.

Evans & Associates, PSC

Evanston Northwestern Healthcare

Exceptional Psychological Services

First Baptist Church of Forest Grove OFB

First in Focus

Floodberg Development, Inc.

Glassman & Stanik, LLC

Grace Lutheran Church

Greystone Park Psychiatric Hospital

* Member of the WAIS–IV Tryout Phase Examiner Review Panel

** Special Participant Representing Examiners in the WAIS–IV Tryout Advisory Panel Meeting

Gulfcoast Neuropsychology Laboratory

Henry Ford Health System-Division of Neuropsychology

Horizon InFocus

Immaculate Heart of Mary

Indiana University of Pennsylvania Center for Applied Psychology

Jesse G. Harris Jr. Psychological Services Center, PSC

LFG & Associates, LLC

Living Days Adult Day Care, Inc.

LSU Epilepsy Center of Excellence

Metropolitan Detroit Research & Education Foundation, Psych Sec

Midwestern Neuropsychology

Minnesota Epilepsy Group, PA

Mississippi State Hospital

Montana Neuropsychological Corp.

Neuropsychology Consultants, LCC

Northside ISD Adult Education

Office of Disability Services

Orion Academy

Perceptive Market Research

Pittsburg State University

Plaza Research, Inc.

Polish Society of Cape Cod & The Islands

Prairie Psychological Services, PA

Private Practice Antonio E. Puente, PhD

Private Practice of Carla Hedeen

Private Practice of Cindy D'Alberto

Private Practice of Dr. Michael Riordan, PsyD, PA

Private Practice of Gary Blagg

Private Practice of Kathryn Ecklund

Private Practice of Paul S. McCollum, PhD

Private Practice of Robert J. Kennerley

Private Practice of Ronald Devere, MD

Private Practice of Tracy Larson

Private Practice of Tracy Thompson

Private Practice Stephen M Huggins, PsyD, PC

Psychological and Neuropsychological Services

Psychological Solutions, Inc.

Resolutions Consulting Group, LLC

Roseville Apartments

Sacred Heart Nutrition Center

Safe Haven

Sandilands, Inc.

SASH Volunteer Service Council

School District of Wabeno Area

School Sister of Notre Dame of St. Louis

Shih Yu-Lang Central YMCA

Shorewood Senior Resource Center, SSRC

South Texas Mensa

St. Andrews UMC

TexCare Adult Day Care

The Family Center/La Familia

The Village at Incarnate Word

The Women's Center

University of Alabama Psychology Clinic

University of Idaho

University of Louisiana Monroe Department of Psychology

University of Louisville Psychological Services Center

USO San Antonio

Visions Within, Inc.

Wayne State University Practice Group

Winston School San Antonio

Yellen & Associates

References

Adair, J. C., Na, D. L., Schwartz, R. L., & Heilman, K. M. (1998). Analysis of primary and secondary influences on spatial neglect. *Brain and Cognition, 37*, 351–367.

Allen, M. J., & Yen, W. M. (1979). *Introduction to measurement theory.* Monterey, CA: Brooks/Cole.

Ambery, F. Z., Russel, A. J., Perry, K., Morris, R., & Murphy, D. G. M. (2006). Neuropsychological functioning in adults with Asperger syndrome. *Autism, 10*(6), 551–564. doi: 10.1177/1362361306068507 http://dx.doi.org/10.1177/1362361306068507.

American Association on Intellectual and Developmental Disabilities. (2007). *User's guide: Mental retardation: Definition, classification and systems of support* (10th ed.). Washington, DC: Author.

American Educational Research Association. (2006). *Standards for reporting on empirical social science research in AERA publications.* Retrieved May 21, 2008 from http://www.aera.net/uploadedFiles/Opportunities/Standards forReportingEmpiricalSocialScience_PDF.pdf

American Educational Research Association, American Psychological Association, & National Council on Measurement in Education. (1999). *Standards for educational and psychological testing.* Washington, DC: Author.

American Psychiatric Association. (2000). *Diagnostic and statistical manual of mental disorders* (4th ed., text revision). Washington, DC: Author.

Anastasi, A., & Urbina, S. (1997). *Psychological testing* (7th ed.). Upper Saddle River, NJ: Prentice Hall.

Angoff, W. H. (1984). *Scales, norms, and equivalent scores.* Princeton, NJ: Educational Testing Service.

Angoff, W. H. (1988). Validity: An evolving concept. In H. Wainer & H. I. Braun (Eds.), *Test validity* (pp. 19–32). Hillsdale, NJ: Erlbaum.

Armour-Thomas, E., & Gopaul-McNicol, S.-A. (1997). Bio-ecological approach to cognitive assessment. *Cultural Diversity and Mental Health, 3*(2), 131–144.

Arnau, R. C., & Thompson, B. (2000). Second-order confirmatory factor analysis of the WAIS–III. *Assessment, 7*(3), 237–246.

Assistance to States for the Education of Children With Disabilities and Preschool Grants for Children With Disabilities; Final Rule. 71 Fed. Reg. 46,540 (August 14, 2006).

Axelrod, B. N., Fichtenberg, N. L., Liethen, P. C., Czarnota, M. A., & Stucky, K. (2001). Performance characteristics of postacute and traumatic brain injury patients on the WAIS–III and WMS–III. *The Clinical Neuropsychologist, 15*(4), 516–520.

Axelrod, B. N., Fichtenberg, N. L., Liethen, P. C., Czarnota, M. A., & Stucky, K. (2002). Index, summary, and subtest discrepancy scores on the WAIS–III in postacute traumatic brain injury patients. *International Journal of Neuroscience, 112*, 1479–1487.

Baddeley, A., & Jarrold, C. (2007). Working memory and Down syndrome. *Journal of Intellectual Disability Research, 51*(12), 925–931.

Balluerka, N., Gómez, J., & Hidalgo, D. (2005). The controversy over null hypothesis significance testing revisited. *Methodology, 1*(2), 55–70.

Banken, J. A. (1985). Clinical utility of considering digits forward and digits backward as separate components of the Wechsler Adult Intelligence Scale–Revised. *Journal of Clinical Psychology, 41*(5), 686–691.

Barkley, R. A., Murphy, K. R., & Bush, T. (2001). Time perception and reproduction in young adults with attention deficit hyperactivity disorder. *Neuropsychology, 15*, 351–360.

Barnhill, G., Hagiwara, T., Myles, B. S., & Simpson, R. L. (2000). Asperger syndrome: A study of the cognitive profiles of 37 children and adolescents. *Focus on Autism and Other Developmental Disabilities, 15*(3), 146–153.

Bate, A. J., Mathias, J. L., & Crawford, J. R. (2001). Performance on the test of everyday attention and standard tests of attention following severe traumatic brain injury. *The Clinical Neuropsychologist, 15,* 405–422.

Beck, A. T., Steer, R. A., & Brown, G. K. (1996). *Beck depression inventory—second edition.* San Antonio, TX: The Psychological Corporation.

Bennett, I. J., Golob, E. J., Parker, E. S., & Starr, A. (2006). Memory evaluation in mild cognitive impairment using recall and recognition tests. *Journal of Clinical and Experimental Neuropsychology, 28,* 1408–1422.

Beres, K. A., Kaufman, A. S., & Perlman, M. D. (2000). Assessment of child intelligence. In G. Goldstein & M. Hersen (Eds.), *Handbook of psychological assessment* (3rd ed., pp. 65–96). Kidlington, Oxford, United Kingdom: Elsevier Science.

Berninger, V. W., Dunn, A., & Alper, T. (2005). Integrated multilevel model for branching assessment, instructional assessment, and profile assessment. In A. Prifitera, D. H. Saklofske, & L. G. Weiss (Eds.), *WISC–IV clinical use and interpretation: Scientist-practitioner perspectives* (pp. 151–185). New York: Academic Press.

Berninger, V. W., & Holdnack, J. A. (2008). Nature-nurture perspectives in diagnosing and treating learning disabilities: Response to questions begging answers that see the forest and the trees. In E. Fletcher-Janzen & C. R. Reynolds (Eds.), *Neuropsychological perspectives on learning disabilities in the era of RTI: Recommendations for diagnosis and intervention* (pp. 66–81). John Wiley & Sons, Inc: Hoboken, NJ.

Berninger, V. W., & O'Donnell, L. (2005). Research-supported differential diagnosis of specific learning disabilities. In A. Prifitera, D. H. Saklofske, & L. G. Weiss (Eds.), *WISC–IV clinical use and interpretation: Scientist-practitioner perspectives* (pp. 189–233). New York: Academic Press.

Berninger, W. B., O'Donnell, L., & Holdnack, J. (2008). Research-supported differential diagnosis of specific learning disabilities and implications for instruction and response to instruction. In A. Prifitera, D. Saklofske, & L. G. Weiss (Eds.), *WISC-IV Clinical assessment.* San Diego, CA: Academic Press.

Binet, A., & Simon, T. (1905). Methodes nouvelles pour le diagnostic du niveau intellectuel des anormaux [A new method for the diagnosis of intellectual level of abnormal persons]. *L'annee Psychologique, 11,* 191–244.

Blaha, J., & Wallbrown, F. H. (1996). Hierarchical factor structure of the Wechsler intelligence scale for children–III. *Psychological Assessment, 8,* 214–218.

Bölte, S., & Poustka, F. (2004). Comparing the intelligence profiles of savant and nonsavant individuals with autistic disorder. *Intelligence, 32,* 121–131.

Bowden, S. C., Lange, R. T., Weiss, L. W., & Saklofske, D. (in press). Invariance of the measurement model underlying the Wechsler Adult Intelligence Scale–III in the United States and Canada. *Educational and Psychological Measurement.*

Bowden, S. C., Weiss, L. G., Holdnack, J. A., & Lloyd, D. (2006). Age-related invariance of abilities measured with the Wechsler Adult Intelligence Scale–III. *Psychological Assessment, 18*(3), 334–339.

Boyle, P. A., Wilson, R. S., Aggarwal, N. T., Tang, Y., Bennett, D. A. (2006). Mild cognitive impairment: Risk of Alzheimer disease and rate of cognitive decline. *Neurology, 67,* 441–445.

Bracken, B. A. (1992). The interpretation of tests. In M. Zeidner & R. Most (Eds.), *Psychological testing: An inside view* (pp. 119–156). Palo Alto, CA: Consulting Psychologists Press.

Brown, T. E. (1996). *Brown attention-deficit disorder scales.* San Antonio, TX: The Psychological Corporation.

Browne, M. W., & Cudeck, R. (1993). Alternative ways of assessing model fit. In K. A. Bollen & J. S. Long (Eds.), *Testing structural equation models* (pp. 136–162). Newbury Park, CA: Sage Publications.

Buehner, M., Krumm, S., Ziegler, M., & Pluecken, T. (2006). Cognitive abilities and their interplay: Reasoning, crystallized intelligence, working memory components, and sustained attention. *Journal of Individual Differences, 27*(2), 57–72.

Bull, R., & Scerif, G. (2001). Executive functioning as a predictor of children's mathematics ability: Inhibition, switching, and working memory. *Developmental Neuropsychology, 19*, 273–293.

Busse, A., Hensel, A., Gühne, U., Angermeyer, M. C., & Riedel-Heller, S. G. (2006). Mild cognitive impairment: Long-term course of four clinical subtypes. *Neurology, 67*, 2176–2185.

Byrne, B. M. (2001). Structural equation modeling: Perspectives on the present and the future. *International Journal of Testing, 1*(3&4), 327–334.

Caffrey, E., & Fuchs, D. (2007). Differences in performance between students with learning disabilities and mild mental retardation: Implications for categorical instruction. *Learning Disabilities Research & Practice, 22*(2), 119–128.

Calhoun, S. L., & Mayes, S. D. (2005). Processing speed in children with clinical disorders. *Psychology in the Schools, 42*(4), 333–343.

Campbell, D. T., & Fiske, D. W. (1959). Convergent and discriminant validation by the multitrait—multimethod matrix. *Psychological Bulletin, 56*, 81–105.

Carroll, J. B. (1993). *Human cognitive abilities: A survey of factor-analytic studies.* Cambridge, England: Cambridge University Press.

Carroll, J. B. (1997). The three-stratum theory of cognitive abilities. In D. P. Flanagan, J. L. Genshaft, & P. L. Harrison (Eds.), *Contemporary intellectual assessment: Theories, tests, and issu*es (pp. 122–130). New York: Guilford Press.

Cattell, R. B. (1941). Some theoretical issues in adult intelligence testing. *Psychological Bulletin, 38*, 592.

Cattell, R. B. (1943). The measurement of adult intelligence. *Psychological Bulletin, 40*(3), 153–193.

Cattell, R. B. (1957). *Personality and motivation structure and measurement.* New York: World Book.

Cattell, R. B. (1963). Theory of fluid and crystallized intelligence: A critical experiment. *Journal of Educational Psychology, 54*, 1–22.

Cattell, R. B., & Horn, J. L. (1978). A check on the theory of fluid and crystallized intelligence with description of new subtest designs. *Journal of Educational Measurement, 15*, 139–164.

Cederlund, M., & Gillberg, C. (2004). One hundred males with Asperger syndrome: A clinical study of background and associated factors. *Developmental Medicine & Child Neurology, 46*, 652–660.

Chertkow, H., Massoud, F., Nasreddine, Z., Belleville, S., Joanette, Y., Bocti, C. et al. (2008). Diagnosis and treatment of dementia: 3. Mild cognitive impairment and cognitive impairment without dementia. *Canadian Medical Association Journal, 178*(10), 1273–1285.

Cohen, B. H. (1996). *Explaining psychological statistics.* Pacific Grove, CA: Brooke/Cole Publishing Company.

Cohen, J. (1952a). A factor-analytically based rationale for the Wechsler-Bellevue. *Journal of Consulting Psychology 16*(4), 272–277.

Cohen, J. (1952b). Factors underlying Wechsler-Bellevue performance of three neuropsychiatric groups. *The Journal of Abnormal and Social Psychology, 47*(2), 359–365.

Cohen, J. (1957a). A factor-analytically based rationale for the Wechsler Adult Intelligence Scale. *Journal of Consulting Psychology, 21*(6), 451–457.

Cohen, J. (1957b). The factorial structure of the WAIS between early adulthood and old age. *Journal of Consulting Psychology, 21*(4), 283–290.

Cohen, J. (1959). The factorial structure of the WISC at ages 7-6, 10-6, and 13-6. *Journal of Consulting Psychology, 23*(4), 285–299.

Cohen, J. (1988). *Statistical power analysis for the behavioral sciences* (2nd ed.). Hillsdale, NJ: Erlbaum.

Cohen, J. (1990). Things I have learned (so far). *American Psychologist, 45*, 1304–1312.

Cohen, J. (1992). Quantitative methods in psychology: A power primer. *Psychological Bulletin, 112*(1), 155–159.

Cohen, J. (1994). The earth is round (p < .05). *American Psychologist, 49*, 997–1003.

Cohen, M. (1997). *Children's memory scale.* San Antonio, TX: The Psychological Corporation.

Colom, R., Rebollo, I., Palacios, A., Juan-Espinosa, M., & Kyllonen, P. C. (2004). Working memory is (almost) perfectly predicted by g. *Intelligence, 32*, 277–296.

Conners, F. A., Rosenquist, C. J., Arnett, L., Moore, M. S., & Hume, L. E. (2008). Improving memory span in children with Down syndrome. *Journal of Intellectual Disability Research, 52*(3), 244–255.

Cox, E., Mager, D., & Weisbart, E. (2008). *Geographic variation trends in prescription use: 2000 to 2006.* Retrieved May 21, 2008 from http://www.express-scripts.com/industryresearch/outcomes/onlinepublications/study/geoVariationTrends.pdf

Crawford, J. R., Johnson, D. A., Mychalkiw, B., & Moore, J. W. (1997). WAIS–R performance following closed-head injury: A comparison of the clinical utility of summary IQs, factor scores, and subtest scatter indices. *The Clinical Neuropsychologist, 11*(4), 345–355.

Crocker, L., & Algina, J. (1986). *Introduction to classical and modern test theory.* Fort Worth, TX: Harcourt Brace Jovanovich College.

Cronbach, L. (1951). Coefficient alpha and the internal structure of tests. *Psychometrika, 16*(3), 297–334.

Cronbach, L. J., & Meehl, P. E. (1955). Construct validity in psychological tests. *Psychological Bulletin, 52,* 281–302.

Crowe, S. F. (2000). Does the letter number sequencing task measure anything more than digit span? *Assessment, 7,* 113–117.

Davis, F. B. (1959). Interpretation of differences among averages and individual test scores. *Journal of Educational Psychology, 50,* 162–170.

de Jonge, P., & de Jong, P. F. (1996). Working memory, intelligence and reading ability in children. *Personality and Individual Differences, 21*(6), 1007–1020.

Delis, D. C., Kaplan, E., & Kramer, J. H. (2001). *Delis–Kaplan executive function system.* San Antonio, TX: Harcourt Assessment.

Delis, D. C., Kramer, J. H., Kaplan, E., & Ober, B. A. (2000). *California verbal learning test–second edition.* San Antonio, TX: Harcourt Assessment.

Demakis, G. J., Sawyer, T. P., Fritz, D., & Sweet, J. J. (2001). Incidental recall on WAIS-R Digit Symbol discriminates Alzheimer's and Parkinson's diseases. *Journal of Clinical Psychology, 57,* 387–394.

Denckla, M. B., & Rudel, R. G. (1976). Rapid "automatized" naming (R.A.N.): Dyslexia differentiated from other learning disabilities. *Neuropsychologia, 14,* 471–479.

Dennis, M., Lockyer, L., Lazenby, A. L., Donnelly, R. E., Wilkinson, M., & Schoonheyt, W. (1999). Intelligence patterns among children with high-functioning autism, phenylketonuria, and childhood head injury. *Journal of Autism and Developmental Disorders, 29,* 5–17.

Devanand, D. P., Habeck, C. G., Tabert, M. H., Scarmeas, N., Pelton, G. H., Moeller, J. R. et al. (2006). PET network abnormalities and cognitive decline in patients with mild cognitive impairment. *Neuropsychopharmacology, 31,* 1327–1334.

Dickinson, D., Iannone, V. N., & Gold, J. M. (2002). Factor structure of the Wechsler Adult Intelligence Scale–III in schizophrenia. *Assessment, 9*(2), 171–180.

Dige, N., & Wik, G. (2005). Adult attention deficit hyperactivity disorder identified by neuropsychological testing. *International Journal of Neuroscience, 115,* 169–183.

Dikmen, S. S., Machamer, J. E., Winn, H. R., & Temkin, N. R. (1995). Neuropsychological outcome at 1-year post head injury. *Neuropsychology, 9*(1), 80–90.

Dikmen, S., Reitan, R. M., & Temkin, N. R. (1983). Neuropsychological recovery in head injury. *Archives of Neurology, 40,* 333–338.

Donders, J. (1997). Sensitivity of the WISC–III to injury severity in children with traumatic head injury. *Assessment, 4,* 107–109.

Donders, J., Tulsky, D. S., & Zhu, J. (2001). Criterion validity of new WAIS–III subtest scores after traumatic brain injury. *Journal of the International Neuropsychological Society, 7,* 892–898.

Doniger, G. M., Dwolatzky, T., Zucker, D. W., Chertkow, H., Crystal, H., Schweiger, A. et al. (2006). Computerized cognitive testing battery identifies mild cognitive impairment and mild dementia even in the presence of depressive symptoms. *American Journal of Alzheimer's Disease and Other Dementias, 21*(1), 28–36.

Dubois, B., Feldman, H. H., Jacova, C., DeKosky, S. T., Barberger-Gateau, P., Cummings, J. et al. (2007). Research criteria for the diagnosis of Alzheimer's disease: Revising the NINCDS-ADRDA criteria. *The Lancet Neurology, 6,* 734–746.

Dudek, F. J. (1979). The continuing misinterpretation of the standard error of measurement. *Psychological Bulletin, 86,* 335–337.

Duncan, J., Burgess, P., & Emslie, H. (1995). Fluid intelligence after frontal lobe lesions. *Neuropsychologia, 33*, 261–268.

Earnst, K. S., Wadley, V. G., Aldridge, T. M., Steenwyk, A. B., Hammond, A. E., Harrell, L. E. et al. (2001). Loss of financial capacity in Alzheimer's disease: The role of working memory. *Aging, Neuropsychology, and Cognition, 8*(2), 109–119.

Economou, A., Papageorgiou, S., & Karageorgiou, C. (2006). Working-delayed memory difference detects mild cognitive impairment without being affected by age and education. *Journal of Clinical and Experimental Neuropsychology, 28*, 528–535.

Elliott, C. D. (1990). *Differential ability scales.* San Antonio, TX: The Psychological Corporation.

Engle, R. W., Tuholski, S. W., Laughlin, J. E., & Conway, A. R. A. (1999). Working memory, short-term memory, and general fluid intelligence: A latent-variable approach. *Journal of Experimental Psychology: General, 128*, 309–331.

Feehan, M., Knight, R. G., & Partridge, F. M. (1991). Cognitive complaint and test performance in elderly patients suffering depression or dementia. *International Journal of Geriatric Psychiatry, 6*, 287–293.

Finkel, D., Reynolds, C. A., McArdle, J. J., & Pederson, N. L. (2007). Age changes in processing speed as a leading indicator of cognitive aging. *Psychology and Aging, 22*(3), 558–568.

Fischer, P., Jungwirth, S., Zehetmayer, S., Weissgram, S., Hoenigschnabl, S., Gelpi, E. et al. (2007). Conversion from subtypes of mild cognitive impairment to Alzheimer dementia. *Neurology, 68*, 288–291.

Flanagan, D. P., & Mascolo, J. T. (2005). Psychoeducational assessment and learning disability diagnosis. In D. P. Flanagan & P. L. Harrison (Eds.), *Contemporary intellectual assessment: Theories, tests, and issues* (2nd ed., pp. 521–544). New York: Guilford Press.

Fletcher, J. M., Coulter, W. A., Reschly, D. J., & Vaughn, S. (2004). Alternative approaches to the definition and identification of learning disabilities: Some questions and answers. *Annals of Dyslexia, 54*(2), 304–331.

Fletcher-Janzen, E., & Reynolds, C. R. (Eds.). (2008). *Neuropsychological perspectives on learning disabilities in the era of RTI: Recommendations for diagnosis and intervention.* Hoboken, NJ: John Wiley & Sons.

Flynn, J. R. (1984). The mean IQ of Americans: Massive gains 1932 to 1978. *Psychological Bulletin, 95*, 29–51.

Flynn, J. R. (1987). Massive IQ gains in 14 nations: What IQ tests really measure. *Psychological Bulletin, 101*, 171–191.

Flynn, J. R. (1999). Searching for justice: The discovery of IQ gains over time. *American Psychologist, 54*, 5–20.

Flynn, J. R. (2007). *What is intelligence? Beyond the Flynn effect.* New York: Cambridge University Press.

Flynn, J. R., & Weiss, L. G. (2007). American IQ gains from 1932 to 2002: The WISC subtests and educational progress. *International Journal of Testing, 7*(2), 209–224.

Fontana, S. (2004). The instructional approach: Improving the performance of a person with moderate mental retardation in a reasoning task. *Journal of Cognitive Education and Psychology, 4*(1), 148–150.

Fry, A. F., & Hale, S. (1996). Processing speed, working memory, and fluid intelligence: Evidence for a developmental cascade. *Psychological Science, 7*, 237–241.

Ganguli, M., Dodge, H. H., Shen, C., & DeKosky, S. T. (2004). Mild cognitive impairment, amnestic type: An epidemiologic study. *Neurology, 63*, 115–121.

Gathercole, S. E., Hitch, G. J., Service, E., & Martin, A. J. (1997). Phonological short-term memory and new word learning in children. *Developmental Psychology, 33*, 966–979.

Geldmacher, D. S., Fritsch, T., & Riedel, T. M. (2000). Effects of stimulus properties and age on random-array letter cancellation tasks. *Aging, Neuropsychology, and Cognition, 7*(3), 194–204.

Gilchrist, A., Green, J., Cox, A., Burton, D., Rutter, M., & Le Couteur, A. (2001). Development and current functioning in adolescents with Asperger syndrome: A comparative study. *Journal of Child Psychology and Psychiatry, and Allied Disciplines, 42*, 227–240.

Giovannetti, T., Lamar, M., Cloud, B. S., Swenson, R., Fein, D., Kaplan, E. et al. (2001). Different underlying mechanisms for deficits in concept formation in dementia. *Archives of Clinical Neuropsychology, 16*, 547–560.

Glutting, J. J., McDermott, P. A., & Stanley, J. C. (1987). Resolving differences among methods of establishing confidence limits for test scores. *Educational and Psychological Measurement, 47*, 607–614.

Golden, Z., Bouvier, M., Selden, J., Mattis, K., Todd, M., & Golden C. (2005). Differential performance of Alzheimer's and vascular dementia patients on a brief battery of neuropsychological tests. *International Journal of Neuroscience, 115,* 1569–1577.

Goldstein, G., & Beers, S. R. (Eds.). (2003). *Comprehensive handbook of psychological assessment: Vol. 1.: Intellectual and neuropsychological assessment.* Hoboken, NJ: Wiley.

Goldstein, G., Beers, S. R., Siegel, D. J., & Minshew, N. J. (2001). A comparison of WAIS–R profiles in adults with high-functioning autism or differing subtypes of learning disability. *Applied Neuropsychology, 8*(3), 148–154.

Goldstein, G., & Hersen, M. (2000). *Handbook of psychological assessment* (3rd ed.). Kidlington, Oxford, United Kingdom: Elsevier Science.

Goldstein, G., Minshew, N. J., Allen, D. N., & Seaton, B. E. (2002). High-functioning autism and schizophrenia: A comparison of an early and late onset neurodevelopmental disorder. *Archives of Clinical Neuropsychology, 17,* 461–475.

Gorlyn, M., Keilp, J. G., Oquendo, M. A., Burke, A. K., Sackeim, H. A., & Mann, J. J. (2006). The WAIS–III and major depression: Absence of VIQ/PIQ differences. *Journal of Clinical and Experimental Neuropsychology, 28,* 1145–1157.

Gottfredson, L. S. (2008). Of what value is intelligence? In A. Prifitera, D. Saklofske, & L. G. Weiss (Eds.), *WISC–IV clinical assessment and intervention* (2nd ed., pp. 545–564). Amsterdam: Elsevier.

Green, R. E. A., Melo, B., Christensen, B., Ngo, L., Monette, G., & Bradbury, C. (2008). Measuring premorbid IQ in traumatic brain injury: An examination of the validity of the Wechsler Test of Adult Reading (WTAR). *Journal of Clinical and Experimental Neuropsychology, 30,* 163–172.

Greiffenstein, M. F., & Baker, W. J. (2002). Neuropsychological and psychosocial correlates of adult arithmetic deficiency. *Neuropsychology, 16,* 451–458.

Groth-Marnat, G. (2003). *Handbook of psychological assessment* (4th ed.). New York: Wiley.

Gualtieri, C. T., & Johnson, L. G. (2006). Reliability and validity of a computerized neurocognitive test battery, CNS vital signs. *Archives of Clinical Neuropsychology, 21,* 623–643.

Guilford, J. P. (1954). *Psychometric methods* (2nd ed.). New York: McGraw-Hill.

Guilford, J. P., & Fruchter, B. (1978). *Fundamental statistics in psychology and education* (6th ed.). New York: McGraw-Hill.

Gustafsson, J. E., & Undheim, J. O. (1996). Individual differences in cognitive functions. In D. C. Berliner & R. C. Calfee (Eds.), *Handbook of educational psychology* (pp. 186–242). New York: MacMillan.

Hale, J. B., & Fiorello, C. A. (2004). *School neuropsychology: A practitioner's handbook.* New York: Guilford Press.

Hale, J. B., Naglieri, J. A., Kaufman, A. S., & Kavale, K. A. (2004). Specific learning disability classification in the new Individuals with Disabilities Education Act: The danger of good ideas. *The School Psychologist, 58,* 6–13, 29.

Hambleton, R. K. (1993). Principles and selected applications of item response theory. In R. L. Linn (Ed.), *Educational measurement* (3rd ed., pp. 147–220). Phoenix, AZ: Oryx Press.

Harcourt Assessment. (2005). *Wechsler individual achievement test–second edition examiner's manual: Update 2005.* San Antonio, TX: Author.

Hart, R. P., Kwentus, J. A., Wade, J. B., & Hamer, R. M. (1987). Digit symbol performance in mild dementia and depression. *Journal of Consulting and Clinical Psychology, 55*(2), 236–238.

Harvey, P. D., Reischenberg, A., Romero, M., Granholm, E., & Siever, L. J. (2006). Dual-task information processing in schizotypal personality disorder: Evidence of impaired processing capacity. *Neuropsychology, 20*(4), 453–460.

Hill, R. D., Storandt, M., & LaBarge, E. (1992). Psychometric discrimination of moderate senile dementia of the Alzheimer type. *Archives of Neurology, 49,* 377–380.

Hinshaw, S. P., Carte, E. T., Sami, N., Treuting, J. J., & Zupan, B. A. (2002). Preadolescent girls with Attention-Deficit/Hyperactivity Disorder II: Neuropsychological performance in relation to subtypes and individual classification. *Journal of Consulting and Clinical Psychology, 70,* 1099–1111.

Hirono, N., Mori, E., Ishii, K., Imamura, T., Shimomura, T., Tanimukai, S. et al. (1998). Regional metabolism: Associations with dyscalculia in Alzheimer's disease. *Journal of Neurology, Neurosurgery, and Psychiatry, 65*(6), 913–916.

Hiscock, M., Inch, R., & Gleason, A. (2002). Raven's Progressive Matrices performance in adults with traumatic brain injury. *Applied Neuropsychology, 9,* 129–138.

Holland, P. W., & Thayer, D. T. (1988). Differential item performance and the Mantel-Haenszel procedure. In H. Wainer & H. I. Braun (Eds.), *Test validity* (pp. 129–145). Hillsdale, NJ: Erlbaum.

Horn, J. L. (1985). Remodeling old models of intelligence. In B. B. Wolman (Ed.), *Handbook of intelligence: Theories, measurement, and applications* (pp. 267–300). New York: Wiley.

Horn, J. L. (1988). Thinking about human abilities. In J. R. Nesselroade & R. B. Cattell (Eds.), *Handbook of multivariate experimental psychology* (2nd ed., pp. 645–685). New York: Plenum.

Horn, J. L. (1991). Measurement of intellectual capabilities: A review of theory. In K. S. McGrew, J. K. Werder, & R. W. Woodcock (Eds.), *Woodcock-Johnson technical manual* (Rev. ed., pp. 197–232). Itasca, IL: Riverside.

Horn, J. L., & Noll, J. (1997). Human cognitive capabilities: Gf-Gc theory. In D. P. Flanagan, J. L. Genshaft, & P. L. Harrison (Eds.), *Contemporary intellectual assessment: Theories, tests, and issues* (pp. 53–91). New York: Guilford Press.

Hu, L., & Bentler, P. M. (1999). Cutoff criteria for fit indexes in covariance structure analysis: Conventional criteria versus new alternatives. *Structural Equation Modeling, 6*(1), 1–55.

Hubbard, R., & Lindsay, R. M. (2008). Why *p* values are not a useful measure of evidence in statistical significance testing. *Theory & Psychology, 18*(1), 69–88.

Hunter, J. E. (1997). Needed: A ban on the significance test. *Psychological Science, 8,* 3–7.

Individuals with Disabilities Education Improvement Act of 2004, Pub. L. 108–446, 118 Stat. 328 (2004).

Iverson, G. L., Turner, R. A., & Green, P. (1999). Predictive validity of WAIS–R VIQ-PIQ splits in persons with major depression. *Journal of Clinical Psychology, 55,* 519–524.

Ivnik, R. J., Malec, J. F., Smith, G. E., Tangalos, E. G., Petersen, R. C., Kokmen, E. et al. (1992). Mayo's older Americans normative studies: WAIS–R norms for ages 56–97. *The Clinical Neuropsychologist, 6*(Suppl.), 1–30.

Jarrold, C., Purser, H. R. M., & Brock, J. (2006). Short-term memory in Down syndrome. In T. P. Alloway & S. E. Gathercole (Eds.), *Working memory and neurodevelopmental disorders* (pp. 239–266). New York: Psychology Press.

Jenkins, L., Myerson, J., Joerding, J. A., & Hale, S. (2000). Converging evidence that visuospatial cognition is more age-sensitive than verbal cognition. *Psychology and Aging, 15*(1), 157–175.

Jenkinson, J. C. (1983). Is speed of information processing related to fluid or to crystallized intelligence? *Intelligence, 7,* 91–106.

Jennett, B. (2002). The Glasgow coma scale: History and current practice. *Trauma, 4,* 91–103.

Jensen, A. R. (1982). Level I/Level II: Factors or categories? *Journal of Educational Psychology, 74,* 868–873.

Jensen, A. R. (1998). *The g factor: The science of mental ability.* Westport, CT: Praeger.

Jöreskog, K. G., & Sörbom, D. (1993). *LISREL 8: User's reference guide.* Chicago: Scientific Software International.

Kail, R. (2000). Speed of information processing: Developmental change and links to intelligence. *Journal of School Psychology, 38,* 51–61.

Kail, R., & Hall, L. K. (1994). Processing speed, naming speed, and reading. *Developmental Psychology, 30,* 949–954.

Kail, R., & Salthouse, T. A. (1994). Processing speed as a mental capacity. *Acta Psychologica, 86,* 199–225.

Kaplan, E. (1988). A process approach to neuropsychological assessment. In T. J. Boll & B. K. Bryant (Eds.), *Clinical neuropsychology and brain function: Research, measurement, and practice* (pp. 129–167). Washington, DC: American Psychological Association.

Kaplan, E., Fein, D., Morris, R., & Delis, D. C. (1991). *WAIS–R as a neuropsychological instrument.* San Antonio, TX: The Psychological Corporation.

Kaufman, A. S. (2000). Seven questions about the WAIS–III regarding differences in abilities across the 16 to 89 year life span. *School Psychology Quarterly, 15*(1), 3–29.

Kaufman, A. S., & Kaufman, N. L. (1993). *Kaufman adolescent and adult intelligence test.* Circle Pines, MN: American Guidance Service.

Kaufman, A. S., & Lichtenberger, E. O. (1999). *Essentials of WAIS–III assessment.* New York: Wiley.

Kaufman, A. S., & Lichtenberger, E. O. (2006). *Assessing adolescent and adult intelligence* (3rd ed.). Hoboken, NJ: Wiley.

Kaufman, A. S., Lichtenberger, E. O., & McLean, J. E. (2001). Two- and three-factor solutions of the WAIS–III. *Assessment, 8*(3), 267–280.

Kavale, K. A., Holdnack, J. A., & Mostert, M. P. (2005). Responsiveness to intervention and the identification of specific learning disability: A critique and alternative proposal. *Learning Disability Quarterly, 28*, 2–16.

Kazui, H., Hashimoto, M., Hirono, N., & Mori, E. (2003). Nature of personal semantic memory: Evidence from Alzheimer's disease. *Neuropsychologia, 41,* 981–988.

Keith, T. Z. (1985). Questioning the K–ABC: What does it measure? *School Psychology Review, 14,* 19–20.

Keith, T. Z. (1990). Confirmatory and hierarchical confirmatory analysis of the differential ability scales. *Journal of Psychoeducational Assessment, 8*(3), 391–405.

Kirk, R. E. (1996). Practical significance: A concept whose time has come. *Educational and Psychological Measurement, 56,* 746–759.

Kirk, R. E. (2001). Promoting good statistical practices: Some suggestions. *Educational and Psychological Measurement, 61,* 213–218.

Koyama, T., Tachimori, H., Osada, H., Takeda, T., & Kurita, H. (2007). Cognitive and symptom profiles in Asperger's syndrome and high-functioning autism. *Psychiatry and Clinical Neurosciences, 61,* 99–104.

Lange, R. T., & Chelune, G. J. (2006). Application of new WAIS–III/WMS–III discrepancy scores for evaluating memory functioning: Relationship between intellectual and memory ability. *Journal of Clinical and Experimental Neuropsychology, 28,* 592–604.

Larrabee, G. J., Largen, J. W., & Levin, H. S. (1985). Sensitivity of age-decline resistant ("hold") WAIS subtests to Alzheimer's disease. *Journal of Clinical and Experimental Neuropsychology, 7*(5), 497–504.

Leckliter, I. N., Matarazzo, J. D., & Silverstein, A. B. (1986). A literature review of factor analytic studies of the WAIS–R. *Journal of Clinical Psychology, 42,* 332–342.

Lezak, M. D., Howieson, D. B., & Loring, D. W. (with Hannay, H. J., & Fischer, J. S.). (2004). *Neuropsychological assessment* (4th ed.). New York: Oxford University Press.

Li, H., Rosenthal, R., & Rubin, D. B. (1996). Reliability of measurement in psychology: From Spearman-Brown to maximal reliability. *Psychological Methods, 1,* 98–107.

Likert, R., & Quasha, W. H. (1995). *Revised Minnesota paper form board test* (2nd ed.). San Antonio, TX: The Psychological Corporation.

Lindenberger, U., Mayr, U., & Kliegl, R. (1993). Speed and intelligence in old age. *Psychology and Aging, 8*(2), 207–220.

Liss, M., Fein, D., Allen, D., Dunn, M., Feinstein, C., Morris, R. et al. (2001). Executive functioning in high-functioning children with autism. *Journal of Child Psychology and Psychiatry, 42*(2), 261–270.

Loewenstein, D. A., Acevedo, A., Ownby, R., Agron, J., Barker, W. W., Isaacson, R. et al. (2006). Using different memory cutoffs to assess mild cognitive impairment. *American Journal of Geriatric Psychiatry, 14*(11), 911–919.

Lucas, J. A., & Addeo, R. (2006). Traumatic brain injury and postconcussion syndrome. In P. J. Snyder, P. D. Nussbaum, & D. L. Robins (Eds.), *Clinical neuropsychology: A pocket handbook for assessment* (2nd ed., pp. 351–380). Washington, DC: American Psychological Association.

Luis, C. A., Loewenstein, D. A., Acevedo, A., Barker, W. W., & Duara, R. (2003). Mild cognitive impairment: Directions for future research. *Neurology, 61,* 438–444.

MacDonald, M. C., Almor, A., Henderson, V. W., Kempler, D., & Andersen, E. S. (2001). Assessing working memory and language comprehension in Alzheimer's disease. *Brain and Language, 78,* 17–42.

Mackintosh, N. J., & Bennett, E. S. (2003). The fractionation of working memory maps onto different components of intelligence. *Intelligence, 31,* 519–531.

MacMillan, D. L., & Forness, S. R. (1998). The role of IQ in special education placement decisions: Primary and determinative or peripheral and inconsequential? *Remedial and Special Education, 19,* 239–253.

Magnusson, D. (1967). *Test theory.* Reading, MA: Addison-Wesley.

Mandelli, L., Serretti, A., Colombo, C., Florita, M., Santoro, A., Rossino, D. et al. (2006). Improvement of cognitive functioning in mood disorder patients with depressive symptomatic recovery during treatment: An exploratory analysis. *Psychiatry and Clinical Neurosciences, 60,* 598–604.

Marchetta, N. D. J., Hurks, P. P. M., Krabbendam, L., & Jolles, J. (2008). Interference control, working memory, concept shifting, and verbal fluency in adults with attention-deficit/hyperactivity disorder (ADHD). *Neuropsychology, 22*(1), 74–84.

Marland, S. P. (1972). *Education of the gifted and talented – Volume 1: Report to the Congress of the United States by the U. S. Commissioner of Education.* Washington, DC:U.S. Government Printing Office. (ERIC Document Reproduction Service No. ED056243)

Matarazzo, J. D. (1972). *Wechsler's measurement and appraisal of adult intelligence* (5th ed.). Baltimore: Williams & Wilkins.

Matarazzo, J. D. (1990). Psychological assessment versus psychological testing: Validation from Binet to the school, clinic, and courtroom. *American Psychologist, 45,* 999–1017.

Matarazzo, J. D., Daniel, M. H., Prifitera, A., & Herman, D. O. (1988). Inter-subtest scatter in the WAIS–R standardization sample. *Journal of Clinical Psychology, 44,* 940–950.

Matarazzo, J. D., & Herman, D. O. (1985). Clinical uses of the WAIS–R: Base rates of differences between VIQ and PIQ in the WAIS–R standardization sample. In B. B. Wolman (Ed.), *Handbook of intelligence: Theories, measurement, and applications* (pp. 899–932). New York: Wiley.

Mathias, J. L., & Wheaton, P. (2007). Changes in attention and information-processing speed following severe traumatic brain injury: A meta-analytic review. *Neuropsychology, 21*(2), 212–223.

Mattson, A. J., & Levin, H. S. (1990). Frontal lobe dysfunction following closed head injury: A review of the literature. *Journal of Nervous and Mental Disease, 178*(5), 282–291.

Mayes, S. D., & Calhoun, S. L. (2003). Analysis of WISC–III, Stanford-Binet: IV, and academic achievement test scores in children with autism. *Journal of Autism and Developmental Disorders, 33*(3), 329–341.

Mayes, S. D., & Calhoun, S. L. (2007). Wechsler Intelligence Scale for Children–Third and Fourth Edition predictors of academic achievement in children with attention-deficit/hyperactivity disorder. *School Psychology Quarterly, 22*(2), 234–249.

McArdle, J. J., & Woodcock, R. W. (1997). Expanding test-retest designs to include developmental time-lag components. *Psychological Methods, 2,* 403–435.

McFie, J. (1975). *Assessment of organic intellectual impairment.* Oxford, England: Academic Press.

McGraw, K. O., & Wong, S. P. (1996). Forming inferences about some intraclass correlation coefficients. *Psychological Methods, 1,* 30–46.

McKhann, G., Drachman, D., Folstein, M., Katzman, R., Price, D., & Stadlan, E. M. (1984). Clinical diagnosis of Alzheimer's disease: Report of the NINCDS-ADRDA work group under the auspices of Department of Health and Human Services Task Force on Alzheimer's disease. *Neurology, 34,* 939–944.

Miller, C. J., Miller, S. R., Bloom, J. S., Jones, L., Lindstrom, W., Craggs, J. et al. (2006). Testing the double-deficit hypothesis in an adult sample. *Annals of Dyslexia, 56*(1), 83–102.

Minshew, N. J., Siegel, D. J., Goldstein G., & Weldy, S. (1994). Verbal problem solving in high functioning autistic individuals. *Archives of Clinical Neuropsychology, 9,* 31–40.

Mitchell, R. E., Grandy, T. G., & Lupo, J. V. (1986). Comparison of the WAIS and the WAIS–R in the upper ranges of IQ. *Professional Psychology: Research and Practice, 17*(1), 82–83.

Morasco, B. J., Gfeller, J. D., & Chibnall, J. T. (2006). The relationship between measures of psychopathology, intelligence, and memory among adults seen for psychoeducational assessment. *Archives of Clinical Neuropsychology, 21,* 297–301.

Na, D. L., Adair, J. C., Kang, Y., Chung, C. S., Lee, K. H., & Heilman, K. M. (1999). Motor perseverative behavior on a line cancellation task. *Neurology, 52,* 1569–1576.

Naismith, S. L., Hickie, I. B., Turner, K., Little, C. L., Winter, V., Ward, P. B. et al. (2003). Neuropsychological performance in patients with depression is associated with clinical, etiological and genetic risk factors. *Journal of Clinical and Experimental Neuropsychology, 25*(6), 866–877.

Nakahachi, T., Iwase, M., Takahashi, H., Honaga, E., Sekiyama, R., Ukai, S. et al. (2006). Discrepancy of performance among working memory-related tasks in autism spectrum disorders was caused by task characteristics, apart from working memory, which could interfere with task execution. *Psychiatry and Clinical Neurosciences, 60,* 312–318.

Nordlund, A., Rolstad, S., Klang, O., Lind, K., Hansen, S., & Wallin, A. (2007). Cognitive profiles of mild cognitive impairment with and without vascular disease. *Neuropsychology, 21*(6), 706–712.

Nunnally, J., & Bernstein, I. H. (1994). *Psychometric theory* (3rd ed.). New York: McGraw-Hill.

Palmer, K., Wang, H. X., Backman, L., Winblad, B., & Fratiglioni, L. (2002). Differential evolution of cognitive impairment in nondemented older persons: Results from the Kungsholmen project. *American Journal of Psychiatry, 159*(3), 436–442.

Park, N. W., Moscovitch, M., & Robertson, I. H. (1999). Divided attention impairments after traumatic brain injury. *Neuropsychologia, 37,* 1119–1133.

Payne, R. W., & Jones, H. G. (1957). Statistics for the investigation of individual cases. *Journal of Clinical Psychology, 13,* 115–121.

Pearson. (in press). *WAIS–IV/WMS–IV advanced clinical solutions.* San Antonio, TX: Author.

Perbal, S., Couillet, J., Azouvi, P., & Pouthas, V. (2003). Relationships between time estimation, memory, attention, and processing speed in patients with severe traumatic brain injury. *Neuropsychologia, 41,* 1599–1610.

Petersen, R. C., Smith, G. E., Waring, S. C., Ivnik, R. J., Tangalos, E. G., & Kokmen, E. (1999). Mild cognitive impairment: Clinical characterization and outcome. *Archives of Neurology, 56,* 303–308.

Petersen, R. C., Stevens, J. C., Ganguli, M., Tangalos, E. G., Cummings, J. L., & DeKosky, S. T. (2001). Practice parameter: Early detection of dementia: Mild cognitive impairment (an evidence-based review). *Neurology, 56,* 1133–1142.

Prifitera, A., Weiss, L. G., & Saklofske, D. H. (1998). The WISC–III in context. In A. Prifitera & D. H. Saklofske (Eds.), *WISC–III clinical use and interpretation: Scientist-practitioner perspectives* (pp. 1–38). San Diego, CA: Academic Press.

Raiford, S. E., Weiss, L. G., Rolfhus, E., & Coalson, D. (2005). General ability index [WISC–IV Technical Report No. 4]. Retrieved April 8, 2008, from http://harcourtassessment.com/hai/Images/pdf/wisciv/WISCIVTechReport4.pdf

Randolph, C. (1998). *Repeatable battery for the assessment of neuropsychological status.* San Antonio, TX: The Psychological Corporation.

Reynolds, C. R. (1997). Forward and backward memory span should not be combined for clinical analysis. *Archives of Clinical Neuropsychology, 12,* 29–40.

Ribaupierre, A. de, & Lecerf, T. (2006). Relationships between working memory and intelligence from a developmental perspective: Convergent evidence from a neo-Piagetian and a psychometric approach. *European Journal of Cognitive Psychology, 18*(1), 109–137.

Ritchie, K., Artero, S., & Touchon, J. (2001). Classification criteria for mild cognitive impairment: A population-based validation study. *Neurology, 56,* 37–42.

Roid, G. H. (2003). *Stanford-Binet intelligence scales, fifth edition, technical manual.* Itasca, IL: Riverside.

Ryan, J. J., Paolo, A. M., Oehlert, M. E., & Coker, M. C. (1991). Relationship of sex, race, age, education, and level of intelligence to the frequency of occurrence of a WAIS–R marker for dementia of the Alzheimer's type. *Developmental Neuropsychology, 7*(4), 451–458.

Ryan, J. J., Sattler, J. M., & Lopez, S. J. (2000). Age effects on Wechsler Adult Intelligence Scale–III subtests. *Archives of Clinical Neuropsychology, 15*(4), 311–317.

Saccuzzo, D. P., Johnson, N. E., & Russell, G. (1992). Verbal versus performance IQs for gifted African-American, Caucasian, Filipino, and Hispanic children. *Psychological Assessment, 4*(2), 239–244.

Saklofske, D. H., Prifitera, A., Weiss, L. G., Rolfhus, E., & Zhu, J. (2005). Clinical interpretation of the WISC–IV FSIQ and GAI. In A. Prifitera, D. H. Saklofske, & L. G. Weiss (Eds.), *WISC–IV clinical use and interpretation: Scientist-practitioner perspectives* (pp. 33–65). New York: Academic Press.

Saklofske, D. H., Weiss, L. G., Raiford, S. E., & Prifitera, A. (2006). Advanced interpretive issues with the WISC–IV full-scale IQ and general ability index scores. In L. G. Weiss, D. H. Saklofske, A. Prifitera, & J. A. Holdnack (Eds.), *WISC–IV advanced clinical interpretation* (pp. 99–138). New York: Elsevier.

Salthouse, T. A. (1996). The processing-speed theory of adult age differences in cognition. *Psychological Review, 103*(3), 403–428.

Salthouse, T. A. (2000). Aging and measures of processing speed. *Biological Psychology, 54*, 35–54.

Salthouse, T. A. (2004). What and when of cognitive aging. *Current Direction in Psychological Science, 13*(4), 140–144.

Salthouse, T. A., & Ferrer-Caja, E. (2003). What needs to be explained to account for age-related effects on multiple cognitive variables? *Psychology and Aging, 18*(1), 91–110.

Salthouse, T. A., & Pink, J. E. (2008). Why is working memory related to fluid intelligence? *Psychonomic Bulletin & Review, 15*(2), 364–371.

Sattler, J. M. (2008a). *Assessment of children: Cognitive foundations* (5th ed.). San Diego, CA: Author.

Sattler, J. M. (2008b). *Resource guide to accompany assessment of children: Cognitive foundations* (5th ed.). San Diego, CA: Author.

Schalock, R. L., Luckasson, R. A., & Shogren, K. A. (with Borthwick-Duffy, S., Bradley, V., Buntinx, W. H. E., Coulter, D. L., Craig, E. M., Gomez, S. C. et al.). (2007). The renaming of mental retardation: Understanding the change to the term intellectual disability. *Intellectual and Developmental Disabilities, 45*(2), 116–124.

Schinka, J. A., Vanderploeg, R. D., & Curtiss, G. (1997). WISC–III subtest scatter as a function of highest subtest scaled score. *Psychological Assessment, 9*, 83–88.

Schumacker, R., & Lomax, R. (2004). *A beginner's guide to structural equation modeling* (2nd ed.). Mahwah, NJ: Erlbaum.

Schweiger, A., Abramovitch, A., Doniger, G. M., & Simon, E. S. (2007). A clinical construct validity study of a novel computerized battery for the diagnosis of ADHD in young adults. *Journal of Clinical and Experimental Neuropsychology, 29*(1), 100–111.

Schweizer, K., & Moosbrugger, H. (2004). Attention and working memory as predictors of intelligence. *Intelligence, 32*, 329–347.

Scruggs, T. E., & Mastropieri, M. A. (2002). On babies and bathwater: Addressing the problems of identification of learning diabilities. *Learning Disability Quarterly, 25*, 155–168.

Shinn, M. R. (2007). Identifying students at risk, monitoring performance, and determining eligibility within response to intervention: Research on educational need and benefit from academic intervention. *School Psychology Review, 36*(4), 601–617.

Shrout, P., & Fleiss, J. (1979). Intraclass correlations: Uses in assessing rater reliability. *Psychological Bulletin, 86*, 420–428.

Siegel, L. S. (1989). IQ is irrelevant to the definition of learning disabilities. *Journal of Learning Disabilities, 22*, 469–478, 486.

Siegel, L. S. (2003). IQ-discrepancy definitions and the diagnosis of LD: Introduction to the special issue. *Journal of Learning Disabilities, 36*, 2–3.

Siegel, D. J., Minshew, N. J., & Goldstein, G. (1996). Wechsler IQ profiles in diagnosis of high-functioning autism. *Journal of Autism and Developmental Disorders, 26*, 389–406.

Silver, N. C., & Dunlap, W. P. (1987). Averaging correlation coefficients: Should Fisher's *z* transformation be used? *Journal of Applied Psychology, 72*, 146–148.

Silverstein, A. B. (1981). Reliability and abnormality of test score differences. *Journal of Clinical Psychology, 37*, 392–394.

Silverstein, A. B. (1982). Two- and four-subtest short forms of the Wechsler adult intelligence scale—revised. *Journal of Consulting and Clinical Psychology, 50*, 415–418.

Slate, J. R. (1995). Discrepancies between IQ and index scores for a clinical sample of students: Useful diagnostic indicators? *Psychology in the Schools, 32*, 103–108.

Sparrow, S., & Gurland, S. T. (1998). Assessment of gifted children with the WISC–III. In A. Prifitera, & D. H. Saklofske (Eds.), *WISC–III clinical use and interpretation: Scientist-practitioner perspectives* (pp. 59–72). San Diego: Academic Press.

Spearman, C. (1904). "General intelligence": Objectively determined and measured. *American Journal of Psychology, 15*, 201–293.

Spek, A. A., Scholte, E. M., & van Berckelaer-Onnes, I. (2008). Brief report: The use of WAIS–III in adults with HFA and Asperger syndrome. *Journal of Austim and Developmental Disorders, 38*, 782–787.

Spruill, J. (1996). Composite SAS of the Stanford-Binet intelligence scale, fourth edition: Is it determined by only one area SAS? *Psychological Assessment, 8,* 328–330.

Spruill, J. (1998). Assessment of mental retardation with the WISC–III. In A. Prifitera & D. H. Saklofske (Eds.), *WISC–III clinical use and interpretation: Scientist-practitioner perspectives* (pp. 73–91). San Diego: Academic Press.

Stanley, J. C. (1971). Reliability. In R. L. Thorndike (Ed.), *Educational measurement* (2nd ed., pp. 356–442). Washington, DC: American Council on Education.

Stanovich, K. E. (1986). Matthew effects in reading: Some consequences of individual differences in the acquisition of literacy. *Reading Research Quarterly, 21,* 360–407.

Stanovich, K. E., & Siegel, L. S. (1994). Phenotypic performance profile of children with reading disabilities: A regression-based test of the phonological-core variable-difference model. *Journal of Educational Psychology, 86,* 24–53.

Steiger, J. H. (1990). Structural model evaluation and modification: An interval estimation approach. *Multivariate Behavioral Research, 25,* 173–180.

Sternberg, R. J. (1995). *In search of the human mind.* Fort Worth, TX: Harcourt Brace College.

Sternberg, R. J. (Ed.). (2000). *Handbook of intelligence.* New York: Cambridge University Press.

Stevens, J. (1996). *Applied multivariate statistics for the social sciences.* Mahwah, NJ: Erlbaum.

Storandt, M. (1994). General principles of assessment of older adults. In M. Storandt & G. R. VandenBos (Eds.), *Neuropsychological assessment of dementia and depression in older adults: A clinician's guide* (pp. 7–32). Washington, DC: American Psychological Association.

Strauss, E., Spreen, O., & Hunter, M. (2000). Implications of test revisions for research. *Psychological Assessment, 12,* 237–244.

Strube, M. J. (1988). Some comments of the use of magnitude-of-effect estimates. *Journal of Counseling Psychology, 35,* 342–345.

Süß, H.-M., Oberauer, K., Wittmann, W. W., Wilhelm, O., & Schulze, R. (2002). Working-memory capacity explains reasoning ability—and a little bit more. *Intelligence, 30,* 261–288.

Swanson, H. L., & Howell, M. (2001). Working memory, short-term memory, and speech rate as predictors of children's reading performance at different ages. *Journal of Educational Psychology, 9,* 720–734.

Swanson, H. L., & Jerman, O. (2006). Math disabilities: A selective meta-analysis of the literature. *Review of Educational Research, 76*(2), 249–274.

Sweetland, J. D., Reina, J. M., & Tatti, A. F. (2006). WISC–III verbal/performance discrepancies among a sample of gifted children. *Gifted Child Quarterly, 50*(1), 7–10.

Taub, G. E., McGrew, K. S., & Witta, E. L. (2004). A confirmatory analysis of the factor structure and cross-age invariance of the Wechsler Adult Intelligence Scale–Third Edition. *Psychological Assessment, 16*(1), 85–89.

Terman, L. M. (1916). *The measurement of intelligence: An explanation of and a complete guide for the use of the Stanford revision and extension of the Binet-Simon intelligence scale.* Oxford, England: Houghton Mifflin.

Thompson, B. (1998). In praise of brilliance: Where that praise really belongs. *American Psychologist, 53,* 799–800.

Thompson, B. (2000). Ten commandments of structural equation modeling. In L. G. Grimm & P. R. Yarnold (Eds.), *Reading and understanding MORE multivariate statistics* (pp. 261–283). Washington, DC: American Psychological Association.

Thorndike, R. M. (1997). The early history of intelligence testing. In D. P. Flanagan, J. L. Genshaft, & P. L. Harrison (Eds.), *Contemporary intellectual assessment: Theories, tests, and issues* (pp. 3–16). New York: Guilford Press.

Tremont, G., Mittenberg, W., & Miller, L. J. (1999). Acute intellectual effects of pediatric head trauma. *Child Neuropsychology, 5,* 104–114.

Tucker, L. R., & Lewis, C. (1973). A reliability coefficient for maximum likelihood factor analysis. *Psychometrika, 38,* 1–10.

Tulsky, D. S., Saklofske, D. H., Chelune, G. J., Heaton, R. K., Ivnik, R. J., Bornstein, R. et al. (Eds.). (2003). *Clinical interpretation of the WAIS–III and WMS–III.* New York: Academic Press.

Tulsky, D. S., Saklofske, D. H., Wilkins, C., & Weiss, L. G. (2001). Development of a general ability index for the Wechsler Adult Intelligence Scale—Third Edition. *Psychological Assessment, 13,* 566–571.

Tulsky, D., Zhu, J., & Prifitera, A. (2000). Assessment of adult intelligence with the WAIS–III. In G. Goldstein & M. Hersen (Eds.), *Handbook of psychological assessment* (3rd ed., pp. 97–129). Kidlington, Oxford, United Kingdom: Elsevier Science.

Unsworth, N., & Engle, R. W. (2007). On the division of short-term and working memory: An examination of simple and complex span and their relation to higher order abilities. *Psychological Bulletin, 133*(6), 1038–1066.

U.S. Bureau of the Census. (2005). *Current population survey, October 2005: School enrollment supplement file* [CD-ROM]. Washington, DC: Author.

Van der Molen, M. J., Van Luit, J. E. H., Jongmans, M. J., & Van der Molen, M. W. (2007). Verbal working memory in children with mild intellectual disabilities. *Journal of Intellectual Disability Research, 51*(2), 162–169.

Verger, K., Junqué, C., Jurado, M. A., Tresserras, P., Bartumeus, F., Nogués, P. et al. (2000). Age effects on long-term neuropsychological outcome in pediatric traumatic brain injury. *Brain Injury, 14,* 495–503.

Vigil-Colet, A., & Codorniu-Raga, M. J. (2002). How inspection time and paper and pencil measures of processing speed are related to intelligence. *Personality and Individual Differences, 33,* 1149–1161.

Visser, P. J., Kester, A., Jolles, J., & Verhey, F. (2006). Ten-year risk of dementia in subjects with mild cognitive impairment. *Neurology, 67,* 1201–1207.

Vukovic, R. K., & Siegel, L. S. (2006). The double-deficit hypothesis: A comprehensive analysis of the evidence. *Journal of Learning Disabilities, 39*(1), 25–47.

Ward, L. C., Ryan, J. J., & Axelrod, B. N. (2000). Confirmatory factor analyses of the WAIS–III standardization data. *Psychological Assessment, 12*(3), 341–345.

Watkins, M. W., Greenawalt, C. G., & Marcell, C. M. (2002). Factor structure of the Wechsler Intelligence Scale for Children—Third Edition among gifted students. *Educational and Psychological Measurement, 62,* 164–172.

Wechsler, D. (1939). *Wechsler-Bellevue intelligence scale.* New York: The Psychological Corporation.

Wechsler, D. (1944). *The measurement of adult intelligence* (3rd ed.). Baltimore: Williams & Wilkins.

Wechsler, D. (1945). A standardized memory scale for clinical use. *The Journal of Psychology, 19,* 87–95.

Wechsler, D. (1955). *Wechsler adult intelligence scale.* New York: The Psychological Corporation.

Wechsler, D. (1958). *The measurement and appraisal of adult intelligence* (4th ed.). Baltimore: Williams & Wilkins.

Wechsler, D. (1975). Intelligence defined and undefined: A relativistic appraisal. *American Psychologist, 30,* 135–139.

Wechsler, D. (1981). *Wechsler adult intelligence scale–revised.* San Antonio, TX: The Psychological Corporation.

Wechsler, D. (1989). *Wechsler preschool and primary scale of intelligence–revised.* San Antonio, TX: The Psychological Corporation.

Wechsler, D. (1991). *Wechsler intelligence scale for children—third edition.* San Antonio, TX: The Psychological Corporation.

Wechsler, D. (1997a). *Wechsler adult intelligence scale—third edition.* San Antonio, TX: The Psychological Corporation.

Wechsler, D. (1997b). *Wechsler memory scale—third edition.* San Antonio, TX: The Psychological Corporation.

Wechsler, D. (2002a). *WAIS–III/WMS–III technical manual, updated.* San Antonio, TX: The Psychological Corporation.

Wechsler, D. (2002b). *Wechsler preschool and primary scale of intelligence–third edition.* San Antonio, TX: Harcourt Assessment.

Wechsler, D. (2003). *Wechsler intelligence scale for children–fourth edition.* San Antonio, TX: Harcourt Assessment.

Wechsler, D. (in press). *Wechsler memory scale–fourth edition.* San Antonio, TX: Pearson.

Wechsler, D., Kaplan, E., Fein, D., Kramer, J., Morris, R., Delis, D. et al. (2004). *Wechsler intelligence scale for children–fourth edition integrated.* San Antonio, TX: Harcourt Assessment.

Werheid, K., Hoppe, C., Thöne, A., Müller, U., Müngersdorf, M., & von Cramon, D. Y. (2002). The adaptive digit ordering test: Clinical application, reliability, and validity of a verbal working memory test. *Archives of Clinical Neuropsychology, 17,* 547–565.

Werner, H. (1937). Process and achievement: A basic problem of education and developmental psychology. *Harvard Educational Review, 7,* 353–368.

Wilkins, C., Rolfhus, E., Weiss, L., & Zhu, J. J. (2005, April). *A new method for calibrating translated tests with small sample sizes.* Paper presented at the 2005 annual meeting of the American Educational Research Association, Montreal Canada.

Willcutt, E. G., Pennington, B. F., Boada, R., Ogline, J. S., Tunick, R. A., Chhabildas, N. A. et al. (2001). A comparison of the cognitive deficits in reading disability and attention-deficit/hyperactivity disorder. *Journal of Abnormal Psychology, 110,* 157–172.

Williamson, D. J. G., Scott, J. G., & Adams, R. L. (1996). Traumatic brain injury. In R. L. Adams, O. A. Parsons, J. L. Culbertson, & S. J. Nixon (Eds.), *Neuropsychology for clinical practice: Etiology, assessment, and treatment of common neurological disorders* (pp. 9–64). Washington, DC: American Psychological Association.

Winner, E. (2000). The origins and ends of giftedness. *American Psychologist, 55,* 159–169.

Wojciulik, E., Husain, M., Clarke, K., & Driver, J. (2001). Spatial working memory deficit in unilateral neglect. *Neuropsychologia, 39,* 390–396.

Woodcock, R. W., McGrew, K. S., & Mather, N. (2001). *Woodcock-Johnson III tests of cognitive abilities.* Itasca, IL: Riverside.

Wylie, S. A., Ridderinkhof, K. R., Eckerle, M. K., Manning, C. A. (2007). Inefficient response inhibition in individuals with mild cognitive impairment. *Neuropsychologia, 45,* 1408–1419.

Yesavage, J. A., Brink, T. L., Rose, T. L., Lum, O., Huang, V., Adey, M., et al. (1982–1983). Development and validation of a geriatric depression screening scale: A preliminary report. *Journal of Psychiatric Research, 17*(1), 37–49.

Young, S., Bramham, J., Tyson, C., & Morris, R. (2006). Inhibitory dysfunction on the Stroop in adults diagnosed with attention deficit hyperactivity disorder. *Personality and Individual Differences, 41,* 1377–1384.

Zachary, R. A. (1990). Wechsler's intelligence scales: Theoretical and practical considerations. *Journal of Psychoeducational Assessment, 8,* 276–289.

Zec, R. F. (1993). Neuropsychological functioning in Alzheimer's disease. In R. W. Parks, R. F. Zec, & R. S. Wilson (Eds.), *Neuropsychology of Alzheimer's disease and other dementias* (pp. 3–80). New York: Oxford University Press.

Zhou, X., & Zhu, J. (2007, August). Peeking inside the "blackbox" of Flynn effect: Evidence from three Wechsler instruments. Poster session presented at the annual meeting of the American Psychological Association, San Francisco, CA.

Zhu, J., & Tulsky, D. (2000). Co-norming the WAIS–III and WMS–III: Is there a test-order effect on IQ and memory scores? *The Clinical Neuropsychologist, 14,* 1–7.